The Global Politics of the Environment

Also by Lorraine Elliott

INTERNATIONAL ENVIRONMENTAL POLITICS: Protecting the
Antarctic

PROTECTING THE ANTARCTIC: Australia and the Minerals
Convention

The Global Politics
of the Environment

Lorraine Elliott

NEW YORK UNIVERSITY PRESS
Washington Square, New York

BMO 7431 - 2/1

First published in the U.S.A. in 1998 by
NEW YORK UNIVERSITY PRESS
Washington Square
New York, N.Y. 10003

This book is printed on paper suitable for recycling and
made from fully managed and sustained forest sources.

Library of Congress Cataloging-in-Publication Data
Elliott, Lorraine M.
The global politics of the environment / Lorraine Elliott.
p.   cm.
Includes bibliographical references and index.
ISBN 0–8147–2163–X (clothbound). — ISBN 0–8147–2164–8 (pbk.)
1. Environmental policy—International cooperation.
2. Environmental degradation.   3. Nature—Effect of human beings on.
I. Title.
GE170.E47 1998
363.7'0526—dc21   97–22763
                                                             CIP

Printed in Malaysia

For Matthew, Loren, Louise and Benjamin

Contents

Acknowledgements

The process of writing an international account of global environmental politics has led me to incur debts to colleagues around the world. Many of these debts have arisen not just in the writing of this specific book, but in the willingness of many to spend time talking with me about global environmental politics generally, providing a supportive community of scholars and enabling me to test ideas through seminars, conference papers and publication. They have, at all times, been encouraging of my work even as they required me to strengthen my own arguments when, as happens, they called me to account for my views. They may not have realised, at the time, that they were contributing in various ways to the development of the ideas that appear in this book, and perhaps neither did I.

In various ways, then, and for various reasons I would like to thank Marc Williams, Julian Saurin, Matt Paterson, Ian Rowlands, Dave Scrivener, Peter Newell, Mark Imber, Hugh Dyer and John Vogler; Lois Lorentzen and Jennifer Turpin; Gwyn Prins; Kristalina Georgieva; Helen Freeman (and the staff at WorldWIDE); Ann Tickner, Maureen Molot, Kim Nossal, Martin Rudner, Stuart Harris, Kate Manzo, Joe Camilleri and Andy Mack; and Ali Bos, Adam Cunningham, Deb Foskey and Johanna Sutherland (the last four, my postgraduates, all of whom are working on environment-related issues). The writing of this book has been woven not just with my research on a range of environmental issues and problems but also with my teaching on this subject matter. Thanks are due therefore to the undergraduate and honours students who have taken my global environmental politics courses over the last four years.

Sue Fraser did a sterling job of checking and, where necessary, chasing up references, a task which required her to read through the whole manuscript (for which I am very grateful: she bears no responsibility for any errors). Steven Kennedy has been a strict but supportive publisher and his encouragement has been central to the completion of this book. I should like also to acknowledge financial support from the Australian National University New Staff Grant scheme and the Australian Research Council Small Grants for some of the research on NGOs which appears in this book.

I've been supported through the tough writing times by a good group of friends, many of whom were also in writing mode. Greg Fry, Paul Keal, Nancy Viviani, Graeme Cheeseman and Jan Jindy Pettman fall into this category. Jo Crawford, Jen Curtin, Heather Devere, Anna George, Diane Stone and Sue Weston have all turned up trumps as the best of friends and deserve thanks simply for that. That they are all so competent and knowledgeable in their various academic and policy work, which has often overlapped with mine, is an added bonus.

This book is dedicated to my nieces and nephews: if there is to be such a thing as intergenerational equity, then it is to the next generation that we first owe that obligation. They deserve better from us than, I fear, we will be able to leave them.

June 1997 LORRAINE ELLIOTT

List of Abbreviations

ACC	Administrative Committee on Coordination
AGBM	Ad Hoc Working Group on the Berlin Mandate
AIJ	Activities Implemented Jointly
ANEN	African NGOs Environment Network
ANGOC	African NGO Coalition
APPEN	Asia Pacific Peoples Environment Network
AOSIS	Alliance of Small Island States
ASEAN	Association of SouthEast Asian Nations
BCSD	Business Council for Sustainable Development
CBD	Convention on Biological Diversity
CCD	Convention to Combat Desertification [short title]
CCOL	Coordinating Committee on the Ozone Layer
CFCs	Chlorofluorocarbons
CH_4	Methane
CHOGM	Commonwealth Heads of Government Meeting
CIDIE	Committee of International Development Institutions on the Environment
CITES	Convention on International Trade in Endangered Species
CNPPA	Commission on National Parks and Protected Areas
CO_2	Carbon dioxide
COFO	Committee on Forestry
COICA	Coordinating Body for the Indigenous Peoples Organisations of the Amazon Basin
COP	Conference of the Parties
CSCE	Conference on Security and Cooperation in Europe
CSD	Commission on Sustainable Development
CSW	Commission on the Status of Women
DC/PAC	Desertfication Control Programme Activity Centre
DFNS	Debt for Nature Swaps
DOEM	Designated Officials for Environmental Matters
EA	Environmental Assessment
EC	European Community
ECE	Economic Commission for Europe
ECOSOC	Economic and Social Council
EEB	European Environment Bureau

EEZ	Exclusive Economic Zone
EIA	Environmental Impact Assessment
EITs	Economies in Transition
EMIT	[GATT Group on] Environmental Measures in Trade
ENB	Earth Negotiations Bulletin
ENDA	Environment and Development Action in the Third World
ENMOD	Environmental Modification Convention [Convention on the Prohibition of Military or any other Hostile Use of Environmental Modification Techniques]
EPA	[US] Environment Protection Agency
ETM	Environmental trade measure
EU	European Union
FAO	Food and Agriculture Organisation
FCCC	Framework Convention on Climate Change
FIELD	Foundation for International Environmental Law and Development
FLS	[Nairobi] Forward Looking Strategies
FoE	Friends of the Earth
FoEI	Friends of the Earth International
FRG	Federal Republic of Germany
G77	Group of 77
GATT	General Agreement on Tariffs and Trade
GDP	Gross Domestic Product
GEF	Global Environment Facility
GEMS	Global Environment Monitoring System
GHG	Greenhouse gas
GNP	Gross National Product
GW	Gigawatts
HCFCs	Hydrochlorofluorocarbons
HFCs	Hydrofluorocarbons
IACSD	Interagency Committee on Sustainable Development
IAEA	International Atomic Energy Agency
IBRD	International Bank for Reconstruction and Development
ICC	International Chamber of Commerce
ICCBD	Intergovernmental Committee on the Convention on Biodiversity

ICP	Industry Cooperative Programme
ICSU	International Council of Scientific Unions
IGBP	International Geosphere-Biosphere Programme
IIED	International Institute for Environment and Development
IISD	International Institute for Sustainable Development
ILO	International Labour Organisation
IMF	International Monetary Fund
IMO	International Maritime Organisation
INC	Intergovernmental Negotiating Committee
INCD	Intergovernmental Negotiating Committee for the elaboration of an international convention to combat desertification in those countries experiencing serious drought and/or desertification particularly in Africa
INFOTERRA	International Referral System for Sources of Environmental Information
INGOF	International NGO Forum
IPAC	International Policy Action Committee
IPCC	Intergovernmental Panel on Climate Change
IPE	International Political Economy
IPF	Intergovernmental Panel on Forests
IPRs	Intellectual Property Rights
IRPTC	International Register of Potentially Toxic Chemicals
ITTA	International Tropical Timber Agreement
ITTO	International Tropical Timber Organisation
ITWAN	International Toxic Waste Action Network
IUCN	International Union for the Conservation of Nature and Natural Resources
IWC	International Whaling Commission
IWGF	Intergovernmental Working Group on Forests
JI	Joint Implementation
JUSCANZ	Japan, United States, Canada, Australian and New Zealand Group
LRTAP	Long-Range Transboundary Air Pollution
MAPW	Medical Association for Prevention of War
MARPOL	International Convention for the Prevention of Pollution from Ships
MDB	Multilateral Development Bank
MNC	Multinational Corporation

N_2O	Nitrous oxide
NAFTA	North American Free Trade Agreement
NASA	National Aeronautics and Space Administration
NATO	North Atlantic Treaty Organisation
NAM	Non-Aligned Movement
NFAP	National Forestry Action Plan
NGO	Non-governmental organisation
NICs	Newly Industrialised Countries
NOZE	National Ozone Expedition
NOx	Nitrogen oxide
OAU	Organisation of African Unity
ODA	Official development assistance
OECD	Organisation for Economic Cooperation and Development
OTA	Office of Technology Assessment
OTP	Ozone Trends Panel
PACD	Plan of Action to Combat Desertification
PNG	Papua New Guinea
ppb	parts per billion
ppm	parts per million
PPP	Polluter Pays Principle
PrepComm	Preparatory Committee
PRIO	Peace Research Institute, Oslo
R&D	Research and Development
SAR	Second Assessment Report
SBI	Subsidiary Body on Implementation
SBSTA	Subsidiary Body on Scientific and Technical Advice
SBSTTA	Subsidiary Body on Scientific, Technical and Technological Advice
SCOPE	Scientific Committee on the Problems of the Human Environment
SIDS	Small Island Developing States
SIPRI	Stockholm International Peace Research Institute
SO_2	sulphur dioxide
SLORC	State Law and Order Council
SPREP	South Pacific Regional Environment Programme
STAP	Scientific and Technical Advisory Panel
SWAGSD	[UNEP] Senior Women's Advisory Group on Sustainable Development
TOMA	Tropospheric Ozone Management Area
TFAP	Tropical Forestry Action Plan

UN	United Nations
UNCED	United Nations Conference on Environment and Development
UNCLOS	United Nations Convention on the Law of the Sea
UNCOD	United Nations Conference on Desertification
UNCTAD	United Nations Conference on Trade and Development
UNCTC	United Nations Centre on Transnational Corporations
UNDP	United Nations Development Programme
UNEP	United Nations Environment Programme
UNESCO	United Nations Educational, Scientific and Cultural Organisation
UNFCCC	United Nations Framework Convention on Climate Change
UNGA	United Nations General Assembly
UNIFEM	United Nations Development Fund for Women
UNNRC	United Nations Natural Resources Committee
USIS	United States Information Service
USSR	Union of Soviet Socialist Republics
UVB	Ultra-Violet B radiation
VOC	Volatile Organic Compound
WCED	World Commission on Environment and Development
WCS	World Conservation Strategy
WEDO	Women's Environment and Development Organisation
WICEM	World Industry Conference on Environmental Management
WMO	World Meteorological Organisation
WRI	World Resources Institute
WRM	World Rainforest Movement
WTO	World Trade Organisation
WWF	World Wide Fund for Nature

Introduction

One of the questions asked by many policy-makers, activists and scholars after the 1992 United Nations Conference on Environment and Development (UNCED) was 'Did we save the earth'? Needless to say, the answers vary: some answer yes, some answer no and some answer maybe but it's too soon to tell. The ideas explored in this book, however, canvass more than responses to that specific, albeit important question. The main purpose of this text is to focus attention on a more fundamental question, 'how *should* we save the earth?', and to examine the often competing answers offered in response. The reasons why these questions should be asked is increasingly obvious.

At the end of the twentieth century, it is clear that human activity is changing the environment, and not for the better, in a way unlike that of any other era. Extensive and excessive resource use, energy-inefficient lifestyles, industrialisation and the pursuit of economic growth are inextricably linked to environmental degradation, within and across state borders. Since the 1950s, world industrial production has increased four-fold (see Sitarz, 1994, p. 38). Energy production has increased exponentially, by a factor of about 4.5 between 1950 and 1985 although that growth rate had slowed by the early 1990s (Porter and Brown, 1996, p. 6). World oil production increased by a factor of almost six between 1950 and 1992 (see Brown et al., 1993, p. 47). Fertiliser use increased ten-fold between 1950 and 1992 (Brown et al., 1993, p. 19). World water use doubled between 1940 and 1980 (MacNeill, 1989–90, p. 6) and by 1996 per capita water supply in developing countries was only one-third of the 1970 level (UNDP, 1996, p. 26). Atmospheric concentrations of carbon dioxide emissions have increased exponentially since the Industrial Revolution and now stand at something in the vicinity of 360 parts per million (ppm), a number which may mean little on its own but which scientific consensus accepts will contribute to interference with the climate system with a rate of change in average global temperatures faster than at any time in the last 10 000 years and sea level rises about three to six times faster than in the last 100 years (see Houghton et al., 1990, p. xxviii). Much of this activity is unsustainable in the way it depletes resources and affects the environment and the livelihoods of the world's peoples, especially in the developing world.

The environmental impacts of this economic activity have been widespread. Land degradation has increased to the extent that as much as one-third of the world's land surface is now threatened by desertification (see Abate and Akhtar, 1994, p. 72). Water scarcity is on the increase, with over 80 countries now facing water shortages, 26 of them officially designated as water-scarce. Air pollution and contamination of waterways and coastal areas have become a standard feature of industrialised and developing country ecosystems. The world's forests, both tropical and temperate, are in decline. Every day, as many as 50 of the earth's species become extinct. Environmental degradation increases the poverty of those who are already poor especially in those parts of the world where livelihoods and lives are closely dependent on terrestrial, river, stream and coastal ecosystems. Desertification and land degradation undermine the agricultural and subsistence practices of peoples in the developing world. Pollution of rivers and streams affects the irrigation of farms in developed and developing countries, it diminishes people's access to clean drinking water and it kills fish upon which local peoples rely for food. Deforestation denies sources of food, medicine and the basics of daily life to millions of forest dwellers and indigenous peoples as well as undermining their cultural and spiritual identity. Increasing scarcity of fuelwood and water increases the burden of the lives of developing world women. In both developed and developing countries hazardous waste dumping and toxic pollution cause death (recall Bhopal) and illness (recall Minimata or Love Canal).

These issues cannot be separated from inequities in cause and impact. While the industrialised world accounts for about one-quarter of the world's population, it consumes 70 per cent of the world's energy, 85 per cent of its wood, 75 per cent of its metals and 60 per cent of its food (UNDP, 1992, p. 35). Yet the local impacts of global environmental decline will be felt first, and disproportionately, in those countries and among those peoples who have contributed less to the causes. Inequities between rich and poor countries, unequal trade and international capital transactions, the paucity of international development assistance in the pursuit of basic human needs, and the ever-growing burden of developing country debt are entwined with environmental degradation in complex cause-and-effect relationships.

Environmental degradation is now a global issue – ecologically, politically and economically. Global environmental problems, it is argued, require global solutions. This simple aphorism hides a multitude of political and economic difficulties, not the least of which is how we should understand the 'global' as an organising principle. The difference between local environmental problems and what we understand as a global problem has come to be often simply a matter of degree. As Wood and colleagues note,

> at the local level, a problem such as deforestation primarily affects slash and burn cultivators and peasants attempting to establish stationary farms. But the same problem, multiplied by thousands of small farms and combined with extensive commercial logging, can exacerbate the global-level issue of accelerated atmospheric warming (Wood *et al.*, 1989, p. 32).

That there are no simple solutions might be a second aphorism. Cooperation among states has become a necessary (but not sufficient) condition for controlling or preventing the causes of environmental degradation and for finding ways to overcome or at least mitigate both the global environmental impacts of local human activity and the local impacts of global environmental degradation.

Yet while there are now many, many thousands of words on paper – in conventions, protocols, declarations, statements of principle, management programmes, action plans, communiqués – environmental degradation continues to worsen. Thus there is a crisis in capacity, a failure of governance, an apparent lack of political will. In seeking to overcome these problems, the first-order questions for many are those related to the kinds of targets and commitments which should be incorporated into international environmental agreements, to how scientific evidence should be translated into policy, how implementation can be ensured, how compliance should be monitored and verified, the nature of liability and accountability, whether to focus on symptoms or causes (or both), whether agreements should attempt to prohibit or control activities and behaviours that are the cause of environmental degradation, and what kinds of institutions should be established to oversee these agreements and to manage global environmental programmes.

For others, including this author, these are second-order questions. The questions to be asked *first* are those which focus attention 'on the underlying structure in which this process is being played out' (Thomas, 1993, p. 2). It is important, as Cox suggests, to appraise the 'very framework for action' (1986, p. 208). In this view, environmental degradation is not simply a 'glitch' (albeit a rather large one) in the otherwise reasonably smooth running of the contemporary political and economic world order. Rather the contemporary political and economic order is quite likely to be part of the problem. At very least, we should not assume that it is not. This introduces a different set of questions. What prospect, for example, is there for effective environmental governance in a decentralised system of sovereign states? Does the liberal international economic order, with its emphasis on freer international trade, modernisation and export-led growth, provide a firm basis for the elaboration of principles and strategies which will overcome global environmental decline, or is the liberal international economic order part of the problem in the first place? Can we achieve environmental security in a militarised world? It is those questions which provide the structure for much of this book.

The purpose here, in examining these questions and the answers to them, is not to persuade readers of a particular point of view. Rather it is to try to make some sense of the different ways in which scholars, commentators and practitioners have sought to understand the global politics of the environment and the means by which we should 'save the earth'. Throughout the book, equal attention is given to the orthodox reformist views which have generally informed the practice of states and many other actors – as well as much academic research and analysis – and to alternative critical perspectives which pose a more radical challenge to the contemporary world order and its guiding principles and values.

Structure of the book

The first three chapters of this text examine the globalising of the environmental agenda. Chapter 1 focuses on two significant events in that globalising process – the 1972 UN Conference on the Human Environment (the Stockholm Conference) and the 1992 United Nations Conference on Environment and Development (the Rio Conference) – as well as exploring the main features of the intervening two decades. The two subsequent chapters explore the expanding agenda of environmental concerns in two stages. Chapter 2 explores what might be called the Stockholm agenda – the transboundary conservation and pollution issues which dominated international environmental debate, dispute and negotiation in the 1970s and 1980s. Chapter 3 focuses on the so-called Rio agenda, those issues (climate change, ozone depletion, desertification, deforestation and loss of biodiversity) which are together identified, sometimes controversially, as the global agenda. While concern and discussion about each of these environmental problems predated the Rio Conference, it was that event in 1992 which (with the exception of ozone depletion) provided the catalyst for not always successful negotiations on comprehensive agreements. While these chapters are primarily descriptive of environmental concerns and the politics of negotiations, they illuminate the political problems, tensions, issues and debates which provide the focus for the rest of the book.

Chapters 4, 5 and 6 focus on various aspects of the processes of and debates about environmental governance. Governance is understood here as something more than simply (or even) the formal, material organisations which exist to address environmental conerns. Rather it includes the broader social institutions, rules and practices which provide the framework for decision-making and cooperation. While there is often agreement that we face some kind of crisis in environmental governance, demands for better governance beg at least two important questions. First, *why* is there a crisis of governance? Second, what are the characteristics of better environmental governance and how, if at all, can this be achieved? In examining these issues further, Chapter 4 examines the existing institutional framework (especially the UN system) in the light of concerns about its efficacy and the adequacy or otherwise of international environmental cooperation based on the principle of state sovereignty. For many, global civil society provides an important counterbalance to what are perceived to be the environmental failures of this state-centric system. In this context, Chapter 5 examines the role in environmental governance and politics of non-state actors, particularly environmental non-governmental organisations. Chapter 6 explores the politics of environmental marginalisation, paying attention to the impact of environmental degradation on women and indigenous peoples, whose voices have so often been at the very edges of the formal structures of environmental governance (if, indeed, they have been heard at all).

Chapters 7 and 8 focus more closely on the international political economy of the environment. The relationship between the structures and processes of the world economy – trade, debt, development – and environmental degradation is complex and in dispute. That relationship is further complicated, and the dispute exacerbated, by the competing interests and concerns of rich and poor countries (as well as rich and poor peoples). Chapter 7 considers the tensions between developing and developed countries which have become a central characteristic of the global politics of the environment. Concerns about inequities in cause and impact are revisited in political debates about commitments, obligations, costs and benefits, the contested meaning of sustainable development (the catch-cry of the post-UNCED era) and the best strategies for achieving it. Those strategies, few of which have yet been put into effect, are explored further in Chapter 8. They range across resource transfers of various kinds, more effective utilisation of trade mechanisms, attempts to address the high level of developing country debt and the application of financial mechanisms at an international level. It will come as no surprise that the usefulness of any of these strategies, and the manner in which they should be given effect, is contested.

Chapter 9 turns to another much used but less-well-understood phrase of the post-Rio era, albeit one which travels in tandem with sustainable development, that of environmental security. In particular, it questions the extent to which this concept should be understood primarily as an 'add on' to a traditional security agenda or whether it invokes a rethinking of accepted wisdoms and practices about that orthodox agenda. Chapter 10, the concluding chapter, specifically addresses the respective merits of the two broad traditions of analysis – a generally orthodox reformist position on the one hand and a more critical perspective on the other – which have shaped the global politics of the environment and which have informed the ideas explored in this book.

1

From Stockholm to Rio

Two events, 20 years apart, framed the globalisation of environmental politics. The 1972 United Nations Conference on the Human Environment (the Stockholm Conference) is frequently described as a watershed in the development of international environmental law, as the beginning of serious international cooperation on the environment, as 'the event where international debate on the environment began' (Tolba, El-Kholy *et al.*, 1992, p. 742). It represented a formal acknowledgment (by industrialised countries in particular) of the importance of multilateral efforts to deal with transboundary environmental problems. Two decades after Stockholm, representatives of governments, international organisations and non-governmental organisations (NGOs) met in Rio de Janiero, in Brazil, for the United Nations Conference on Environment and Development (UNCED), known also as the Rio Summit or the Earth Summit. That meeting was hailed as firm evidence that environmental concerns had moved to occupy a central place in the agenda of world politics.

Prior to the Stockholm Conference and especially before the 1960s, environmental problems were more likely to arise within, rather than across, state borders. They were most often defined in scientific and technical terms with rather less attention paid to political, economic or social impacts. Much of the debate was expert-driven, absent a high degree of public concern or interest. Where agreements were reached between states, they were most often reactive rather than precautionary. Nevertheless, as the 1960s progressed, scientific developments and public concern about environmental degradation contributed to a slow development of international environmental law and an equally slow democratisation of international environmental policy-making. In the two decades between Stockholm and Rio scientific knowledge and public concern about environmental degradation and its impacts grew along with a sense of planetary crisis and demands for international cooperation to halt and then reverse the environmental impact of human activity. The result was an increase not only in the number and scope of environmental concerns on the international agenda but also the number of multilateral treaties adopted to respond to those concerns. In the years from 1921 to 1959, only 20 multilateral environmental agreements were signed. This number rose to 26 in the 1960s alone. It increased to 49 in the 1970s with a similar number of agreements also negotiated in the 1980s (see Soroos, 1994b, p. 304).

Before Stockholm

Lynton Caldwell has usefully located most of the pre-1972 international environmental concerns and agreements in one of three categories: wilderness and wildlife conservation, maritime pollution and issues related to the spread of nuclear-weaponry (see Caldwell, 1991, p. 6). These categories reflect a broadening of the environmental agenda from territorial issues, where state jurisdiction over particular kinds of behaviour was usually clear, to concerns for the high seas outside the reaches of national jurisdiction, to issues such as nuclear pollution likely to affect the planet as a whole. Conservation concerns probably have the longest history. As far back as 1872, the Swiss government proposed an international commission to protect migrating birds. In 1900 the European colonial powers signed a convention for the preservation of animals, birds and fish in Africa. The *North Pacific Fur Seal Treaty* was adopted in 1911 and the *Convention on Nature Protection and Wildlife Conservation in the Western Hemisphere* in 1940 (see Brenton, 1994, p. 16). One of the earliest global conservation agreements still in force is the 1946 *International Convention for the Regulation of Whaling*, although its membership was initially small and its primary purpose was the regulation of an economic activity to prevent resource-depletion rather than the conservation of whale species *per se*. Wildlife conservation also gave rise to efforts to preserve ecosystems, efforts reflected, for example, in the 1971 Ramsar *Convention on the Conservation of Wetlands*. Agreements were also reached on the prevention, or at least control of oil pollution at sea in response to a number of maritime disasters. The 1954 *International Convention for the Prevention of Pollution of the Sea by Oil* (usually agreed to have been a fairly ineffectual agreement) is one such example. The 1958 *Convention on the High Seas* (a forerunner to the 1982 *Convention on the Law of the Sea*) also contained provisions on maritime pollution. The third of Caldwell's categories, those agreements intended to limit or protect against the use and testing of atomic weaponry, is not explored in any detail in this book. One might look, however, to the 1959 *Antarctic Treaty* – which banned the testing of *all* kinds of weaponry and the dumping of nuclear waste in the Antarctic thus effectively creating the world's first nuclear free zone (even though this was not the Treaty's primary purpose) – or to the 1963 *Partial Test Ban Treaty*.

While much of this multilateral activity was dominated by states and governments, non-governmental environmental and conservation organisations (discussed further in Chapter 5) became increasingly concerned with and activist on transboundary and international environmental issues. NGO membership grew in the 1960s. In the US, for example, membership of the Sierra Club and the National Audubon Society, both long-standing organisations concerned primarily with wilderness conservation, went from the few tens of thousands to 140 000 and 200 000 respectively by the early 1970s (Brenton, 1994, p. 19). New NGOs were also established, ones with a more activist focus and a wider agenda of environmental concerns. A split in the Sierra Club in the late 1960s, after a serious difference of opinion over tactics and strategy, gave rise to Friends of the Earth. Greenpeace was founded in 1969, following a campaign against atomic testing at Amchitka.

Intellectual developments in the years prior to 1972 also set the scene for the Stockholm Conference. Much of the influential work invited a reappraisal of the values of industrialisation, modernisation and development and sought to rethink the impacts of human activity on the environment and, in turn, the impact of a degraded environment on human society. The view that human health could be severely affected by pollutants was further confirmed by incidents such as the revelations of mercury poisoning at Minamata Bay in Japan in 1959. The 1962 publication of Rachel Carson's book *Silent Spring* was, as so many commentators have noted, a major factor in this debate. While Carson, a biologist, was concerned specifically about the impact of the use of pesticides, her book generated a questioning of the effects of human activity on the environment. Carson's work was one of a number of influential pieces written by scientists – often biologists – as the science of ecology developed. There was a strong doomsday trend in many of the predictions. This sense of impending disaster, of a shrinking planet, of a planet reaching its carrying capacity, was reinforced by photos of the earth from the moon and from space (via the Apollo spacecraft) which seemed to emphasise the fragility of the earth and gave rise to the image of 'spaceship earth' with humans as its passengers.

In 1968, in a much quoted (and often misquoted) piece in the reputable journal *Science*, biologist Garrett Hardin likened the unregulated use of the oceans and atmosphere to the historical overuse of the English commons, arguing that the outcome would be a 'tragedy of the commons' in that 'freedom in a commons brings ruin to all' (Hardin, 1968, p. 1244). Where there is no individual ownership, he argued, everyone has an incentive to use the resource to their own advantage, resulting in resource overuse. However Hardin's concern in this piece was not primarily environmental: rather it was for the overall sub-optimal effects of unrestricted population growth, for which his solution (drawing on the metaphor of enclosure of the commons) was mutual coercion and the 'relinquishing of the freedom to breed' (Hardin, 1968, p. 1248). He returned to this issue in his later work – such as his 1974 piece 'Living on a Lifeboat' (Hardin, 1974) – in which he argued, among other things, that food aid to Third World countries should be discontinued to compel those countries to limit their populations.

Others were also concerned about population. Paul Ehrlich, in his seminal piece *The Population Bomb* (Ehrlich, 1968) located his analysis of unrestrained population growth in the context of the impact of inequitable consumption, noting that the environmental impact of one American (that is someone who lived in the United States of America) was the same as that of two Swedes, three Italians, 13 Brazilians, 35 Indians or 280 Chadians or Haitians (see Brenton, 1994, p. 14). In 1972, in *The Limits to Growth* – an influential report for the Club of Rome – Donella Meadows and her colleagues argued for the imperatives of cutting back on resource-intensive industrial activity based on resource carrying-capacity predictions arising from their global-systems computer modelling (Meadows *et al.*, 1972). The carrying capacity and limits scenario were challenged in works by scholars such as John Maddox, *The Doomsday Syndrome* (1972) and the collection, *The resourceful Earth*, edited by Julian Simon and Herman Kahn (1984), which argued that a variety of factors, such as the human capacity to invent and find substitutes, and the market valuing of scarce resources would ensure that the carrying capacity and limits to growth could be overcome.

The cumulative outcome of this increase in awareness of environmental degradation and concern about resource scarcity and population growth was pressure for collective action. In a 1969 speech, U Thant, Secretary-General of the United Nations, suggested that

> members of the United Nations have perhaps ten years left in which to subordinate their ancient quarrels and launch a global partnership to curb the arms race, to improve the human environment, to defuse the population explosion (cited in Brenton, 1994, p. 28).

This, then, was the background to the UN Conference on the Human Environment.

The United Nations Conference on the Human Environment

In Resolution 2398, which established the Conference, the General Assembly anticipated a consciousness-raising exercise to provide a 'framework for comprehensive consideration within the United Nations of the problems of the human environment in order to focus the attention of governments and public opinion on the importance and urgency of this question' (cited in Rowland, 1973, p. 34). A second resolution (Resolution 2581) ensured that the conference would generate a more vigorous and activist outcome and would serve 'as a practical means to encourage and to provide guidelines for action by governments and international organisations' (see Brenton, 1994, p. 36).

In the two years before the conference the 27-member Preparatory Committee (PrepComm) met four times and received over one hundred national reports from members states. The Communist bloc countries withdrew from the preparatory process (and did not attend the final conference) on ideological and political grounds, angry that East Germany was prevented from participating and confident that environmental degradation was a capitalist problem. Developing countries were cautious about the Conference, wary that 'Northern' concerns with pollution and nature conservation would take precedence over poverty and underdevelopment. There were tensions also over issues of responsibility for environmental degradation, appropriate levels of development assistance, funding, technology transfer and population. These concerns were voiced at a meeting of developing country scientists and experts in Founex in 1971. The report of that meeting – the Founex Report – emphasised the importance of continued development and made clear developing country opposition to any strategies which would slow industrialisation or place environmentally-motivated restrictions on aid, investment and trade (see Brenton, 1994, p. 38).

The Stockholm Conference, 5 to 16 June 1972, was attended by about 1200 delegates from 114 countries. Only two heads of government attended – Olaf Palme from the host government and Prime Minister Indira Gandhi of India. There was a parallel, formal NGO conference (which set a precedent for what has become a standard feature of UN thematic diplomacy) and an informal People's Forum. Accredited NGOs were able to present formal statements to the Conference and had access to delegates for lobbying purposes. There were three substantive outcomes of the Conference process: a declaration, an action-plan and an organisational framework for addressing environmental concerns within the United Nations system. Maurice Strong, the Canadian who was appointed Secretary-General of the Conference, favoured a declaration which would establish the 'rights and obligations of citizens and governments with regards to the preservation and improvement of the human condition' (Strong, 1972a). The Stockholm Declaration, a non-binding declaration of 26 principles, did not meet the test Strong had set. It was a compromise which balanced the *shared* interests of states in maintaining the principle of state sovereignty and the *competing* interests of developed and developing countries. The Declaration balances the importance of a global commitment to protect resources and limit pollution against the importance of economic development. It emphasises, in principles 9 to 12, the importance of aid, technology and other assistance in overcoming the underdevelopment which is identified as the cause of most environmental problems in developing countries. The most quoted principle is principle 21 which asserts a state's sovereign rights over its resources as well as responsibility for environmental damage beyond its borders, but which gives no guidance as to how these two potentially competing purposes might be reconciled. Palmer says of the Declaration that it was a 'wish list of items that were inconsistent with one another and the overall result was to some extent intellectually incoherent' (1992, p. 266).

The Conference adopted a less well known Action Plan – 109 recommendations relating to human settlements, resource management, pollution, development and the social dimensions of the impact of environmental degradation on the human environment. Maurice Strong identified the Action Plan as a 'blueprint' for a continuing environmental work programme (1972b) but its relative brevity makes it a catalogue of concerns rather than a strong basis for environmental progress. Brenton's (1994, p. 46) view is, albeit with considerable hindsight, representative: he argues that there is little concrete in the Action Plan and that its long-term impact has been difficult to assess.

The third major outcome of the Stockholm Conference was institutional, paving the way for the General Assembly to establish the United Nations Environment Programme (UNEP). While the creation of UNEP ensured that the UN system would become the major site for international environmental diplomacy and the future development of international environmental law, political factors constrained UNEP's potential contribution to global environmental protection. Developed countries were generally cautious about any institution which would require substantial funding. Developing countries were reluctant to accept an institution whose decisions might place restrictions on their development and existing UN agencies were intent on jealously guarding their existing environment-related prerogatives. Thus UNEP was established as a programme, with a role as coordinator and catalyst, rather than a specialised agency with an operational mandate. It has a large governing council (58 members) and is headquartered in Nairobi rather than one of the usual UN locations of New York, Geneva or Vienna. Its operating budget was (and remains) small, to be supplemented by voluntary contributions to an environmental fund.

In his opening statement to the Conference, Maurice Strong suggested that Stockholm would launch a 'new liberation movement' (1972a). Yet Stockholm was not the liberation movement Strong had hoped for and, while it addressed some of the systemic issues of poverty and underdevelopment, there was little real practical commitment to halting and reversing the causes of environmental degradation. The major achievement of the Stockholm conference was that it brought together governments to debate international environmental issues and that it provided a basis for the slow development of international environmental law in the years to follow. Its success, then, was primarily political rather than environmental.

Stockholm to Rio: The In-Between Years

The report of the Stockholm Conference was submitted to the General Assembly at the end of 1972. The years following Stockholm were characterised by further development of scientific knowledge about environmental degradation and its causes, an increase in the activities and expertise of environmental NGOs and a greater recognition that environmental problems required not just scientific and technical solutions but attention to the complexity of causes and their social, economic and political consequences. There were many international environmental conferences and a number of international environmental agreements were adopted. In spite of this, progress in halting and reversing environmental degradation was incremental and piecemeal. Brenton has described this post-Stockholm period as one of relapse after the 'high point in Western public attention to the environment' (1994, p. 51). There was a lot of activity but not much real action.

Scientific knowledge was disseminated to policy-makers and the public through a number of publications and expert conferences. In 1977, UNEP convened an Ad Hoc Committee of Experts which formulated a World Plan of Action on the Ozone Layer. In 1979 the First World Climate Conference was convened under the auspices of the World Meteorological Organisation (WMO) in Geneva. In 1980, UNEP and the International Union for the Conservation of Nature (IUCN) launched the World Conservation Strategy (WCS) and in 1982 the UN General Assembly adopted a World Charter for Nature although its scope was limited to the conservation and use of living natural resources. In 1984 the International Council of Scientific Unions (ICSU), which in 1970 had established the Scientific Committee on Problems of the Human Environment (SCOPE), sponsored the International Geosphere-Biosphere Programme (IGBP). The purpose of this programme was to understand the relationship between the Earth's systems and to assess the extent of change in those systems as a result of human activity. It was followed, in 1987, by the Human Dimensions of Global Change Programme.

Public concern about environmental problems, in the West at least, heightened in response to a series of disasters with environmental consequences. The 1976 dioxin leak at Seveso in Italy, the 1978 Amoco Cadiz oil spill and the 1979 partial melt-down at the Three Mile Island nuclear power plant in Pennsylvania all grabbed headline space in the media. In 1984, the methyl isocyanate gas leak at Bhopal in India, which killed 2000 and injured 200 000, drew attention to the activities of multinational corporations, especially in developing countries. In the same year, 30 tons of toxic chemicals were washed into the Rhine following a fire at a Sandoz warehouse in Switzerland.

The explosion at the Chernobyl nuclear power station in the then Soviet Ukraine, in 1986, reminded people once again of the transboundary nature of pollution (the radiation spread across 21 countries in Europe) and raised questions about state responsibility, accountability and liability. Such accidents were increasingly perceived not as isolated incidents, but as evidence of the potential dangers of unregulated industrialisation and industrial pollution.

In response to scientific reports and public concern, governments adopted a number of agreements (some of which are discussed in subsequent chapters) designed to mitigate or control transboundary environmental degradation. In the 1970s, following Stockholm, there was a series of agreements on oceans pollution (the 1972 *London Dumping Convention* and the 1973 *International Convention for the Prevention of Pollution from Ships* – the *MARPOL* agreement), on endangered species (the 1973 *Convention on International Trade in Endangered Species*) and on acid rain (the 1979 *Geneva Convention on Long-Range Transboundary Air Pollution*. In 1989, 116 countries adopted the Basel *Convention on the Control of Transboundary Movements of Hazardous Wastes and their Disposal*. The first major agreement on the degradation of the global atmosphere, the Vienna *Convention for the Protection of the Ozone Layer,* was adopted in 1985. Two years later, before that Convention had come into force, governments established reduction targets in the Montreal *Protocol on Substances that Deplete the Ozone Layer*.

There was, however, little attempt until the mid-1980s to revisit the broader questions which had been deemed so important at Stockholm. In 1983, the UN General Assembly (UNGA), in resolution 38/161, established a special independent commission to formulate a 'long-term agenda for action' (UNGA, 1983, para 8(d)). The World Commission on Environment and Development (WCED), known as the Brundtland Commission after its chairperson Gro Harlem Brundtland, the Prime Minister of Norway (and former Norwegian Environment Minister), comprised 23 members from 22 countries, each serving in their independent and expert capacities. More than half (13 of the 22 if one includes the Vice-Chair) came from developing countries, ranging from China, India and Brazil to the Ivory Coast, Guyana and Zimbabwe. Those from the 'developed' world included individuals from most, but not all of the G7 countries (there was no-one from France or the UK) as well as from the then socialist bloc. Most had backgrounds in politics, academia or international public service (and sometimes all three). The Commission appointed a number of expert Special Advisers and three Advisory Panels (on energy, industry and food security). One of the hallmarks of the Commission's work was the series of public hearings held throughout the world between March 1985 and February 1987, enabling Commissioners to hear from a wide variety of interested people and organisations (from government and non-government sectors). The Commission's report, *Our Common Future* (WCED, 1987 – which is discussed in greater detail in Chapter 7) placed the concept of 'sustainable development' firmly into the global environmental lexicon.

The year following publication of the WCED report, 1988, was described by Mostafa Tolba (at the time director of UNEP) as the year in which environmental concerns (finally) became a top item on the international agenda (see Soroos, 1991, p. 1). In January 1988, scientists, policy-makers and representatives of intergovernmental and non-governmental organisations met in Toronto for the *Changing Atmosphere: implications for global security* conference, adopting voluntary targets for greenhouse gas emissions. In the same year, the World Meteorological Organisation (WMO) and UNEP established the Intergovernmental Panel on Climate Change (IPCC), involving over 1000 scientific, legal and policy experts from over 60 countries. The momentum of 1988 was maintained in subsequent years. Twenty-four heads of government met in the Hague in March 1989 at a conference convened by the Prime Ministers of France, the Netherlands and Norway and adopted a declaration which acknowledged the seriousness of threats to the atmosphere and the inadequacy of existing machinery of environmental governance. However, neither the United States or the Soviet Union was invited for fear that they would resist any declaration or recommendations which seemed to undermine state sovereignty. Environmental concerns were inscribed on the agenda of the G7 meeting in Paris in July that year, the first time any serious attention had been given to such concerns in this forum. The seven wealthiest industrialised countries argued that 'decisive action is urgently needed to understand and protect the earth's ecological balance' (cited in Fairclough, 1991, p. 96).

Late in 1989 (22 December to be exact), the UN General Assembly (UNGA) adopted a number of resolutions on the global impact of environmental degradation. Resolution 44/207 – Protection of the Global Climate for Present and Future Generations of Mankind [sic] – acknowledged an urgent need to address climate change (which was described as an issue of common concern) (UNGA, 1989a). A second resolution – 44/224 – declared that deterioration of the environment was 'one of the main global problems facing the world today' (UNGA, 1989b). A third resolution – 44/228 (UNGA, 1989c) – paved the way for what was intended to be the environmental highlight of the 1990s – the United Nations Conference on Environment and Development, known also as the Rio Summit, the Earth Summit, or just UNCED.

United Nations Conference on Environment and Development

Resolution 44/228 expressed concern at the 'continuing deterioration of the state of the environment and the serious degradation of the global life-support systems' (UNGA, 1989c, preamble). It recognised the global character of environmental problems and identified unsustainable patterns of production and consumption, particularly in industrialised countries, as the cause of much of that deterioration. It stressed the importance of international cooperation, scientific research and access to technology and new and additional financial resources for developing countries. The resolution identified a number of major environmental concerns – protection of the atmosphere, freshwater and oceans resources, land resources, biological diversity and biotechnology, waste management (including toxic wastes) and issues related to urban settlements, poverty and human health conditions. The Conference was to elaborate 'strategies and measures to halt and reverse environmental degradation in the context of increased national and international efforts to promote sustainable and environmentally sound development in all countries' (UNGA, 1989c, Part I, paragraph 3), an objective which was supplemented by a long list of more specific purposes (UNGA 1989c, Part I, paragraph 15, sub-paragraphs (a) to (w)).

The Conference preparatory committee was established as a committee of the General Assembly (a strategy supported by the G77), chaired by Ambassador Tommy Koh of Singapore. The conference secretariat, headquartered in Geneva with support units in New York and Nairobi, was headed by Maurice Strong as Secretary-General. In Koh (who had chaired the Law of the Sea negotiations) and Strong (who had been the first Executive Director of UNEP and a member of the Brundtland Commission after his time as Secretary-General of the Stockholm Conference), UNCED had extensive diplomatic experience and considerable corporate memory on the difficulties of reconciling environment and development concerns. The preparatory process was to be funded through the regular budget of the UN but a voluntary fund was also established to assist developing countries ('in particular the least developed among them' in the words of resolution 44/228) to participate in the Conference and PrepComms. UNEP and other UN bodies were asked to 'contribute fully' to the preparations. All States were invited to take an active part in preparations, including submission to the Secretariat of national reports, albeit in a timely manner and as appropriate. NGOs with consultative status with the UN Economic and Social Council (ECOSOC) were also requested to contribute 'as appropriate' to the conference.

The PrepComm held an organisational session in New York in March 1990, followed by three substantive sessions (one in Nairobi and two in Geneva) and a final session in New York to 'prepare draft decisions for the Conference and submit them to the Conference for consideration and adoption' (UNGA 1989c, Part II, para. 8(c)). Decision-making was to proceed by consensus. Cross-sectoral issues, such as financial assistance, technology transfer, the international economic system, were addressed in plenary sessions and were not, for the most part, resolved during the preparatory process. Other issues were addressed by three working groups. The first two – one on atmosphere, land resources (including deforestation, desertification and drought) and biodiversity/biotechnology and one on oceans, seas, coastal areas, freshwater resources, waste management and trade – were established at the first PrepComm. The third, on legal and institutional issues, was established at the second substantive Prep-Comm. The three main working groups often broke into smaller groups (see Halpern, 1992) known in UN-speak as the 'formals' (those meetings at which delegations could make official statements and which were open to NGOs), the 'formal-informals' (informal meetings, often open to NGOs, with proceedings translated but not transcribed) and the 'informal-informals' (small meetings, often conducted in English and open only to government representatives). It was at these latter meetings that final compromise decisions were often made. Some of the smaller delegations were cautious about this process, because of the difficulties of attending many simultaneous meetings. Environmental NGOs, who were typically excluded from the informal-informals, were also concerned at a lack of transparency.

The early PrepComms drew up an agenda and negotiating proce-dures and sought to identify issues of dispute and difference, but they made little real progress on the substantive agreements to be presented to the Conference. Negotiations began in earnest at Prep-Comm III but the bulk of the negotiation did not begin until the fourth and final PrepComm in New York – the five-week 'New York Marathon' where agreement was finally reached on a declaration of principles and about 85 per cent of the programme of action that would be presented to the Conference. Halpern suggests that much of the work was completed during the last days before the session closed at 5.10 a.m. on 4 April. The draft declaration of principles was only agreed to at 3.30 a.m. on that morning and only, she suggests, after Tommy Koh had three days earlier ordered delegates to select a new panel of negotiators and to compile a new working draft (see Halpern, 1992).

The Conference was held in Rio de Janiero in Brazil from 3 to 14 June 1992, following two days of procedural consultations (including the election of the 39 conference Vice-Presidents!). There were 178 national delegations and over 1400 officially accredited NGOs. There was a strong media presence although the exact number of journalists may never be known. Haas, Levy and Parson (1992, p. 7) say there were 8000; Halpern says there were 'tens of thousands' (1992). At the same time but almost 40 kms away at Flamengo Park over 30 000 people attended the parallel NGO conference – the Global Forum.

The work of the conference proceeded in two main bodies – the Plenary (the forum for so-called general debate, mainly country statements) and the Main Committee. It was in the Main Committee (and its subsidiary groups) where substantive negotiations took place. The final two days of the Conference were set aside for the summit of heads of government and state with over 100 such leaders in attendance. The Conference agreements – the Rio Declaration, Agenda 21 and the Statement of Forest Principles – were formally adopted in those final two days and two separately negotiated conventions – that is, the *UN Framework Convention on Climate Change* (UNFCCC) and the *Convention on Biological Diversity* (CBD) – were opened for signature. The UNCED reports were submitted to the 47th session of the General Assembly at the end of 1992. The General Assembly endorsed the Rio Declaration, Agenda 21 and the Statement on Forests, established a standing agenda item on implementation of decisions and recommendations of the UNCED and decided to convene, not later than 1997, a special session for the purposes of an overall review of Agenda 21.

Maurice Strong had envisaged the main task of the Conference as moving 'environmental issues into the centre of economic policy and decision-making' (Strong, 1991, p. 290). It would, he said, focus largely on the 'changes that must be made in economic behaviour to ensure global environmental security' (1991, p. 293). The conference, he hoped, would also 'establish the basis for the new dimensions of international cooperation that will be required to ensure "our common future"' (Strong, 1991, p. 297) a task to be achieved through the elaboration of principles, the development of a programme for action and the strengthening of environmental governance. Many of the outcomes of the Rio Conference, and the extent to which they met Strong's expectations, are discussed in more detail in later chapters. The Statement on Forests along with the Climate Convention and the Convention on Biological Diversity are discussed in Chapter 3. The Commission on Sustainable Development, the major institutional outcome of Agenda 21, is examined in Chapter 4. The Global Environment Facility, whose role as the major financial mechanism for environmental assistance to developing countries was strengthened by UNCED, a move initially resisted by developing countries, greeted with caution by many and outright criticism by others, is explored further in Chapter 8. Given this, the discussion here focuses on the Rio Declaration and Agenda 21.

The Rio Declaration on Environment and Development

The Rio Declaration – 27 principles to guide governments in their pursuit of sustainable development – was eventually adopted in the same form as it came from the Preparatory Committee. The Declaration was initially envisaged as an Earth Charter, but developing country concern that such a document would favour environmental rather than developmental concerns resulted in a watering down of initial proposals. Commentators suggest that there were difficulties in reaching agreement on a 'broader, more philosophical approach' (Fletcher, 1992, p. 2).

The Declaration's stated goal is the establishment of 'a new and equitable global partnership through the creation of new levels of cooperation among States, key sectors of societies and people' (UNCED, 1992a). Principle 1 establishes 'human beings' at the centre of concerns for sustainable development, rather than elaborating a prior and fundamental concern for protection of the planetary ecosystem. The second principle reasserts principle 21 of the Stockholm Declaration, elaborating states' sovereign rights over resources as well as recalling their transboundary responsibilities. The political and economic concerns of developing countries informed several of the principles. The right to development (controversial in human rights debates) is asserted in principle 3. Principle 5 emphasises the importance of eradicating poverty, principle 6 requires that the special needs of developing countries should be given priority and principle 7 reinforces the common but differentiated responsibilities of developed and developing countries. Principle 8 calls for a reduction in, and elimination of, unsustainable patterns of production and consumption as well as the promotion of 'appropriate demographic policies', a rather oblique and finessed response to debates over population growth.

The Declaration is more inclusive than its predecessor at Stockholm. Individuals are to have access to information; public awareness and participation is to be encouraged (principle 10). Women, youth and indigenous communities are recognised as important participants in the pursuit of sustainable development. Principle 23, the subject of some controversy, calls for the environment of people under oppression, domination and occupation to be protected, an injunction that Israel resisted as an intrusion into Middle Eastern politics. It was accepted in the Rio Declaration on the understanding that the wording would not be used in Agenda 21. Principle 12 calls for the further promotion of a 'supportive and open international economic system'. The Declaration reasserts the precautionary principle (principle 15), arguing that 'lack of full scientific certainty shall not be used as a reason for postponing cost effective measures' and the polluter pays principle (in principle 16) which encourages the full internalisation of environmental costs. The Declaration also draws attention, in principle 24, to warfare as inherently destructive of sustainable development and notes that 'peace, development and environmental protection are interdependent and indivisible' (principle 25). In a final flourish, states are to solve their environmental disputes peacefully (principle 26) and states and peoples are to cooperate in good faith and a spirit of partnership in fulfilling the principles in the Declaration (principle 27).

Assessments of the Rio Declaration focus on whether it really provides a set of principles to shape international action on environment and development, to forge a global partnership and to provide the basis for a global ethic of sustainable development. It is unclear whether the Declaration elaborates anything new, or whether it simply collates and codifies existing principles and statements. In general, assessments have not been favourable, suggesting that

governments and peoples cannot look to the Declaration for guidance and inspiration. Parson and his colleagues are rather muted in
their criticism, suggesting only that the Declaration is 'less inspiring
and coherent than originally proposed' (1992, p. 12). Davison and
Barns, on the other hand, argue that it 'fails to provide the kind of
framework needed to deal with global environmental problems'
(1992, p. 6). Johan Holmberg, from the Institute of Environment
and Development, suggests that the document was heavily compro-
mised during negotiations (1992b, p. 4) and Ileana Porras, who was
an adviser to the Costa Rican government during the conference,
argues that rather than integrating environment and development,
the Rio Declaration is driven by development concerns. She characterises the agreement as a 'text of uneasy compromises, delicately
balanced interests and dimly discernible contradictions' (Porras,
1993, p. 23). Rowlands (1992, p. 214) suggests that the failure of
the Declaration to integrate environment and development is sugges-
tive of a broader failure of the UNCED process.

These observations expose two concerns which are explored in later
chapters. First, the Declaration and its principles are shaped by and
reinforce the imperatives of state sovereignty rather than global
stewardship. Second, the Declaration illuminates the difficulties of
reconciling environment and development concerns in the concept of
sustainable development, a concept which is nowhere defined in the
agreement.

Agenda 21

Agenda 21 (UNCED, 1992b) is, like the Rio Declaration, a non-
binding agreement. It sets out a detailed plan of action for implementing the principles of the Declaration and for achieving sustainable development. It has 40 chapters – grouped together in a
preamble (chapter 1) and four sections – and is about 800 pages
long. The description here, therefore, can only touch on the major
themes. Each chapter adopts the same format – identification and
elaboration of the issue, a description of the proposed programme
and a cost estimate. Section one of the Agenda, on social and
economic dimensions, includes chapters on combating poverty, changing consumption patterns, managing demographic dynamics, human
health and human settlements. The second section is the environmental issues section. Under the broad heading 'Conservation and
Management of Resources for Development' this section contains

chapters on atmosphere, land resources, deforestation, desertification and drought, sustainable agriculture and rural development, biodiversity, biotechnology, oceans, freshwater resources and various aspects of waste management. Section three (chapters 23–32) focuses on strengthening the role of what are called the major groups – women, children and youth, indigenous peoples, NGOs, local authorities, trade unions, business and industry, science and technology, and farmers. The final section – means of implementation – covers financial resources and mechanisms, technology transfer, institutional arrangements and legal instruments as well as less contentious chapters on science, education and capacity building.

Fifteen per cent of Agenda 21 went to the Conference bracketed (that is, without consensus). Each of those chapters on which agreement had not yet been reached – atmospheric protection, high seas fisheries, biotechnology safety concerns, technology transfer, institutional arrangements, poverty and consumption and financial resources – was dealt with by one of eight contact groups. The Main Committee ran out of its allotted time at 6.00 a.m. on Thursday 11 June and disputes on the content of three chapters – forests, finance and atmosphere – still had not been resolved. Final consensus was reached only after discussion at ministerial level.

The final wording of the preamble (chapter 1) includes several ingenious compromises. As a result of extensive bargaining, references to the 'particular circumstances facing the economies in transition' (the EITs) were retained but all other references to the EITs in the Agenda were removed in response to developing country concerns that too extensive a recognition of the former Soviet bloc countries could jeopardise their own development needs. All references to 'peoples under occupation' which, as noted above, were seen by Israel as interference in Middle East politics, were removed from the Agenda as a trade-off for them remaining in the Declaration: the preamble states only that Agenda 21 is to be carried out in full respect of all principles in the Declaration. All of chapter 9, on atmospheric issues, had been bracketed at the final plenary of PrepComm IV by the Yemeni delegation (acting on behalf of the Arab Group) concerned about what they perceived as an over-emphasis on energy efficiency and a general antipathy to fossil-fuels. Differences revolved around commitments to renewable energy resources (resisted by the Saudi delegation) and references to 'environmentally safe and sound energy systems', which some took to embody an anti-nuclear bias. The solution was to include a footnote statement in the preamble that all references in the Agenda to environmentally sound energy sources, systems, supplies and technologies should be read to mean 'environmentally safe and sound' (see UNCED, 1992b). The Saudi delegation, which had wanted the whole of chapter 9 removed, entered a formal reservation to the chapter because of its references to renewable energy, although this reservation has little practical significance given the non-binding nature of the Agenda.

Chapter 33, which deals with financial resources and mechanisms, also incorporates some careful diplomatic compromises. Donor governments 'reaffirm' their commitment to the United Nations official development assistance target of 0.7 per cent of donor country Gross National Product (GNP), a reaffirmation that means little in the absence of any real deadlines (although there had been an attempt to set 2000 as the target year). Few countries had met this target and others, such as the United States, had never accepted it. There was no agreement on the forthcoming replenishment of the International Development Agency of the World Bank – although the idea of an 'Earth increment' had been proposed by Lewis Preston, President of the Bank in his address to plenary – and there was no consensus on any increased funding for the Global Environment Facility (GEF) although chapter 33 does acknowledge developing country demands for the GEF to be restructured to make it more democratic and transparent.

A number of other difficult issues were finessed through diplomatic language, or diverted to other fora. Such was the case with the problem of straddling and migratory fish stocks (those which move between territorial waters and high seas). In the absence of any agreement on how to balance sovereign rights with high seas freedoms, the issue was referred to a separate UN conference. No specific commitments could be reached on technology transfer – chapter 34 simply suggests that such access should be 'promoted, facilitated and financed as appropriate' (UNCED, 1992b, para. 34.11). The environmental impact of military establishments proved a sticking point for chapter 20 on hazardous wastes. The United States claimed national security interests and the chapter requires governments only to ensure that militaries should conform to national norms on the treatment and disposal of hazardous waste (see Parson *et al.*, 1992, p. 15).

For some, Agenda 21 made a substantial contribution to the pursuit of sustainable development. In his closing address (reproduced in Johnson, 1993, p. 522), Maurice Strong said that although Agenda 21 had been weakened by compromise and negotiation, it was still the most comprehensive programme of action on environmental concerns ever sanctioned by the international community. Haas *et al.* suggest that it 'reflects a far more sophisticated appreciation of the ecological links that must be addressed to achieve sustainable development than did the Stockholm Action Plan' (1992, p. 32). Others are more cautious. Susskind suggests that it is flawed as an agenda for action because 'it contains no priorities of any kind' (1994, p. 41). Holmberg characterises Agenda 21 as an agreement which 'contains many useful ideas but [ones which] must be further elaborated and disaggregated to the country level to have much practical meaning' expressing concern that it remains largely unfinanced (1992b, p. 4). Still others argue that the Agenda is too mired in existing power structures and paradigms to provide any useful framework for action.

Conclusion

Not surprisingly, given the differences of opinion on the Declaration and Agenda 21, judgements of the Rio Conference itself are mixed. Haas *et al.* argue that UNCED has laid a strong foundation for continuing commitment and momentum on environmental issues (1992, p. 32). Holmberg argues that it would be wrong to judge this huge conference only in the light of its short-term achievements, or lack thereof. It was, he suggests, a 'momentous exercise in awareness-raising at the highest political level' and should be judged not 'by its immediate outcomes but by the processes it set in motion' (1992b, p. 4). He argues that while the conference result falls well short of stated intentions, it is doubtful if those intentions could ever be met. Andrey Vavilov, who was head of external relations for the Conference, takes a similar view. 'Miracles', he suggested, would 'not be achieved in Rio. Nor should they be expected' (1992, p. 118).

Others, however, are less persuaded by this emphasis on progress and process as a measure of success, concerned instead at the extent to which the conference advanced global environmental protection. Sir Crispin Tickell, a former British ambassador to the United Nations, has diplomatically called the Rio Conference an 'interesting mix of some success and *much failure*' (1993a, p. 80; emphasis added). Alberto Szekely, a member of the International Law Commission, argues that the 'appalling poverty of the legal achievements of the Rio Conference provides very little scope for optimism' (1994, p. 66).

Governments have been criticised for failing to meet either of Rio's twin goals of elaborating a firm basis for defining and achieving sustainable development, and of halting and reversing global environmental degradation. There are, Koy Thomson argues, 'no leaps towards a sustainable future' (1992, p. 4). Even Maurice Strong in his closing address pointed out that commitments on funding, technology transfer and elimination of poverty had been insufficient (in Johnson, 1993, pp. 522–3).

Many of the issues that were unresolved at Rio had been on the agenda of Stockholm 20 years earlier, and went unresolved there as well. While the agenda of environmental problems expanded in the 'in-between' years, it is not clear that the political will to meet those concerns had kept pace. Indeed it is fair to suggest that it had not.

2

The Transboundary Agenda: Conservation and Pollution

Introduction

Transboundary conservation and pollution issues have been fundamental to the globalising environmental agenda, sparking international concern about conservation of species, protection of living resources and management of pollution. Wildlife protection takes on a transboundary dimension when wildlife either crosses or is transported across state borders and national jurisdictions, and it is international to the extent that concern is shared among countries or that collective action is deemed necessary in the management and protection of endangered wildlife. Conservation of living resources – marine living resources in the case explored here – is both transboundary and international in that neither fish stocks nor the sources of depletion confine themselves to any one national jurisdiction, thus requiring international cooperation if those stocks are to be managed sustainably. Pollution becomes transboundary through the dispersal of pollutants from one state to another through air or ocean currents, or through pollution displacement, that is the deliberate transportation of pollutants from one country to another, or to areas beyond national jurisdiction.

Transboundary environmental problems have been met with demands for multilateral cooperation. However, as Gündling (1991, p. 99) points out, an obligation to negotiate does not mean that the negotiations will produce results. While the environmental issues explored here are selective they demonstrate a number of features which have come to characterise the international and then global politics of the environment and which are relevant to the main themes of this book. They point to the difficulties of securing effective environmental protection in a decentralised world of sovereign states when agreements are sparse on enforcement and compliance mechanisms, engendering a reliance on what Soroos calls 'good faith efforts' (1986, p. 314). They reveal the gap between commitments on paper and the political and financial commitments required to ensure the effective implementation of those agreements. They also show how transboundary environmental problems, and the search for solutions to those problems, are embedded in the global political economy and, in particular, the relationship between the industrialised countries of the North and the poorer countries of the South. The agreements discussed in this chapter have all been criticised for their vague language, their limited response to the problems they were intended to address and for their permissive approach to environmental management. Responses have been sectoral, ad hoc, often not well-coordinated and driven by political and economic interests as much as by environmental ones. The 'better than no agreement at all' syndrome has often prevailed: the very fact that an agreement exists has been claimed as some measure of success. Yet in spite of this, and in spite of often poor environmental achievement, there has also been a slow development of new concepts and ideas in international environmental law and management, ideas such as that of critical loads or prior informed consent (PIC), and a slow move (in some but not all cases) from regulation to prevention.

Protecting Wildlife and Conserving Living Resources

The protection of wildlife and the conservation of living resources have invoked two distinct and often competing approaches to non-human species and to individual creatures. Preservationist concerns focus on the inherent value and 'right to life' of non-human species. The extinction or endangering of individual species by humans, with a particular but not exclusive emphasis on terrestrial and marine mammals and some bird species, is therefore understood as a denial of that right to life and also as a loss for humanity. This runs counter to the 'resource conservation' ethos, where the primary imperative for action is to maintain the economic viability of a species especially those which have a food or other commodity value for humans.

Protecting Wildlife

Individual species may be endangered to the point of extinction through a range of direct and indirect economic pressures, including exploitation for commercial gain or for food, or as the unintended consequences of changes in and sometimes destruction of habitats through altered land use or use of water resources. The loss in individual species numbers has, in some instances, been substantial. Barbier reports that in the 1980s, elephant numbers in Africa halved from 1.2 million to just over 600 000 (1995, p. 3) although in some countries, according to UNEP figures, up to 90 per cent of the populations have been lost (UNEP 1994d, p. 1). Tiger numbers in the 14 tiger range countries (that is those states in which the species is found) are now estimated to be no more than something between 4600 and 7700 (UNEP, 1994a) and three of the original eight sub-species are believed to be extinct (UNEP, 1994b, p. 2). Rhinoceros numbers in Africa have been depleted by 97 per cent in the last 35 years (UNEP, 1994d, p. 1). Chimpanzee numbers in Western Africa had, by the early 1990s, declined from a peak population of over one million to about one-tenth of that number and the number of wild mountain gorillas was estimated at no more than 350 (Karno, 1991, p. 990).

As Miller points out, the 'conservation of living resources [sic] has been a global endeavour at least since the First International Congress for Landscape Protection held in Paris in 1909' (1983, p. 243). Much of that effort has focused on the *in-situ* conservation and protection of species and habitats under individual state jurisdiction. International cooperation, monitoring and information exchange has proceeded under the auspices of institutions such as the International Union for the Conservation of Nature and Natural Resources (IUCN), that organisation's Commission on National Parks and Protected Areas (CNPPA) and the United Nations Environment Programme (UNEP). Non-governmental organisations, such as the WorldWide Fund for Nature (WWF), the Sierra Club, the Audubon Society and the US-based Nature Conservancy, have been active contributors to scientific monitoring programmes and to policy-making. Regional and international agreements have focused on the protection of habitats or important ecosystems through the designation of biosphere reserves (under UNESCO's 1970 *Man [sic] and the Biosphere* programme), national parks or world heritage sites under the 1972 *Convention Concerning the Protection of the World Cultural and Natural Heritage* (the World Heritage Convention), or in support of the IUCN's *World Conservation Strategy*. The rationale for much of this activity was, as the World Conservation Strategy put it, conservation in the interests of 'human use of the biosphere and of the ecosystems and species that compose it, so that they may yield the greatest sustainable benefit to present generations while maintaining their potential to meet the needs and aspirations of future generations' (cited in Miller, 1983, p. 250).

Recent international action to save species from extinction has focused on coordination of expertise and resources. In March 1994, for example, 12 of the 14 tiger range states met to establish a global tiger forum. In the same month, nine countries in eastern and southern Africa began negotiations to establish an African wildlife task force to support cooperative enforcement operations directed at illegal trade in wild fauna and flora. The agreement was initiated by African wildlife officers in an attempt to overcome the difficulties of uncoordinated national attempts to halt poaching and smuggling of endangered species. Negotiations culminated in the adoption of the Lusaka Agreement in September 1994 (see UNEP, 1994g).

While international effort has focused primarily on support for action on the protection of species, habitat and ecological processes *within* national jurisdictions, there have also been attempts to manage the transboundary aspects of species protection. The transboundary imperatives for protection of individual species arise, first, because of the migratory patterns of birds and animals (and those who hunt them) and, second, because of the cross-border trade in such species. There are also potential transboundary aspects to the destruction of crucial habitat but those issues are not explored here. On the first issue, the *Convention on the Conservation of Migratory Species of Wild Animals* (the Bonn Convention) was adopted in 1979 to provide protection for endangered migratory species. Species listed in Appendix I of that agreement are to be given strict protection. Species listed in Appendix II are to be the subject of further multilateral agreements. Although the Convention came into effect in 1983 progress has been 'disappointingly slow' (Bowman, 1991, p. 137).

It has been the second issue, the trade in endangered species, which has attracted most international attention. Both live creatures and their products (fur, ivory, organs) are traded. The economic value of legal trade in wildlife is estimated at somewhere between $US5 billion and $US17 billion a year (Favre, 1993, p. 887). The value and extent of illegal trade is even more difficult to determine but estimates from US government agencies suggest a figure of $US100 million in illegal plant and animal trade into the US alone (cited in Favre, 1993, p. 888). Other sources suggest that this represents only the value of illegal goods actually seized upon entry into the US each year (Karno, 1991, p. 999) which suggests that the real amount may be much higher. Interpol estimates that illegal trade is worth $US5 billion annually (Anon., 1994p, p. 307). The wildlife trade endangers species not only by the taking of individual animals or birds but also (especially if poaching or smuggling is involved) because the death of infants or mothers or disruption to breeding ensures an incidental death rate greater than the numbers of animals traded or smuggled (see, for example, Karno, 1991, pp. 991–2 on the taking of chimpanzees or Barbier, 1995, pp. 4–6 on elephants).

Convention on International Trade in Endangered Species (CITES)

CITES was adopted in March 1972 and came into effect in July 1975. Those species, including plant species, which are to be protected through trade regulations and restrictions are listed in appendixes to the Convention. Appendix I species are those which are determined to be vulnerable to or endangered by existing or potential trade. Commercial trade in these species is prohibited and any non-commercial transaction requires permits from both importing and exporting countries. The species listed under Appendix II are those which *might* become threatened because of large volumes of trade: any cross-border movement requires only a permit from the exporting country. Appendix II also covers species for whom it is difficult to distinguish between an endangered and non-endangered sub-species so as to prevent a rare or endangered animal being passed off as a more common member of the species. Appendix III species are those which are protected in the sponsoring country and where international cooperation is of assistance in maintaining this protection through, in this case, requiring importing countries to obtain an export permit. The guidelines for species listing or delisting were updated in 1994. Parties are required to establish supporting national legislation, which may be more stringent than the Convention, and to designate management and scientific authorities responsible for implementation and permit procedures. However, the Convention contains no provisions for sanctions in the case of non-compliance. Penalties for smuggling or contravention of the agreement is the province of individual governments. Parties may also enter reservations to listings which absolve them of compliance with restrictions.

Scientific specimens, specimens collected before the Convention came into force and those taken as personal effects (including trophies) are exempted from the provisions. Article VII(4) also allows limited trade in Appendix I species if they have been bred in captivity.

The adequacy of CITES' contribution to wildlife conservation and the protection of endangered species is under scrutiny in two ways. The first has to do with commitment to and compliance with the agreement. The second questions whether trade bans are an appropriate tool for species protection. On the first, there has been little commitment from industrialised countries to providing financial assistance to the range states of listed species to assist them to manage either habitats or their general obligations under the Convention. Parties have been slow to adopt national implementing legislation. A 1994 survey revealed that fewer than 20 per cent of the Parties had fully adequate law in support of the Convention (see Anon., 1995d, p. 89). National reporting to CITES has been lax with suggestions that up to 45 per cent of all CITES transactions go unreported (see Karno, 1991, p. 1004). CITES provisions have been circumvented through smuggling and re-exporting from non-parties and through misrepresentation of animals as bred in captivity. Circumvention has also arisen because of loopholes which allow trade either for non-commercial purposes or in cases where it is determined that trade will not be detrimental to the survival of the species, a determination that is difficult to make and which can be open to abuse. Karno argues that circumvention is 'rampant among both members and non-members' (1991, p. 1000). On the second point, that of the utility of trade bans, Appendix I listings and restrictions on trade are seen as 'too little, too late' responses to the problem of species protection on the one hand, and as potentially counterproductive and an incentive to illegal trade and increased poaching on the other. CITES does not, for example, provide for restrictions on trade in species which might be endangered for non-trade-related reasons. Under the agreement, a species cannot be listed until it can be shown that it is vulnerable to, or likely to be endangered by trade.

These debates came to a head over the protection of the African elephant. The ban on ivory trade, enacted in 1989 through the relisting of the African elephant from Appendix II to Appendix I status, has been controversial and the extent to which it enhances or undermines elephant conservation efforts has been seriously questioned. The widely held view is that CITES has failed to save the elephant but differences arise on whether this is because the agreement has been poorly implemented or because the basic approach is flawed. Wilder points out that continued trade in ivory, and therefore continued pressure on elephant numbers, has been possible through circumvention of the CITES provisions and the ineffectiveness of the Ivory Export Quota System (1995, pp. 63, 66–7). Others, such as Barbier (1995) and Swanson (1992), question the logic of trade bans in the first place. Barbier (1995, p. 9) suggests that increases in the price of ivory, reflecting scarcity under a trade ban, could provide an incentive for illegal trade and increased poaching. Trade bans could also deny to range states potential income for conservation programmes from sustainably managed trade. The trade ban is also criticised for not recognising differences between those countries where elephant numbers are severely depleted and those, such as South Africa, where populations are healthy but where selective culling may be required to keep numbers within the range that can be supported by the habitat.

There has been increasing pressure for some form of controlled wildlife utilisation in developing countries as a means to generate income for further conservation efforts and to undermine illegal trade. A key group of elephant range states, including Zimbabwe, Botswana, Malawi and Namibia, have sought either a resumption in non-ivory elephant products or a transfer of their elephant populations to Appendix II status. At the 1994 CITES meeting, South Africa tabled (and then withdrew) a proposal to resume trade in sustainably-culled non-ivory elephant products in order to generate further income for conservation activities. Swanson (1992) and Barbier (1995) argue in favour of such a sustainable use principle which, they suggest, *is* compatible with the provisions and purpose of CITES. CITES resolutions now accommodate ranching proposals, which allow for the downlisting of particular species in selected countries for sustainable resource management, and the establishment of species quotas which set strict limits for the taking of a named species to be distributed among range states. The ranching strategy was adopted, for example, for the Zimbabwean population of the Nile crocodile and a species quota approach has been applied to a number of species including the African leopard and four crocodile species (see Swanson, 1992, p. 61; see also Wilder, 1995, pp. 61–2, 69) on quotas for leopard skins and for crocodiles). These innovations have, however, been subject to problems because of the difficulties of elaborating effective control structures within producer states (Swanson, 1992, p. 61).

These debates have also been characterised by tensions between range states and non-range states over the listing of species and what are sometimes perceived to be attempts by industrialised countries to impose Northern environmental concerns on developing countries. On the issue of elephants, for example, range states have attempted, thus far unsuccessfully, to have the listing process changed to give them an effective veto. However the main issue which bedevils this debate is whether the '*economic* value of wildlife, as realised through international trade [should be] fostered and encouraged through the CITES process in order to realise the goal of protection and recovery of listed species' (Favre, 1993, p. 883; emphasis added). In other words, can the killing of wildlife, under a sustainable-use regime, be compatible with the imperatives of protecting that same wildlife?

Conserving or Protecting Ocean 'Resources'

This tension between protecting wildlife and conserving resources has also shaped debates over protection of the oceans, which cover about 70 per cent of this planet we call Earth. Daniel Sitarz argues that 'the world's oceans are in trouble – serious and potentially catastrophic trouble' (1994, p. 144). The fisheries are being overfished and marine mammals are, in many cases, severely threatened. Pollution of the oceans threatens marine and coastal ecosystems and may undermine the contribution the oceans make to the planetary ecosystem.

Marine mammals continue to suffer decline in numbers although there have been some recoveries in individual species numbers. Threats to marine mammals such as whales and seals come from direct hunting activities as well as from the indirect effects of disruption to the marine food chain. Seal populations off the coast of Namibia, for example, collapsed when their food supply was depleted by overfishing (Brown *et al.*, 1993, p. 111). Other marine mammals, such as dolphins, have not necessarily been threatened in terms of overall numbers but their deaths as bycatch to commercial fishing operations have attracted public concern. As Weber (1994, p. 51) points out, many endangered marine species are now subject to conservation agreements and national laws. Yet again there are tensions between the imperatives of protecting wildlife and the counter-claims of the economic imperatives of continued exploitation, perhaps no more so evident than in the debates over protection of whales. The 1946 *International Convention for the Regulation of Whaling*, which established the International Whaling Commission

(IWC), was initially intended as a management regime for a severely depleted resource, although Reader (1993, p. 82) suggests that the Convention had the opposite effect and that more whales were taken *after* the entry into force of the agreement than when whaling was unrestricted. In the 1970s wildlife conservation efforts, mobilised by non-governmental organisations and non-whaling countries, became the dominant theme at the IWC and, in 1982, the Commission adopted a moratorium on whaling (with exceptions only for taking whales for scientific purposes) to come into effect at the end of 1985. The moratorium was upheld in 1993, and in 1994 the IWC established a whaling sanctuary in the waters of the Southern Ocean and Antarctica.

The moratorium has been strongly opposed by whaling countries – Iceland, Norway and Japan – who argue not only that the whaling industry is of economic importance (and, in some cases, that whale meat is culturally significant) but also that for some species, such as the minke whale, sustainable harvesting is possible. All three have continued to take whales under the scientific purposes provisions and all three have either entered formal objections to the moratorium provisions or have proposed to recommence commercial whaling outside the provisions of the IWC. The IWC contains no formal sanctions and has therefore come to rely on publicity from NGOs and general public and international outcry to keep whaling nations in line.

Depletion of fish stocks has generated far less public concern than the taking of marine mammals although it is an equally serious problem. The world's fish catch is no longer increasing and the Food and Agricultural Organisation (FAO) estimates that all major fish stocks are at their limits (cited in Weber, 1994, pp. 41, 52). Of the 9000 or so species which are harvested, only about 20 support major commercial fisheries (Sitarz, 1994, p. 154) and they are therefore vulnerable to overfishing which has increased with development of sophisticated detection and catch technology. The loss is not only a commercial one: as well as the flow-on effect for the robustness of the marine food chain and therefore marine ecosystems, fish accounts for about 16 per cent of the world's total protein consumption (Sitarz, 1994, p. 154) a dependence that is even higher in the developing world.

As Wilder points out, the 'development of principles for the conservation of international fisheries has been slow' (1995, p. 76). There are now a number of regional fisheries commissions but attempts to establish a global and comprehensive agreement on fisheries management have been constrained, not so much by differences over wildlife versus resource values as by political differences between coastal states seeking to exercise sovereign rights over coastal waters and maritime states which maintain long-distance fishing fleets. The establishment of Exclusive Economic Zones (EEZ) under the provisions of the 1982 *UN Convention on the Law of the Sea* (UNCLOS) (which finally came into effect in November 1994) extends to 200 nautical miles the maritime zones over which coastal states have national jurisdiction and sovereign rights to resources. This has further complicated the transboundary aspect of any negotiations on managing the living resources of the seas. Much of the world's commercial fish harvest is taken in coastal waters and EEZs. Only about 5 per cent comes from the high seas. Yet managing fish resources requires international cooperation to regulate long-distance fishing fleets which fish outside their own territorial waters, and to regulate access to highly migratory and straddling stocks which move between territorial waters or across the boundaries between high seas and EEZs. Although it is not discussed in any detail here, debates over fisheries management have also focused on appropriate regulatory strategies. There have been several issues of dispute. Should international agreements attempt to control equipment and fishing techniques? Should they restrict access to fishing grounds or focus on limiting or regulating catches and, if the latter, should this be done on an individual species basis or should it take into account the ecosystem impacts of species depletion? Should restrictions adopt a total allowable catch or a distributed quota system?

Debates over high seas fishing rights and likely impacts on fisheries within EEZs (and therefore under national jurisdiction), issues which had been contentious at the UNCLOS negotiations, re-emerged at UNCED and have continued to shape debates. While Agenda 21 includes an extensive chapter on oceans and coastal management (chapter 17) it proved impossible to get agreement on the management of marine living resources especially straddling and highly migratory stocks. In a compromise move, the issue was deferred to a later international conference – the UN Conference on Straddling Fish Stocks and Highly Migratory Fish Stocks. In August 1995, after four substantive meetings during which negotiations were 'tense and at times bitter' (Anon., 1995g, p. 179), parties adopted an agreement which reaffirms the provisions of UNCLOS as the basis for conserving and managing straddling and migratory fish stocks.

Transboundary Pollution: Dispersal and Displacement

As the scope of environmental concerns expanded in the 1970s and 1980s, greater attention was paid to the transboundary aspects of pollution, as pollutants moved across state borders either through air or oceans currents, or were physically displaced through trade or dumping. Attempts to manage pollution issues have been shaped by differences between polluter states and victim states on the extent of the problem, the extent of regulation required, and the nature of implementation, compliance and verification. The pollution agreements adopted for both the atmosphere and oceans, the two issues explored here, were slow to be implemented and were often piecemeal and sectoral.

Long-Range Transboundary Air Pollution (LRTAP)

Concerns about air pollution within countries is not new. The problem of cross-border air pollution did not, however, generate a great deal of public concern until the 1960s and was not inscribed formally on the international agenda until the 1970s. It remains an issue addressed primarily by the industrialised countries. The pollutants which have been of most concern are sulphur dioxide (SO_2) and nitrogen oxide (NOx) which are released when oil and gas are burned. About two-thirds of sulphur dioxide emissions in Europe come from coal-fired power stations (Porter and Brown, 1991, p. 72) and nitrogen oxide emissions come primarily from power-plants and automobile emissions. The irony is that this transboundary aspect of air pollution is the outcome of national laws mandating an increased height in smokestacks (up to 500 feet) to facilitate the 'dispersal of pollutants that would otherwise be concentrated at dangerous levels in localised areas' (Soroos, 1986, p. 296). The term acid rain (first coined by Robert Smith, a Scottish chemist) refers to the acids formed by these oxides in chemical reaction with water vapour and sunlight, acids which are then deposited 'in precipitation or in dry form' (Levy, 1993, p. 79). Acid rain causes damage not only to buildings but also to lake, river and terrestrial ecosystems. Damage to human health from long-range air pollution is more likely to arise from the impact of what are now referred to as Volatile Organic Compounds (VOCs). VOCs, along with nitrogen oxides, are precursors of ground-level (tropospheric) ozone which is damaging to human and plant health, in contrast with its crucial protective role in the stratosphere. Levy observes that scientific evidence now accepts that ground-level ozone 'is just as harmful to forests and agricultural crops' as are sulphur emissions (1993, p. 94). Halting acid rain and its effects requires reductions in source emissions: the problem with transboundary fluxes is that the source emissions are in one country and the impact in another. Thus some form of multilateral cooperation is necessary.

The Scandinavian countries were the first to express concern about the detrimental environmental impacts of long-range air pollution. In the late 1960s a Swedish scientist, Svante Oden, claimed that an increasing acidification of precipitation (acid rain) was damaging the lakes and fisheries of Scandinavian countries. The source of the pollutants, he claimed, was industrial sulphur emissions in the United Kingdom and Central Europe, a charged denied by the UK and the Federal Republic of Germany which argued that there was no evidence that pollutants of this kind could be dispersed over such distances. A Swedish government report on the acid rain issue tabled at the Stockholm Conference was given little attention at the time. However Sweden and Norway were able to pressure the Organisation for Economic Cooperation and Development (OECD) to inaugurate a programme in 1972 to identify and measure long-range air pollution. The results, which were published in 1977, provided confirmation of the long-range dispersal of pollutants. By the 1980s the problem was recognised as serious enough to warrant discussion on mitigation efforts. The 1982 Stockholm Conference on Acidification of the Environment concluded not only that control measures were required to prevent further deterioration of soil and water (Wettestad, 1995, p. 169) but also that 'forest ecosystems may be at risk as well' (Levy, 1993, p. 92). The data on forest death (*waldsterben*) presented at the conference suggested that as much as one million hectares of central European forest was at risk, with about 10 per cent of that already dying (Levy, 1993, p. 93). Recent figures suggest that up to three-quarters of all European forests receive damaging levels of sulphur deposition (cited in Brown *et al.*, 1993, p. 108) with consequent economic losses of $US35 billion per year (UNDP, 1996, p. 26).

Negotiations among the countries of Europe on how to manage the sources of long-range air pollution have taken place under the auspices of the United Nations Economic Commission for Europe (ECE). The major cleavage of interests in the ECE negotiations was that between net-importer and net-exporter states. The former are the victim states, those who suffer greater effects of acid deposition than might be expected given their emissions of pollutants. For example, over half of the sulphur deposits in Finland, Norway, Sweden, Austria and Switzerland are from foreign sources (Schwarzer, 1993, p. 14). The latter, conversely, are the source states, those whose emissions are dispersed and who therefore suffer less than would be commensurate with their level of emissions. While the victim states have consistently supported stringent regulations, the polluter states have favoured only minimum commitments. Negotiations in 1978 and 1979 for a convention were burdened by differences between the Nordic countries and members of the EC. Sweden, Finland and Norway, all of whom had been affected by the impact of acid rain, argued for specific targets, including a freeze on both sulphur dioxide and nitrogen oxide emissions to be followed by cuts of up to 50 per cent. They were opposed by the United States and the United Kingdom, with some support from France, Belgium and Denmark. Indeed, Schwarzer (1993, p. 16) suggests that most participating governments wanted little more than a declaratory agreement and Levy (1993, p. 84) argues that at the time only Norway and Sweden thought that acid rain was a serious problem.

Convention on Long-Range Transboundary Air Pollution

In November 1979, 35 countries, including Eastern bloc countries and the United States and Canada, adopted the *Convention on Long-Range Transboundary Air Pollution* (the Geneva Convention). The Convention recognises airborne pollutants as an environmental problem but it does little more. Parties are required only to 'endeavour' to limit and if possible reduce air pollution. The Convention emphasises exchange of information and research as the basis for further consultation on appropriate strategies. By doing so it locked the then Eastern bloc countries into the monitoring and reporting programmes established for Western Europe. The Geneva Convention was, in effect, one more compromise agreement. Porter and Brown have characterised it as a 'toothless agreement that failed to effectively regulate emissions or transboundary fluxes of acid rain' (1991, p. 72). Gündling argues that the Convention indicates that 'states tried to avoid too stringent provisions' (1991, p. 95) and Wexler notes that it had only vague commands and no substantive guidelines (1990, p. 6). The Convention did not come into effect until 1983 and Schwarzer suggests that it had little impact on practice within the polluting countries (1993, p. 16).

There were, however, subsequent attempts to negotiate reduction targets and the LRTAP regime now includes a number of pollutant-specific protocols. The 1985 Helsinki *Protocol on the Reduction of Sulphur Emissions* followed earlier unsuccessful attempts by Norway and Sweden to persuade parties to commit to reductions. It was influenced also by the 'normative pressure [placed] on reluctant states' (Levy, 1993, p. 94) by the so-called 'Thirty Percent Club', initially a group of ten countries which had pledged, at a meeting in Ottawa in 1984, to reduce their own sulphur dioxide emissions by 30 per cent. The Helsinki Protocol established reduction targets for sulphur dioxide emissions and transboundary fluxes of at least 30 per cent of 1980 levels by 1993 at the latest. Wettestad suggests that in spite of growing scientific acceptance of the nature of long-range air pollution, the choice of 1980 as a baseline and the reduction target of 30 per cent were arbitrary (1995, p. 170). The Protocol came into force in October 1985. However, three major polluters, the US, the UK and Poland, which together contribute over 30 per cent of global sulphur dioxide emissions (Porter and Brown, 1991, p. 74), did not sign the agreement.

The 1988 Sofia Protocol on nitrogen oxide emissions commits parties to a freeze on nitrogen oxide emissions at 1987 levels by 1994 allowing, in fact, for a potential *increase* in emissions in the interim. Specific targets were to be subject to further negotiation. The Eastern bloc countries were opposed to specific reduction targets. Outdated automobile technology meant there was little likelihood of meeting any targets: indeed nitrogen oxides emissions were increasing. Differences between Western European countries over reduction of car emissions was driven by the different research programmes undertaken by automobile industries in Germany and the UK (German technology favoured catalytic converters; UK industry had focused on lean burn engines). Twelve European countries adopted a declaration pledging to reduce nitrogen oxide emissions by 30 per cent by 1998. Five countries – Sweden, Switzerland, Austria, The Netherlands and, in a change of heart motivated by the increasing damage from acid rain to its forests, the Federal Republic of Germany – were prepared to commit to a 30 per cent reduction by 1995. In 1991 (the year the Helsinki Protocol finally came into effect) the parties adopted a third protocol to deal with Volatile Organic Compounds (VOCs) with varying commitments to freeze VOC emissions or reduce them by 30 per cent by 1999 (but with different baseline years) either at a national level or within designated tropospheric ozone management areas (TOMAs). In general, these reduction targets are considered to be too low (Schwarzer, 1993, p. 19).

The Helsinki Sulphur agreement was revised in June 1994. This agreement recognises differing economic and technical capacities for emission reductions and is based not on a percentage reduction but on critical loads. A critical load formula takes account of the resilience threshold of the environment in establishing an emission level (which will vary from location to location) below which no damage to the ecosystem should occur. Thus a different emissions target is calculated for each party. While the advantages of a critical loads approach are that it emphasise equity over equality, it can also be time-consuming and difficult to agree on those loads (see Gündling, 1991, p. 99). Schwarzer has suggested that the loads are exceeded in almost all parts of Europe (1993, p. 21).

The impact of these agreements has been mixed. Compliance with reporting requirements is uneven (Levy, 1993, p. 91). However almost all parties to the original sulphur protocol had achieved their 30 per cent reduction targets by 1993 and eleven had exceeded those targets (see Schwarzer, 1993, p. 19) although Levy queries whether this was in response to the protocol or other factors such as domestic health concerns or redirection of energy generating capacities away from sulphur producing processes (1993, pp. 118–27). By 1994, and the renegotiation of the Helsinki Protocol, overall sulphur emissions had been reduced by 40 per cent (Anon., 1994m, p. 231). However an increase in nitrogen oxide emissions meant that 'damage to forests, soils, inshore waters and historical monuments' continued to worsen (Schwarzer, 1993, p. 21). Brown *et al.* (1993, p. 109) suggest that even with the best technology available, an emphasis on reductions and critical loads will not solve the problem. What is required, they argue, is a major reassessment of the energy infrastructure, with a strong emphasis on conversion to renewable sources of energy production. It is doubtful whether that can be mobilised under the Geneva Convention and its protocols.

Oceans Pollution: Protecting the Commons

The pollution of the oceans was, for so long, paid little attention in international circles. The oceans were deemed to have unlimited capacity as a dumping ground and environmental impact was therefore not considered to be a problem. Accidents such as the Torrey Canyon oil spill in 1967, however, sharpened public concern about ship-based pollution of coastlines and coastal wildlife. The trans-boundary dimension of oceans pollution arises through dispersal and displacement. In the first case, pollutants are carried by ocean currents across jurisdictional boundaries both between high seas and territorial waters and across states' sea-based territorial bound-aries. About 70 per cent of marine pollution is from land-based sources which includes agricultural run-off (pesticides and ferulisers), sewage, oil and hydrocarbons, synthetic compounds and a range of heavy metals (see Sitarz, 1994, p. 145). Pollution from rivers not only damages coastal ecosystems and disrupts coastal fisheries but can extend well into the oceans. Pollution plumes from the Amazon River, for example, can extend up to 2000 kilometres from the mouth of the river (Holdgate cited in Soroos, 1986, p. 297). In the case of pollution displacement, pollutants are dumped either in the oceans or coastal regions (usually of other states) through deliberate or acci-dental discharge from ships. Something between 600 000 tons (Sitarz, 1994, p. 145) and one million tons (Mitchell, 1993, p. 189) of oil are discharged into the oceans each year from ship-based sources, although this contributes only about one-third of the oil entering the oceans (Mitchell, 1993, p. 189).

In 1972 the Stockholm Conference adopted *General Principles for Assessment and Control of Marine Pollution* as guidance for future agreements (see Thacher, 1991, p. 446). Part XII of the 1983 UN *Convention on the Law of the Sea* contains provisions 'for the protection and preservation of the marine environment . . . [includ-ing] measures to prevent the pollution of the oceans by pollutants carried through the atmosphere' (Ramakrishna, 1990, pp. 431–2). By the end of the 1980s there were over 70 multilateral agreements addressing various aspects of marine environmental protection (Wood *et al.*, 1989, p. 32) although the general view is that their success has been, at best, mixed. Weber suggests that the 'interna-tional community [has been] reluctant to call for specific global agreements or standards that would cross the traditional line of national sovereignty over coastal waters' (1994, p. 55). While both the Law of the Sea Convention and chapter 17 of Agenda 21 urge states to take action to prevent, reduce or control land-based sources of oceans pollution, 'major global treaties have largely overlooked the pressing issues of land-based sources of pollution [and] habitat destruction' (Weber, 1994, p. 54). For the most part, states were urged to comply with UNEP's 1985 non-binding *Montreal Guidelines for the Protection of the Marine Environment Against Pollution from*

Land-Based Sources and to promote (where appropriate) regional arrangements in support of UNEP's regional seas programme. Only since UNCED have governments met, under the auspices of UNEP, to draft a Programme of Action on the protection of the marine environment from land-based sources of pollution. The Programme was finally adopted in late 1995.

International agreements on ship-based sources of marine pollution date to the 1950s although negotiations have been dominated by the interests of maritime states (those with long-distance shipping capabilities) and the shipping industry. Agreements have, for the most part, adopted a regulatory approach through the use of discharge restrictions and equipment standards. The 1954 *International Convention for the Prevention of Pollution of the Sea by Oil* established restricted discharge zones, although the provisions were generally ineffective (see Mitchell, 1993, p. 202). Amendments to the Convention, which extended the restricted discharge zones and placed equipment requirements on new tankers, effectively reversed a permissive approach by prohibiting discharges except under certain conditions rather than allowing discharge except in prohibited zones (Mitchell, 1993, p. 208).

The two main agreements on the prevention of ship-based sources of marine pollution are the 1972 *Convention on the Prevention of Marine Pollution by Dumping of Wastes and Other Matters* (the London Dumping Convention, sometimes just referred to as the London Convention) and MARPOL 73/78, that is the 1973 *International Convention for the Prevention of Pollution from Ships* and its 1978 protocol. The London Dumping Convention deals with the dumping of dangerous substances at sea through a list process – a blacklist of prohibited wastes and a graylist of those substances, such as lead, arsenic and copper, for which permits are required and with which special care must be taken. The dumping of highly toxic pollutants and high-level radioactive wastes in the oceans is banned. In 1985, a two-year non-binding moratorium on the dumping of low-level radioactive waste was extended for an unlimited duration against, Lang (1991a, p. 157) suggests, the interests of the major dumping countries, France, the United Kingdom and the United States. In 1993, the parties adopted an unconditional ban on dumping of any nuclear wastes in the seas (see Moody-O'Grady, 1995, p. 700). In spite of this progressive tightening of the rules on dumping, Lang suggests that the obligations are considerably weakened by caveats which require parties only to take 'practicable steps' to prevent pollution and to take 'effective' measures only in accordance with their 'scientific, technological and economic capabilities' (1991a, p. 156). Wapner (1996, p. 23) notes that fewer than two-thirds of the parties have submitted reports on their dumping activities and Stairs and Taylor (1992, p. 122) suggest that in many respects the LDC has come to be viewed as a 'dumpers club'.

MARPOL was intended to address more general ship-based pollution, to eliminate international pollution of the marine environment and to minimise accidental discharge of pollutants from ships and tankers. It was, as Mitchell suggests, broader in scope than earlier agreements. It covered a range of maritime vessels including oil platforms as well as a wider range of controlled substances including oil, liquid chemicals, sewage, garbage and harmful packaged substances (Mitchell, 1993, p. 210). The agreement also imposed tougher equipment standards than had hitherto been the case and expanded verification and inspection procedures. It did not, however, come into effect until 1983, ten years after its adoption. In 1978, however, the parties negotiated a protocol to the original 1973 agreement which tightened equipment standards and extended the verification regime to allow for unscheduled inspections (see Mitchell, 1993, p. 215). However, there is little evidence to suggest that there is anything but a low level of compliance with the provisions on discharge standards although compliance with equipment standards is judged to be more extensive (Mitchell, 1993, pp. 218–19). As with the London Convention, the extent of compliance may be difficult to determine with accuracy because, as Wapner (1996, p. 23) points out, only 30 per cent of MARPOL signatories have ever submitted monitoring reports.

Managing Hazardous Waste

The environmental and human health problems of hazardous substances came to public attention through a number of chemical-related accidents in the 1970s and 1980s including the Seveso chemical plant explosion in Italy in 1976, the fatal Bhopal toxic gas leak in 1984, and a major chemical fire and toxic spill into the Rhine at Basel in 1986. In the late 1980s, this concern was heightened by incidents such as the journey of the *Khian Sea*, which spent over two years looking for a dumping site for its cargo of toxic incinerator ash (misleadingly labelled as fertiliser ash). The ship was turned away from the Bahamas and then asked to leave Haiti after dumping part of its cargo. The ship was finally traced to Singapore where it was empty (see Godwin, 1993, p. 196). Tests on the ash disposed of in Haiti showed high levels of cadmium, arsenic, mercury and dioxins (Howard, 1990, p. 224). This coincided with a general increase in the transboundary transportation of hazardous wastes as industrialised countries adopted stringent waste disposal regimes which 'encouraged' waste producers to seek to dispose of their waste in countries where environmental regulations were more permissive, or where the costs of doing so were lower than in the country of production.

The amount of hazardous waste generated annually is not known, but estimates are in the vicinity of some 400 million tonnes (see Rummel-Bulska, 1994, p. 13). Most of the waste, around 95 per cent, is produced by the developed world. The United States accounts for about 85 per cent of the total (although this includes diluted waste waters) (Anon., 1993c, p. 14) and the amount of hazardous waste produced in the US increased from 9 million tons in 1970 to 238 million tons in 1990 (Puckett, 1994, p. 53). While only a small proportion is exported out of producing countries, that waste includes non-nuclear industrial waste, pesticide sludge, chemical wastes, uranium mining waste and incinerator ash. The total amounts exported are difficult to determine with accuracy. The US Environment Protection Agency points out, for example, that perhaps only one-eighth of waste exported from the United States alone is actually reported (Biggs, 1994, p. 335).

While not all hazardous waste movement is between industrialised and developing countries, it is that movement which has attracted most attention. The amounts which are transported to developing countries are difficult to ascertain. UNEP estimates that as much as 20 per cent of hazardous waste trade goes to developing countries (cited in Murphy, 1994, p. 30) although generally the US exports less of its waste than do European countries (Kiss, 1991, p. 522). Greenpeace estimates that between 1986 and 1988 three million tonnes of such wastes was dumped in developing countries (cited in Howard, 1990, p. 225). Since the end of the Cold War, former Central and Eastern European countries have also become major hazardous waste disposal sites. Illegal waste is often transported covertly and highly sophisticated technology is required to determine the contents of waste (Nanda, 1991, p. 509). Technical facilities for safe disposal of such wastes are often minimal in developing countries. Disposal in developing countries therefore often means dumping – in used mines, on the surface or in poorly managed landfills where seepage into soils and waterways is not uncommon. The environmental and human impacts can be disastrous for local communities and the costs of cleanup high. Contamination of the food chain, increases in cancers and birth defects and shortened life spans are some of the possible consequences.

For exporters of waste, the lower costs of disposal and less stringent environmental regulations in developing countries can often be an attractive reason for transporting waste. In 1991, then chief economist for the World Bank, Lawrence Summers, argued that 'the economic logic behind dumping a load of toxic waste in the lowest wage country is impeccable . . . underpopulated countries such as Africa [sic] are vastly under-polluted' (cited in Puckett, 1994, p. 53). Developing countries can be also attracted by the revenue involved. For example, Puckett (1994, p. 53) suggests that the government of Guinea-Bissau agreed to accept over 15 millions tons of toxic waste for payment of $US600 million, an amount four times its annual Gross National Product. The figures are difficult to confirm. George Ndi (1993) also provides information on toxic waste shipments of industrial and pharmaceutical waste to Guinea-Bissau from the UK, USA and Switzerland, a total amount of 15 million tons over five years. He suggests this included 10 million drums of waste from a UK firm which had obtained a 10-year disposal licence in return for a payment of $1.6 million (Ndi, 1993, p. 27). Godwin (1993, p. 196), however, confirms the figure of $600 million (citing it as twice Guinea-Bissau's foreign debt and 35 times the value of its annual exports).

Until the late 1980s, the movement of hazardous wastes was managed primarily through national or regional legislative initiatives such as the 1984 *Hazardous and Solid Waste Amendments* to the US *Resource Conservation and Recovery Act* and the EC *Directive on the Transfrontier Shipment of Hazardous Waste* adopted in the same year (see Nanda, 1991, p. 507). OECD recommendations on the transfrontier movement of hazardous wastes, adopted in 1984 and 1986, were a precursor to UNEP's 1987 *Cairo Guidelines and Principles for the Environmentally Sound Management of Hazardous Waste*. At the time the Cairo Guidelines were adopted the Executive Director of UNEP convened an Ad-Hoc Working Group to negotiate an international legal instrument on hazardous wastes.

One of the main issues addressed during negotiations was whether a regime should be regulatory or preventative, that is whether it should seek to control and regulate the movement of hazardous wastes or whether it should seek to prohibit the movement of wastes as a means of limiting waste production in the first place. A second issue was whether an agreement should provide for technical assistance, especially monitoring technology, to developing importing countries.

Convention on the Control of Transboundary Movements of Hazardous Wastes and their Disposal (the Basel Convention)

The Basel Convention was adopted by 116 countries at a Conference of Plenipotentiaries on 22 March 1989, although only 35 countries actually signed the Convention at that time. Non-signatories included members of the Organisation of African Unity (OAU) which had sought (unsuccessfully) to strengthen the Convention through amendments on liability, comparable standards and technology, and verification procedures (see Nanda, 1991, p. 510). The Convention urges that the generation and movement of hazardous waste should be minimised and that any such waste should be disposed of as close as possible to its source. While waste is defined rather broadly as substances and objects which are either disposed of, or intended or required to be disposed of (article 2(1)) the Convention also classifies wastes according to source (such as clinical wastes or wastes produced in chemical production processes), constituent parts (including arsenic, cadmium, mercury, asbestos, phenols and organohalogen compounds) and characteristics (see Kiss, 1991, p. 536). Radioactive wastes are excluded because they are the responsibility of the International Atomic Energy Agency (IAEA). Hazardous wastes dumped from ships are also excluded because they come under the provisions of the London Dumping Convention. Parties may export waste only if they do not have the facilities to dispose of the waste in an environmentally sound manner (a term which is not defined) and only if they can be certain that it will be disposed of in such a manner in the importing country. If that proves not to be possible, the exporting state is obliged to re-import the waste. Movement of hazardous wastes may not proceed unless and until the exporting state has received, in writing, the prior informed consent of the importing state and any transit states. Movement of wastes between parties and non-parties is prohibited unless it is covered by a bilateral or regional agreement. This is no less stringent than the Convention which also recognises the sovereign right of states to prohibit the import of hazardous waste. Any movement of waste which does not meet the provisions of the Convention is deemed to be illegal and parties are required to introduce legislation to prevent and punish such trade. The Convention came into effect on 5 May 1992. Neither the EC nor the United States, the two largest producers of hazardous waste, were among the parties ratifying at that time. Mostafa Tolba, then Executive Director of UNEP, characterised this as an 'unreasonably long period in which to transform strong words and good intentions into real action' adding that it was 'high time that some of these countries announce openly that they are taking steps now to ratify' (cited in Anon., 1993c, p. 14).

Developing countries have sought to strengthen the Convention, often supported by NGOs working through the International Toxic Waste Action Network (ITWAN). At the first Conference of Parties in Uruguay in December 1992, one of the most contentious issues was whether Parties should adopt a ban on the export of all hazardous wastes from OECD to non-OECD countries. Support came primarily from developing countries and some European countries (see Puckett, 1994, p. 55) although Germany and the United Kingdom remained opposed (see Godwin, 1993, p. 205). The issue was clouded because neither the United States nor the EC had completed ratification of the Convention. The compromise decision placed an effective ban on export and import of hazardous wastes for final disposal but permitted export for recycling purposes. At the 1994 meeting the parties agreed to a full ban on trade for final disposal between industrialised and developing countries (although the Convention itself was not amended to take this into account until 1995), and advocated the phasing out of trade for recycling purposes by 1997.

The Convention has been characterised as an 'effective starting point' (Howard, 1990, p. 227) containing 'many useful features in protecting human health and the environment' (Sens cited in Nanda, 1991, p. 508). For others the Convention added 'nothing new to the existing rules' with little expectation that it would 'impact seriously upon the burgeoning international hazardous waste trade' (Williams cited in Godwin, 1993, p. 203). Kiss has suggested that the Convention was only at the 'very beginning' of necessary international action and reflected a general inability of states to respond to 'rapidly changing scientific knowledge regarding hazardous wastes' (1991, p. 539).

The Convention has also been heavily criticised for its slippery language and loopholes and for legitimising 'a horrible business'

(Puckett cited in Nanda, 1991, p. 508). The Prior Informed Consent (PIC) principle has come under particular scrutiny. The principle does not, for example, take account of economic disparities between developed and developing countries whereby developing countries may have little choice but to 'consent' to receiving hazardous waste. PIC also assumes that the appropriate authority in the importing state will act in the interests of local communities where the disposal or dumping occurs, an assumption which is potentially flawed. Indeed Puckett argues that PIC can 'undermine local democracy and institute a system of decision-making that is wide open to abuse' (1994, p. 54). Under article 6(4) parties can also waive the prior consent requirement (see Nanda, 1991, p. 508). The provisions which permit export for recycling have also been contentious, not the least of which because they are open to abuse in the form of sham and dirty recycling. In the first case, waste is misleadingly labelled as recyclable when there is in fact no recuperation or reprocessing intended. In the second case, there may be a genuine recycling or further use component, but the process involves the release of highly polluting contaminants and heavy metals, dangerous to recycling workers and to the environment. Waste trading firms, in an attempt to take advantage of the recycling provisions, have been offering financial investment in power plants in places like Sierra Leone or Belize if hazardous waste will be accepted to fuel the plants (see Clapp, 1994, p. 508).

A range of subsequent agreements suggests continued dissatisfaction with the Basel Convention. In 1988, prior to the adoption of the Convention, the OAU had adopted a resolution which condemned dumping of toxic wastes in African countries and called for a ban on importing of such wastes into the continent (see Kiss, 1991, pp. 532–3). In 1991, the members of OAU, most of whom did not sign or ratify the Basel Convention because of their concerns that it was not stringent enough and would not protect them from the environmental and human impacts of hazardous waste, adopted the Bamako Convention (in full, the *Convention on the Ban on the Import into Africa and the Control of Transboundary Movement and Management of Hazardous Wastes within Africa*). This agreement banned the import of all forms of hazardous and nuclear wastes into Africa (except Morocco and South Africa), prohibited the conclusion of bilateral agreements on the import of such waste and established liability provisions. Agreements have also been adopted or are under negotiation in Central America, South America, South-East Asia (under the auspices of ASEAN) and the South Pacific (under the auspices of the

South Pacific Forum). Rosencranz and Eldridge characterise this lack of consensus as demonstrative of a 'fundamental disparity between the objectives of developed countries (along with certain multinational industries)' who 'seek to legitimise the continued generation and disposal of hazardous waste' and 'developing countries (along with environmental groups)' whose purpose is to 'reduce and ultimately eliminate the production and dumping of such waste' (1992, pp. 318–19).

It is, as yet, unclear how much the Basel Convention has done to control the movement in hazardous waste. Greenpeace, which runs a toxics campaign, has been particularly active in monitoring toxic waste shipments, legal and illegal, and providing information on the toxicity levels of waste, information often not available to the importing country. Between 1989 and 1994 they identified over 500 export proposals (338 of them identifying former Eastern bloc countries as the recipient) for an aggregate 200 million tonnes of hazardous waste movement from OECD to non-OECD countries (see Puckett, 1994, p. 54) although the amount actually exported seems to have been much smaller. Puckett suggests, nevertheless, that an average of 3700 tonnes of toxic wastes are exported to Asia every day (1994, p. 54). Rummel-Bulska (1994, p. 13) cites OECD estimates that a contingent of hazardous wastes crosses an OECD frontier every five minutes. Concern remains that the Basel Convention regulates rather than prohibits hazardous waste, in spite of its stated objective to minimise the generation of waste, and that the disparities in protective standards between developed and developing countries continue to be exploited. Rosencranz and Eldridge (1992, p. 321) argue, in effect, that this places a differential value on the environment and health of people in developed and developing countries. Problems continue in the lack of an adequate control and verification system, especially for monitoring or preventing illegal trade, and the lack of technical expertise in developing countries with limited commitment from industrialised countries to transfer either disposal or detection technology. Biggs argues that the Convention remains an 'imperfect solution to an escalating, intractable environmental problem' (1994, p. 366). It remains to be seen how many parties will actually ratify and therefore be bound by the amendment which enacts the 1997 ban on trade for recycling purposes, and whether the ban will affect the extent of hazardous waste movement from developing to non-developing countries in any significant way, or whether it will drive the trade underground.

Conclusion

Transboundary conservation and pollution issues – the Stockholm Agenda – demonstrate the difficulties of negotiating and adopting comprehensive environmental protection agreements. The process is almost always a slow one and, in the cases explored here, has almost always been reactive rather than precautionary. Implementation has relied very much on national action and the success of the strategies adopted and compliance with various agreements is at least open to dispute. Opt-out clauses, reservations and cautious language characterise these agreements. Negotiations and implementation problems point to the importance, especially for developing countries, of funding and technology and the difficulties of getting real commitments from developed countries. In spite of all this, the period following Stockholm did witness a further elaboration of principles of international environmental law, such as that of transboundary responsibility and prior informed consent. Strategies, such as the 'freeze and roll back' which was to prove central to the ozone negotiations, or the use of trade provisions, were refined. Negotiations also demonstrated the importance of scientific knowledge and 'evidence', the possible value of adopting a framework convention followed by issue-specific protocols, and the impact on environmental provisions of coalitions of states who were prepared to commit to more stringent action than that mandated by a particular agreement. These developments provided some basis for international environmental diplomacy and law when it came to addressing a range of global environmental issues. The global agenda and the agreements adopted thereon are explored in the next chapter.

3

The Emergence of a Global Agenda

The environmental problems explored in this chapter – ozone depletion, climate change, deforestation, loss of biodiversity and desertification – have all, in some way, been characterised as part of the global environmental agenda, although the way in which these problems have been understood as global differs. It is for that reason that this chapter has been divided, perhaps a little arbitrarily, into three sections. The first section deals with ozone depletion and climate change. These are problems of the global commons, in this case the atmosphere. The impacts of these particular environmental problems will be felt planet-wide, regardless of whether a country has contributed to the problem. Indeed, impacts may often be out of proportion to contribution. The second two issues, deforestation and loss of biodiversity, also have potential planet-wide or global consequences. Both demonstrate tensions over the claiming of national 'resources' as the global or common heritage of humankind as well as the connections between local causes and the workings of the world economy. The final issue, described in the third section of this chapter, is desertification. Although the causes of desertification are linked with deforestation and, potentially, climate change, its impacts are for the most part local. The 'global' nature of desertification, therefore, lies not in its impact on a global commons, nor its relevance to a common heritage but rather in a (sometimes reluctant) recognition of common concern for those countries, usually developing countries, which faced extensive land degradation.

All five of these issues have been the subject of not always successful negotiations for global agreements, that is, agreements with open membership and with a focus on managing the problem at a planetary rather than just a national or regional level. With the exception of ozone depletion, UNCED provided a focus or catalyst for those negotiations. In all cases, negotiations for a legally binding and global agreement built on a range of earlier declarations, management programmes and scientific inquiries. Political action often followed scientific concern (this is particularly so with ozone depletion and climate change) and, although it is discussed further in Chapter 5 rather than here, pressure for action from non-governmental environmental organisations. The problems and difficulties in the negotiations echo and magnify those demonstrated in Chapter 2: competing interests, the imperatives of sovereignty, compromises between substantive agreements and declaratory frameworks, resistance to targets and firm commitments, and permissive compliance and verification procedures. There was also, in the case of ozone depletion and climate change in particular, an increasing emphasis on precautionary action, even in the absence of complete scientific certainty, although there are many doubts as to whether the principle of precaution was given any real effect in the specific provisions of the agreements adopted.

The Global Commons of the Atmosphere: Ozone Depletion

Ozone depletion was the first major environmental issue with a planetary dimension to challenge the scientific and diplomatic communities. Negotiations on ozone depletion are generally regarded as the most successful example of international environmental cooperation to date and as the best model for the further development of international environmental law.

Ozone, which is made up of three atoms of oxygen, was discovered in 1840. In the stratosphere – that is, the lower atmosphere about 10 to 50 kms above the earth's surface – it performs the important function of filtering harmful ultraviolet B radiation (UVB) even though it exists there only in a few parts per million. Stratospheric ozone is, however, vulnerable to destruction in chemical reaction with chlorine and bromine gases. The anthropogenic (that is, human-made) sources of those gases are found in chlorofluorocarbons (CFCs) (which are used as propellants for aerosols, refrigerants, solvents for cleaning electrical components and the manufacture of rigid and flexible foam products), in the organic solvents carbon tetrachloride and methyl chloroform, in methyl bromide (which is used primarily as a fungicide) and in halons which are found primarily in fire extinguishers. There is also a possible natural contribution to ozone depletion through the release of chlorine as a by-product of volcanic eruptions and biomass burning. The stability of sources – CFCs, for example, can remain in the atmosphere for up to 120 years before breaking down – has resulted in increased stratospheric concentrations of ozone-depleting gases which has, in turn, resulted in accelerated destruction of ozone and an increase in UVB rays. Chlorine concentrations increased from 0.6 parts per billion (ppb) in pre-Industrial times to about 1.5 to 2 ppb in the 1970s and 3 ppb in 1985 (Benedick, 1991, pp. 129–30). A 1 per cent decrease in stratospheric ozone is thought to cause a 2 per cent increase in surface UVB radiation. The likely effects of an increase in UVB radiation include an increase in skin cancers and cataracts, suppression of the immune system in both humans and animals with a resultant increase in vulnerability to infectious diseases and a decrease in the productivity of plants and phytoplankton, the basis of the marine food chain (and also a carbon dioxide fixer). A 1 per cent drop in ozone has been predicted to cause as much as a 4 to 6 per cent increase in skin cancers (Shea, 1989, p. 82). Rowlands (1991, p. 101) cites a US Environment Protection Agency (EPA) report which argued that, if no steps were taken to reverse ozone depletion, there could be an increase in cancer numbers of between 163 million and 308 million in the generations born up to 2075 in the US alone, of which 3.5 to 6.5 million could be fatal.

Much of this knowledge is relatively new. In the 1960s, debates about damage to stratospheric ozone focused on the possible consequences of supersonic air transport, although the culprits here were water vapour and nitrous oxide. In 1974, two US scientists, Mario Molina and Sherwood Rowland, hypothesised that accumulated chlorine gases could lead to depletion of stratospheric ozone (Molina and Rowland, 1974), work for which they, along with Paul Crutzen, have recently been awarded the Nobel Prize for Chemistry. In 1977 a UNEP-convened meeting of experts drew up a World Plan of Action on the Ozone Layer which emphasised the further scientific research. The Coordinating Committee on the Ozone Layer (CCOL) established by that meeting met annually from 1977 to 1985. In 1981, at the urging of its Executive Director, Egyptian scientist Mostafa Tolba, UNEP's Governing Council convened an Ad Hoc Legal and Technical Working Group to draft an ozone protection convention. Negotiations began in 1982.

Convention for the Protection of the Ozone Layer (the Vienna Convention)

The Vienna Convention was adopted by 20 countries plus the EC on 22 March 1985 following the quaintly-titled Conference of Plenipotentiaries. It is a framework convention of 21 articles, most of which are procedural and administrative. It contains no firm targets or controls, only general obligations emphasising the importance of cooperation and scientific research. Difficulties in reaching agreement on specific commitments arose because of unilateral actions already taken by some of the negotiating parties in the 1970s and early 1980s. The US, Canada, Finland, Norway and Sweden (collectively known as the Toronto Group) had enacted bans on non-essential aerosol uses of CFCs and therefore favoured such a strategy in the convention. The European Community countries argued that a production cap, which the EC had adopted in 1980, would be easier to monitor. Industry opposition to reductions in either consumption or production was also, Benedick (1991, pp. 30–4) suggests, stronger in Europe than in the United States. Despite its generality, the Convention's revolutionary potential lay in its precautionary nature: at that stage there was no scientific certainty on the causes or impacts of ozone depletion and thus the agreement departed from usual past reactive practices of international environmental law.

In 1985, a team of British Antarctic Survey scientists, working at Halley Bay station under the leadership of Joe Farman, reported readings which indicated that since 1979 there had been up to a 40 per cent reduction in springtime ozone over the Antarctic, results which were initially treated with some scepticism because none of the atmospheric models had predicted such an outcome (either freak measurements or faulty equipment was initially thought responsible). A July 1985 report by a team of 150 scientists working under the auspices of the National Aeronautics and Space Administration (NASA) and UNEP concluded that the ozone layer was already damaged. Two subsequent NASA-sponsored expeditions to the Antarctic (National Ozone Expedition (NOZE) I and II) demonstrated the 'undoubted chemical cause in destruction of ozone by atmospheric chlorine' (Rowlands, 1991, p. 106). Ozone depletion was, therefore, no longer theory. By 1988, there was strong evidence of an increase in ozone depletion over middle latitudes. NASA's Ozone Trends Panel (OTP) reported, in March of that year, that

between 1969 and 1986 there had been a total decrease in stratospheric ozone of between 1.7 and 3.0 per cent in latitudes between 30
and 60 degrees north (see Shea, 1989, p. 81). In the same month,
chemical giant Du Pont, which accounted for about 25 per cent of
global CFC production, announced that it would phase out CFC
production, although only three weeks before, prior to the release of
the OTP report, the company had argued that the 'scientific evidence
does *not* point to the need for dramatic CFC reductions' (see
Benedick, 1991, p. 111; emphasis added). In the context of a resolution adopted at the Vienna meeting calling for further negotiations,
this scientific evidence and a weakening of industry influence facilitated the adoption of reduction targets.

*Protocol on Substances that Deplete the Ozone Layer (Montreal
Protocol)*

On 16 September 1987 (before the Vienna Convention had come into
effect) 24 countries plus the EC adopted the Montreal Protocol. The
Protocol established consumption control measures and reduction
targets, through a freeze and roll back strategy, for two groups of
ozone depleting substances. Group I substances – five fully-haloge-
nated CFCs – were to be cut to 50 per cent of 1986 levels by 1999.
Group II substances, halons, were to be frozen at 1986 levels by the
end of 1992. The value of setting a 1986 baseline meant that there
would be no advantage to governments in delaying their accession to
the Protocol. The Protocol included a number of other provisions
designed to support these control measures. There were restrictions
on trade with non-signatories in controlled substances and products
containing controlled substances (article 4). Scientific information
was to be the catalyst for further review of the schedules of controlled
substances. A modified amendment procedure ensured that, once
adopted, amendments to existing schedules would automatically
come into effect within six months, thus circumventing often lengthy
domestic ratification processes.

While the Protocol was hailed as a successful piece of environmental
diplomacy and an important step in addressing ozone depletion, it
contained exceptions, loopholes and flaws which undermined its
success as an environmental agreement. Developing countries were
granted a 10-year grace period for compliance with the provisions of
the Protocol, as long as their annual consumption did not exceed 0.3
kg per capita (an amount about one-quarter of US per capita

consumption), a level exceeded by only a few developing countries – Bahrain, Malta, Singapore and the United Arab Emirates (see Gehring and Oberthür, 1993, p. 9). Exceptions were also made to accommodate the planned economies of the then Eastern bloc countries (article 2.6; see Benedick, 1991, p. 83), to allow limited transfer of production for industrial rationalisation purposes (article 2.5) or for CFC production increases to meet the import demands of developing countries (articles 2.1 to 2.4; see Benedick, 1991, p. 81). There were no enforcement or verification procedures except for national reporting provisions. Not all ozone-depleting substances were covered, and reduction goals were emission- rather than concentration-driven. Further, the substitutes that were being developed and which were not at that stage covered by the Protocol – hydrochlorofluorocarbons (HCFCs) – were, like CFCs, still ozone-depleting and greenhouse-enhancing gases. Those substitutes that were not ozone-depleting, the hydrofluorocarbons (HFCs), still had a very high greenhouse potential. The US Office of Technology Assessment (OTA) estimated that if only the original signatories complied with the Protocol's provisions, consumption of CFCs and halons could increase by as much as 20 per cent by 2009 (see Morrisette, 1989, p. 818). The US EPA calculated that full global participation in the Protocol could still result in a threefold increase in stratospheric chlorine concentrations by 2075 (Caron, 1991, p. 762). At best, the Protocol would not arrest depletion, merely slow its acceleration (see Shea, 1989, p. 94).

One of the major obstacles to the future success of the Protocol was the non-participation of developing countries. While the industrialised countries, accounting for less than 25 per cent of the world's population, contributed about 88 per cent of ozone consumption and were rightly required to shoulder much of the responsibility for reductions, consumption of ozone-depleting substances in developing countries was likely to increase in the future. Neither China nor India, two essential participants if future emissions and concentrations were to be controlled, were signatories at that stage. Developing countries took the view that ozone depletion was a problem created by, and therefore to be solved, by the industrialised countries, arguing also that they were not prepared to forego the benefits of existing investment in technology, even if it were ozone depleting, when alternative substances and technologies were so expensive.

Since the Protocol entered into force on 1 January 1989, after being ratified by at least 11 countries representing two-thirds of global consumption of halons and CFCs, the parties have met regularly under the review procedures to revise and ratchet existing schedules, to adopt new schedules and to increase the coverage of controlled substances. Some parties have also committed unilaterally to more stringent reductions. In March 1989, for example, the EC announced its commitment to phase out CFC use by 85 per cent as soon as possible, with a total phaseout by 2000, a position also adopted by the United States and Canada. The first meeting of parties was held in Helsinki in May 1989, but the first amendments were not adopted until the second meeting in London in June 1990. The London amendments required a total phaseout of CFCs (including some newly added to the schedules), halons and carbon tetrachloride by 2000. Intermediate targets for CFCs required a 50 per cent cut by 1995, and an 85 per cent cut by 1997. Methyl chloroform was to be phased out by 2005. The London meeting also agreed to establish an interim multilateral fund for financial and technology transfer to assist developing countries meet their obligations. The fund was to function under the day-to-day administration of UNEP, the United Nations Development Programme (UNDP) and the World Bank, with overall guidance provided by a probably larger than administratively necessary executive committee of seven developed and seven developing countries. The initial commitment of $US160 million was to be increased to $US240 million if and when China and India became parties to the Protocol. At the 1991 meeting in Nairobi, the fund was increased to $US200 million following China's accession, although there were already problems with non-payment of contributions (especially from France and the new Russian Federation).

Further targets were adopted at the 1992 review, the fourth meeting of parties in Copenhagen. The complete phaseout on halons was ratcheted to 1994 with reductions on CFCs, methyl chloroform and carbon tetrachloride ratcheted to 1996. Reduction schedules were finally adopted for HCFCs (although the phaseout date was set to 2040) with a complicated 1996 consumption cap calculated on a baseline of the aggregate of 1989 consumption plus 3.1 per cent of 1989 consumption of CFCs. In a precautionary move, restrictions were placed on bromine-containing hydrocarbons even though the substances had not yet been marketed. However the only agreement that could be reached on methyl bromide was a freeze on production and consumption at 1991 levels by 1995. While the US favoured a tight phaseout, the EC was constrained by some of its member countries who used methyl bromide as a commodity fumigant and pesticide. Israel, a major producer and exporter of methyl bromide, was strongly opposed to any restrictions. Procedures on non-compliance were also adopted at this meeting but no consensus could be reached on replenishment of the Fund, either for 1994 or the following three years.

At the fifth meeting in Bangkok in November 1993, concerns were raised at the slow rate of ratifications of amendments, delays in reporting and the level of outstanding contributions to the Fund (see Anon., 1994e, p. 67). Only nine parties had ratified the Copenhagen amendments, only 23 of 99 parties had submitted 1992 reports and only $53 million of the $114 million pledged for 1993 had been received. Informal commitments made at the Bangkok meeting included a commitment by 22 countries (but not the US) to phaseout HCFCs 15 years more quickly than required, and a voluntary declaration by 16 signatories to cut methyl bromide consumption by 25 per cent by 2000. The major accomplishment, though, was agreement on replenishment of the Fund in the sum of $US510 million for a three year period.

The parties did not adopt any further amendments to the schedules at their sixth meeting in Nairobi in 1994. They did, however, confirm a small number of specific-use exceptions to the CFC schedules (for metered-dose inhalers and for the US shuttle programme) as well as confirming that no exceptions would be permitted for halon targets in developed countries because technically- and economically-feasible alternatives were available. A series of further freeze and roll-back steps were taken at the seventh meeting of parties in December 1995 (the so-called Vienna Adjustments) after Elizabeth Dowdeswell called for further action on methyl bromide and HCFCs. Parties adopted a revised phase-out date of 2020 for HCFCs for developed countries and 2040 for developing countries. A full phaseout of methyl bromide by 2010 was adopted, although quarantine, pre-shipment and critical agricultural-use applications were exempted from this and developing countries were required only to commit to freeze requirements. At least one commentator has characterised these amendments as 'extremely weak' (Leubuscher, 1996, p. 186) and many parties signed two non-binding declarations on HCFCs and methyl bromide at that meeting, expressing concern about the continued limited action on those two substances. The eighth meeting of parties in Costa Rica in November 1996 agreed to a $US466 million replenishment of the Multilateral Fund for the 1997–9 triennium (although the Nordic countries had argued for a replenishment of $US510 or even higher). There was no further adjustment on the methyl bromide phaseout.

A number of political problems, particularly those relating to funding and technology transfer, and tensions between developed and developing countries, remain on the agenda of the Protocol. Further, while the Protocol has had some impact on emissions and concentrations it has been a slow impact. Figures available at the 1993 Bangkok meeting showed that the 'average reduction of ozone-depleting substances by developed countries was 45 per cent' (although the 1995 developed country phaseout target for CFCs has been met) but that only 'nine developing countries had shown a decrease in their consumption of controlled substances and three had shown an increase of more than 80 per cent' (Anon., 1994e, p. 67). In 1994, the Protocol's Scientific Assessment report concluded that the rate of chlorine loading (but not the level of concentrations) had finally slowed, but that depletion would continue for at least another 50 years, with a slow recovery in ozone loss not anticipated until about 2045 (Anon., 1995a, p. 22). Those predictions were, however, based not only on the assumption that there would be no new threats to the ozone layer but also on the assumption of full compliance with the Montreal Protocol and its amendments. Concerns therefore remain, as Leubuscher points out, about 'continued and worsening ozone depletion caused by poor compliance' as well as a 'disturbing volume of illegal traffic in controlled substances' (1996, p. 186), issues which continue to undermine the Protocol and efforts to halt and reverse ozone depletion.

The Global Commons of the Atmosphere: Climate Change

If Benedick was able to refer to the Montreal Protocol as 'the impossible accord' (1991, p. xiii) it was nothing compared with the difficulties of addressing climate change. Scientific uncertainty, economic interests and costs, political tensions and the fundamental question of equity between developed and developing countries all came to bear on an issue which one diplomat has called perhaps 'the most complex public policy issue ever to face governments' (Reinstein, 1993, p. 79).

The greenhouse effect is a natural phenomenon. Atmospheric gases – carbon dioxide (CO_2), methane (CH_4), nitrous oxide (N_2O), tropospheric ozone (and water vapour) – as well as CFCs and their substitutes which do not occur naturally in the atmosphere, absorb infra-red radiation which is reflected from the earth's surface as heat. Without this, average global temperatures would be about 33°C cooler than they are now. The problem arises when the trapping effect is enhanced by increased concentrations of those gases (with the exception of water vapour which is not increased anthropogenically). The sources of greenhouse gas emissions are varied. CO_2 emissions arise primarily from the burning of fossil-fuels and from deforestation. Methane, which is a very efficient greenhouse gas, is a by-product of agriculture, especially rice paddy and livestock, and is also released as leakage during the extraction and transportation of fossil fuels. Nitrous oxides arise from biomass burning, fertiliser use, fossil fuel combustion, land clearing and deforestation.

Since pre-Industrial times (the late 1700s), atmospheric concentrations of CO_2 have increased at least 20 to 25 per cent (see Rosswall, 1991, p. 567; Grubb, 1990, p. 68). Research suggests pre-Industrial CO_2 concentrations averaged 280 ppm. By the 1980s that had increased to approximately 330 ppm (Solomon and Freedburg, 1990, p. 87) and by the 1990s the level had reached 360 ppm (IPCC, 1995, para 2.2). Concentrations of methane have doubled in the last 200 years (Kelly and Karas, 1989, p. 19) and nitrous oxide concentrations have increased by about 10 per cent in the same period (Mintzer and Leonard, 1994b, p. 7). By 1991, global CO_2 emissions had increased for eight consecutive years and were at their highest level since formal records began in 1950 although the rate of growth was thought to be declining (see Anon., 1995c, p. 3).

While there is agreement on the measurements, there is much less scientific certainty on the likely effects of those increased concentrations. The difficulty in predicting impacts arises from a number of factors. It has proved difficult to model the relative contribution of gases. While carbon dioxide is the most important greenhouse gas in terms of the total amount emitted, it is an inefficient trapper of heat. One molecule of methane, for example, is 32 times more efficient than carbon dioxide (see Arrhenius and Waltz, 1990, p. 4): thus a small increase in methane will contribute more to the greenhouse effect in the short term than the same molecular increase in carbon dioxide. While methane has a much shorter atmospheric life span than carbon dioxide its impact is also affected by the presence of carbon monoxide which, while not a greenhouse gas, inhibits the action of free radicals, chemical agents which are important because they attack and destroy methane in the atmosphere (see Arrhenius and Waltz, 1990, pp. 3–6). Therefore, as carbon monoxide increases so too does methane. The complex interaction of positive and negative feedbacks and the still only partially understood impact of carbon sinks (those parts of the biosphere such as the oceans and forests which absorb carbon dioxide) have also been difficult to determine. Positive feedbacks, such as the release of methane from thawing tundra, result in a further enhancing of the greenhouse effect. Negative feedbacks, by contrast, are processes such as reforestation which may help retard the greenhouse effect. Scientists are also uncertain about the threshold level for concentrations and about whether, when that threshold level is reached, the inherent resiliency of the climate system might be overwhelmed (see Arrhenius and Waltz, 1990, p. 10).

Scientific research therefore confirms trends rather than proof, emphasising probable rather than certain outcomes. Nevertheless, there is a high degree of consensus within the climatological community on those likely outcomes, expressed most clearly in the reports of the Intergovernmental Panel on Climate Change (IPCC). In spite of some uncertainties, the balance of probabilities favours an enhanced global warming (see Plant, 1990, p. 418): the no-climate-change scenario is considered the least likely. Predicted climate-related impacts include increases in average global temperatures, rises in sea levels and an increase in the frequency and intensity of extreme weather conditions.

Climatological history indicates that the planet has always been subject to temperature fluctuations and changes in sea levels (see, for example, Brown, 1989a, p. 62): it is the rate and degree of contemporary change that is cause for concern. Grubb (1990, p. 68) reports that by the year 2030, average global temperatures could be higher than at any time in the last 120 000 years. By the late 1980s, research indicated that global temperatures had increased by 0.5 to 0.7°C in the previous 100 years, and that the hottest years of the twentieth century had all been in the 1980s (see Solomon and Freedburg, 1990, p. 89). Arrhenius and Waltz (1990), in a report for the World Bank, note that average temperatures rose only 0.5 to 0.7°C in the nineteenth century and have probably not varied more than 1 to 2°C in the last 10 000 years, or perhaps no more than 6 to 7°C in the last million years. They note that the whole development of 'human social and cultural infrastructures over the last 7000 years has taken place entirely within an average global climate neither 1°C warmer nor colder' than at present (Arrhenius and Waltz, 1990, p. 2). Yet the

IPCC has predicted that with a business-as-usual approach (that is, with no action taken to limit emissions or concentrations) average surface temperatures could increase by as much as 1°C by 2030 and by 3°C by 2100 (compared with a 1990 baseline) (Houghton *et al.*, 1990, p. xxiii). Temperature changes are also likely to be uneven with minimal changes close to the equator and changes as much as 8°C near the poles. The consequent thermal expansion of the oceans (water expands as it heats), accompanied in the first instance by the melting of non-polar glacial ice, could result in sea level rises of up to 6 cm per decade (Rosswall, 1991, p. 568) with even the IPCC conservatively estimating as much as 20cm by 2050 and 65cm by 2100 (Houghton *et al.*, 1990, p. xxx). The IPCC estimates that such a rise would be three to six times faster than in the previous 100 years (Houghton *et al.*, 1990, p. xxviii).

The impacts will be widespread. Sea-level rises will result in inundation of often densely-populated coastal areas, possibly displacing up to 1 billion of the world's people. Coastal erosion and salt water intrusion of inland waterways could, in conjunction with changes in climate zones, affect up to one-third of the world's croplands. Shifts in climate and agricultural zones may occur more rapidly than will the adaptive capacity of plants or animals, resulting in a loss of biodiversity and a diminution of crop yields, thus affecting world food supplies. Those peoples who are likely to be worst hit are in those parts of the world which are already ecologically and often economically marginal – peoples and countries which have, for the most part, contributed little or nothing to the problem. Countries such as Bangladesh, Egypt, Gambia, Indonesia, Mozambique, Pakistan, Senegal, Surinam and Thailand are high risk countries because of their coastal concentrations. Low-lying island states such as Tuvalu, Tonga, Kiribati, the Marshall Islands and the Maldives might become uninhabitable and, at worst, simply cease to exist.

Strategies for addressing the greenhouse effect have been contentious because, as Paterson and Grubb point out, they will 'reach into the heart of countries' political and economic structures' (1992, p. 294). The elaboration of appropriate strategies is, therefore, not simply a scientific and technical exercise. It is a highly political and politicised one. The first area of dispute has been the objectives of strategies and debates which have focused on the need to stabilise and if possible reduce concentrations through reducing emissions. These are hardly simple tasks. The IPCC estimated that to stabilise concentrations at 1990 levels, emissions would need to be reduced by over

60 per cent for CO_2, 15–20 per cent for methane and 70–80 per cent
for nitrous oxide (Houghton *et al.*, 1990, p. xxiii) and 70–75 per cent
for CFC-11, 75–85 per cent for CFC-12 and 40–50 per cent for
HCFC-22 (Houghton *et al.*, 1990, p. xviii). David Pearce calculates,
however, that given the long-term impact of present concentrations,
stabilising all greenhouse gases at 1990 levels would only reduce the
0.3°C increase in global temperature per decade to 0.23°C (cited in
Hanisch, 1992, p. 64). Reductions in carbon dioxide emissions are
possible. They can be achieved through a variety of strategies including increased energy efficiency, development of alternatives, changing
the mix of fossil fuels to avoid the more dirty, high emitting sources,
using penalties or financial mechanisms such as carbon taxes or
tradeable permits, slowing deforestation or putting efforts into re-
afforestation. Arrhenius and Waltz (1990, p. 12) cite research which
estimates that a $10 billion investment in cost-improvements in
electricity end-use could offset an anticipated $50 billion demand
for 22 GigaWatts (GW) of new generating capacity. Nuclear energy is
potentially a less-useful reduction strategy given costs and the difficulties of dealing with nuclear waste. Kelly and Karas (1989, pp. 23–
4) cite studies which indicate that each dollar invested in energy
efficiency in the US displaces seven times as much CO_2 as a dollar
invested in nuclear power. As Prins notes, only about 10 per cent of
CO_2 emissions are from fixed power-generating stations and nuclear
power could therefore substitute to only a small extent (1990, p. 718).
A 1988 study for the EC Commission demonstrated that the full costs
of photovoltaic and wind power would be lower than either nuclear
or fossil fuel, assuming that the full costs of the latter options were
internalised (Jain, 1990, p. 560). Yet the industrialised countries
(along with traditional energy industries) have been generally reluctant to adopt these strategies.

The second area of dispute has been that of responsibility to act.
Countries vary not only in their contributions to greenhouse emissions, but also in the ease with which they can reduce emissions, in
their capacity to pay for response policies and in their degree of
resilience or vulnerability to impacts. The allocation of responsibility
and obligation on a country-by-country basis is controversial. It
depends on which gases are counted and how they are counted: on a
total output basis, a per capita basis, or a per GNP basis; on the basis
of current levels of exploitation, historical contributions or projected
future emissions. Nevertheless, developed industrialised countries
cannot escape the major burden of responsibility. The OECD

countries, approximately one-quarter of the world's population, contribute about three-quarters of global radiative forcing. The developing world's average per capita emissions of fossil CO_2 are about one-tenth the OECD average and average per capita emissions on the Indian sub-continent and Africa are about one-twentieth those of the US (Paterson and Grubb, 1992, p. 297). Grubb (1990, p. 74) estimates that if China and India emitted carbon at the same per capita level as the US, world emissions would nearly treble. He also calculates that if all economic activity were to be conducted at the per GNP emission level of Japan (an unlikely scenario, given the technological sophistication required) current emissions would be *reduced* threefold. Greenhouse emissions from the developing countries are, however, predicted to increase and to contribute a greater percentage than at present to overall radiative forcing, especially when the contribution of methane from rice and livestock agriculture is taken into account. Future increases in CO_2 emissions are predicted to account for only half of future temperature increases (Rosswall, 1991, p. 567). Some developed industrialised countries – and the US has been chief among them – have argued therefore that reductions in CO_2 emissions on their part will be futile if developing countries do not also commit to reduction targets for both CO_2 and methane. Developing countries have strongly resisted this logic, arguing that it smacks of environmental colonialism and is an attempt by developed countries not only to shift the blame and to avoid their own responsibilities but also to restrain the development and economic growth of developing countries (see Agarwal and Narain, 1991; McCully, 1991a). It is an analysis that, as Henry Shue observes, also ignores or downplays the differences between luxury emissions (those from unrestricted energy use, for example) and survival or subsistence emissions (Shue, 1993).

The manner in which scientific uncertainty should be factored into any agreement has become a third area of contention. The United States in particular has cautioned against extensive commitments in the absence of further scientific research, arguing for 'no regrets' policies, actions which are justified on other than climate change grounds and which will incur minimal cost if the predictions turn out to be inaccurate. Yet many developing countries interpret this as a strategy by which developed countries could extricate themselves from meeting obligations based on historical and current contributions as well as the rather selfish actions of countries which are better placed, economically and technologically, to deal with the impacts of climate change.

Making policy

Atmosphere and general climate issues were addressed at a series of scientific conferences in the 1970s and early 1980s, including the First World Climate Conference convened by WMO in 1979, the 1972 Stockholm Conference on the Human Environment (see recommendation 70 of the Action Plan), the UN World Food Conference in 1974, the UN Water Conference in 1976 and the UN Desertification Conference in 1977. However, it was not until the rather ponderously titled International Conference on Assessment of the Role of CO_2 and other GHGs [Greenhouse Gases] in Climate Variation and Associated Impact, held in Villach, Austria in 1985, that scientific concern began to translate into concerted demands for political responses on an international level. The Villach meeting recommended that UNEP, WMO and ICSU should take action to 'initiate, if deemed necessary, consideration of a global convention' (cited in Bodansky, 1994, p. 48). The Villach Conference was followed by workshops in Bellagio, Italy in 1985 and 1987. In June 1988, over 300 scientists and policy-makers from 46 countries along with another 100 or so people from non-governmental organisations, the UN and other intergovernmental organisations, met in Toronto, Canada for the Conference on the Changing Atmosphere: Implications for Global Security. The conference statement recommended a 20 per cent reduction in CO_2 emissions by 2005 (the so-called Toronto target), called for an international convention and action plan and advocated the establishment of a World Atmosphere Fund to be funded, in part, by a levy on fossil fuel consumption in industrialised countries.

The most important contribution to scientific consensus, and to the process of negotiating an international agreement on climate change, has been the work of the Intergovernmental Panel on Climate Change (IPCC). This expert body was established in 1988 (just before the Toronto conference) by the WMO and UNEP. Its work proceeded in three working groups. Working Group I was mandated to assess the scientific information on climate change. Working Group II focused on the environmental and socioeconomic impacts of climate change and the third working group was charged with formulating response strategies. The IPCC released its first major assessment in August 1990. The predictions of Working Group I, the scientific assessment panel, have been noted above. While Working Group II was more cautious in its interpretation of the scientific evidence, it did draw attention to the expected disproportionate environmental and socioeconomic impacts on regions already under stress (see Tegart *et al.*, 1990). Working Group II noted the limitations faced by the developing countries as a result of debt and limited resources in their attempts to adapt to changes and to limit their own emissions. It suggested that such countries would need assistance from developed ones and argued that 'global warming and impacts must not widen the gap between developed and developing countries' (IPCC, 1990, p. 32). In spite of the concerns expressed by Working Groups I and II, Working Group III on policy responses offered no priority list or detailed action guide for policy.

While the IPCC groups were deliberating, the General Assembly passed resolution 43/53 in December 1988 requesting the WMO and UNEP, through the IPCC, to begin to think about the possible elements of a convention on climate change (UNGA, 1988). As the possibility of formal negotiations increased, governments became increasingly cautious in their commitments. At a Ministerial Conference in Noordwijk in the Netherlands in 1989, delegates debated a Dutch proposal that industrialised countries should stabilise their CO_2 emissions by the year 2000. Neither the US nor Japan would agree to such a specific commitment, and the Declaration articulated only the general aim of limiting or reducing emissions (see Bodansky, 1994, p. 55). In November 1990, the WMO convened the Second World Climate Conference. Some governments were prepared to support a final statement which would commit industrialised countries to stabilisation of CO_2 emissions at 1990 levels by 2000. US resistance again resulted in vague language on targets and national strategies (see Reinstein, 1993, p. 83). In December, under resolution 45/212, the UN General Assembly formally established the Intergovernmental Negotiating Committee (INC) for the negotiation of a climate change convention, effectively removing this task from the auspices of UNEP and the IPCC (UNGA, 1990).

The Committee – officially known as the Intergovernmental Negotiating Committee for a Framework Convention on Climate Change (INC/FCCC) – was given 18 months to produce a convention in time for signature at the Rio Conference in June 1992. The INC met five times – in Chantilly, Virginia (in the US) in February 1991, in Geneva in June, Nairobi in September and Geneva again in December 1991. In February 1992 it met in New York, a session which resumed at the end of April with a large number of brackets remaining in the draft text. The negotiations were chaired by Jean Ripert of France, former chair of the IPCC Committee on the Special

Circumstances of Developing Countries and proceeded in two major working groups, one to deal with commitments, financial resources, technology transfer and the special needs of developing countries, and a second working group to consider institutional and legal mechanisms for implementation. Negotiations were described by the head of the INC Secretariat, Michael Zammit Cutajar, as a 'process of two steps forward and one step back' (United Nations INC/FCCC, 1991, p. 2). As expected, they were driven as much by political and economic interests as by environmental imperatives. Indeed, the first two sessions did little else but deal with procedural matters.

Participating governments coalesced into a series of interest-based coalitions. Although there was a 'North–South' dimension to the negotiations, political cleavages went beyond this simple bifurcation. Identifiable groups included the 37-member Alliance of Small Island States (AOSIS) which had formed at the Second World Climate Conference, the oil producing and exporting countries, the Newly-Industrialised Countries (NICs) who were dependent on energy-intensive patterns of production, the Economies in Transition of the former Soviet bloc and the OECD countries, although for some commentators (see Pulvenis, 1994, p. 85 and Sands, 1992b, p. 271) the United States stood apart from its industrialised counterparts in a bloc on its own. Nor was there always agreement within these blocs. For example, while there was general agreement among the OECD countries (with the exception of the US) on the need for targets, there was disagreement on what those targets should be (see Reinstein, 1993, p. 89). Hanisch suggests also that the EC, Japan and the US were unlikely to agree to anything which would affect the trade balance between them or 'endanger their competitive ability' (1992 p. 72). The oil producing countries and the US favoured only a framework convention (the Vienna model). Other developed countries and AOSIS supported a convention which would include specific commitments and implementation measures, although there were, Agarwal and Narain (1991), suggest serious fears among developing countries that the convention would limit their development opportunities by placing restrictions on energy use and agricultural practice.

UN Framework Convention on Climate Change

The UN *Framework Convention on Climate Change* (UNFCCC) was finalised at 6.10 p.m. on Saturday, 9 May 1992 (after days of negotiating when delegates often met until 3.00 or 4.00 in the morning). It is not a long document: a preamble, 26 articles and two annexes (United Nations INC/FCCC, 1992). The principles which shape the Convention (article 3) include precaution, equity (both inter- and intra-generational), cooperation and sustainability of development. The Convention's objective is the stabilisation of atmospheric greenhouse gas concentrations at levels that will prevent human activities from interfering dangerously with the global climate system, within 'a time frame sufficient to allow ecosystems to adapt naturally to climate change, to ensure that food production is not threatened and to enable economic development to proceed in a sustainable manner' (United Nations INC/FCCC, 1992, article 2). This goal is to be achieved through limiting emissions, enhancing sinks and protecting reservoirs. However, the Convention contains no authoritative targets or deadlines, in large part because of US opposition (Paterson, 1992, pp. 268–9) with support from the oil-exporting countries. Article 4.2(a), which Sands calls possibly 'the most impenetrable treaty language ever drafted' (1992b, p. 273), refers only to the value of returning emissions to 'earlier levels' by 2000. Developed countries, including those undergoing transition to a market economy, are encouraged but not required to aim, individually or jointly, to bring their emissions of gases not controlled by the Montreal Protocol to 1990 levels (article 4.2(b)). This is, in effect, a voluntary goal, one which is less stringent than the 1988 Toronto target and nowhere near the 60 per cent reduction which the IPCC suggested would be necessary to stabilise concentrations.

The issue of equity between developed and developing countries is mediated through the principle of 'common but differentiated responsibilities and respective capabilities' (article 3.1). Developed countries are required to take the lead in mitigating climate change and report on the strategies they adopt. The Convention also recognises their general obligations on the transfer of financial resources and technology to assist developing countries to meet their commitments (which do not at this stage include reducing emissions) and to prepare for and adapt to the adverse effects of climate change. The Convention recognises a range of other vulnerabilities (including those of countries with low-lying, coastal, arid and semi-arid areas) and special circumstances, especially those of countries which are highly dependent on either the production or consumption of fossil fuels.

Much of the Convention is given over to institutional and procedural mechanisms. The Conference of Parties (COP) is to be the 'supreme body of this Convention' (article 7.2) supported by a

Secretariat (article 8). Two subsidiary bodies – on Scientific and Technical Advice (SBSTA) and on Implementation (SBI) – are to assist, provide advice to and report to the COP (articles 9 and 10). Article 11 establishes a financial mechanism for the Convention and article 21 entrusts the Global Environment Facility with the responsibility of operating the mechanism 'on an interim basis'. Also here, buried in article 21, is the terse but significant injunction, albeit one slightly finessed, that 'the Global Environment Facility *should* be appropriately restructured and its membership made universal' (United Nations INC/FCCC, 1992, article 21; emphasis added), an issue addressed in more detail in Chapter 8.

Chadwick calls the Convention 'pathbreaking' (1994, p. xiii) and Sands suggests that 'taken as a whole, the Convention marks an important new phase in the development of international environmental law' (1992b, p. 271). Mintzer and Leonard call it a 'powerful force for change in North–South relations' (1994b, p. 21). Ted Hanisch (1992, p. 67) (who was a member of the Norwegian delegation to the INC) argues that the Convention is successful because it establishes a first step in building a regime for climate change even though, as he acknowledges, it will not stop the trend of increasing global emissions and concentrations by the end of the decade. Yet it is precisely those flaws which have led others to be much harsher in their judgment, suggesting that the Convention is an internally contradictory agreement and that it does not address in any satisfactory way the problem of climate change. Greenpeace lobbyists Jeremy Leggett and Paul Hohnen (1992, p. 76) argue that the Convention fails to establish targets which would enable its own stated objectives to be met. Farhana Yamin (n.d., p. 5), writing for the Foundation for International Environmental Law and Development (FIELD), a nongovernmental organisation which worked closely with the AOSIS during the negotiations, suggests that the present continuation of emissions is inconsistent with the objectives and obligations accepted by the Parties to the Convention. She notes also that the Convention contains no reference to energy efficiency, even though chapter 9 of Agenda 21 clearly elaborates this as an important strategy.

The Convention was opened for signature at the Rio Conference (UNCED) on 4 June where it was signed by 154 countries and the EC. The necessary fiftieth ratification was deposited on 21 December 1993, and the Convention entered into force on 21 March 1994. The INC met a further six times after the Convention was opened for signature to prepare for implementation. The first meeting of Parties was held in Berlin in March 1995. As well as a number of procedural issues, the Berlin meeting focused on the adequacy of commitments, especially after the year 2000, replaying earlier disagreements. The AOSIS and the EU favoured more stringent targets and AOSIS submitted a draft protocol which would have required developed countries to reduce their CO_2 emissions to 20 per cent below 1990 levels by 2005. Other developed countries, especially Japan, the US, Canada, Australia and New Zealand (the JUSCANZ group), were reluctant to accept further obligations and focused instead on the imperatives for developing countries to adopt commitments within a comprehensive approach which would include sources, sinks and reservoirs. The majority of OECD countries were not, as Rowlands (1995b, p. 153) notes, on track to meet even their vague commitments under the FCCC. China and the Group of 77 (G77) continued to emphasise developed country responsibility and the oil-exporting countries remained opposed to any action at all. In the face of no consensus on specifics, the COP adopted the so-called 'Berlin Mandate' to address the commitments issue. The Mandate recognises that commitments in the Convention are inadequate and sets in train a process to elaborate a protocol or other legal instrument on further commitments, although it contains no target dates beyond 2000 or specific directives as to the content of a protocol, except for general references to the need for a comprehensive approach. The Mandate became the responsibility of an ad hoc working group (the AGBM) which was required to have a draft prepared for adoption at COP-3 in 1997.

The Joint Implementation issue, whereby 'one country can fulfil its obligations by helping to reduce greenhouse gas emissions, enhance carbon sinks or preserve reservoirs in another country' (Rowlands, 1995b, p. 148) was also controversial at Berlin. Concerns were raised about whether developed countries would endeavour to meet their obligations, not by taking action 'at home', but by funding cheaper options in developing countries, thereby not only potentially determining reduction priorities for developing countries but also reducing future options for those developing countries when their own commitments were invoked at some future stage. In the end, a pilot phase (to be known as AIJ or Activities Implemented Jointly) was adopted on the basis of voluntary participation with no credits, at this stage anyway, for emissions reductions.

The IPCC completed its second full assessment (SAR) in December 1995. This report, drawing on all three working groups, confirmed a likely continued increase in atmospheric GHG concentrations, based on current emission trends, and a growth in the magnitude of interference with the climate system (IPCC, 1995, para 1.7). It reinforced, with some modifications, its impact predictions of 1990. The particular importance of this report lay in its confirmation that climate change is happening. The Panel's experts noted that the increase in global mean surface temperature of between 0.3 and 0.6°C since the late nineteenth century was 'unlikely to be entirely natural in origin' and that the 'balance of evidence . . . suggests a discernible human influence on global climate' (IPCC, 1995, para 2.4). The second SAR followed an interim report released at the end of 1994 in which the IPCC noted that, even with a stabilisation of current emissions, concentrations of CO_2 would continue to increase for at least two centuries (see Oberthür and Ott, 1995, p. 145). In what has been called an 'extraordinary move', the World Energy Council (peak body for the world's energy industries) countered that the Panel's recommendations were based on 'shaky evidence' (Anon., 1996f, p. 175) and were (to quote the Council) 'unrealistic and influenced by academics seeking to attract funding for their work' (cited in Anon., 1996f, p. 175).

The IPCC Report, and responses to it, provided the context for the second Conference of Parties (COP2) in Geneva in July 1996. A number of issues relating to administrative and procedural debates were also on the agenda: the meeting ended with final agreement on a Memorandum of Understanding between the COP and the GEF, but with no final agreement on COP rules of procedure. Parties were divided in their response to the IPCC SAR with the oil-exporting countries, with the support of Russia, arguing that there were still too many uncertainties to use the report as the basis for recommendations for urgent action (see Oberthür, 1996b, p. 196). In a major shift, the US government committed its support for the Berlin Mandate and the need for legally-binding targets, although this seems to have been linked to its preference for the introduction of a system of tradeable permits. The parties were unable to agree on a formal decision in response to the latest scientific information. In the absence of a consensus, and in the face of opposition from a small number of 'laggard' states (Oberthür, 1996b, p. 200), the meeting was only able to 'note' the (non-binding) Ministerial Declaration – the Geneva Declaration – which endorsed the IPCC conclusions and called for legally binding objectives and significant reductions in GHG emissions.

At time of writing, therefore, many of the issues that were central to the negotiations for the Convention have not yet been resolved in the COP process. Technology transfer remains a difficult issue and will be the subject of a roundtable at COP-3 (to be held in Kyoto in December 1997). If discussions proceed on schedule, the AGBM will table a draft negotiating text on binding targets at COP-3 but the extent of support for targets and the extent to which those targets will address environmental rather than diplomatic concerns is, on past performance, open to doubt. One of the most contested issues in the Mandate negotiations has come to be whether reduction targets should be based on a percentage reduction (favoured by the EU and AOSIS) or upon differentiation – the setting of targets to take account of different capabilities – a strategy favoured by the US, Australia and New Zealand among others. In the meantime, the significant reductions in emissions that the IPCC has identified as necessary even to stabilise concentrations of GHGs are nowhere in sight.

Global Heritage or Sovereign Resources: Biodiversity

The second convention opened for signature at UNCED was the Convention on Biological Diversity. Concern about the loss of biodiversity developed from the species and habitat conservation agenda of the 1960s and 1970s. For many commentators, the transformation from 'species' to 'biodiversity' in the 1980s was accompanied by a process of commodification (see, for example, C. von Weizsäcker, 1993). Tensions and differences during the negotiation of the convention were driven not so much by questions of appropriate strategies for protection of species and ecosystems as by questions of ownership of and intellectual property rights to genetic material and biotechnology.

Biodiversity is colloquially used as a synonym for the number of species, but it encompasses not only the diversity of species but also genetic diversity *within* species. Biodiversity is not, as Shiva (1990, p. 44) notes, uniformly distributed throughout the world. Rather it is concentrated in the tropical countries of the Third World. Over half of all species live in the 6 per cent of the earth's land surface that is covered by tropical forest (Brenton, 1994, p. 198). Of the 12 'megadiverse' countries, 11 are in the developing world – Brazil, China, Columbia, Ecuador, India, Indonesia, Madagascar, Malaysia, Mexico, Peru and Zaire (see Brenton, 1994, p. 201; Shine and Kohona,

1992, p. 278). Australia is the only developed megadiverse country. The megadiversity of tropical countries is reflected, for example, in the statistics that one river in Brazil alone contains more fish species than are to be found in the whole of the United States and a small reserve in Costa Rica contains more plant species than the whole of the United Kingdom (WRM, 1990, p. 16).

The loss in diversity of and within species has a number of causes. Destruction of habitats through processes such as drainage of wetlands, pollution of and damage to coral reefs through sedimentation and the direct and indirect impacts of climate change contributes to species loss. Green Revolution technology resulted in loss of genetic diversity within crop species. The introduction of or invasion by exotic species can threaten indigenous fauna and flora. Quantitative information on the extent of species loss and on rates of extinction is difficult to determine simply because we do not know how many species there are in the world. Recent estimates, based on a variety of scientific extrapolations, have revised numbers upwards and suggestions stand at anything from 8 million to 30 million (and, indeed, perhaps even much higher). Only about 1.5 million species have been identified and classified. In spite of this uncertainty, there is agreement that species extinction is increasing. Walter Reid (1992, p. 1090) argues that the rate of extinction could be higher than at any time in the last 65 million years. Murray (1993, p. 70) suggests that, at present rates, up to 8 per cent of all species could become extinct in the next 25 years. Bragdon (1992, p. 382) cites scientific opinion that perhaps 50 species become extinct each day and suggests that, at this rate, 25 per cent of all species could become extinct within the next 50 years. Whichever of these estimates is closest to the mark, the extinction rate is much faster than the natural rate – the World Rainforest Movement (1990, p. 27) estimates that it could be 400 times higher and Porter and Brown (1991, p. 15) suggest possibly up to 1000 times faster. This loss is irreversible.

Much of the contemporary debate about the impact of species and biodiversity loss focuses on the utility value of biodiversity, especially with respect to pharmaceutical and medicinal purposes. The commercial value of plant- and insect-derived medicines is estimated at $US43 billion per annum (Murray, 1993, p. 75). Plants in particular also hold medicinal value for indigenous peoples and local communities. The World Health Organisation lists over 21 000 plants used in traditional medicines (Murray 1993, p. 75). Biodiversity, and especially diversity within species, is also valuable for agriculture: diversity enhances the disease- and pest-resistance of domesticated plant crops whereas genetic uniformity can result in widespread and costly vulnerability to disease. In 1970, US farmers lost approximately $US1 billion as disease decimated genetically uniform and highly susceptible corn varieties (see Reid, 1992, p. 1092). Reliance on genetically uniform crops can result in severe genetic erosion. Reid (1992, p. 1092) also suggests that over 1500 local rice varieties have become extinct in Indonesia alone since the mid-1970s. Biodiversity also has an intrinsic value, based on the idea that *all* species, not just humans, should be respected in and of their own right. Finally there is the ecosystem value of biodiversity: we cannot predict how the loss of a species (or many species) might affect the balance of the ecosystem nor how long it might take an ecosystem to recover from this damage. Berlin and Lang note that 'palaeontologists have estimated that it took the environment 20 million years to heal fully after the last great episode of mass species extinction' (1993, p. 37).

Genetic diversity issues were raised at Stockholm where, even then, they were divisive. The Stockholm Action Plan contained six recommendations on the preservation of the world's genetic resources, activities in which the Food and Agricultural Organisation was expected to take a lead role. The first suggestions for a biodiversity convention date to 1974 (see Brenton, 1994, p. 200). UNESCO's 1976 Man [sic] and the Biosphere Programme and the 1980 World Conservation Strategy (WCS) drawn up by the IUCN contributed to general efforts on species protection, with the WCS including the preservation of genetic diversity among its objectives (see Boyle, 1994, p. 112). In 1983, the FAO passed a non-binding *Undertaking on Plant Genetic Resources* which established that such resources were the 'heritage of mankind [sic]' and should be 'available without restriction' (see Hendrickx *et al.*, 1993, p. 258), although this did not mean they should be free. In 1985 the World Bank established a Task Force on Biodiversity (see Shiva, 1990, p. 44), which resulted in the drafting of a Biological Diversity Action Plan by UNEP, IUCN, the World Resources Institute and WWF–US, a plan followed in February 1992 by the Global Biodiversity Strategy. Thus there were a number of preliminary, albeit for the most part non-binding instruments in place when the IUCN began work on a draft convention in 1987, a process taken over by UNEP when it convened an Ad Hoc Working Group of Experts on Biological Diversity in November 1988. Formal negotiations for a legal instrument officially began in 1990 with the Ad Hoc Working Group of Legal and Technical Experts, the third session of which was constituted as the Intergovernmental Negotiating Committee. The Committee met another five times and the Convention was adopted at an 'extremely bad-tempered and confused' (Brenton, 1994, p. 203) final session in Nairobi in May 1992.

The issues which caused the 'harshest discussions' (Hendrickx *et al.*, 1993, p. 250) during the negotiations were not those of conservation strategies but those related to the ownership of genetic resources, to intellectual property rights and to the distribution of benefits from genetic exploitation, with countries cleaved between the gene-rich South and the (bio)technology-rich North. Genetic resources had traditionally been treated by the North at least as a 'common heritage' or, if not owned by all in common, then owned by no-one. In this way, however, companies in developed countries were able to utilise the species and genetic resources of developing countries as a free resource, a process which Shiva (1990) likens to gene robbery. Developing countries argued that genetic resources were not a global heritage but sovereign national resources to be utilised by them as they saw fit in accordance with their own development and environmental priorities. They argued that Northern concern for the protection of (mainly) Southern biodiversity and the continued emphasis on biodiversity as a 'global' issue were driven by eco-imperialist and economic concerns rather than environmental ones. Developing countries suggested that if Northern companies were to continue to exploit the species and genetic resources of the South, an equitable sharing of benefits was in order to compensate for the problem of unequal exchange and, further, that they should have access to Northern biotechnology to exploit their own genetic resources (see Brenton, 1994, p. 203). The response of developed countries and the biotechnology industry was, in summary, that, '[i]t is not the products found in plants that are offered for sale, but derivatives which have been isolated and synthesised at considerable expense . . . legal protection is needed to safeguard the large investments required for future work' (Murray, 1993, p. 79). Thus the question of who 'owned' extracted genetic material was made a legal one, complicated by political tensions and economic imperatives, and one which contributed to the difficulties in reaching agreement. Redgwell (1992, p. 265) notes that at one stage the draft convention was 46 pages long with 350 pieces of bracketed text, more bracketed text, she suggests, than agreed text.

Throughout this process, not a great deal of attention was paid to indigenous peoples' concerns. Chatterjee and Finger (1994, p. 43) suggest that the voices of local communities which often sustain and depend on biodiversity for foods, medicine and way of life were simply not heard nor, in any substantive way, sought. Indeed, Boyle (1994, p. 117) notes that Brazil objected to draft wording to the effect that biodiversity was the common concern of 'all peoples' on the grounds that it might be taken to confer rights on indigenous peoples. Little attention was paid to the important contribution to the biotechnology industry of indigenous peoples' knowledge about traditional medicines, knowledge for which no compensation or recognition had ever been given. Nor was the issue of intellectual property rights for indigenous peoples addressed in any detail. Soto argues that it is an irony that for many Southern countries 'the loss of biodiversity has often come as a result of new technologies (such as the Green Revolution) and forms of exploitation provided by the North at the expense of indigenous practices that helped sustain genetic diversity' (1992, p. 694).

The Convention on Biological Diversity

The Convention has a fairly lengthy preamble, 42 articles and two annexes, one on identification and monitoring and one on arbitration and conciliation. The Convention's objectives, set out in article 1, are the conservation of biological diversity, the sustainable use of its components, and the fair and equitable sharing of the benefits arising from the utilisation of genetic resources. The reasons for doing so: because biological diversity has 'intrinsic . . . ecological, genetic, social, economic, scientific, educational, cultural, recreational and aesthetic values' (elaborated in the first paragraph of the preamble) and because, the preamble rather curiously suggests, 'the conservation and sustainable use of biological diversity will strengthen friendly relations among States and contribute to peace for humankind' (UNEP, 1992, preamble). Obligations are, nevertheless, to be pursued at the national level, 'as far as possible and as appropriate', through the development of national strategies, plans and programmes (article 6), identification and monitoring (article 7), *in-situ* (article 8) and *ex-situ* (article 9) conservation and impact assessment (article 14).

The Convention reinforces sovereign rights over resources (article 3): the preamble identifies the conservation of biodiversity as a common *concern* (not a common heritage!) of humankind. No specific rights to genetic resources are guaranteed, although states are encouraged not to impose any restrictions on access that would 'run counter to the objectives' of the Convention (article 15.2). Access to genetic resources has to be on terms mutually agreed (among states) and has to be based on informed prior consent (again the consent of states). The results of research are to be shared with the aim of doing so in a 'fair and equitable way' (article 15.7). Technology for the conservation of biodiversity and the use of genetic resources is to be 'provided and/or facilitated' by developed countries (see article 16). 'Effective' participation in biotechnology research for parties who provide genetic resources (likely to be developing countries) is to be facilitated 'as appropriate' (article 19.1). Intellectual property rights (IPRs) and patents are to be adequately and effectively protected (see articles 16.2; 16.3; see also McNeely *et al.*, 1995, pp. 46–7). Boyle (1994, pp. 124–5) suggests, however, that this leaves unresolved the question of whether IPRs are intended to benefit the providers or users of genetic resources. It also leaves unresolved the question of whether IPRs are appropriate tools for the protection of indigenous knowledge. The preamble 'recognises' the traditional dependence of indigenous and local communities on biological resources and the 'desirability' of equitable sharing in benefits from the use of traditional knowledge, but the Convention includes little in the way of specific provisions to ensure that this dependence is protected and those benefits distributed, leaving it up to individual governments.

Institutional articles provide for a conference of parties (article 23), secretariat (article 24), a subsidiary body on scientific, technical and technological advice (SBSTTA) (article 25) and a financial mechanism (article 21). As with the FCCC, developing countries opposed the GEF as the financial mechanism for the Convention, lobbying instead for a separate Biodiversity Fund with compulsory contributions. Developed countries favoured a voluntary contributory mechanism, although the Convention provides that developed countries *shall* provide new and additional financial resources (article 20). In a strategy similar to that adopted in the Climate Change Convention, the CBD provides for the GEF to operate the financial mechanism on an interim basis, provided it has been appropriately restructured (article 39).

Elizabeth Dowdeswell, Executive Director of UNEP, called the Convention a 'unique opportunity for achieving a new contract between people and nature . . . a contract characterised by solidarity, independence and equity' (UNEP, 1994f). McNeely *et al.* (1995, p. 33) suggest that it is a comprehensive agreement and praise it for its attention to equity concerns. Others are not so sanguine. While

Boyle calls it an 'important new development' (1994, p. 111) he also accepts that it 'displays serious flaws' (1994, p. 112) noting that it is a convention driven by 'human use' rather than preservationist principles (1994, p. 115). Redgwell calls the obligations 'soft' (1992, p. 265). Chatterjee and Finger refer to the Convention as 'just one of many typical examples where the concern for exponential destruction has been perverted into a preoccupation with new scientific and (bio)-technological developments to boost economic growth' (1994, p. 42). They argue that it focuses too much on profits, patent rights, access and control and not enough on the main causes of the destruction of biodiversity. Brenton argues that the Convention is 'vague in the extreme' (1994, p. 204) as far as its conservation obligations are concerned, 'defective' and nothing more than a 'minimal first step' (1994, p. 205). This view is reinforced by Raustiala and Victor who describe the Convention as a 'pastiche of vague commitments, ambiguous phrases and some awkward compromises' (1996, p. 19).

The *Convention on Biological Diversity* was opened for signature at UNCED in June 1992 and came into effect on 29 December 1993. By the end of the Rio conference it had been signed by over 150 countries. The US was not among them, although in a statement which referred to the recommendations on biodiversity in Agenda 21 but made no reference at all to the Convention the US government called for a comprehensive international survey of plants, animals and natural resources (and the establishment of a multidisciplinary scientific committee to guide this effort) (see USIS, 1992b). The US did not sign on the grounds that the provisions went beyond legitimate biodiversity protection goals and that the Convention would unduly restrict the biotechnology industry. This decision was reversed by the new Clinton administration on 21 April 1993 although at time of writing ratification is still being held up in the US Senate.

In May 1993, UNEP's Governing Council established the Inter-governmental Committee on the Convention on Biodiversity (ICCBD) to prepare for the first COP which was held in the Bahamas from 28 November to 9 December 1994 with much of the agenda focusing on the basic machinery for the Convention's implementation. Debate continued on whether the GEF should be the funding mechanism, on the need for and purpose of a clearing-house mechanism and on the administration, budget and location of the Secretariat. The UK, in particular, was adamant that the COP should not be authorised to make decisions on the size or frequency of country contributions to the GEF for its biodiversity programme (see Anon.,

1994n, p. 265). Conservation issues under discussion included the importance of an ecosystem approach to species conservation, the need to address biodiversity conservation in the context of forests, agricultural production and fisheries management, and the general difficulties of defining sustainable use of biodiversity resources. Other substantive issues, including indigenous peoples' rights and the negotiation of a biosafety protocol, were deferred until later in the medium-term work programme established by the COP.

The second Conference of Parties convened in Jakarta, Indonesia, from 6 to 17 November 1995 under the theme *Biodiversity for Equitable Welfare of all People*. This meeting addressed what the *Earth Negotiations Bulletin* called both the 'internal affairs' and the 'external relations' of the CBD (see IISD, 1995b) although it tended to be dominated by 'scientific, technical and technological issues' (Glowka, 1996, p. 72). Decisions were made on many of the issues that seemed to have been hastily put to one side at COP-1: Montreal was designated as the location for the permanent secretariat (to be run by UNEP); there was agreement to negotiate a biosafety protocol; the GEF was redesignated as the continuing (but still interim) financial mechanism. Substantive conservation issues, including those of marine and coastal biodiversity, were also on the agenda and there was agreement to address the contentious issue of forests and biodiversity, including the COP input to the Commission on Sustainable Development's new Intergovernmental Panel on Forests (IPF).

The Parties met again for COP-3 in Buenos Aires, in November 1996, a meeting characterised by efforts to further the Convention's 'aspiring role as a focal point' on biodiversity issues (IISD, 1996h). The emphasis was thus on implementation of earlier decisions with the Parties adopting a fairly detailed work programme and agreeing to hold an intersessional meeting on indigenous issues. They also took steps to elaborate further the position of the COP *vis-à-vis* other international fora, such as the WTO and the World Intellectual Property Organisation on intellectual property issues, and the FAO and the Intergovernmental Panel on Forests on plant genetic resources and forest biodiversity.

Global Heritage or Sovereign Resources: Deforestation

Deforestation has been rather dryly defined as a change in land use from forest to non-forest purposes (an approach adopted by FAO and UNEP – see Thomas, 1992b, p. 240). The extent of present-day tropical forest loss is unclear, because no fully accurate baseline information is available. Estimates vary from 11 million hectares (Thomas, 1992b, p. 242) to 17 million hectares (Chatterjee and Finger, 1994, p. 46) to 20 million hectares (Fairclough, 1991, p. 91) per year, something in the vicinity of 1.8 to 2 per cent of tropical forest cover annually. Over the last 30 years, 40 per cent of rainforests have disappeared and the rate of deforestation may well be on the increase. Murray (1993, p. 72) notes that in 1980 about 113 000 square kilometres of tropical forest was cleared. By 1990 annual clearance was 169 000 square kilometres. A study in *The Economist* (Anon., 1994h, p. 29) reports that the rate of forest clearance in Asia has roughly trebled since the early 1960s. The replenishment of this 'renewable' resource is often marginal. Drawing on the Brundtland Report, MacNeill (1989–90, p. 6) observes that in 1950 Ethiopia was 30 per cent forested but by the late 1980s that figure was down to 4 per cent. India's forest cover has gone from 50 per cent 75 years ago to about 14 per cent now. In 1961 over half of Thailand (53 per cent) was covered in forest: by 1986 the figure was 29 per cent.

The pattern of deforestation is also changing. In a report for Friends of the Earth, Norman Myers suggested that three countries – Brazil, Indonesia and Zaire – comprise about 50 percent of tropical timber deforestation with another seven – Burma, Columbia, India, Malaysia, Mexico, Nigeria and Thailand – adding another quarter to that total (see Thomas, 1992b, pp. 242–3). The rate of deforestation is now on the decrease in Brazil, but on the increase in the Philippines and Vietnam. Deforestation has also decreased in Thailand since a Royal decree placed restrictions on logging in that country but logging activity, often illegal, has been displaced into Burma. Yet is worth remembering that while the contemporary emphasis is on deforestation in tropical regions, prior to World War II much of the world's deforestation took place in temperate regions. The World Rainforest Movement suggests that Western Europe, for example, has lost 70 per cent of its forests since Roman times and argues that fully one-third of 'temperate broadleaved forests have been lost since the dawn of agriculture' (1990, p. 21).

The causes of deforestation are varied and patterns of forest use and forest destruction will also vary from region to region. One of the primary causes of deforestation is the conversion of forest land to agricultural land, both for large-scale agriculture (including ranching and cash cropping) and for subsistence agriculture. Large-scale conversion is often related in the first instance to the production of elite wealth, which has in the past often been supported by fiscal incentives. In Brazil, for example, ranching attracted subsidies and zero tax rates on income, thus making land conversion, often without subsequent use, an attractive financial proposition. The policy was abolished in 1989 but cattle ranching accounted for 38 per cent of all deforestation in Amazonia in the years between 1960 and 1976 (Woodliffe, 1991, p. 61). Forest land has often been cleared in support of mono-cropping, frequently for the production not of food stuffs for local consumption, but for export in the service of debt. Land cleared in Thailand, for example, has been used to grow cassava for feedstock in the EC and soybeans grown on once-forested land in Amazonia are destined for overseas markets rather than to feed local populations (see Opschoor, 1989, pp. 139–40). Land clearance and forest loss arises also from internal colonisation initiatives, the two best known of which are the Indonesian Transmigration Scheme, which was funded partly by the World Bank, and the Brazilian Polonoroeste Programme.

The slash-and-burn agriculture traditionally practised by shifting cultivators – up to 10 per cent of the world's population – is based on ecologically sound principles. It minimises threats to the forest by leaving land fallow over periods of time long enough for regeneration. The numbers of peoples engaged in slash-and-burn agriculture has been increased by what Norman Myers calls the 'shifted cultivator' (1992, p. 444), landless peasants who have been forced from their own lands. Increases in the number of people pursuing such a subsistence lifestyle contributes to deforestation through further encroachment on forest lands and reductions in fallow-times. Caution is required here, however, not to cast as culprits those who are forced into more unsustainable uses of forest land as less land becomes available through land accumulation for large-scale agriculture and mono-cropping. Uneven land tenure contributes even further to this problem – 75 per cent of people in developing countries depend on agriculture for their livelihood, but do not own the land they farm (Thomas, 1992b, p. 247) making them vulnerable to land clearance and development programmes.

Commercial logging – both legal and illegal – is another source of deforestation although there are regional differences in the extent of that contribution. Porter and Brown (1991, p. 97) suggest that logging is responsible for about 20 to 25 per cent of annual forest loss. The World Rainforest Movement (1990, p. 51) suggests a lower figure, in the vicinity of 10 per cent, but notes that logging is the major cause of primary rainforest destruction in SouthEast Asia and Africa. This has been accompanied by an increase in what Colchester calls 'South–South colonialism' (1994a, p. 52) where the foreign companies which are awarded logging concessions in tropical regions are not Northern-based companies but companies from the Newly Industrialised Countries (NICs) of Malaysia and South Korea.

Fuelwood demand is another cause of deforestation although its contributions may have been overstated. In many developing countries, fuelwood is still a major source of energy. Even in an oil-rich country like Nigeria, 82 per cent of energy demands in the 1980s were met by fuelwood (Thomas, 1992b, p. 250). Urban preferences for charcoal, which is less energy-efficient than 'unadulterated' wood, exacerbates fuelwood demand. Nevertheless, in rural communities in developing countries, on the other hand, much of the fuelwood that is collected for domestic use – primarily by women – rarely involves the destruction of large stands of trees. Firewood collection primarily affects open forests and fallow land rather than closed forests (see WRM, 1990, p. 79). Pollution and pollution-related diseases are one more cause of deforestation or 'forest death' (waldsterben). A study by the Economic Commission for Europe (ECE) estimated that in some European countries, up to two-thirds of all trees showed some degree of pollutant-related damage (see WRM, 1990, p. 22).

Forests are ecologically, economically and culturally important at a local and global level and the loss of forests therefore has a number of impacts. Forests help prevent soil erosion and impede water flows. They contribute to the regulation of local climate systems. The ecological consequences of deforestation therefore include soil erosion, nutrient loss, siltation of watershed and downstream ecosystems, possible increase in floods and droughts, and changes in local and regional weather patterns. Forest destruction also contributes to climate change in what Peters calls a 'double assault' (1989–90, p. 73): deforestation contributes to the release of stored CO_2 as well as removing an important carbon sink, although the pattern and extent of carbon release and sequestering is as yet unclear. Mature forests, for example, are thought to have a minimal CO_2 fixation rate (see Thomas, 1992b, p. 260). However the most widely quoted figures suggests that forest destruction contributes up to one-third of annual global CO_2 emissions (see Woodliffe, 1991, p. 58). Forest destruction through burning contributes also to nitrous oxide emissions. A further indirect 'side-effect' is the potential increase in methane emissions from agricultural practices which supplant forest use. As noted earlier, loss of forests is also a major factor in loss of biodiversity: tropical forests, approximately 6 per cent of the world's land surface (Woodliffe, 1991, p. 59) contain at least 50 per cent and possibly up to 90 per cent of the world's species (WRM, 1990, p. 16). In Madagascar alone, for example, at least 1000 and possibly up to 2500 endemic plants have been lost because of deforestation (Thomas, 1992b, p. 256).

Forests also provide an economic resource. While tropical timber makes up about only 10 per cent of the world timber trade and is worth about $US7.5 billion per annum (see Anon., 1994f, p. 69), the price of tropical timber has risen by over 50 per cent since 1991 (Anon., 1994h, p. 29). There is little disagreement over the damage caused by most commercial logging. As Thomas observes, 'to date and almost without exception, logging has been undertaken in an environmentally harmful, economically unsustainable and socially destructive fashion' (1992b, p. 252). Unsustainable logging results in a loss of future economic resource. A study for the World Bank has predicted that of 'thirty-three developing countries that were exporting forest products in the mid-1980s . . . only ten will be doing so by the year 2000' (cited in Woodliffe, 1991, p. 61). Logging undermines the regenerative capacity of the forest and leads to erosion, loss of fauna and forest canopy (see Colchester, 1994a, p. 47) and contributes to 'collateral' forest damage through the opening up of access roads which facilitates settler movements and further conversion of land to agricultural purposes.

Deforestation results also in a loss of habitat and identity for indigenous forest dwellers through loss of land and, sometimes, forcible removal and resettlement. Approximately 50 million indigenous peoples plus another 90 million forest dwellers rely on forests not only for food, fodder, building materials and medicines but also for cultural and spiritual identity (see World Rainforest Movement, 1990, p. 18). As Colchester notes, the 'land rights of forest dwellers have consistently been denied and native leaders [have been] bought off or eliminated' (1994a, p. 48). The most well-publicised cases of destruction of indigenous forest habitats have been those of the Penan in Sarawak and the Yanomami Indians in the Brazilian Amazon but the pattern is repeated in a number of other countries.

Prior to UNCED, international action on forests was the realm of the 1983 International Tropical Timber Agreement (ITTA) and the 1985 Tropical Forestry Action Plan (TFAP). The ITTA, which entered into force in 1985, is primarily a commodity agreement focusing on trade in tropical timber products. The Agreement established the International Tropical Timber Organisation (ITTO), a forum for producers and consumers of tropical timber, which began operational activities in 1987. The ITTO has two, possibly mutually exclusive objectives. The first is to promote the expansion and diversification of international trade in tropical timber; the second is to maintain the ecological balance of the timber producing regions. The Agreement was initially welcomed as a real opportunity to curb the excesses of the timber industry but more recently it has been strongly criticised as little more than a lobbying group for timber interests (Colchester, 1990, p. 166) which promotes trade at the expense of conservation. Target 2000, the Organisation's (non-binding) attempt to reconcile its trade and conservation objectives by requiring that all tropical timber entering the international trade should come from sustainably-managed forest sources by the year 2000 has had little impact on logging practices. Indeed, the Organisation estimates that less than one-half of 1 per cent of all logging is managed on a sustainable basis (Porter and Brown, 1991, p. 101). Proposals to certify logs as sustainably grown, or attempts to restrict imports from countries which do not practice sustainable logging techniques, have run into difficulties within the free-trade ITTO with Malaysia leading the producer states in resisting restrictions on exports. Consumer states such as Japan, which is the largest source of ITTO funding and the major 'vote-holder' on the Council, have also opposed such proposals. The Coordinating Body for Indigenous Peoples Organisations of the Amazon Basin (COICA, 1991), has called the ITTO an 'anti-indigenous crime' for what is seen as endorsement of 'trespass' by logging companies on indigenous lands and its emphasis on the commercial timber value of the forest rather than (as representatives of the Native Peoples of Sarawak put it) the 'survival, social and cultural significance [of forests] to the local people' (Native Peoples of Sarawak, 1991). The successor agreement to the original ITTA was adopted in January 1994, but it is little changed from its predecessor, in spite of some hopes that it would extend coverage to temperate forests and require tropical timber products to come from sustainably managed forests.

The Tropical Forestry Action Plan was established in 1985 by the World Bank, UNEP, the FAO and World Resources Institute under the coordination of the forestry department of the FAO. It has, as its primary focus, the sustainable management of the forestry industry rather than of forests *per se*. It emphasises financial flows, technical assistance and policy advice to recipient countries for the development of National Forestry Action Plans (NFAPs). For some, the Plan was a mechanism to harmonise development assistance for forestry; for others it was to serve as a vehicle for addressing the fundamental causes of deforestation (see Thomas, 1992b, p. 261). It is not clear that it has fulfilled either expectation. The World Rainforest Movement identifies it as 'an attempt to legitimise the commercialisation of the world's tropical forests' and one which fails to address the primary causes of deforestation (WRM 1990, pp. 76–8). By 1990, annual funding for TFAP had reached $US1 billion per year, yet little of its budget, only about 9 per cent, has been spent on conservation (see Thomas, 1992b, p. 262). There is little procedural transparency and little consultation with local communities or with NGOs.

More recent attempts to forge a comprehensive and binding global forests agreement have been unsuccessful. In 1990, FAO's committee on forestry (COFO) and the FAO Council discussed the possibility of treaty negotiations although some participants, including the UK and the US, favoured an international agreement but were reluctant to see such negotiations proceed under the auspices of FAO. The 1990 G7 summit in Houston called for a convention on the protection of the world's forests to be negotiated for signature at Rio. Johnson notes the 'general air of weariness and pessimism' (1993, p. 108) associated with the forest negotiations during the Rio PrepComms. Preliminary discussions on a convention broke down after tropical timber producer countries, led by Malaysia, objected to any agreement which would infringe upon their sovereign rights to manage their resources, including their forests, as they saw fit in accordance with their own development priorities rather than Western-dominated environmental priorities. The chief Malaysian negotiator at UNCED took the view that 'forests are clearly a sovereign resource . . . we cannot allow forests to be taken up on global forums' (cited in Brenton, 1994, p. 216). Developing countries were concerned that the emphasis on a forests convention was a way of diverting attention from the issue of developed country commitments on climate change. Further difficulties arose in trying to get agreement on what kinds of forests should be covered in any international agreement – the developing countries argue that it is discriminatory for agreements to refer only to tropical forests – and how questions of responsibility and compensation should be addressed. Producer countries argued that if they were to forgo short-term gain from forest resources as a contribution to a greater global good, then compensation would be in order. As one Brazilian politician has claimed, 'if the Amazon is a world resource, the world will have to pay for it' (cited in Woodliffe, 1991, p. 69). There have also been differences of opinion as to whether sustainable forest management is primarily an economic or an ecological concept and whether strategies should focus on minimising the causes or alleviating the symptoms of deforestation.

UNCED Statement of Forest Principles

In the absence of any agreement on a convention, but unwilling to leave the matter altogether, participants sought to negotiate a weaker statement of principles. The text that went to Rio from the Prep-Comms was in a 'state of disarray' according to the Earth Summit report, with 73 instances of bracketed text (see Johnson, 1993, p. 109). What was finally agreed at Rio was, to give it its full title, a *Non-legally binding authoritative statement of forest principles for a global consensus on the management, conservation and sustainable development of all types of forests.* The statement is based on the concept of multiple value: it acknowledges forests as both ecological and economic resources which should be 'sustainably managed to meet the social, economic, ecological, cultural and spiritual human needs of present and future generations' (UNCED, 1992c, principle 2(b)). On the whole, though, the statement is little more than a series of general guidelines addressing, with no detail or commitment, a range of political concerns brought to the negotiations by the various parties. It reinforces states sovereign rights to resources (principles 1(a) and 2(a)). It emphasises the importance of international coop-eration, the imperatives for equitable sharing of the costs of forest conservation and sustainable development, the impact of external indebtedness and poverty on the ability of developing countries to manage their forests, the need for new and additional financial resources and the transfer of technology on concessional and pre-ferential terms. It reinforces the principle that trade in forest pro-ducts should be based on non-discriminatory and multilaterally agreed rules. It also pays some attention to the importance of full participation in decision-making and implementation of national strategies by indigenous people, local communities, forest dwellers and women.

The Statement of Principles (along with chapter 11 of Agenda 21, titled Combating Deforestation) has been criticised by Greenpeace as a further step 'towards legitimising the policies of those actors – the transnationals, the multilateral development banks, UN agencies etc – that have to date contributed to a large extent to the crisis of the tropical, temperate, and boreal forests' (cited in Chatterjee and Finger, 1994, p. 47). Alberto Szekely, a member of the International Law Commission, argues that the Forest Statement 'falls one hundred percent short of providing even the most elementary basis for an international regime for the protection of the world's forests' (1994, p. 67). The statement makes no reference to the relationship between deforestation and climate change, or forests and loss of biodiversity. Chapter 11 of Agenda 21 is primarily managerial in tone with an emphasis on programme areas which will support sustainable forest management and effective utilisation of the goods and services provided by forests, forest lands and woodlands.

The Forest Principles suggest that the issue of further international cooperation on forests (the words 'international convention' are not used) should be kept under assessment. Chapter 11 is slightly more direct in its suggestions that governments should consider the need for an international agreement on forests. Since Rio a number of other fora, both intergovernmental and non-governmental have sprung up to discuss and confer on forest issues, although none has yet emerged as any kind of precursor to formal negotiations on a convention. After its 1995 sectoral review, the Commission on Sustainable Development (CSD) (see Chapter 4) established the Intergovernmental Panel on Forests (one more open-ended ad hoc body to add to the list). The IPF is mandated to 'pursue consensus and coordinated proposals for action to support the management, conservation and sustainable development of forests' and to have policy recommendations available for CSD-5 in 1997, although its first meeting in September 1995 seems to have been dominated by procedural issues (see IISD, 1996d). A jointly-sponsored Malaysian/Canadian initiative – the Intergovernmental Working Group on Forests (IWGF) (initially 'Global Forests') – was established with the specific purpose of focusing on the 1995 CSD review of forests and the Agenda 21 commitments. However, the IWGF provides opportunities only for discussion, not negotiation. A 'Working Group on Criteria and Indicators for the Conservation and Sustainable Management of Temperate and Boreal Forests' (the Montreal Process for short) was established in 1993, and in February 1995 completed its task of developing a 'scientifically rigorous [but non-binding] set of criteria and indicators' to measure forest management at a national level (see IISD, 1996a). Another forum, the Helsinki Process, had already begun work in 1990 to develop guidelines on the sustainable management of forests in Europe, a process which has been progressed through a series of ministerial and expert meetings (IISD, 1996b). The major non-governmental forum for discussion on forest issues, and one which may well have some input into the 1997 CSD review on forests, is the World Commission on Forests and Sustainable Development. This Commission was first convened in June 1995 (although the initial idea was proposed in 1992) under the auspices of the InterAction Council of Former Heads of State and Government. Many of the tensions which characterised UNCED negotiations on forests and deforestation have continued to shape debates in these fora, particularly those pursued under the auspices of the IPF prior to the 1997 CSD5 review. Humphreys summarises those tensions and issues thus: the future of the criteria and indicators process, the certification and labelling of timber products, the role of the FAO and the whole issue of a forests convention (1996a, pp. 244–51).

Common Interest and Global Burden Sharing: Desertification

The extent to which desertification, in both its causes and impacts, is a transboundary problem is open to dispute. Nevertheless even if it is not transboundary in the usual sense there are, as Abate and Akhtar suggest, still good reasons for addressing desertification issues in a global regime, not least of which are the 'principles of burden-sharing and a common interest in the global environment' (1994, p. 77). The negotiations on desertification resulted in the first post-UNCED convention mandated by the Rio conference although international deliberations on this issue date to the 1970s.

Desertification is the reduction in or loss of the biological productivity of land (land degradation) particularly in drylands ecosystems. Conventional wisdom is that desertification is on the increase and that it now threatens about between 25 and 35 per cent of the earth's land surface and between one-sixth and one-quarter of the world's population (Abate and Akhtar, 1994, p. 72). Chapter 12 of Agenda 21 (UNCED, 1992b, para 12.2) suggests that about 70 per cent of the world's drylands and one-quarter of the total land area of the world are affected, degradation that, according to UNEP (1995e), directly affects 250 million people and directly puts at risk another one billion, many of them already living in poverty.

The causes of desertification include human activities and climatic variations. Changing land-use patterns and ecologically unsustainable agriculture – including overcultivation, planting of inappropriate crops, heavy use of fertilisers and chemicals – contribute to the kind of soil erosion and land degradation that results in desertification. Overgrazing of stock is another possible cause. As with deforestation, such practices are often the unintended consequences of development programmes, inequitable land tenure and enforced unsustainable use of marginal lands rather than the result of conscious and deliberate negligence by local communities. Changes in climate patterns, as a result of anthropogenic interference as well as natural climate cycles, chronic drought and dessication also contribute to desertification (see Hulme and Kelly, 1993). UNEP (1995b) points out that the relationship between population pressures and land degradation is not clear cut, noting that in some cases a decline in population can result in non-caring for the land, and citing examples of high population density not resulting in land degradation.

The ecological impacts that help to define desertification include decline in soil fertility and soil structure, loss of biodiversity, degradation of irrigated cropland and loss of arable land. The socioeconomic effects include food insecurity and loss of subsistence livelihoods with flow-on effects of exacerbation of poverty, malnutrition, starvation and forced movements of peoples. There are also extensive economic costs: UNEP (1995c) estimates the direct loss of annual income through desertification at about $US42 billion per year but is reluctant to put an estimate on indirect costs.

The United Nations Environment Programme has taken the institutional lead in mobilising action and negotiations on this issue but a general lack of funding and political will limited the success of early attempts to address desertification. In 1977, UNEP convened the UN Conference on Desertification (UNCOD) from which came the Plan of Action to Combat Desertification (PACD). Two years later the Governing Council of UNEP called on governments to contribute to a special fund set up by the Secretary-General to counter the spread of deserts. The Plan was less than successful even though over 30 National Action Plans were prepared and overseen by the Desertification Control Programme Activity Centre (DC/PAC) (see Anon., 1994d, p. 60). A 1992 report by UNEP suggested that low priority by funding agencies, lack of funds within developing countries, a lack of integration of desertification programmes with other socio-developmental programmes, failure to include local populations and the domination of political and economic problems over environmental concerns were explanatory factors (see IISD, 1993a). Attempts in the mid-1980s to manage and halt desertification in Africa, including the establishment in 1984 of a four-year drought and desertification control programme for the mid-Sahel and, in 1985, the Cairo programme for African cooperation on desertification issues, were faced with similar problems.

The resolution which established UNCED also called for 'high priority' to be given to drought and desertification control and called upon the Conference to consider *all means necessary* to halt and reverse the process of desertification (UNGA, 1989c, para. 15(g); emphasis added). It was the G77 countries which argued that 'all means necessary' should include a desertification convention. At a regional preparatory meeting for UNCED, in November 1991, representatives of African countries adopted the African Common Position on Environment and Development along with the Abidjan Declaration which called, among other things, for a convention to combat desertification to be one of the specific outcomes mandated in Agenda 21 (see IISD, 1993a). The industrialised countries, particularly the EC and the US, were less persuaded that desertification was an international issue and no negotiations for a convention were set in train prior to UNCED. Chapter 12 of Agenda 21 – the chapter on combating desertification and drought – remained bracketed until the final PrepComm. It sets out six programme areas which emphasise both mitigation and response strategies, focusing not only on specific anti-desertification plans but on integrated programmes for the eradication of poverty. It also requests the General Assembly to convene negotiations on a desertification convention (UNCED, 1992b, para. 12.40).

At the end of 1992, General Assembly resolution 47/188 established what was formally known as the intergovernmental negotiating committee for the elaboration of an international convention to combat desertification in those countries experiencing serious drought and/or desertification particularly in Africa – known (thankfully) as the INCD for short. The Committee, under the chair of Ambassador Bo Kjellén of Sweden, held a preliminary organisational session and five substantive negotiating sessions working through the issues in two main working groups supported by an interim secretariat. A special voluntary fund was established to provide assistance for developing countries to participate in the negotiations.

There were a number of difficult issues but the negotiations seem to have been less acrimonious than those on biodiversity or forests. However, the United States and the EC continued to oppose the identification of desertification as a global problem rather than a regional issue of concern only to affected countries. The nature of solutions was also fundamental – should the convention address causes or symptoms, should strategies be reductive or adaptive, did natural climatic factors place limits on strategies and should drought be considered on an equal footing with desertification. Debate on commitments focused on the extent to which affected countries (mainly developing countries) should be required to take action to halt or reverse desertification and the degree of obligation of developed countries to provide assistance. Industrialised countries argued that any financial assistance should be conditional upon a complementarity of commitment. Developing countries, while seeking to maintain sovereign rights, were also keen that a convention acknowledge the importance of economic growth, social development and the eradication of poverty as relevant strategies for which they required assistance. The Africa Group (representing that part of the world most affected) called not only for new resources but also for debt relief and commitments to the UN target of 0.7 per cent of GNP to be committed to official development assistance (ODA). One of the most difficult issues, on which negotiations almost stalled at the first substantive INCD in 1993, was that of the elaboration of regional instruments as annexes to the convention. The INCD's initial mandate was to negotiate an annex on Africa, with annexes on Latin America/Caribbean and Asia to be attended to once the convention had been agreed. Non-Africa regional groups emphasised the importance of extending this mandate to include other regions in the draft Convention and in 1993 the General Assembly adopted a resolution which did just that.

UN Convention to combat desertification in those countries experiencing serious drought and/or desertification, particularly in Africa (CCD)

The Convention was finalised in June 1994 and opened for signature in Paris on 14–15 October 1994. Four regional annexes (for Africa, Latin America/Caribbean, Asia and the Northern Mediterranean) are appended to the Convention: the African annex is the most 'elaborate in form and content' (Anon., 1994l, p. 229). At the June meeting, the INCD adopted a resolution on urgent action for Africa, recommending a range of further measures including the establishment of partnership arrangements between African countries and developed countries (see UNEP, 1994e). The preamble to the Convention identifies desertification as having a 'global dimension' (in that it affects all regions of the world) thus requiring joint action. The rather awkwardly-phrased objective of the Convention (article 2) is to:

> combat desertification and mitigate the effects of drought in countries experiencing serious drought and/or desertification, particularly in Africa, through effective action at all levels, supported by international cooperation and partnership arrangements, in the framework of an integrated approach which is consistent with Agenda 21, with a view to contributing to the achievement of sustainable development in affected areas. (UNEP, 1994h)

Actions on desertification should, according to the Convention, be informed by the principles of participation, including local participation, cooperation at international, national and local levels, and consideration of the special needs of affected developing countries. Both affected countries and developed countries have obligations under the Convention, the former to give priority to desertification and to enact or strengthen laws, policies and action programmes in support of this and the latter to provide support and financial resources and facilitate access to technology, knowledge and know-how.

In contrast with the precedent set by other negotiations, this Convention is more than a framework agreement: as well as the usual statements of principle and procedural and institutional articles, the Convention contains detailed provisions for action. Much of the Convention is concerned with the development of action programmes at national, subregional and regional levels, scientific and technical cooperation and supporting measures such as capacity building, education and public awareness. The Convention places particular emphasis on participation (including that of local communities, indigenous peoples and women), decentralisation and 'bottom-up' planning.

The INCD continued to function prior to entry into force, meeting twice in 1995 and twice again in 1996 in preparation for the first

Conference of the Parties. Progress has been made on procedural matters relating to scientific and technical cooperation, but financial issues, especially those relating to the Global Mechanism and its likely host institution, remain unresolved (see IISD, 1996e, 1996f). Reports indicate that steps are already underway with respect to implementation of the Annex and recommendations relating to urgent action in Africa (CCD, 1996). The requisite fiftieth ratification (from Chad) was deposited on 27 September 1996 and the Convention came into effect on 26 December 1996. As with other conventions discussed in this chapter, the CCD is a compromise. Nevertheless, this Convention has been received with more optimism (albeit still cautious) than other global agreements: as one commentator notes 'few were totally pleased with the outcome . . . most were hopeful that this Convention could have some positive impact' (Anon., 1994l, p. 230). It is more activist in content than other agreements discussed here although it remains to be seen how its provisions, especially those on participation, implementation and cooperation, will translate into practice now that the Convention is in force.

Conclusion

The agreements and issues covered in this chapter have continued to dominate the global environmental agenda since the end of the UN Conference on Environment and Development. As suggested in the analysis here, they have been greeted with both optimism and pessimism. In the former case, the processes of negotiation and the adoption of an agreement, especially those which seem to give voice to the principles of sustainable development and precaution, have determined the criteria for success. In the latter, the fact that most of these agreements are declaratory, with little in the way of specific targets or agreements and little in the way of effective provisions for implementation, verification and compliance is taken as evidence that they will do little to mitigate the environmental problems they purport to address.

The description of the negotiations and agreements in Chapter 2 and in this chapter have focused primarily on difficulties specific to each of these environmental concerns. Clearly, however, there are patterns of dispute which they share in common. It is those patterns and the questions to which they give rise which are examined more closely in the following chapters of this book – questions of govern-ance and participation, questions about the international political economy, the pursuit of sustainable development and tensions be-tween developed and developing countries, and questions on the fundamental understanding and purpose of environmental security. It will come as no surprise that the answers to those questions and, indeed, the very framing of the questions in the first place, are contested and in dispute.

4

The State and Global Institutions

Introduction

As environmental problems become transboundary and global in nature, they require international agreements which are not only precautionary and take into account often-incomplete but changing scientific information, but which also establish environmental standards and means by which those standards can be met and verified. Environmental agreements and the procedures by which they are negotiated need to account for the interests of a range of 'stakeholders' including environmental non-governmental organisations, grass-roots movements, indigenous peoples, industry, financial institutions, scientific bodies and intergovernmental organisations as well as states and governments. Environmental governance, therefore, must at minimum be cooperative and collective.

Yet as chapters in the previous section have suggested, environmental treaties and international environmental institutions, where they exist, have often been less effective than the environmental tasks at hand require. They either lack formal competence, because states are reluctant to give it to them, or they lack real powers, often for the same reason. Existing institutions are often poorly funded with little political clout. Nor has there been much beyond a rhetorical commitment to important cross-sectoral issues of financial and technology transfer, debt, unequal trading relationships or poverty alleviation. In general, the 'unprecedentedly high degree of international cooperation and mutual understanding' (Fairclough, 1991, p. 83) that is required has not been forthcoming.

Despite the declarations, resolutions, conventions and protocols that have been adopted in the years since Stockholm, the overall state of the environment continues to deteriorate. As Shanna Halpern bluntly put it just after the Rio Conference, 'the global environment is worse now than it was two decades ago – not one major environmental issue debated in Stockholm has been solved' (1992). Lester Brown takes a similar view: 'the health of the planet has deteriorated dangerously during the twenty years since Stockholm' (1992, p. 174). In his opening statement to UNCED (reproduced in Johnson, 1993, p. 50), Maurice Strong argued that 'despite significant progress made since 1972 in many areas, the hopes ignited at Stockholm remain largely unfulfilled'. Mostafa Tolba, at that stage still Executive Director of UNEP, also observed at UNCED that none of the problems of Stockholm had been solved (cited in Cropper, 1992, p. 314). Two years later, Strong admitted that 'the momentum of Rio has been lost at the government level and the fundamental changes need to head off impending disaster are no closer to reality than they were – in fact things have gone backwards if anything' (cited in Kirwin, 1994, p. 24).

Thus we have a crisis in and perhaps even a failure of international environmental governance which is, as the introduction to this book pointed out, something more than formal decision-making structures and processes. It includes the norms, principles and political practices which inform decision-making. Analyses of the crisis in governance and responses to it fall, perhaps a little untidily, into two broad categories – a reformist approach which seeks to work within and improve existing international frameworks and a critical approach, which questions the usefulness of those institutions and the values which underpin them, seeking a sometimes radical transformation in the structures and practices of international politics.

For many, the failure of environmental governance arises because existing international practices are no longer adequate, if they ever were, when it comes to dealing with transboundary and environmental degradation. Koy Thomson argues that 'environmental diplomacy seems too immature to find a way through the many impasses' (1992, p. 4). Susan Bragdon suggests that 'the traditional orientation of international law . . . is ill-suited to address global environmental problems' (1992, p. 383). Hilary French (1992, p. 157) points out that international institutional development is not keeping pace with increasing interdependencies. Thus governance is understood as a procedural and institutional problem and solutions to the crisis in environmental governance can be found in reform. For those who adopt a more critical approach, the crisis in environmental governance has a more fundamental cause. It arises because there is an incongruence between problems which arise from the interconnected nature of the global ecosystem and solutions which are sought in the framework of a geopolitical system based on the state. As the World Commission on Environment and Development observed, 'the Earth is one but the world is not' (1987, p. 27) – and that is part of the problem. This chapter turns first to those debates about the inadequate state and, by extension, the inadequate state system before exploring the range of options offered for better, stronger, or even global governance.

The Inadequate State?

Global environmental problems call into question the adequacy and authority of the state, the reality and utility of sovereignty as a fundamental international norm, and the nature of international governance which, together, the state and sovereignty engender. Transboundary environmental degradation presents a challenge to the internal autonomy and authority, that is the sovereignty, of the state. In Brenton's view, the 'emergence of the [environmental] agenda is plainly a symptom of the diminishing authority of the nation-state' (1994, p. 7). The causes of environmental degradation in any one state often lie outside that state and the impacts do not recognise the porous borders of sovereign states. Clearly, then, as a report on environmental security published by the Peace Research Institute, Oslo (PRIO) and UNEP puts it, 'the notion of sovereignty is difficult (if not impossible) to maintain within an ecological frame of reference' (PRIO, 1989, p. 18). Further, the state cannot 'defend' its territory against externally sourced environmental threats and is therefore incapable of fulfilling the social contract to provide security for its citizens. Elise Boulding (1991) argues, for example, that the state is at best an ambivalent defender of environmental security. Gwyn Prins goes even further: we live, he suggests, in the era of the incapable state, an era characterised by the 'waning ability of state power to engage with the environmental security agenda' (1990, p. 722). In such circumstances, unilateral action by states is likely to be ineffective as a response to transboundary or global environmental degradation. The principle of self-help is of limited use.

There are also doubts as to the extent of cooperation and collective action that can be achieved, through diplomacy, international law and the development of international institutions, in a system of international governance in which the sovereignty of states remains a fundamental organising principle. Hurrell and Kingsbury, for example, question whether 'a fragmented and often highly conflictual political system made up of over 170 sovereign states and numerous other actors [can] achieve the high (and historically unprecedented) levels of cooperation and policy coordination needed to manage environmental problems on a global scale' (1992b, p. 1). One of the primary principles of international law is that states, as sovereign actors, cannot be bound without their consent. Thus environmental diplomacy proceeds on the basis of consensus, which has value in that all parties can agree to the final instrument (although this does not prevent them from then refusing to sign, as happened with the Biodiversity Convention). It also results in lowest common denominator agreements shaped as much if not more by political and economic compromises as by environmental concerns. Consensus demands also ensure that the negotiation process is often lengthy with final agreements cobbled together hurriedly in the final hours of the final days. Inordinate amounts of time are often given over to procedural matters, such as the setting of the agenda, the focus and composition of working groups, the election of officers, the nature of seating arrangements, to ensure that no one country or group of countries feels disadvantaged in the subsequent substantive negotiation. The sovereignty imperative means also that states are reluctant to adopt international environmental agreements which would involve an abrogation of authority to an international institution on issues such as standard setting, monitoring or enforcement. Thus institutional frameworks are rarely authoritative. Environmental agreements rarely incorporate sanctions, extensive verification procedures, compliance mechanisms or dispute settlement mechanisms. Such agreements might meet the test of success of words on paper but their success as environmental instruments is open to question.

National sovereignty, or at least the claiming of it, is therefore interpreted as a barrier to global environmental cooperation and the achievement of the kinds of agreements that are required to address environmental degradation successfully. Of course, there is an irony here. If states were willing to relinquish whatever degree of sovereignty might be required in the interests of a common future, then the reasons for them needing to do so in the first place, that is to overcome the competitive self-interests which are the basis of the (environmental) tragedy of the commons, would cease to be relevant. At the very least what is proposed as a response to the crisis in governance is some kind of 'reality fix' to take account of ecological interdependence. Hilary French sums up this position when she argues that 'stronger international governance will evolve . . . from better utilisation of existing mechanisms and, over time, through the development of new ones' (1992, p. 157). Those mechanisms of governance include international environmental law which is explored here before the chapter turns to a more extensive consideration of the nature of international institutions.

International Environmental Law

UNCED was mandated to promote the 'further development of international environmental law', including the 'feasibility of elaborating general rights and obligations of States' (UNGA, 1989c, Part I, 15(d)). Thus the General Assembly accepted that states were the subjects of international law. The focus of the Conference, and of chapter 39 of Agenda 21 on international legal instruments and mechanisms, was primarily on effective participation (by states) in international law-making, implementation mechanisms, dispute resolution and general standard-setting. There was little substantive attention to the nature or content of legal principles (except for a long paragraph which sought to ensure that standards should not be trade distorting). UNCED therefore reinforced the status quo with respect to international environmental law. There is, however, an ever-growing body of work which questions whether 'the existing international legal order [is] fundamentally and inherently inimical to environmental protection, requiring wholesale rejection and re-invention' (Sands, 1993, p. xviii). A detailed analysis of that international legal order and the principles which inform it is beyond the scope of this book. Yet the emphasis on state sovereignty in the traditional model of international law is argued to have led to 'generally decentralised rule enforcement' (Springer, 1983, p. 32) and an unwillingness among states to exercise guardianship over the global environment (Sands, 1989, p. 393). Not everyone agrees with these propositions. Birnie takes the view that 'ample techniques derived from traditional sources of international law are available for development of regulations to protect the environment' (1992, p. 82). At one level, then, the problems of international environmental law are identified as procedural and institutional – Palmer, for example, argues that the existing *processes* of making international law are 'slow, cumbersome, expensive, uncoordinated and uncertain' (1992,

p. 259) – and the emphasis on 'further development of international law' is on improving regulatory techniques and the processes for making international law. At another level, that exemplified by Sands (and others), the problem is more fundamental, and the 'further development of international law' requires a new legal ethic which incorporates not only new principles but which also involves other actors besides states, particularly non-governmental organisations, as legitimate subjects of international law.

Within a reformist tradition, attention has been paid to elaborating and reformulating the legal doctrine of state responsibility and liability. Principle 21 of the Stockholm Declaration – that oft-quoted principle that reinforces sovereignty over resources – also requires that states should not cause damage to the environment of other states or to areas beyond national jurisdiction. While this would seem to establish the basis for a principle of state responsibility and, therefore, liability, especially as it builds on earlier arbitrations, it has proved more difficult to put into practice. Certainly it is open to question whether, in spite of references to transboundary responsibility in many environmental declarations and other texts, there is little more than fragmentary evidence that such principles have become customary international law – that would require evidence of general state practice and that, it would seem, is not yet the case. Along with responsibility and liability comes the issue of whether states have a duty to inform and consult other states with respect to detrimental environmental impact of their activities (a contentious issue at the Stockholm Conference) and what legal remedies might be available in the case of transboundary or potentially global environmental degradation. The issues of liability and compensation have been under scrutiny by the International Law Commission, by a group of legal experts convened by the World Commission on Environment and Development, and by a UNEP expert meeting held prior to UNCED (see Palmer, 1992). UNCED itself did not really come to grips with these issues, suggesting only (in chapter 39 of Agenda 21) that future action could include an 'examination of the feasibility of elaborating general rights and obligations of States' (UNCED, 1992b, para. 39.5) which simply repeated the wording of resolution 44/228. The Conference, Peter Sand argues, 'brought no basic changes in the mechanisms of international law-making or dispute resolution' (1993, p. 388).

International environmental law has, however, provided a focus for the elaboration of new principles such as the polluter pays principle

(PPP) and the precautionary principle. The polluter pays principle, which is discussed further in Chapter 8, is not, as often thought, primarily a principle on compensation. Rather it was developed as an economic principle under the auspices of the OECD and was designed to prevent public subsidisation of environmental repair or preventive action. In other words, all costs should be borne by the polluter, in order that polluters should not otherwise have any unfair commercial advantage. Principle 16 of the Rio Declaration may give some further effect to the customary intent of the polluter pays principle although it is rather vague in its wording and injunction. The principle says, in full, that '[n]ational authorities should endeavour to promote the internalisation of environmental costs and the use of economic instruments, taking into account the approach that the polluter should, in principle, bear the cost of pollution, with due regard to the public interest and without distorting international trade and investment' (UNCED, 1992a).

The precautionary principle, which is intended as a response both to scientific uncertainty and to the imperatives of anticipating environmental degradation rather than relying on reactive action and international law, has evolved through various processes, including the ad hoc International North Sea Conferences (see Birnie, 1992, p. 80), building on domestic application in what was then West Germany. It has been incorporated into international conventions such as the Framework Convention on Climate Change and adopted in principle 15 of the Rio Declaration which states that 'the precautionary approach shall be widely applied by States according to their capabilities' (UNCED, 1992a). However, the exact content of the precautionary principle and what it means in practice is open to debate. NGOs, for example, have taken it to mean a reversing of the burden of proof – that is, that until and unless it can be determined that an action (for example, the dumping of wastes at sea) does not cause environmental damage, then that action should be prevented or restricted. In more conventional use, it has been interpreted as encouraging and perhaps even requiring action to be taken even when there is a degree (and the degree is unspecified) of scientific uncertainty – thus it is a precautionary action. One of the difficulties here is whether the precautionary principle is to be invoked only as a response to scientific uncertainty or whether the principle has more general applicability, requiring that any action be precautionary in content – that is, a cautious action which prevents further environmental damage. The application of the precautionary principle is complicated further because many environmental agreements also incorporate an 'acceptability' principle, suggesting that some impact on the environment *is* acceptable but that any actions which are intended or might be expected to cause long-term, severe or irreversible damage are not.

The elaboration of more specific rights and obligations for states and the development of regulatory techniques is, for some, insufficient to strengthen international environmental law and its contribution to international governance. Rather, new concepts such as the common heritage of humankind, intergenerational equity and the idea of environmental rights must be incorporated into international law, both as principle and as specific provisions designed to give effect to those principles. These principles seek not only to incorporate into law an ethic of justice but also challenge, in effect, traditional state-centric jurisdictions as well as widening the scope of those to whom obligations are owed in international law beyond states and present generations.

The common heritage of humankind principle articulates the view that common spaces – areas beyond national jurisdiction such as the high seas, outer space, Antarctica – should be regulated for the benefit of the international community as a whole rather than being subject to the first-come, first-served law of open spaces. The legal and customary content of the common heritage concept is unclear. It has been partially accepted with respect to the high seas, through the UN Convention on the Law of the Sea which has now come into effect, but it has certainly been challenged with respect to the Antarctic, and probably not tested at all with respect to outer space. It is also the case that the elaboration of the principle in UNCLOS was intended primarily to address issues of common management of resource exploitation rather than stewardship of the environment. Efforts have been made to articulate the common heritage principle with respect to the atmosphere and the climate system although the Climate Change Convention acknowledges only that change in the Earth's climate (and its adverse effects) are a common *concern* of humankind. Attempts to apply this principle to biodiversity and tropical forests – areas (or 'resources') which are clearly under national jurisdiction – has been contentious, as Chapter 3 has demonstrated, especially if the implication is therefore that such areas must be managed either by an international body, or by a state or group of states acting as trustees or stewards for the benefit of the international community.

The idea of a heritage invokes the principle of intergenerational equity which suggests that future generations have a right to inherit a planetary environment in at least as good a condition as previous generations have enjoyed. Thus present generations have an obligation to ensure that they do not damage the planetary ecosystem in such a way that this right is denied. The Stockholm Declaration suggested in principle 1 that we have a solemn responsibility to protect and improve the environment for present and future generations. The concept of sustainable development elaborated by the Brundtland Commission (on which more in Chapter 7) embodies some element of intergenerational equity – that is, it relies on meeting the needs of the present generation without compromising the needs of future generations (see WCED, 1987, p. 8). The idea of some degree of intergenerational responsibility would seem to be accepted in general and wording of this nature is often incorporated in environmental agreements. The difficulty, legal academic arguments about the content of a right held by generations as yet unborn notwithstanding, is how to give effect to this and how an obligation to future generations can be tested and operationalised.

The issues of 'rights' includes not only intergenerational equity but also intragenerational equity (an issue addressed in more detail in Chapters 7 and 8) as well as the question of whether there is such a thing as an human right to 'environment'. As Shelton (1991, pp. 103–4) notes, some international agreements, such as the UN Convention on the Rights of the Child, do refer to environmental rights, and the UN Commission on Human Rights has asserted a link between preservation of the environment and the promotion of human rights. The Stockholm Declaration declares that people have a 'fundamental right to freedom, equality and adequate conditions of life, in an environment of a quality that permits a life of dignity and well-being' (principle 1), implying that the exercise of other human rights require basic environmental health (see Shelton, 1991, p. 112). The 1989 Hague Declaration recognises, in paragraph 5, that environmental degradation affects the 'right to live in dignity in a viable global environment'. While Sands identifies the potential difficulties in bringing together environmental concerns and human rights, in that 'a distinction may be drawn between environmental rights, which are collective, and human rights, which under the current regime are characterised as individual' he also accepts that it is 'not farfetched to consider the right to a healthy environment as a human right' (1989, p. 416). Nevertheless, what is not clear from the debates on the existence or elaboration of a human right to environment is whether such a principle is intended to contribute to environmental protection goals, or whether protection of the environment is effectively subsumed to the imperatives of protecting a variety of other human rights.

Institutional Reform

As noted earlier in this chapter, better environmental governance involves, at minimum, some reassessment of the commitment to national sovereignty. Nevertheless, as Maurice Strong argues, 'the concept of national sovereignty has been an immutable, indeed sacred, principle of international relations . . . that will yield only slowly and reluctantly to the new imperatives of global environmental cooperation' (1991, pp. 297–8). Given this, one solution has been to seek to make the state system more effective and to modify rather than overturn sovereignty. International cooperation is thus to be achieved 'not by a denial of sovereignty but by new and effective means of enabling nations to exercise . . . sovereignty collectively where they can not longer exercise it effectively alone' (Strong, 1973, p. x). Thus the imperatives for better governance have been cast as a managerial problem, one which requires better negotiating processes and more effective international institutions.

There is a growing body of literature on environmental diplomacy and negotiation. Some of this work analyses the general features of successful environmental diplomacy (see, for example, Young, 1989 and Benedick, 1991) whereas other work, most specifically Susskind (1994), draws on negotiation theory to offer specific strategies for improving the negotiation process. Young (1990) explores the problems of cooperation in solving the collective action problems presented by global environmental degradation with particular emphasis on the importance of institutional bargaining and leadership. Lang seeks also to identify the 'distinctive attributes of negotiations on the environment' (1991b, p. 343), including coalition activity, the influence of the media and the potential importance of individuals. These factors were also elaborated by Benedick (1991) in his analysis of the ozone negotiations. He stresses, in his concluding chapter, the importance of strong leadership by a major country (1991, p. 205), the desirability of 'pre-emptive action in advance of a global agreement' (1991, p. 206) and the value of 'firmness and pragmatism' (1991,

p. 208). Yet it is not clear just how such circumstances are to be achieved and nor is it clear whether they are not only necessary but also sufficient conditions for the achievement of better environmental governance.

This reformist debate also leads to the question of what characterises an effective institution if, as Levy *et al.* argue, 'international institutions . . . necessarily follow the principle of state sovereignty' (1992, p. 13). Levy and colleagues, working within the limits of a sovereignty paradigm and recognising the state as the 'sole legitimate source of public policy' (1992, p. 36) suggest that effective institutions 'nudge countries further along [the] continuum of commitment and compliance', they 'promote concern among governments [and] enhance the contractual environment by providing negotiating forums' (1992, p. 14). Better governance is to be pursued not through coercion or enforcement but through finding ways of encouraging states to cooperate more effectively. There is a paradox here: if existing institutions are shaped by sovereignty, and if the state and sovereignty are at the root of the crisis in governance, then how can such institutions ever be made effective, an issue returned to later in this chapter.

The cast of (state-centred) institutional characters is large and growing larger all the time. Many of the issue-specific environmental bodies have been discussed in previous chapters – the various secretariat, working groups, conference of parties, scientific and technical assessment panels which have been established to monitor and advise on the implementation of individual agreements and treaties. The European Community (now the European Union) has long focused on environmental imperatives and the development of environmental law in Europe. Other regional groupings, such as the Association of South East Asian Nations (ASEAN) or the environment-specific South Pacific Regional Environment Programme (SPREP), have facilitated environmental agreements and declarations to address regional concerns relevant to their member states. The Secretariat of the Commonwealth of Nations (the 'heir' to the British Commonwealth) has responded to the environmental concerns of its members. The OECD and the G7, the two major representative groupings of industrialised countries, have accommodated environmental concerns in their respective agenda. The G77, a product of the UN system in that it dates its formative years to the first UN Conference on Trade and Development (UNCTAD) in 1964, has provided a focus within environmental negotiations for the interests of developing countries. Ad hoc and interest-specific coalitions of states have arisen within UN-sponsored negotiations (the Toronto Group in the ozone negotiations is one such example) and have, in some cases, acquired a more permanent character. This is the case, for example, with the Alliance of Small Island States, a coalition which formed during the Second World Climate Conference in 1990 but which has since developed an institutional momentum outside that forum, most specifically at the climate negotiations INC and the conference on the sustainable development of small island states.

For those working in a generally reformist tradition, stronger environmental governance, a kind of collective sovereignty, can best be achieved and indeed perhaps can only be achieved within the institutions of the United Nations. Strong argues that the UN is 'the only multilateral organisation that is universal in its membership and global in its scope' (1991, p. 297). If it did not exist, he suggests, we would have to invent it. Others agree. Maurice Williams (1992, p. 23) suggests that the UN is 'uniquely positioned' to help governments in the pursuit of environmental security because of its extensive experience and its multidisciplinary capabilities. As earlier chapters have shown, a considerable amount of environmental activity has proceeded under UN auspices especially since the 1972 Stockholm Conference. Indeed, while institutions outside the United Nations contribute to research and debate on environmental issues and to the body of both soft-law (that is, non-legally-binding declarations and resolutions) and hard law on international environmental concerns, it is now difficult to think of an environmental issue with global relevance (with the exception perhaps of the Antarctic) which is not in some way governed primarily under the auspices of the United Nations. It is therefore helpful at least to consider how the United Nations has responded to the imperatives of global environmental governance.

The United Nations

The management of environmental issues is dispersed throughout the United Nations system. Environmental concerns are debated in and resolutions adopted by the General Assembly. The Economic and Social Council (ECOSOC) and its various commissions have taken up environmental concerns, even when those issues do not fall directly within its mandate (for example the Commission on the Status of

Women has addressed environmental and development issues as they impact on the world's women). The specialised agencies address environmental issues in accordance with their own mandates. The Food and Agricultural Organisation focuses on agriculture, forestry and marine resource issues and has been the task manager for the Tropical Forestry Action Plan. The World Meteorological Organisation has been activist in mobilising debate on atmospheric and climate issues, specifically in convening the World Climate Conferences and as one of the lead parties in establishing and maintaining the Intergovernmental Panel on Climate Change. The International Maritime Organisation (previously the Intergovernmental Maritime Consultative Organisation) continues to focus on marine pollution. The United Nations Development Programme has a mandate which encompasses the environmental impact of development activities and the relationship between poverty, maldevelopment or underdevelopment and environmental degradation. Indeed, the UNDP is an important actor within the UN system in terms of addressing the cross-sectoral complexities of environmental insecurity. Environmental governance also extends to those institutions, such as the World Bank, which are not directly responsible to the UN organisation but which are nevertheless considered part of the broad UN 'family'. However, within the UN system, the institution most *directly* mandated to address environmental issues is the United Nations Environment Programme.

The United Nations Environment Programme (UNEP)

UNEP was a product of the Stockholm process. It was established in 1973, in accordance with General Assembly resolution 2997 of December 1972. UNEP was a compromise, the product of politics. As noted in Chapter 1, developed countries were reluctant to agree to a new institution that would require further funding commitments from them. Developing countries, concerned that the Stockholm environmental agenda was being defined by the industrialised countries, were reluctant to agree to any new body which they thought could place constraints on their development. UN agencies which were already undertaking a range of environment-related tasks were generally suspicious of a new specialised agency which might challenge or undermine their responsibilities and competences. UNEP was therefore established not as a specialised agency, but as a programme within the UN system. A secretariat is charged with the day-to-day running of the programme under the guidance of an Executive Director, but overall policy responsibility lies with a 58-member Governing Council which reports to ECOSOC and through it to the General Assembly. UNEP is headquartered in Nairobi. While there were less expensive locations, and ones which might well have been logistically more sensible, the decision was a concession to developing countries. Administrative expenses for the Council and Secretariat come from the UN general budget, but all programme activities are to be funded from a Voluntary Fund established for that purpose.

UNEP has no executive powers. Its mandate, elaborated by the General Assembly following the Stockholm Conference, has been to monitor, coordinate and catalyse. Nevertheless, as Gray (1990, p. 294) points out, this mandate is vague. UNEP's main areas of activity derive from the functional components of the Stockholm Plan: global environmental assessment, environmental management activities and supporting measures. UNEP has been highly activist in pursuit of its mandate, especially under the lengthy leadership of its second executive director, Egyptian scientist Mostafa Tolba. Through its successful Earthwatch programme, UNEP collects, assesses and monitors information about the environment. Component parts of that programme include GEMS (the Global Environment Monitoring System), INFOTERRA (the International Referral System for Sources of Environmental Information) and IRPTC (the International Register of Potentially Toxic Chemicals). UNEP has forged partnerships with other intergovernmental and non-governmental organisations, working in partnership with, for example, the WMO to sponsor the World Climate Conferences, the 1987 Bellagio and Villach workshops on climate change, the 1988 Toronto Conference and to convene the IPCC. UNEP and the IUCN took the lead in the development of the 1980 World Conservation Strategy. As previous chapters have shown, negotiations for a number of international environmental agreements have taken place under its auspices, including the Vienna Convention and Montreal Protocol on ozone depletion (following the UNEP sponsored World Action Plan on the Ozone Layer) and the desertification negotiations.

Gray argues that UNEP's achievements have been 'substantial, even remarkable, considering the inherent limitations in its mandate and powers, the jealously guarded state sovereignty . . . and the sheer complexity and enormity of the problems at hand' (1990, p. 297). UNEP has suffered from a paucity of funding, from lack of political support by governments and from geographical isolation within the UN system. Hurrell and Kingsbury suggest that 'states [have been] singularly parsimonious in their contributions' to UNEP (1992, p. 31). Contributions to the voluntary fund have been parlous making, as Thacher notes, a 'mockery of the mandate that governments gave [UNEP] in 1972' (1991, p. 429). In 1992, for example, the year in which governments committed themselves to the global partnership of Agenda 21, only 75 out of 179 UN member states made contributions to the Voluntary Fund, an amount which that year totalled only $62 million and led to suggestions that core programme activities would have to be cut back to something in the vicinity of $120 million for the 1994–5 budget (see Anon., 1993e, p. 119).

Despite the important contribution made by UNEP and perhaps because of the limitations placed upon it, the United Nations increasingly came to be perceived in the latter half of the 1980s as minimally effective in its pursuit of environmental security and in providing a lead in environmental governance. For many, the reasons lay in the UN structure. In this view, the UN had become unwieldy, unresponsive and underfunded, characterised by demarcation and duplication of responsibilities. Maurice Williams argues that 'the organisation has become too complex . . . proliferation has produced too many bodies . . . with overlapping agenda and fragmentation of efforts. As a result, authority and responsibility have become blurred and coordination almost an end in itself' (1992, p. 24). Environmental governance was increasingly seen to be hostage to intra-UN politics and claims to issue sovereignty among UN bodies, leading one British diplomat to describe UNEP as a 'minnow in the piranha-filled UN pond' (Brenton, 1994, p. 48).

In this elaboration of the problem, the challenge for the United Nations becomes one of institutional reform and better coordination. There has been no scarcity of suggestions about how to reform and strengthen the institutions of the UN. Some have focused on strengthening UNEP through providing it with more resources, reforming its mandate to give it more political authority, or through strengthening or reforming the role of the Executive Director, perhaps as a Special Commissioner for the Global Environment (on the latter, see PRIO, 1989, p. 22). Nevertheless, upgrading UNEP to a specialised agency might create as many problems as it would solve. It would have to generate its own budget, which the record of the Voluntary Fund suggests might be difficult. Member-states would choose whether to become members or not, a process which, depending on the choices of individual governments, could undermine UNEP's already precarious financial and political status.

Other proposals have focused on the broader UN system, calling for environmental threats to be incorporated into the mandate of the Security Council, or for the Security Council to convene special sessions on environmental insecurities, in much the same way that it holds special sessions on disarmament, or for the security focus of the United Nations to be extended with the establishment of an Environmental Security Council. It has also been suggested that the Trusteeship Council, now well towards the end of its useful life, could be revamped as an Environmental Trusteeship Council. This suggestion seems to have been first made by the President of the World Federation of United Nations Associations (see Palmer, 1992, p. 279) but was also taken up by UNCED Secretary-General Maurice Strong (see Imber, 1994, p. 106). Whether it would be accepted as such by developing countries, given its neo-colonial history, and whether this would be possible under its existing mandate, is another matter.

Still other proposals seek to strengthen General Assembly competence over environmental issues by reconstituting one of its committees as an 'environmental committee' or by creating a new committee – sustainable development and the Rio agenda are presently the responsibility of the Second Committee. Yet the committee system mirrors General Assembly state-centric politics and neither the committees nor the Assembly have executive authority. Suggestions have also been made for a standing commission on the environment and development or an international environmental ombuds-office (Schrijver, 1989) which could receive petitions from individuals and NGOs and possibly even have the authority to establish multilateral inspection teams for environmental fact-finding and monitoring. The New Zealand government, in 1989, proposed the establishment of an Environmental Protection Council (see Palmer, 1992, p. 279). The UN Expert Study Group on Military Resources to the Environment recommended the establishment of the 'Green Berets' in the form of an international environmental relief team (see Theorin, 1992, p. 12), a proposal also made by the then Soviet Foreign Minister, Eduard Shevardnadze, in 1988. A proposal for 'Green Helmets' to function as a kind of dispute resolution team was made by Austria at the Sixth Committee in 1989 (see Anon., 1994j, p. 221). UNEP has since established a small-scale centre for emergency environmental assistance (see Hurrell and Kingsbury, 1992b, p. 34). The World Commission on Environment and Development called for greater responsibility and accountability on the part of UN agencies in support of sustainable development and better coordination among those agencies. It outlined recommendations for strengthening UNEP and for better and more effective interagency coordination (WCED, 1987, pp. 316–23). This issue of institutional reform was revisited at UNCED.

UNCED and the Governance Test

The UN Conference on Environment and Development was intended to herald a new era in international environmental governance. Resolution 44/228, which formally established the conference, emphasised the 'need to strengthen international cooperation' (UNGA, 1989c, Part I, para. 13). Conference objectives included the 'further development of international environmental law' (UNGA, 1989c, Part I, para. 15(d)) and the 'review and [examination] of the role of the United Nations system in dealing with the environment and possible ways of improving it' (UNGA, 1989c, Part I, para. 15(q)). The Conference provided an opportunity to improve environmental diplomacy and institutional effectiveness and to move towards a collective sovereignty in the interests of global governance. Yet, as foreshadowed in Chapter 1, it is doubtful that UNCED forged the global partnership that it was intended to. To some extent UNCED was a more open, participatory and transparent process. Yet Susskind argues that 'the results of the Earth Summit and the events preceding it offer conclusive evidence of the weaknesses of the existing environmental treaty-making system' (1994, p. 41). Negotiations were, in spite of their greater openness to non-governmental organisations, still dominated by a win–loss mentality, by last minute compromises reached in the final hours of the final days and by the maintenance of a commitment to the concerns of sovereign states.

Institutional reform, one of the tests of better environmental governance, was contentious at UNCED. Views on reform were divided between those who favoured a strengthening of UNEP rather than the creation of a new institution and those who wanted a new UN organisation which would provide a specifically post-Rio focus (see Hurrell and Kingsbury, 1992b, p. 34; Brenton, 1994, pp. 217–18). Chapter 38 of Agenda 21, on international institutional arrangements, seeks to clarify UNEP's mandate and suggests, *inter alia*, that

UNEP should be better provided with financial resources. Chapter 38 also recommended the establishment of a new UN body, the Commission on Sustainable Development, in a 'spirit of reform and revitalisation of the United Nations system' (UNCED, 1992b, para. 38.1). There is, however, some doubt as to the extent of revitalisation and the value of the reforms adopted at Rio. As former UK Ambassador to the UN, Crispin Tickell, argues 'it seems unlikely' that the institutional mechanisms 'laid down at Rio . . . will prove sufficient for their task' (1993b, p. 23).

Commission on Sustainable Development

While general details on the Commission were outlined in paragraphs 38.11 to 38.14 of Agenda 21, its terms of reference, its composition, guidelines for participation of NGOs and relationship with other UN bodies were elaborated in General Assembly resolution 47/191. The Commission is comprised of 53 member governments, elected by ECOSOC on a regional representation basis. It reports to ECOSOC and through it to the General Assembly. The CSD has two broad areas of responsibility which are to be executed fully-guided by the principles of the Rio Declaration. The first is to monitor and examine progress of the UNCED agenda, especially the implementation of Agenda 21 and any problems arising therefrom, a task which is to be undertaken primarily through consideration and analysis of information provided by governments in national reports. More specifically CSD is mandated to review progress on financial resource and technology transfer commitments, on commitments to the UN target of 0.7 per cent ODA/GNP and on the adequacy of funding mechanisms. The Commission has no powers of enforcement, however, if it finds that progress has been slow or non-existent. The second area of responsibility for the Commission is to facilitate the integration of environment and development concerns within the UN system and among governments.

To date, the Commission has held five substantive sessions, the first from 14–25 June 1993, the second in May 1994, the third from 11–28 April 1995, the fourth from 18 April to 3 May 1996 and the fifth from 7–25 April 1997. At its first substantive session, the Commission adopted a thematic program of work as a means of monitoring the implementation of Agenda 21, with particular clusters of Rio issues to provide the focus for each meeting. Subsequent substantive meetings of the Commission have focused on both sectoral and cross-sectoral issues in Agenda 21 and the Rio commitments more generally. Early in 1994, the Commission convened two ad hoc open-ended working groups, one on financial flows and mechanisms and the other on technology transfer and cooperation and, in 1995, established the Intergovernmental Panel on Forests. The fourth meeting in 1996 completed the cycle of the thematic programme of work, as well as taking up a number of issues including progress on the Programme of Action for the Sustainable Development of Small Island States. The fifth meeting was essentially a preparation for the UN Special Session. As well as discussing a draft programme of work for CSD for 1998–2002, and conducting dialogue sessions with all the major groups, delegates worked on preparing a draft final document for the Special Session, in the hope that it would include some kind of statement of commitment. Despite much activity (which has included many intersessional meetings and ad hoc working groups) substantive progress has still to be made on states' commitments to the cross-sectoral concerns of financial and technology resources, poverty alleviation or changes in patterns of production and consumption.

As with UNEP 20 years before, the CSD was a compromise and it is doubtful if it meets any of the expectations for a substantive body elaborated in the various reform proposals discussed above. There are doubts whether CSD has been able to move in any effective way from rhetoric and speech-making to dialogue and action. Haas and his colleagues predict that, 'to long time observers of UN politics . . . the possibility that the Commission [on Sustainable Development] might be held hostage by petty bureaucratic squabbles or become a venue for patronage or cronyism is all too obvious' (1992, p. 11). Rowlands suggests that it has been 'so weakened that it is fated to be an ineffective body' (1992, p. 223). Brenton predicted that the CSD was likely to become nothing more than a 'new UN talking shop with very limited impact on the world outside' (1994, p. 221). Reports from CSD-4 suggest that, despite four years' work, 'a clear consensus on the purpose of the Commission has not emerged' (Anon., 1996e, p. 152). Indeed, at that meeting CSD Chair, Henrique Cavalcanti from Brazil, suggested in a frank admission to an NGO meeting that 'he was not sure the CSD would be around after 1997' (in Doran, 1996, p. 100) and the General Assembly's Special Session review of the CSD as part of its review of the UNCED agenda and commitments. Under-Secretary-General for Policy Coordination and Sustainable Development, Nitin Desai, has argued that the success of the Commission would depend on the 'political weight given to it by governments' (in Anon., 1995e, pp. 163–4). There is little evidence that governments have been prepared to give the Commission that necessary political weight.

Improving Coordination

The Brundtland Report and chapter 38 of Agenda 21 called for better interagency coordination within the United Nations. Yet coordination on environmental issues has become increasingly confused since Rio, comprehensible only to the most assiduous observer or the most experienced UN insider. Coordination among various UN bodies and agencies was initially the responsibility of the Environment Coordination Board established following Stockholm. It was wound up in 1977 (see Brenton, 1994, p. 50; Thacher, 1991, p. 440) and its responsibilities taken over by the Administrative Committee on Coordination (ACC). Other coordinating bodies have included the Designated Officials for Environmental Matters of the United Nations (DOEM) and the CIDIE, the Committee of International Development Institutions on the Environment. The latter, which was established in 1980, includes representatives of UNEP, the International Bank for Reconstruction and Development (IBRD), UNDP and 11 other intergovernmental financial institutions.

Chapter 38 identified the need for 'a coordination mechanism under the direct leadership of the Secretary-General' (UNCED, 1992b, para. 38.16), recommending that the task be given to the ACC but recommending also that there should be a high level advisory body to provide expert advice on sustainable development issues (UNCED, 1992b, para. 38.18). At the end of 1992, the Secretary-General announced the creation of a Department for Policy Coordination and Sustainable Development to staff the CSD which is itself, in turn, subject to the coordinating efforts of ECOSOC and the ACC. The ACC has also created a new sub-committee – the Interagency Committee on Sustainable Development (IACSD) (see Imber, 1994, p. 115). In 1993, the General Assembly reconstituted and reorganised the UN Natural Resources Committee (UNNRC, first established in 1970) to advise ECOSOC on natural resource issues, especially water and mining. Imber's suggestion that 'the UN's way of streamlining itself can move grown men to tears' (1994, p. 116) – presumably women are made of sterner stuff – seems apt.

Sovereignty Reinforced

In spite of the rhetoric of a 'global partnership' for the environment, UNCED demonstrated that the sovereignty principle is alive and well in the UN. Despite the participation of non-state actors, it remains states which determine the nature of the partnership. The Rio agreements reinforced the 'rhetoric of responsible states' (Davison and Barns, 1992, p. 10) and sustained rather than challenged the primacy of national sovereignty. Rowlands argues also, for example, that it was 'concerns about sovereignty [which] neutered UNCED's most important product [CSD]' (1992, p. 223). The principle of national sovereignty, elaborated in the Stockholm Declaration, is everywhere affirmed. To recall, principle 21 of the 1972 Declaration provides that:

> States have, in accordance with the Charter of the United Nations and the principles of international law, the sovereign right to exploit their own resources pursuant to their own environmental policies, and the responsibility to ensure that activities within their jurisdiction or control do not cause damage to the environment of other States or of areas beyond the limits of national jurisdiction.

This has now become principle 2 of the Rio Declaration with the added emphasis of sovereignty over developmental as well as environmental policy. It appears in the preambles of the Vienna Convention, the Desertification Convention and the Climate Change Convention (which also reaffirms the 'principle of the sovereignty of states in international cooperation to address climate change'(UN INC/FCCC 1992, preamble). It stands as principle 1(a) in the Forest Principles and as article 3 of the Biodiversity Convention, which also provides that states have sovereign rights over their own biodiversity resources. The dominance of sovereignty concerns was also reinforced rather than challenged by continued tensions between the developed and developing countries. In the absence of any firm commitments from the developed countries on financial and technology transfer, or assistance to address causes and impact, the developing countries have reasserted sovereignty to protect their right to development.

Moving Beyond Reform: The Critical Position

If, as Davison and Barns argue, UNCED did not respond to a 'growing pressure for a more effective system of world governance' (1992, p. 10) the question is why did it not do so? Where do the problems lie? Is it, as Thacher suggests, because of 'shortcomings in institutions, political will and resources' (1991, p. 435) or is there a more fundamental problem? The reformist position suggests, to borrow from Levy *et al.* (1992, p. 36) that it is possible to mitigate environmental problems without changing the underlying political and economic factors responsible for environmental degradation. For others, this is inadequate as a response to the crisis of environmental governance. Kildow argues that 'there can be no breakthroughs as long as the current international infrastructure remains . . . the nation-state and anachronistic perceptions of sovereignty impede reform' (1992, pp. 1077–8). Or, as Mische puts it, 'existing concepts of state sovereignty' (which she calls a persistent and resilient myth) are not only incongruent with but also 'antithetical to the prerequisites for global ecological security' (1989, pp. 394–5).

In this view, then, the reason that the UN has not been able to respond to growing pressure for change in a more effective way is that it cannot do so and that expectations otherwise are misplaced and unwarranted. If global governance is to mean something more than better international cooperation among states then the UN is not the place to expect such a transformation. Kildow's critique (1992, pp. 1077–8) is representative of these arguments. She argues that the UN is an inward-looking, cumbersome body, echoing a distant past of 50 years ago, encumbered with employees whose tenure nearly matches the age of the UN. It is, she continues, dominated by older men, by an old-boy network, a cultural resistance to change and is characterised by appointment on the basis of politics not merit at a time when brilliance is needed. This is, she argues, an organisation which simply cannot effect a mandate for change and we should not expect it do to so. The United Nations remains the tool of states and therefore, as Gareth Evans, Australia's former Foreign Minister noted, it can 'at the end of the day . . . do no more than . . . its member states allow it to do or give it the resources to do' (1994, p. 1). Perhaps, then, it is surprising not that the UN has achieved so little, but that it has achieved as much as it has.

In this critical view, institutional reform is, to borrow Nicholas Hildyard's (1993) metaphor for the UNCED process, rather like leaving the foxes in charge of the chickens. Demands for global environmental governance based on collective sovereignty and institutional reform are interpreted as a device for protecting existing power structures rather than changing them – a 'globalisation from above' (see Brecher *et al.*, 1993). Lohmann (1990, p. 82) argues that causes of environmental degradation and the crisis in environmental governance are not analysed if to do so would put the current power structure in an unfavourable light, and that proposed solutions (including institutional reform) leave the main causes of the trouble untouched. Calls for 'global governance' are therefore seen not as a genuine attempt at transformation but as designed to prop up existing power structures and elite interests. Rather than engendering a transformation, claiming 'global' as the organising principle for environmental governance has re-visioned the environmental crisis into a reason for strengthening the institutional and normative status quo (see, for example, Shiva 1993).

From a critical perspective better governance requires that those underlying political and economic factors responsible for environmental degradation are addressed (and this proposition is explored also in later chapters). Without this, institutional reform can only ever be a partial and incomplete response to the environmental crisis. Better governance requires also that the concept of state sovereignty be reconceptualised and that the practice of global governance be decentralised and democratised. Reconceptualising sovereignty as the basis for environmental governance is a difficult task. Reeves puts it well: this should not be about giving something up, but about creating something that we lack (cited in Mische, 1989, p. 402). The state should be displaced (not, note, replaced) as the '*sole* legitimate source of public policy' (Levy *et al.*, 1992, p. 36; emphasis added). Sovereignty would thus become a multilayered, multifaceted concept and practice incorporating concern for planetary sovereignty and the sovereignty of peoples. In practice, this requires a greater democratising of environmental governance to incorporate not just greater participation but also to pay greater attention to and respond more effectively to local voices and local concerns rather than seeing the state as the sole arbiter of competing interests in the determination of public policy. The rationale for this is that the global, as it is presently constructed, does not represent universal human interests, but rather 'a particular local and parochial interest which has been globalised through the scope of its reach' (Shiva, 1993, p. 150) where that 'parochial interest' reflects the concerns of the most powerful industrialised countries and the world's elites. What is required, then, is that environmental governance is humane governance, based on a bottom-up democratisation that emphasises participation (rather than the more narrow notion of liberal representative democracy). The basis for environmental governance should therefore be an earth democracy but this, Shiva argues, cannot be realised 'as long as global domination is in the hands of undemocratic structures' (1993, p. 155). The processes of democratisation and the revitalisation of civil society as a key component of global environmental governance provide the focus for the next two chapters.

5

Non-State Actors: Science, Commerce and Global Civil Society

One of the hallmarks of the global politics of the environment has been the growth in number, scope and activity of a range of non-state actors, including scientific organisations, industry and business, environmental and conservation organisations, grass-roots movements and indigenous peoples' organisations, who have sought in various ways to influence environmental policy or who have become crucial environmental actors. Section III of Agenda 21 acknowledged this broadening of the list of stakeholders, anticipating roles in environmental governance and the pursuit of sustainable development for a variety of sectors of society, collectively defined as the 'independent sector' or the major groups. While some mention is made in this chapter of the role of the scientific community and multinational corporations (MNCs), the main focus here is the growth of global civil society through non-governmental organisations.

Science and Environmental Governance

Science and the scientific community (in as much as it is possible to speak of a 'community' which covers such a range of scientific endeavour) has become increasingly important to environmental governance in several ways. First, science and scientists have helped to mobilise debate and action by governments on environmental problems. Second, on many environmental issues scientific expertise is necessary to assist policy-makers in the elaboration of environmental agreements. Third, once in place, the reassessment of environmental standards and targets is usually to proceed on the basis of best available scientific information and thus further scientific research becomes an important factor in determining the level of commitments by governments. Finally, scientific research and scientists themselves have a potential role to play in encouraging compliance with international agreements. There is also a broader issue, which is really beyond the scope of this book, about whether scientists and the scientific community have a moral responsibility with respect to the 'applications to which science is put' (von Weizsäcker, 1994, p. 190).

As demonstrated in Chapters 2 and 3, the imperatives for environmental action were often grounded in scientific inquiry and demands from within the scientific community for political action. There is not space enough here to list again all the scientific organisations and the range of expert working groups, programmes, scientific conferences and reports which have contributed, in various ways, to the process of environmental governance. A number of environmental regimes have established scientific committees or various expert subsidiary bodies whose purpose is to provide scientific advice to decision-making bodies. Scientists within government agencies, within intergovernmental organisations (such as the WMO, IMO, UNEP and others) and within non-governmental scientific organisations (perhaps the International Council of Scientific Unions (ICSU) has the highest profile) have had a role to play in the development of international agreements and in the dissemination of information and knowledge about environmental problems. It is now standard practice for scientific organisations to be granted observer status at environmental conferences and institutions. In this way scientists have become transnational actors, pursuing policy advocacy and generating knowledge which, once accepted by both the scientific and diplomatic communities, becomes the environmental orthodoxy.

Science and the scientific community have become politicised in two ways. First, as noted above, scientists themselves have become part of the political process, contributing to and becoming involved in decision-making. The Brundtland Report summarised this role thus: 'identifying risks . . . assessing environmental impact and designing and implementing measures to deal with them' (WCED, 1987, p. 326). Haas has pointed to the importance, in environmental governance, of scientists as epistemic communities – 'transnational networks of knowledge based communities that are both politically empowered through their claims to exercise authoritative knowledge and motivated by shared causal and principled beliefs' (1990, p. 349). This is not always a disinterested participation. As Stairs and Taylor note, 'scientists are a lobby group in their own right' (1992, p. 122) sometimes pursuing their own advantage or particular interests which may be related to funding or disputes within the scientific community. Second, science has become politicised as the results of scientific research, often subject to uncertainties and differences within the scientific community, have been appropriated by policy-makers in the pursuit of political and economic interests. As Rosenau points out 'perhaps no issue area on the global agenda relies more heavily on scientific proof as the means through which persuasion and influence is exercised' (1993, p. 81) although Susskind and Ozawa (1992, p. 160) suggest that this can undermine the integrity of scientific analysis. As Chapter 3 indicated with respect to climate change, resistance by some policy-makers to environmental targets has been based on the absence of full scientific certainty. Yet as Litfin demonstrates, with respect to ozone depletion, 'even within a relatively narrow range of scientific uncertainty, nations can easily interpret the available knowledge according to their perceived interests' (1993, p. 100). Richardson draws attention to a further context in which the scientific community is politicised when he points out that much of the scientific research that is undertaken in support of or in contribution to environmental governance is conducted by 'the nationals of developed countries', suggesting that 'developing countries may on occasion tend to be suspicious of assertions of scientific authorities that also happen to serve developed-country interests' (1992, p. 177).

The importance of science and the role of the scientific community in environmental governance is not without scrutiny. Gudynas, for example, is critical of what he terms the 'scientific superiority complex' (1993, p. 172). Scientists, he suggests, have claimed for themselves a mandate to 'determine the viable management of nature' by which the construction of environmental problems as 'strictly scientific and technical' serves not only to marginalise the social and political connotations of environmental degradation, but as a consequence privileges scientific knowledge and the scientific community (Gudynas, 1993, p. 172). Breyman (1993, p. 132) takes a similar line, arguing that the model of 'value-free' information provided by 'neutral scientists' as the basis for environmental decision-making is an aging one. In his exploration of the relationship between science and technology, von Weizsäcker argues that the sciences (by which he means something different from individual scientists themselves) can 'also be held responsible for some of the destructive changes occurring on Earth' (1994, p. 176). This question of responsibility and destruction is relevant also to business and industry.

Business, Industry and Environmental Governance

While corporate interests in general have become a key aspect of environmental politics much of the attention at a global level has focused on the role of multinational corporations (MNCs) as contributors to environmental degradation and as major stakeholders in environmental negotiations. MNCs have been and continue to be a major direct and indirect cause of environmental decline through their substantial control of decisions over resource use, through pollution and land degradation, through what is often continued resistance to strengthening of environmental standards and through their control of global wealth and, therefore, their influential role in the world economy. There is no doubt that, economically, MNCs are powerful international actors. As many sources note, the top 500 control 70 per cent of world trade, 80 per cent of foreign investment (Chatterjee and Finger, 1994, p. 106; Miller, 1995, p. 35) and 30 per cent of world GDP (Miller, 1995, p. 35). Collectively, and often individually, they have budgets much larger than many developing countries. Miller points out, for example, that Shell Oil's 1990 gross income was more than the combined incomes of nine African and South Asian countries which together represented about 10 per cent of the world's population (1995, p. 35).

The contribution of MNCs to global pollution and to resource depletion is significant. As Hildyard puts it, commercial interests have 'sacrificed local livelihoods and environments in order to obtain raw materials, transform them into commodities, market them and dispose of the wastes' (1993, p. 24). Thomas notes that MNCs are 'the largest users of raw materials globally' and the top 500 MNCs 'generate more than half the greenhouse gas emissions produced annually' (1993, p. 19). Twenty of them control almost 90 per cent of global pesticide sales (see Chatterjee and Finger 1994, p. 106) and Porter and Brown (1996, p. 63) suggest that 73 per cent of that market is controlled by only ten MNCs. These interests have encouraged continued pesticide use, with consequences for the long-term fertility of agricultural land, for marine pollution as a result of run-off and for human health. MNCs control 80 per cent of land under cultivation for export crops (Miller, 1995, p. 36), a control which (as

Chapter 3 has demonstrated with respect to deforestation and land degradation) has implications for the use patterns of lands not controlled by them. In Brazil, for example, the land owned by transnational corporations is greater than that owned by the country's peasants (Miller, 1995, p. 37; Hildyard, 1993, p. 30). As Chapter 2 indicated, developing countries have long been concerned about the role of multinational companies in the transport and dumping of hazardous wastes. Multinational corporations, particularly but not exclusively Japanese-based, have also been the major contributors to deforestation in South East Asia (see Porter and Brown, 1996, p. 64) and Asian-based MNCs now 'dominate rainforest logging worldwide' (Gray, 1996, p. 20). The extent to which MNCs are able to engage in environmentally destructive behaviour is a product also of their ability to influence poor governments (and sometimes not so poor governments) with respect to minimising environmental standards and regulations (see Miller, 1995, p. 35).

MNCs, and corporate interests generally, thus have a major stake in the kinds of rules that are adopted nationally and internationally to control pollution and resource depletion. Organising around corporate interests and environmental concerns is not new. MNCs and industry organisations have lobbied domestically and internationally to influence governments' negotiating positions (and have often had representatives on national delegations). They have sought both to influence international rules and standard setting and to limit the impact upon them of any domestic legislation enacted to give effect to international commitments. As Chapters 2 and 3 have demonstrated, they have often been influential in determining the kinds of standards set (or, in some cases, not set) to manage environmental concerns. Porter and Brown argue that corporations have worked 'to weaken several global regimes' (1996, p. 59). The agrochemical industry, for example, has a well-established history not only of lobbying on pesticides issues but also, as Paarlberg (1993) notes, working closely in a semi-official capacity with the FAO to support pesticide use in developing countries, particularly through the Industry Cooperative Programme (ICP). He suggests that industry interests were able to rely on strong political allies in a number of powerful Western country governments who were prepared to support their opposition to tighter regulations (Paarlberg, 1993, p. 320). Miller also suggests that the agrochemical industry has had a direct influence on the scientific research agenda and on government policies through building alliances with 'research institutes, agricultural colleges, regulatory agencies, government ministries and aid agencies' (1995, p. 36).

There are many other policy studies which explore how corporate and MNC interests have sought to exercise influence over environmental policy-making. US CFC producer and user industries, for example, lobbied through the Alliance for Responsible CFC Policy in 1980 to oppose regulation on ozone depleting substances (see Parson, 1993, p. 36). The willingness or otherwise of major CFC producers such as ICI or DuPont to invest in substitutes was an important factor in the Montreal Protocol negotiations. Levy examines the role of industry groups in LRTAP meetings (see Levy, 1993, p. 86). Mitchell (1993, p. 192) describes the ways in which oil companies and shipping interests strongly resisted regulatory mechanisms to control maritime oil pollution, suggesting that industry was able to ignore existing rules and demand new rules that were least costly to their interests. Hildyard (1993, p. 29) discusses the role of the oil industry in the climate change negotiations and the biotechnology industry in the biodiversity negotiations. Biotechnology companies had strong commercial interests to protect in the biodiversity negotiations. Most of the world's biotechnology patents are held by multinational companies and, as Miller (1995, p. 111) notes, substantial profits have accrued to these companies through the exploitation of genetic material, usually with little or no compensation to governments or to indigenous peoples from whom the knowledge is often derived. The energy industry, particularly that engaged in fossil fuel extraction, has taken a strong interest in the climate change negotiations and has, as Chapter 3 indicated, often spoken out against the scientific community on these matters.

Corporate interests have established not only an international presence but also a supporting international structure. The International Chamber of Commerce, which was founded in 1919 and which has consultative status with the UN, has become a key peak body for the pursuit of business environmental interests at a global level, particularly through the efforts of its Commission on the Environment, founded in 1978. The Commission on the Environment 'devises environmental policy for industry' and 'seeks to influence government policy by presenting business comments on proposed intergovernmental measures' (see Bergesen and Parmann, 1996, p. 264). As part of its support for global business interests, the ICC has convened two World Industry Conferences on Environmental Management, the first (WICEM I) in 1984 in conjunction with UNEP and the second (WICEM II) in 1991, as part of industry preparation for UNCED.

Despite their willingness to establish an international presence, MNCs have generally resisted public scrutiny of their activities. In a 1994 report on corporate environmental disclosure the United Nations Centre on Transnational Corporations (UNCTC) concluded that the 'quality of information provided' on environment-related matters in reporting and financial statements had 'not improved' since the Centre's previous report two years earlier (UNCTC, 1994, p. 1). Increased environmental awareness in the 1970s and especially the 1980s, the impact of a number of environmental accidents and disasters in which MNCs were implicated (see Chapter 1) and public pressure on governments to implement policies to contain environmental damage had some effect, although some would suggest a minimal effect, on MNCs and business interests in general. Business and industry moved to improve their environmental credentials and their image of good corporate citizenship, moves designed also to give credence to their claims that self-regulation and voluntary codes of conduct are more effective and efficient than government imposed regulations or command-and-control regimes. Tolba and El-Kholy document various initiatives in this 'greening of the corporate boardroom' (1992, pp. 682–3), many of which have focused on responsible care, recycling, cleaner production, waste minimisation and the introduction of environmental audits (see also Starke, 1990, pp. 92–101). Companies responded also to the growth in public demands for green and ethical investment opportunities as well as the burgeoning market in green technology.

One of the major expressions of international 'green corporatism' has been the Business Charter for Sustainable Development which was promulgated by the ICC in 1990 and which has now been adopted by over 1100 firms worldwide, many of them large MNCs (Miller, 1995, p. 148). More recently Stephan Schmidheiny, in co-operation with the Business Council for Sustainable Development (see below), has published *Changing Course*, which expresses a commitment to environmentally sound corporate practice located within the logic of sound business sense. In general, environmentally sound practices have been cast as 'opportunities and good investment' (Schmidheiny, 1992, p. 4). Business and industry have continued to advocate not only self-regulation (which Schmidheiny identifies as cheaper and more effective in reorienting corporate behaviour than command-and-control mechanisms (1992, pp. 20–1), but also an open international trading system. As Schmidheiny puts it, a 'system of open, competitive markets' is the 'cornerstone of sustainable development' (1992, p. 14). These were the basic propositions that the corporate sector took to the UNCED process.

MNC activity at UNCED was coordinated through the Business Council for Sustainable Development (BCSD), a group of 48 corporate leaders drawn together in 1990 by Swiss industrialist Stephan Schmidheiny who was also appointed personal adviser to Maurice Strong. MNCs were also, through the BCSD, major 'corporate sponsors' of the UNCED process, providing funds through the EcoFund operation to the Trust Fund established by the conference secretariat (for more on this see Chatterjee and Finger, 1994, pp. 117–20). Chatterjee and Finger suggest that up to one-fifth of funding for the secretariat came from corporate interests. Many commentators suggest that by the time of the UNCED conference, MNCs had become not simply one part of the 'independent sector' but partners with governments in the dialogue on sustainable development.

Certainly their activities were subject to little formal scrutiny and there was little discussion on corporate pollution at UNCED (Chatterjee and Finger, 1994, p. 106). ECOSOC had commissioned the UNCTC to provide to UNCED a study and series of draft recommendations on the regulation of MNCs. Those recommendations included 'proposals for greater accountability, a 10-year goal for harmonising of company-level environmental accounting and reporting procedures, and environmental pricing' (Grubb *et al.*, 1993, p. 38). While the G77, with the support of some Northern countries such as Sweden, was keen for these recommendations to go to the early PrepComms and to the conference in Rio, the recommendations and references to MNCs were effectively dropped at PrepComm IV (see Thomas, 1993, p. 19). So too was the UNCTC which (depending on perspective) was either axed (see Chatterjee and Finger, 1994, p. 134) or merged in an internal reorganisation (see Grubb *et al.*, 1993, p. 38) just before the Rio conference.

Few with environmental concerns at heart were satisfied with the outcomes of UNCED with regard to MNCs. Hildyard argues that the final documents not only treated MNCs with 'kid gloves' but also 'extolled them as key actors' in the pursuit of sustainable development (1993, p. 22). Chapter 30 of Agenda 21 articulated a rationale for strengthening the role of business and industry, referring to the importance of the corporate sector in the pursuit of social and economic development. The chapter praises voluntary initiatives and self-regulation, and emphasises the importance of economic interests and free market mechanisms as the framework within which business and industry can make the most effective contribution to sustainable development. Businesses are encouraged to adopt 'enlightened' practices such as cleaner production and responsible entrepreneurship. Thus MNCs, and business and industry generally, are cast as an important part of the solution rather than a major contribution to the problem. Thomas' position, which is shared by many others, is that corporate interests were able to argue successfully for self-regulation (and, indeed, to avoid any serious scrutiny) because they 'had powerful allies in the richest states' (1993, p. 4). Grubb and colleagues also suggest that many governments, particularly those which were less powerful, were 'reluctant to engage such powerful interests' (1993, pp. 38–9).

Yet many environmental NGOs, along with other commentators, dispute both the extent of MNCs' commitment to environmental protection and the adequacy of self-regulation. Chatterjee and Finger point out that many of the MNCs which provided funds for UNCED and were hailed by the BCSD as examples of green corporatism had and continued to have poor environmental records. They also suggest that a close study of many environmental issues might suggest that corporate changes have in fact been motivated by government legislation and not as a result of voluntary improvements in behaviour (see Chatterjee and Finger, 1994, p. 132). Thomas (1993, pp. 19–20) also provides examples of the poor record of the BCSD companies and raises doubts as to the extent to which self-regulation can be a reliable environmental strategy, especially if it is seen by companies to undermine rather than enhance their competitiveness. Miller argues that, in effect, 'the basic characteristics of the corporate culture remain unchanged' (1995, p. 37).

For the most part, then, MNCs have been able to avoid extensive scrutiny of their environmental actions and, where that scrutiny has been forthcoming (often mobilised by environmental NGOs), corporate interests have been able to lobby governments and employ strategic alliances to ensure that self-regulation and voluntary codes of conduct have provided the environmental framework within which they function at a global level. Yet for many the continued contribution of corporate and MNC activities to environmental degradation suggests that a 'code of conduct for [MNCs] is even more necessary today than it was when environmental issues were first considered in UN forums decades ago' (Miller, 1995, p. 148). A focus only on better corporate practice, however, may also divert the debate about MNCs from any serious engagement with the environmental impact of industrialisation and modernisation, or the practices of a liberal international economic order, issues which are addressed further in Chapter 10.

Global Civil Society

The primarily reformist approach to global environmental governance which was explored in Chapter 4 focused on the state and interstate/intergovernmental relations in the pursuit of collective sovereignty. Yet one of the characteristics of post-Stockholm global environmental politics has been the growth of non-governmental environmental organisations and grassroots movements whose focus has turned from national to transnational issues and arena. As a result, as Durning suggests, the 'foundations of a new international environmental movement are in place. Local and national groups are extending tentative feelers out around the world, forming effective communication channels around issues of common interest' (1989, p. 168). This phenomenon is now most often referred to as the growth or development or revitalisation of civil society at a global level.

Explorations of the role of global civil society in environmental governance and the global politics of the environment have involved two not entirely unconnected themes. The first is primarily institutional, emphasising international pluralism and the addition of new, non-state players to international governance. Agenda 21 devotes several chapters to what are there defined as the 'major groups' or the 'independent sector' (a phrase which echoes the managerial and institutionalist ethos of that programme for action) identifying for such actors and sectors of the community an important role in the pursuit of sustainable development. This participation of non-state actors is deemed to be important to environmental governance for reasons based on efficiency and democracy. Decision-making by governments and the implementation of environmental agreements is argued to be more effective if all stake-holders are represented and if other actors besides states are recognised as having legitimate interests and a legitimate role to play. In a speech in 1987, Gro Harlem Brundtland argued that a political system that secures effective participation in decision-making is a major prerequisite to sustainable development (cited in Starke, 1990, p. 64). Pluralist analyses of global civil society and participatory sustainable development tends to focus on environmental non-governmental organisations, the roles they play and the strategies they adopt as they seek to influence international environmental policy and its implementation.

The second framework for analysis emphasises the significance of global civil society as a site of political action rather than just an institutional phenomenon whose importance is understood mainly in terms of its relationship with a primarily state-centric system of environmental governance. Analyses of this kind have tended to emphasise the dynamic nature of global civil society in which the whole is greater than the sum of its organisational parts. Durning draws our attention to an 'expanding latticework of human organisations' which together form an overall movement (1989, p. 154). Conca and Lipschutz point out that 'social movements and networks of non-state actors' have a role not just in concert or competition with the state but 'perhaps . . . as an alternative organising principle for world politics, based on new constitutive rules and institutional forms' (1993, p. 9). Global civil society, in this view, is something more than an aggregate of non-governmental organisations and community groups. It is both evidence of and reinforcing of the politics of resistance, contestation and transformation. The growth of global civil society, and of non-governmental organisations and grassroots movements, is thus understood as a response to statism and the inadequacies of a geopolitical order which has proved of limited success in addressing global environmental degradation, and which has also marginalised local concerns and the voices of the disadvantaged. Indeed, the latter (marginalisation) is offered as an explanation for the former (that is, limited success).

For many scholars and participants in environmental governance, the development of global civil society represents an enlargement of human possibilities in which NGOs and other social movements are 'bearers of ecological values' (Falk, 1992, p. 189). Falk perceives global civil society as a 'vehicle for human-centred and earth sensitive values and approaches' (1995, p. 199). Shiva claims that in global civil society a 'new consciousness is emerging' (1989a, p. 203) a consciousness in which the 'solutions to environmental problems are to be found in fundamental social changes' (Hontelez, 1988, p. 765). Global civil society is claimed also as the expression of a post-modern politics, as indicative of a 'post modern consciousness' (Falk, 1992, p. 36) or as a 'manifestation of the transition from conventional modernity to a yet to be defined post-modern state' (Caldwell, 1990, p. 92). This is not to say, of course, that many non-governmental organisations are not strongly committed to the modernist project, seeking to influence policies based on managerial and technocratic solutions, emphasising the importance of objective science and understanding nature in the service of human species.

Thus NGOs are seen not simply as participants in global environmental politics but also as part of the move towards 'decentred globalism' or a 'pluralistic world order' (Gerlach, 1991, p. 122). This is essentially an optimistic and hopeful approach, one which may or not be misplaced. Global civil society thus becomes the expression of alternative visions of political practice and environmental governance, visions which are consciously normative and transformative. In theory at least, those visions emphasise democratisation, participation and the empowerment of marginalised voices, justice and equity and a reclaiming of the local to counter the centralising tendencies of a reformist, institutionalist approach to global governance. Shiva argues that 'the roots of the ecological crisis at the institutional level lie in the alienation of the rights of local communities to actively participate in environmental decisions' (1993, p. 155). Citizen participation is therefore understood as fundamental to new forms of environmental governance which emphasise decentralisation, democratic values and the 'effective control of change by those most directly affected' (Hontelez, 1988, p. 762) rather than simply as a source of efficiency or effectiveness. Shiva refers to this form of governance as an 'earth democracy' (1993, p. 155) and Tinker suggests that the development of global civil society represents a 'return to the sovereignty of the people' (1993, p. 15). A more participatory and inclusive form of environmental governance is not only more democratic but is seen as essential to the pursuit of a more equitable and just ecological world order. These values have often informed the policies advocated by non-governmental organisations and grassroots movements. They have also shaped political practice within many (but not all) of those organisations and movements.

Non-Governmental Organisations: Movements to Save the Planet?

NGOs and transnational associations provide institutional expression and a potential route to political influence for new social movements and global civil society. Claims are made for their importance not just as participants in environmental governance but as a voice for the grassroots, so often marginalised from environmental governance, and as a voice for social change. Those claims are investigated further here.

A Brief History

As observed above, the growth in the number and influence of non-governmental organisations has been one of the notable features of international and global environmental politics since the Stockholm Conference. The term 'non-governmental organisation' dates to the conferences which established the United Nations. Section 71 of the UN Charter provides that the 'Economic and Social Council may make suitable arrangements for consultation with non-governmental organisations which are concerned with matters within its competence'. While environmental NGOs are often identified as a comparatively new feature of the political scene, there is a long history of private organisation around conservation and environment issues. The history of environmental NGOs is usually written as a western or Northern history, sometimes on the assumption either that there is no similar non-governmental history in the South or that any observations and propositions derived from a Northern analysis are universally relevant. Wapner (1996, p. 16), for example, suggests that his understanding of Northern NGOs will shed light upon all transnational groups, although he acknowledges that this premise may turn out to be false. Chatterjee and Finger (1994, p. 66), on the other hand, argue that movements and NGOs in the North and the South have evolved separately around quite different issues and Hontelez points out that 'the environmental movement in the Third World faces a different situation from that in the West' (1988, p. 765).

In the European world, environmental NGOs developed around local conservation and nature preservation issues in the latter part of the nineteenth century and the early twentieth century. McCormick (1989, p. 5) identifies the earliest organisation as the Commons, Footpath and Open Spaces Preservation Society, founded in the UK in 1865. The Royal Society for the Protection of Birds in the UK dates to 1891, the Sierra Club was founded in the US in 1892 followed by the National Audubon Society in 1905 and the National Wildlife Federation in 1936. This trend was reproduced in other settler societies – in Australia for example, the Wildlife Preservation

Society was founded in Sydney in 1909. These were mainly middle-class organisations with an emphasis on the preservation of nature and natural wilderness areas in the face of the impacts of the Industrial Revolution in Europe and increased settlement, especially in North America. They were not concerned with preservation and conservation *per se*, but rather sought to ensure that such areas and the 'nature' contained therein could be enjoyed by people. What was perhaps the first 'international' environmental organisation – the International Union for the Protection of Nature (now the International Union for the Conservation of Nature and Natural Resources, often referred to as the World Conservation Union) – was founded in 1948, a hybrid body with government and non-government members. In the 1960s and 1970s, as the environmental agenda grew to encompass pollution, nuclear concerns, resource depletion and waste management, issues that were not just about preservation and conservation but about mitigating and preventing the detrimental impacts of human activity, the focus of NGOs also expanded. In this period membership of environmental NGOs grew exponentially and new NGOs were formed with an emphasis on political activism and change. Friends of the Earth (FoE) was founded in the US in 1969 as a result of a split within the Sierra Club (see Burke, 1982). FoE International (FoEI) was established in 1971, the same year as Greenpeace was founded out of opposition to nuclear testing at Amchitka. In the late 1970s and early 1980s, this new breed of NGOs became transnational and international, responding to but also mobilising a changing environmental agenda.

In what we now call the developing world, non-governmental environmental organisations were first established prior to decolonisation, with a conservationist concern for the protection of birds and animals. In post-colonial times, however, non-governmental organisations have rarely been simply 'environmental' in their focus. Rather they have been more broadly-based grassroots organisations, concerned about underdevelopment as well as immediate local environmental decline. As Ekins notes, these peoples' organisations 'tend to combine poverty alleviation with environmental concern because it is precisely through the regeneration of environmental resources that they hope to alleviate their poverty' (1992, p. 39). These 'second generation' NGOs, as Chatterjee and Finger call them (1994, p. 74), strived for self-reliance and emphasised development from the bottom-up, as a challenge to the top-down modernisation approach to development of the major donor countries and lending institutions.

A number of influential Third World NGOs date to the 1970s. Environment and Development Action in the Third World (ENDA), for example, was founded in 1976, Sahabat Alam Malaysia (Friends of the Earth Malaysia) in 1977, the year in which women in Kenya mobilised the GreenBelt Movement. The African NGO Coalition (ANGOC) was founded in 1979. Even those which were established as peak or umbrella organisations maintained a local focus. In the 1980s, Chatterjee and Finger suggest, the emphasis on participatory development as a way of managing local environmental issues seemed to be having little success in the face of continuing modernisation programmes. This gave rise to 'third generation' NGOs for whom local initiatives were now increasingly located within national and international environment and development frameworks (see Chatterjee and Finger, 1994, p. 75). For example, the Asia Pacific Peoples Environment Network (APPEN) was established in 1983 with a range of objectives: to collect and disseminate information, to publish and to set up specialised task forces to support lobbying of governments and international institutions (Shiva, 1989a, p. 203). Nevertheless, as Shiva notes, the Network was never intended to substitute for real work at the grassroots level (1989a, p. 203). The Third World Network, now an influential transnational NGO, was founded in 1985 as a voice for many of the protest movements of the South (Chatterjee and Finger, 1994, p. 77).

Grassroots involvement has continued to be a defining theme of environmental activism in the developing countries in concert with a focus on the integral relationship between poor development practices and destruction of both the ecosystem and people's livelihoods and lifestyles. For example, the Declaration adopted at the Inter-Regional Consultation on People's Participation in Environmentally Sustainable Development, held in the Philippines in June 1989, argues that the principle that 'sovereignty resides with the people, the real social actors of positive change' is basic to people-centred development (in Starke, 1990, p. 81). Martin Khor, from the Third World Network, predicts that this 'growth of environmental consciousness and activism will emerge even more and grow more rapidly in many parts of the Third World' (1988, p. 27).

Contemporary Environmental NGOs

The number of environmental NGOs is difficult to estimate. In 1982, UNEP's best guess of the number of national NGOs was something over 15 000, with about 85 per cent of those located in Europe and North America (McCormick, 1993, p. 133). Wapner cites figures which suggest that worldwide there may now be over 100 000 environmental NGOs or what he terms 'citizen-organised activist groups' (1996, p. 2) although there is little information in either case to suggest how environmental NGO is defined. Regardless of how many environmental NGOs there are, diversity is clearly the hallmark of the contemporary environmental movement. The NGO movement is hardly homogeneous and there have been clear political tensions within the environmental community, differences which have at times been played out over a range of issues, between institutionalised and bureaucratised lobbying organisations and community-based, grass-roots organisations as well as between Northern and Southern NGOs. As Breyman notes, the term (he refers to ecology movements) 'can mask very real differences' in philosophical grounding and strategic approach (1993, p. 124).

NGOs are diverse in scope, in size, in activity, in philosophy, in their degree of institutionalisation and in the range of issues they address. This diversity makes it difficult to categorise them easily. While most Northern NGOs are often membership-based organisations they nevertheless range from small, localised community organisations with precarious funding and little in the way of full-time staff to large, well-funded organisations operating (as McCormick (1989, p. x) puts it) out of designer offices. Some NGOs are constituted primarily as research institutes or think-tanks, others focus on lobbying and pressure group activity and a third and very broad category is activist at a local level, emphasising project management and grass-roots activity. Some NGOs, of course, will fall into all three categories. The best known research institutes would perhaps include the World Resources Institute (WRI) and the WorldWatch Institute, both based in Washington, along with the International Institute for Environment and Development (IIED) and the Foundation for International Environmental Law and Development (FIELD), both of which are headquartered in London, or the New Delhi-based Centre for Environment and Science. Yet so-called environmental think-tanks seek also to lobby governments and intergovernmental decision-makers and, at times, are effective decision-makers themselves. WRI, for example, has also been a lead agency in forging coalitions with governmental organisations to establish programmes such as the Tropical Forestry Action Plan. Others, such as the IIED, also have a strong development assistance and project management component, in partnership with developing country NGOs. Many environmental NGOs in developing countries are strongly involved in grassroots activity and project management even as they also engage in lobbying activity. Other NGOs function primarily as clearing-houses, facilitating information exchange, coordination and network-ing. One might place in this category the Environment Liaison Centre International in Nairobi, established in 1977 to provide a focus for NGO engagement with UNEP and the recently-closed Centre for Our Common Future which was established in Geneva to monitor and encourage follow-up, especially within the NGO community, to the Brundtland Report.

Most environmental NGOs are local or national organisations. There are few with a truly international character. Greenpeace International, Friends of the Earth International and World Wide Fund for Nature are probably the best known in that latter category. In each case, in their international incarnation, they are not member-ship-based organisations. Rather they have institutional relationships with national organisations which bear the same name and are, in effect, affiliates. Greenpeace and Friends of the Earth International maintain their respective international secretariats in The Nether-lands, although the size and purpose of each is quite different. Greenpeace is a highly centralised organisation and the international secretariat has a lead role in policy formulation and coordination of campaigns. FoEI, on the other hand, is much smaller and serves primarily in the role of information exchange among its national 'affiliates' which have much greater autonomy than those of Green-peace. WWF – the World Wide Fund for Nature – is headquartered just outside Geneva in Switzerland. It was established in 1962 to be, in effect, the fundraising arm for the IUCN but its path since then has been, McCormick (1993, p. 134) suggests, more of a parallel than an auxiliary course.

While few NGOs are truly international, one of the hallmarks of contemporary NGO activity is the extent of coalition activity not just within countries but at a transnational level. This kind of activity helps to strengthen the knowledge base and political influence of environmental and grassroots organisations, something that is of benefit to them given the complexity of many of the issues under consideration (see McCormick, 1993, p. 136). NGOs can pool in-formation, expertise and other resources. Coalitions may be ad hoc or formal, they may be issue-oriented (such as the Antarctic and South-ern Ocean Coalition or the Climate Action Network) or they may be constructed around more general environmental or development issues, as is the case with the Third World Network. They may have a national format, such as the US Global Tomorrow Coalition or the Indonesian Environmental Forum, or they may be regionally-based coalitions such as the African NGOs Environment Network (ANEN), the Asia-Pacific Peoples Environment Network (APPEN) or the European Environment Bureau (EEB).

This transnational character of environmental NGOs arises either because of the kinds of issues upon which energies are focused (that is those with a transboundary or global impact) or because activities cross state borders, or both. There is, however, also a global dimension to the environmental movement which arises from the potential cumulative influence of locale-specific activism and which helps to define global as something different from international. Thus Shiva suggests that the 'real ecological space of global ecology is to be found in the integration of all locals' (1993, p. 155). Small community and grassroots organisations, for example, may focus on local concerns such as water pollution, waste management or environmental repair, but they do not do so in isolation. Their work draws on the experience of similar groups working on similar problems in other countries. Such local community and grassroots organisations form part of an overall global movement, sharing similar concerns and values and contributing to what Durning refers to as a 'thickening web' (1989, p. 168). The global movement is therefore the 'result of hundreds of decentralised and locally autonomous initiatives' (in Shiva, 1989b, p. 218).

One of the great strengths of environmental NGOs in all parts of the world and one which contributes to this thickening web is their expertise and knowledge which can be brought to bear on attempts to influence policy or in addressing environmental problems at a local level. Stairs and Taylor suggest that NGOs can count among their attributes 'flexibility, imagination, resiliency, lack of bureaucracy, specialised expertise and independence' (1992, p. 135). Durning adds to this the 'ability to tap local knowledge and resources, to respond to problems rapidly and creatively and to maintain institutional flexibility in changing circumstances' (1989, p. 155). Many of the larger NGOs are now able to commission or undertake independent scientific research or draw on legal expertise to develop draft alternative conventions or provide critical analysis of intergovernmental proposals. Barnes characterises NGOs as important 'sources of real expertise . . . and the originators of important new ideas and concepts'

(1984, p. 173). Developments in technology have facilitated communication between local groups, enabling them to share information about their own activities and the activities (including those which are environmentally degrading) of their governments. Indeed, environmental NGOs have been something of a vanguard in using electronic mail for communication and the Internet for information dissemination. Many of the larger international NGOs are also very well financially resourced. Greenpeace International's 1996 budget, for example, was $US25.9 million (Bergesen and Parmann, 1996, p. 263) and the Sierra Club's total 1995 budget was $US42 million (Bergesen and Parmann, 1996, p. 272) although clearly few other NGOs could match or come anywhere near these amounts.

NGOs and Participation

The Brundtland Report, *Our Common Future*, observed that environmental NGOs have 'played an indispensable role since the Stockholm Conference' (WCED, 1987, p. 326). It is therefore worthwhile spending a little time exploring that role, the kinds of activities in which NGOs engage and the strategies they adopt in pursuit of their goals. While those goals are not always clearly articulated, they frequently focus on the importance of change – in policy, in behaviour, in values and norms – seeking, as Caldwell (1990, pp. 65–6) puts it, change not only in institutional priorities but also in social perspectives. Thus one of the main goals of environmental NGOs and grassroots movements has been not simply to democratise decision-making but to do so for a purpose, to mobilise for change. To characterise NGOs simply as lobby groups or pressure groups in pursuit of this purpose would be to present an incomplete picture. Kamieniecki (1991) identifies the role of NGOs in political mobilisation and agenda building. Stairs and Taylor (1992) explore NGO activities in lobbying, international law-making, scientific research, analysis and data collection. Sands (1992a) pays particular attention to the importance of NGOs in monitoring and seeking to enforce compliance with environmental legislation at both a national and international level. Yet another commentator describes one NGO, the WWF, as 'banker, advocate, instigator, teacher, advisor, diplomat, planner and communicator' (Anon., 1989, p. 124).

The participation of NGOs in multilateral environmental diplomacy dates to the Stockholm Conference and now involves more than pressure group activity on the fringe of diplomatic conferences and international policy-making. Representatives from NGOs are now sometimes included on national delegations (although this is still not a widespread practice and is less common than the inclusion of business and industry representatives). The more usual involvement, and one that contributes to what might be called 'insider' status, is the involvement of organisations as accredited observers either at negotiating or decision-making conferences (such as UNCED) or at regular consultative meetings or conferences of parties convened under specific treaties (such as the International Whaling Commission, the Antarctic Treaty Consultative Meetings, the Montreal Protocol and others). Observer status usually grants the right to table documents, to speak at plenary and other sessions, and often, now, to participate in working and expert groups which also provides opportunities for NGOs to raise issues that have been left off the government agenda. However it rarely involves participation in the small and informal groups in which key compromises are often worked out and final decisions made. NGOs also have less easy access to important economic organisations such as the World Bank, the IMF or the WTO, organisations whose decisions on developing lending and trade have a crucial impact on the processes of global environmental degradation (see Chapter 8). Officially accredited NGOs at environmental negotiations will also pursue a range of activities including direct lobbying of delegates and the exercise of indirect pressure through media activity (such as press conferences) and information dissemination. NGO expertise has often proved valuable to smaller countries who may themselves have limited resources upon which to draw. For example, the Foundation for International Environmental Law and Development (FIELD) has worked closely with the Alliance of Small Island States (AOSIS) in providing legal and related advice, including draft documents and negotiating language, and the preparation of background briefing papers for the climate change negotiations and since.

While some governments have resisted this broadening of participation (for example, the issue of accreditation of NGOs was a contentious issue in the early UNCED PrepComms) it would now be most unusual for environmental diplomacy to proceed in the absence of NGO observers. It would also be unusual for those conferences to proceed without the publication of the environment NGO journal *ECO*. This NGO journal was first published at the Stockholm Conference to provide a daily commentary on the proceedings and as a vehicle to inform the interested public. It was, as

Burke notes, 'widely read by delegates, NGO representatives and journalists, often . . . breaking news ahead of the main media' (1982, p. 116). Since then *ECO* has, in some form, been published at all major environmental conferences (at UNCED as the *Earth Summit Bulletin*). It has also become a valuable source of information for smaller delegations who are unable to attend all of the small working groups at a conference. Mintzer and Leonard note of the climate change negotiations that

> the most widely read source of information . . . was the daily NGO publication called *ECO* . . . [which] not only served to keep the NGOs (and some delegation members) informed about the progress of the negotiations but . . . also provided a sanctioned opportunity for NGO representatives to interact regularly with delegates. (1994b, p. 30)

The most extensive participation of non-governmental organisations in multilateral environmental decision-making to date was, of course, that at UNCED. As noted above, the participation of NGOs was something of a contentious issue at the early PrepComms, with some delegations seeking to limit accreditation only to those NGOs which already had ECOSOC consultative status. The basis for consultative status with ECOSOC (now under review) has been such that it excluded many NGOs with a local or grassroots focus as well as those who were considered to be too radical. UNCED Secretary-General Maurice Strong, on the other hand, was intent on broadening the formal and informal participation of NGOs. In the final analysis, accreditation was accorded to those NGOs which could show that their interests were directly relevant to the UNCED agenda – about 1400 non-governmental bodies were officially accredited to the Conference. Although the focus here is on environmental NGOs, other non-governmental actors including, as noted earlier in this chapter, representatives of the business community were participants at UNCED. NGOs attended PrepComms, where they sought to have some influence on the draft agreements, and also pursued their own preparatory process, one which led to some tension within the NGO movement about representation and strategy (see, for example, Simms, 1993; Rowlands, 1992; Chatterjee and Finger, 1994).

At UNCED, some 30 000 people – from non-governmental organisations, community groups, indigenous peoples organisations and women's groups among others – also participated in the Global

Forum, the NGO and people's event held at the same time as but separate from the official summit. From that process NGOs produced 30 alternative treaties – the NGO and social movements treaties – which were adopted through the International NGO Forum (IN-GOF) which was, however, organisationally separate from the Global Forum. The purpose of the treaties was to invoke commitments to action by the individuals and groups who signed them. They were conceived as a 'means to promote understanding and cooperation' and to 'provide the vision, the alternatives and the commitments to action that the governments were unlikely to offer' (Anon., 1992b, p. 1) although Chatterjee and Finger point out that the 'main problem with the treaties' was that 'no one seemed to know exactly what they would "do" with them' (1994, p. 99).

NGOs and Activism

As noted above, the growth of the contemporary environmental movement in the 1960s and 1970s emphasised activism. Direct action of various kinds has always been one component of this activism, sometimes as an effective strategy to mobilise public concern and to put pressure on governments and sometimes because no other avenue of influence is open to them. Internationally, Greenpeace is probably best known for this kind of direct engagement. NGO activism is not, however, confined solely to the goals of seeking to influence governments and intergovernmental organisations in the development and implementation of specific environmental policies and international law. Indeed, as Lipschutz suggests, one of the hallmarks of global civil society is that it is a 'system that increasingly engages in a transnational politics characterised by a surprising degree of autonomy from the state' (1993, p. 8). There are many other kinds of activism and many stories of local and transnational activism for damage limitation and environmental regeneration (see Ekins, 1992, p. 142) in both the North and South. For organisations like Friends of the Earth, this emphasis on local action is seen as the best way to inform and mobilise the public (Hontelez, 1988, p. 762). In one sense NGOs are 'providing services that governments are unable to' (Starke, 1990, p. 65) although perhaps one should question whether it is that governments are not so much unable as unwilling. At another level these activisms, collectively, reinforce the global nature of the environmental movement and demonstrate the development of global civil society in its opposition to programmes and policies which undermine the environment.

The number of examples is enormous and it is impossible to do justice here to the range of organisations and activities. A few will have to suffice. In Brazil, Kayapó Indians have protested against the Altimira Dam project; in Sarawak, the Penan peoples with the support of environmental NGOs have established blockades to bring a halt to logging in Sarawak; a 100-mile human chain was formed by 100 000 people in (then) Czechoslovakia, Hungary and Austria as a protest against a proposed hydroelectric project; the Pesticides Action Network has publicised the sale of hazardous chemicals in the Third World. Other groups, again in both North and South, have been involved in tree-planting, training programmes on sustainable agriculture, reversing soil erosion, building reservoirs and improving irrigation and a range of other environmental regeneration programmes. One might look, for example, to the tree planting activities of the GreenBelt Movement in Kenya, or the extensive environmental support work undertaken by Haribon in the Philippines. NGO activity also takes place in partnership arrangements across state borders. The IIED has worked as a project partner with community groups in developing countries. The US-based Environment Defense Fund has worked with Southern NGOs and grassroots organisations in opposition to a range of government policies, including the Indonesian Transmigration Programme. WWF has been an important source of innovative action in facilitating debt-for-nature swaps, an increasingly controversial environmental repair strategy which is explored further in Chapter 8. The African NGO Environmental Network (ANEN) has worked with UNEP since 1986 on a desertification programme which enables it to provide small grants to community groups in Botswana, Burkina Faso, Kenya and Senegal.

Impact and Influence

What, however, is the significance of these various kinds of activisms – lobbying, monitoring, resistance, environmental management – for environmental governance, particularly in the face of competing interests? NGO presence at and participation in environmental governance can contribute to improved transparency and accountability and, as Tinker argues, can be a 'check and balance on unbridled state sovereignty' (1993, p. 14). Sands suggests that 'since 1972 . . . NGOs have played an important role in contributing to the massive increase in international environmental legislation' as well as revealing 'the inadequacies of the traditional legal process' (1992a, p. 29). Williams, from the Society for International Development, suggests that NGOs have been 'singularly effective in highlighting environmental problems and in mobilising public opinion and support for sustainable development' (1992, p. 26). Rowlands claims that they create channels of communication, inform public opinion, help to create new international norms and contribute to the scientific debate (1991, p. 113). As suggested above, non-governmental organisations have become increasingly important in the monitoring and compliance of international environmental agreements, often drawing public and government attention to instances of non-compliance and placing pressure on governments and corporate interests.

Studies suggest that NGOs *have* been able to influence the content of environmental agreements and practice on particular issues. Stairs and Taylor (1992), for example, examine the role of NGOs in protection of the oceans, concluding that NGOs have been effective and influential in that regime. Elliott (1994) argues that NGOs were important in the rejection by governments of the Antarctic minerals agreement and the subsequent negotiation of an environmental protocol to the Antarctic Treaty. Benedick (1991) draws attention to the influence of NGOs on the Montreal Protocol negotiations, suggesting that NGO participation is an important factor in getting better environmental agreements. Tolbert explores the ways in which NGOs have sought to influence the climate change negotiations, arguing (at that stage prior to the adoption of the UNFCCC) that their impact 'is not to be underestimated and is likely to be quite substantial' (1991, p. 108).

Views are mixed, however, on the impact and influence of NGOs at UNCED. The knowledge- and information-based activities of NGOs at the conference itself clearly contributed to awareness-raising. Johnson, for example, points out that Strong made special tribute to the work of the *Earth Summit Bulletin*, the NGO paper produced at UNCED, in his final speech, and notes that his own (that is Johnson's) account of UNCED 'would have been far less comprehensive than it is' without it (1993, p. 3). Despite some tensions among participating NGOs, the Global Forum process strengthened networks and information exchange among a range of groups with environmental concerns, especially those from the South. This further development of global civil society, as something different from the influence of specific NGOs on the state-centric policy-making process, is one potential important outcome of UNCED. When it comes to an assessment of the impact on formal outcomes, judgements are cautious. Preston argues that 'quantitatively the presence of nongovernmental organisations at Rio was overwhelmingly positive, but qualitatively their effect was more ambiguous' (1994). Access did not necessarily translate into influence. Chatterjee and Finger (1994, pp. 112–13) suggest that, generally, the NGOs at UNCED were effectively outflanked by the corporate sector. Mark Valentine from the US Citizen's Network suggests that 'most NGOs would have to concur that [we] barely scratched the surface of the official documents' (cited in Chatterjee and Finger, 1994, p. 96). Larry Williams, from the Sierra Club, argues that 'we had almost no impact . . . we failed in the effort that we set out to accomplish' (cited in Simms, 1993, p. 99).

Charles de Haes from WWF argues that at least the 'UNCED process has led to a strengthening and broadening of the role and capacities of NGOs in international negotiations' (cited in Simms, 1993, p. 99). Even on this issue there is disagreement. Chatterjee and Finger (1994, p. 104) take the view that the green movement emerged *weaker* rather than stronger from UNCED. Their concern is that by seeking to work primarily within the system and to lobby governments on policy issues, environmental NGOs have been co-opted and have given legitimacy to a system of environmental governance that is flawed. Historically, they argue, 'the environmental movement has been in opposition to the system . . . over the years parts of the movement have become bureaucratised and part of the establishment themselves' (Chatterjee and Finger, 1994, p. 65). Chatterjee and Finger are particularly trenchant in their criticism of what they call the 'Big 10', the major US environmental organisations who are 'basically mainstream [and] limit themselves to lobbying the political system by calling for more efficient environmental management' (1994, p. 68). Elsewhere, Finger argues that

> NGOs are now trapped in a farce: they have lent support to governments in return for some overall concessions on language and thus legitimised the process of increased industrial development. The impact of lobbying was minimal while that of compromise will be vast, as NGOs have come to legitimise a process that is in essence contrary to what many of them have been fighting for years (1993, p. 36).

Conclusion

Princen suggests that the potential influence of NGOs is strengthened because of their ability to 'position themselves within both top-down and bottom-up approaches to international environmental policy-making' (1994, p. 38) thus, in effect, linking the global and the local. NGOs *can* play an important role in offering alternative approaches and in broadening the horizons of the debate. Barnes, for example, suggests that NGOs bring a 'global perspective' to negotiations and debate and that they are 'often the only groups talking about the long-term view, or bringing up difficult concept[s] [such as] the rights of future generations' (1984, p. 173). Banuri argues that NGOs have 'begun to articulate a genuinely alternative vision of development' (1993, p. 58). Williams suggests that 'active NGO participation . . . is playing an increasingly important role in a constructive vigilance concerning human values and unmet needs' (1992, p. 26). In this view, then, non-governmental organisations should 'be conceived as not only being nongovernmental bodies but as providing a voice for grassroots movements' (Gudynas, 1989, p. 199).

As noted earlier in this chapter, this emphasis on democratisation is a central theme in global civil society. Barnes argues that 'the international NGO phenomena provides the cutting edge of the common interest' (1984, p. 175). The President of Botswana, in a speech in December 1993, argued that 'NGO participation in international affairs buttresses democracy' (in Preston, 1994). Questions are raised, however, about how best to understand the representative nature of NGOs. Some question the claims to representation (and therefore participation) on the grounds that NGOs are not, for example, elected or necessarily accountable to the peoples whom they claim to represent (an observation which rather skirts the fact that a substantial proportion of the world's governments are not freely elected either!). Others, including Chatterjee and Finger, raise different concerns about representation, arguing that many of the NGOs who participate in international environmental diplomacy, for example, represent particular interests within the NGO community, often those of the environmental managerialists, and that 'very few real grassroots or community groups went to Rio or joined the two-year process' (1994, p. 104). Banuri raises concerns that INGOF seemed 'too strongly dominated by Northern NGOs' (1993, p. 64). As a note in the *Harvard Law Review* observes, participatory rights at intergovernmental organisations are 'meaningful primarily for well-organised, well-financed and well-informed NGOs' (Anon., 1991a, p. 1589). Yet it may be, as Tinker argues, that it is 'the voice of new and minority and non-traditional NGOs . . . [that] the international system *most* needs to hear to solve global problems which are increasingly international, interdependent and non-responsive to traditional power politics' (1993, p. 11; emphasis added). The extent to which some of those voices are (or are not) heard is the subject of Chapter 6.

6

Voices from the Margin: Women and Indigenous Peoples

As suggested in the previous chapter, the importance of global civil society lies not just in its potential to improve the participatory or democratic nature of environmental governance, in which case the goal is better policy-making, but also in opening a political space for the expression of marginalised voices and those for whom environmental degradation is symptomatic of a broader structural oppression and silencing. This chapter explores the voices of women and of indigenous peoples in the global politics of the environment. At one level, the participation of women and indigenous peoples in environmental governance is demanded as a condition for the adoption of better policies and for the successful pursuit of sustainable development. At another level, demands for their voices to be heard in the processes of environmental governance are representative of a broader concern with political expression and emancipation.

Holding the Keys: Women and the Environment

The Executive Director of the UN Population Fund has observed that, if 'energy, land and water are the keys to survival, [the] keys are held by the women of the World' (cited in WorldWIDE Network, 1992, p. 4). Women are the 'managers and conservers of natural resources' (WEDO, 1992, p. 14). However, as former Minister for Natural Resources and Tourism in Zimbabwe, Victoria Chitepo, has observed, 'international agencies and governments everywhere have ignored the vital part that women play in caring for the environment. Their voice, like their knowledge and experience is simply not heard' (cited in Dankelman and Davidson, 1988, p. ix). The difference and diversity in women's voices and experiences cannot be overestimated or ignored and women's relationships with their environment 'need to be understood within women's varied social, economic, cultural, political and class contexts' (Asian and Pacific Women's Resource Collection Network, 1992, p. 2). Women also, however, '*share* [their] "otherness", [their] exclusion from decision-making at all levels' (WEDO, 1992, p. 7; emphasis added). It is difficult also to separate 'women and the environment' from the impact of development on women, especially in the Third World (about which much has been written) or from the gender bias that continues, to a greater or lesser degree, to characterise all contemporary societies. Three propositions provide the framework for discussion here. The first is that women are disproportionately disadvantaged by environmental degradation. The second, to borrow from Jacobson (1992), is that this gender bias is a roadblock to sustainable development and the third is that women's participation is essential to the pursuit of sustainable development.

Bearing the Burden

Women, Shiva argues, 'bear the ecological costs of progress and development' (1989b, p. 7). This is especially so for developing world women. A considerable proportion of the daily lives of rural women in developing countries especially is spent in the gathering, growing and harvesting of food (including seafood) and the collection of water and sources of fuel and energy. This is so even where women are increasingly part of the formal economy. In some parts of Africa, for example, women produce 80 per cent of the food and in India about 60 per cent of the farmers are women. In parts of the developing world, women spend up to four or more hours a day collecting water and fuelwood (Dankelman and Davidson, 1988, p. 32). Therefore where the key components of the ecosystem – energy, land and water – are degraded it is women's lives which are more like to be adversely and directly affected. This is further complicated because women are disproportionately found amongst the world's poor, and it is the poor who are hardest hit by environmental degradation and who have fewer resources to deal either with causes or impacts.

Environmental degradation, and the development-related causes of that degradation, make already burdensome tasks more difficult. Clearance of forest land for large-scale agriculture and mono-cropping (an economic activity which has little benefit for women) ensures that smaller amounts of often marginal land are available as a source of food and fuel. Jacobson (1992, pp. 7–8), for example, explores the ways in which women in Ghana have been affected by the privatisation of commons land for cash cropping. As Momsen notes

> the expansion of cash-cropping and production for export has not been accompanied by the trickle down of benefits to the poor, especially poor women, while at the same time it has led to water pollution, soil erosion, destruction of firewood resources and loss of genetic diversity of plant and animal stocks (1991, pp. 93–4).

The local impacts of global problems such as climate change and ozone depletion on both cash and subsistence crops will make the production and collection of food more difficult. Desertification and deforestation exacerbate land degradation, water scarcity and fuelwood scarcity, all of which increase the subsistence burden which is disproportionately borne by women. Women have to work harder to compensate for soil erosion and loss of soil fertility in the production of food. Women have to walk further to collect water and increasingly scarce fuelwood supplies. Where fuelwood is scarce, they have to use alternatives (such as dried dung), alternatives which are less energy efficient and which also deny a source of soil enrichment. (Although women have primary responsibility for collecting fuelwood, they traditionally collect dead wood and are therefore rarely major contributors to deforestation.)

An unequal allocation of resources reinforces a gender bias in the impact of environmental degradation and development policies on women and their lives. Women are so often denied access to credit or to land ownership. Women's customary rights to commons land is being eroded in the 'modernising' of developing country societies (see Jacobson, 1992, p. 27). Women and girl-children eat less well and less frequently than their male counterparts and will continue to do so in the face of food scarcities. Women and girl-children are more likely to be denied access to education. The work women do is undervalued, even when their working hours are longer than those of men (which holds true in almost every country in the world). These factors contribute further to women's poverty and to their lack of access to resources for sustainable development.

Women in developed countries are affected by environmental degradation in different and often less immediate ways than women in the developing world. Nevertheless here too women's lives are more closely tied to household energy, food and water choices or in managing the impacts of environmental damage, such as illness resulting from water or air pollution. Policy responses and strategies which do not take into account the daily responsibilities of women's lives may be inappropriate not only for women but for the reversal of environmental decline. Mitigation strategies such as energy conservation measures, taxes on energy use or changes to public transport often ignore women's roles within the community and the greater extent of poverty among women. For example, something as seemingly straightforward as reduction in street lighting as an energy efficiency measure may affect women's safety and their feelings of security. Stringent restrictions on private car use may impact on women for whom, still, much of car use is in support of household responsibilities such as shopping or taking children to school or the doctor.

Where are the Women?

The articulation of women's concerns about and views on environmental degradation, as well as their expertise, are poorly represented in the institutional arena of environmental governance. Women are rarely to be found in the corridors of power, whether international, national or local. At an international level, few of those making decisions on the environment are women. Of course, this lack of women in international decision-making fora mirrors their under-representation in national governments. According to WEDO (n.d.), in 1994 women accounted for only 11 per cent of members of legislature worldwide. Only three countries had women presidents (Iceland, Ireland and Nicaragua) and only five had women prime ministers (Bangladesh, the Dominican Republic, Norway, Pakistan and Turkey). In 100 countries there were no women in cabinet. Of 181 member states of the United Nations, only seven had women heading their missions to the United Nations, and there were only three women in the senior UN grades of under-secretary-general.

The absence of women is evident also in the extent to which decision-makers ignore or simply do not think to consider the perspectives, views and needs of women. Bella Abzug points out 'everywhere women are catalysts and initiators of environmental activism. Yet policy-makers continue to ignore the centrality of women's roles and needs' (see WorldWIDE Network, 1992, p. 3). Jacobson points out also that 'women are rarely involved in designing or carrying out development programmes' (1992, p. 8). She notes, for example, that most agricultural extension workers in Africa are men even though most of the farmers are women, a pattern which is repeated in other parts of the world (1992, p. 30) and that forestry management programmes rarely include women or consider women's experiences despite their 'prominent role as users and managers' of forest resources (1992, p. 38). Consequently such programmes do not address women's needs and experience but are also, she suggests, likely to fail for this very reason. Thus 'countless programmes to reverse deforestation have failed because their planners did not think to consult village women who are the primary managers and harvesters of forest products in their communities' (Jacobson, 1992, p. 8). Yet that participation is essential, not only to benefit women but to incorporate vital experience and knowledge in the pursuit of sustainable development. As Maurice Strong has suggested, there is a 'pressing need to continue to centralise women's issues and to ensure the incorporation of their collective perspectives, experiences and contribution to sustainable development' (cited in UNIFEM, 1993, p. 3). Jacobson reminds us that

> if women in subsistence economies are the major suppliers of food, fuel and water for their families, and yet their access to productive resources is declining, then more people will suffer from hunger, malnutrition, illness and loss of productivity. If women have learned ecologically sustainable methods of agriculture and acquired extensive knowledge about genetic diversity (as millions have) yet are denied partnership in development, then this wisdom will be lost (1992, p. 47).

With an emphasis also on the emancipatory potential of global civil society, Ynestra King argues that the connection between women and nature provides a 'vantage point for creating a different kind of culture and politics that would ... transform the nature/culture distinction itself and ... envision and create a free ecological society' (1983, p. 123).

For some, the role that women have to play in sustainable development arises not just because of their experiences but as a result of their very woman-ness. In this view women are, because of their reproductive and nurturing roles, closer to nature than men. This essentialist argument suggests that women's insights will be different and, indeed, superior to those of men. This is so because, in this view, women's experience of the life-giving properties of Nature and their inherent caring and nurturing provide them with a sensitivity which stands separate from the combative, mechanistic view of Nature which is the source of environmental destruction. Others resist this kind of biological determinism (seeing in it the source of much of women's oppression), arguing rather that it is women's *experiences* of environmental degradation and ecosystem management that have given them a particular knowledge and ensured that this knowledge and expertise is crucial to the pursuit of sustainable development. In this view, as Shiva (1989b, p. 42) explains, women's access to what she refers to as the sustaining principle has an historical and cultural basis.

Attention in official circles to the gendered nature of environmental degradation and environmental governance is a product of the late 1980s. Neither the impact of environmental degradation on women nor their role in environmental governance were articulated at the Stockholm Conference and, indeed, the Stockholm agreements not only ignore women but are also highly gendered in their language. Within the UN system, UNEP has taken a lead in acknowledging and responding to the linkages between environmental degradation and women's lives. In 1986 UNEP established a committee of senior women advisors on sustainable development (SWAGSD). Between 1989 and 1991, and prior to the UNEP-convened Global Assembly on Women and the Environment (the Partners in Life conference) in November 1991, UNEP sponsored four regional assemblies on women and the environment as part of its programmatic response to the Forward Looking Strategies (FLS) which were adopted at the 1985 Nairobi Conference to review the UN Decade for Women. While the FLS did note that 'environmental degradation is . . . a contributing factor to deplorable conditions endured by many women' (see UNICEF/UNFPA, 1991, p. 3), the link between women and environment had not been a major theme at the Nairobi Conference (see Rodda, 1991, p. 5). The Brundtland Report, while progressive in many ways with its emphasis on social justice as a fundamental theme of sustainable development, devoted almost no time to women or gender concerns at all. Gender issues were also given little attention in the early PrepComms for UNCED and the issue was only taken up after intense lobbying from women and after Filomina Chioma Steady, from Sierra Leone, was appointed a special adviser on women in environment and development to the conference Secretary-General. Even then, most of those doing the deciding at UNCED were men, or elite men to be more accurate. There were far fewer women than men on the delegations at UNCED. Of the heads of state or government attending the final two-day summit, only two were women – Gro Harlem Brundtland of Norway and President Finnbogadottir of Iceland. Women were, of course, not the only ones who were barely noticeable in the corridors of power. Indigenous peoples are also rarely to be found on national delegations or in the secretariat of UN organisations.

Recognising the 'Vital Role'

Principle 20 of the Rio Declaration states that 'women have a vital role to play in environmental management and development. Their full participation is therefore essential to achieve sustainable development' (UNCED, 1992a). Agenda 21 devotes a full chapter to the role of women, the rather awkwardly titled chapter 24, 'Global action for women towards sustainable development'. Chapter 24 says that effective implementation of a range of international programmes already in place for the 'full, equal and beneficial integration of women in development activities' will depend on the 'active involvement of women in economic and political decision-making and will be critical to the successful implementation of Agenda 21' (UNCED, 1992b, para. 24.1). Together, principle 20 and chapter 24 give voice to a recognition that governance should be inclusive of women (the democratisation argument) and that the participation of women in environmental governance and the pursuit of sustainable development is vital (the efficiency argument). They also implicitly acknowledge that women's participation has not been full or equitable in the past.

Chapter 24 calls on governments to recognise women's roles and to facilitate their participation in economic and political decision-making for the benefit of women *and* the effective pursuit of sustainable development. It also places some emphasis on the importance of societal change: on eliminating violence against women, improving women's access to property rights, reducing their heavy workload, ensuring equal employment opportunities and eliminating negative stereotypes and prejudices against women. Chapters on other sectoral and intersectoral issues in Agenda 21 also address the role of women, elaborating the disadvantages which women face and the importance of a range of rights in improving the status of women (see UNIFEM, 1993). UNIFEM's executive director called Agenda 21 a 'tribute to the solidarity of a global women's caucus which has played a strong role in helping to define a document which promises a world of better opportunities for women' (UNIFEM, 1993, p. 2). Yet this judgement may well overestimate the promise of Agenda 21, especially as it is non-binding and relies on the actions and commitments of governments, many of whom have shown little inclination to overcome legal or structural discrimination against women. The Rio Declaration and chapter 24 articulate concerns about the efficient management of sustainable development. They were not driven primarily by concerns to alleviate the burden on women except inasmuch as such alleviation would contribute to better environmental policy-making and practice. Indeed, Joan Martin-Brown argues that 'events at UNCED did not succeed in fundamentally altering perceptions about either the roles and capacities of women or their relationship to the achievement of sustainable development' (1992a, p. 706). Agenda 21 has, however, provided a focus for other organisations and institutions with a primary concern with the status of women. The Commission on the Status of Women (CSW), for example, has urged the full participation of women in the sustainable development institutions of the United Nations and called for greater attention to women's contributions to environmental protection and management (see UN Economic and Social Council, 1993, p. 2).

Empowerment

Women are not simply victims of environmental degradation but, as Shiva argues, 'voices of liberation and transformation' (1989b, p. 47). Women must therefore be viewed as 'innovators, activists, conservationists, natural resource managers and agents of change at all levels of society' (Asian and Pacific Women's Resource Collection Network, 1992, p. 6). The Women's Action Agenda 21, a product of the 1991 World Women's Congress for a Healthy Planet, argued that 'women are a powerful force for change' (WEDO, 1992, p. 16) and that 'by acting together, by organising cooperatives and by managing credit and financial institutions, [women] can help change policy, protect the environment, improve their standards of living and challenge current economic analyses' (WEDO, 1992, p. 15).

In stark contrast to the absence of women in the formal, state-centred structures of environmental governance and decision-making (and the relative neglect of women's experience and concern in such fora) women have been active and effective participants in non-governmental organisations and in grassroots movements. As Durning points out, a 'noteworthy characteristic of community movements is the central role that women play' (1989, p. 158). Much of the organisational energy for environmental work comes from women, an activity which brings them into close contact with the realities of environmental degradation and which further strengthens the potential for collective empowerment. The best known movements mobilised by women are probably the GreenBelt Movement in Kenya, begun by the National Council of Women in 1977 and the Chipko Movement which began in Northern India as a grassroots opposition to logging and forest destruction. But there are many other examples of women working together to protect and repair the environment. The examples here are drawn from women's environment and development projects which were presented as success stories at the Partners in Life Conference in Miami in 1991. Women have worked to combat soil erosion in Ghana, to focus on pollution control on Lake Maruit in Egypt and to oppose toxic waste dumping in the Bay of Bengal in Bangladesh. Women have lobbied in support of organic farming practices in Barcelona, built NGO coalitions for environment and development in the Netherlands, and encouraged sea-turtle conservation in Brazil. They have fostered alternative methods of waste collection in Peru and campaigned against hazardous waste in the US.

In this way, women and their activisms contribute to the development of a global movement of women working for environmental protection and to alternative environmental and political practices, alternatives which emphasise grassroots and bottom-up forms of governance. Women's activism is not confined to local initiatives. International gatherings of women, such as the 1991 World Women's Congress for a Healthy Planet convened by the Women's International Policy Action Committee (IPAC) and organised by the Women's Environment and Development Organisation (WEDO), 'forge links among activists all over the globe' (WEDO, 1992, p. 4). Indeed, that the UNCED agreements address gender concerns in any way was a result of the lobbying effort which coalesced around the Women's Action Agenda 21 which was produced, as noted above, by the Congress.

The grassroots activism of women is not simply a response to marginalisation from formal structures of governance. It must also be explored as a positive act of agency by which women reclaim their rights as subjects in environmental governance rather than as objects of environmental management programmes. Their collective activism brings to global civil society and to the debates about environmental governance a consciously-articulated alternative vision, one which challenges accepted wisdoms and paradigms. The women who 'lead ecology movements in the Third World', Momsen argues, 'are offering a new view of development' (1991, p. 95). Nowhere are these challenges and new views more apparent than in documents such as the Women's Action Agenda 21 or the Draft Plan of Action adopted by the Asian and Pacific NGO Working Group at a conference in the Philippines in 1993, both of which were the result of consultations among women from many countries. The Women's Action Agenda was defined as a 'blueprint for incorporating the woman's dimension into local, national and international environment and development decision-making from now on into the next century' (WEDO, 1992, preface). Its themes were transformation and emancipation. The policy proposals and programmes for action that were adopted were guided by the principles of global equity, resource ethics, the empowerment of women, disarmament and challenges to militarism. Thus, at the conference at which the Agenda was finalised, Peggy Antrobus urged her audience to 'make the links between decisions reached in far off boardrooms and military headquarters, and the worldwide subordination of both women and nature' (WEDO, 1992, p. 1).

The Draft Plan of Action demanded 'radical transformations in the existing reality of the international economic order'. It argued that development should be people-centred, that the rights and needs of all people (including women, the poor and indigenous communities) should be at the 'core of all policies and programmes' and that all people should be 'empowered and centralised in the processes of planning and decision-making' (Asian and Pacific NGO Working Group, 1993, p. 2). The Plan called for the 'infusion of an alternative, feminist morality into development thinking', one which places 'respect for life and the intrinsic worth of all human beings at the core' (Asian and Pacific NGO Working Group, 1993, p. 3). Thus the demand was for a new paradigm, for 'new modes of environmental sustainability *and* social equity' (Asian and Pacific NGO Working Group, 1993, p. 3; emphasis added). This articulation of a new paradigm, based on sustainability and equity, was supported by specific policy initiatives to address the causes of environmental degradation and the causes of inequity in order to develop and promote sustainable livelihoods for women. These policies included the halting of resource extraction and depletion by multinationals, land reforms to address the rights of women to land entitlement, recognition of women as co-heads of households, non-discriminatory credit policies, priority access to resources for sustainable livelihoods for women as local producers and women's access to common land for water, food, fodder and fuel (Asian and Pacific NGO Working Group, 1993, p. 5).

In the context of these alternative voices, questions arise as to whether participation in decision-making and implementation of the kind anticipated in Agenda 21 is an adequate response to women's disproportionate environmental burden. While full participation is clearly required on equity grounds, it does not necessarily ensure that the disproportionate impact of environmental degradation on women will be overcome. Indeed, incorporation and participation in a structure that has systematically marginalised women may be counterproductive if the underlying gender inequities and power relationships within those structures are not acknowledged and addressed at the same time. For women, then, the 'full participation' recommended by principle 20 is more than a simple counting exercise. Nor is it simply that 'women's issues' should be given full attention in decision-making. Both are necessary but not sufficient conditions in the pursuit of sustainable development. Women challenge not only their lack of participation in decision-making, and the lack of attention given to their concerns, but also the structures and values which have resulted in 'unacceptable ecological and human costs . . . [including] massive environmental degradation' and which have 'reinforced old inequities and generated new inequities' (Asian and Pacific NGO Working Group, 1993, p. 1). Thus gender equity, rather than simply women's concerns, becomes an integral component of sustainable development.

Humanity's Hope? Indigenous Peoples and the Environment

Indigenous peoples are on the front line of the ecological crisis. They are the first victims, yet they may also be humanity's hope for the future.

These words, taken from the back cover of the *Gaia Atlas of First Peoples* (Burger, 1990), characterise the ways in which indigenous peoples, because of their close cultural, spiritual and economic relationship with their lands, have most often been located in the global politics of the environment – as victims and as saviours. Both tend towards the simplistic, but they have ensured that much of the debate about indigenous peoples and the environment within the formal structures of international governance, if it occurs at all, defines indigenous peoples as objects to be acted upon, to be empowered from above or from outside, or as a source of knowledge which can be appropriated and incorporated into the global discourse as and when needed.

Some 200 million people in over 70 countries are identified or identify themselves as indigenes (see Colchester, 1988, p. 443). Other phrases are sometimes used – tribal peoples, first peoples, first nations, the Fourth World – with indigenous peoples also having their own ways of describing themselves, such as tangata whenua for the Maori in New Zealand, or Innu for indigenous peoples in the Arctic regions (names which are often translated into English as 'people' or 'people of the land'). Indigenous Survival International defines 'indigenous peoples' as

> distinct cultural communities with unique land and other rights based on original and historical use and occupancy. These are peoples whose cultures, economies and identities are inextricably tied to their traditional lands and resources (cited in Yap, 1989–90, p. 92).

Traditional lands (and related ecosystems, including rivers, streams, coastal waters) are often held communally and it is in these lands and resources that indigenous communities find their meaning and identity as 'cohesive social and cultural groups' (Colchester, 1988, p. 444).

While there is often a tendency to think of indigenous peoples as being located only in the developing world (so called), indigenous peoples and communities are also found within the political boundaries of contemporary settler societies such as New Zealand, Australia, the United States and Canada. However, as the World Council on Indigenous Peoples notes, indigenous peoples do not control the national government of the countries in which they live (cited in Clad, 1988, p. 333). Indeed, indigenous nations do not always coincide with the political borders of states. For example, the Innu are located in the United States, Canada, Greenland and the Arctic regions of the countries of the former Soviet Union. The Fulani of West Africa 'extend across eight countries' (see Burger, 1990, pp. 18–19).

The impact of environmental degradation upon indigenous peoples and communities arises directly out of the damage inflicted upon traditional lands and resources, and indirectly through local and global development activities which are the cause of such degradation. In both cases, the traditional lifestyles and cultural strength of indigenous peoples is threatened and indigenous communities are dispossessed of their lands. As Burger notes, 'indigenous peoples live in fragile environments and are the first to suffer from the effects of . . . war on the ecosystem. Their close relationship with the natural world leaves them particularly vulnerable' (1990, p. 120). For indigenous peoples, environmental security is, however, not simply an issue of environmental management. Rather, it cannot be separated from land rights issues, human rights issues, the fight for self-determination, the impact of development and internal colonisation and, in the final analysis, potential cultural and physical extinction. As Shutkin argues on the latter point, 'cultural extinction is a genuine possibility for indigenous communities threatened by environmental degradation' (1991, p. 490).

As a result of deforestation and the environmental degradation that accompanies it, indigenous peoples (50 million of whom are forest dwellers) are denied a source of food (plants and game), shelter and medicines. They are also denied the forest as a source of spiritual and cultural identity and as a focus for traditional lifestyles. Deforestation is closely linked to loss of biodiversity in many parts of the world peopled by indigenous communities, a loss which further undermines a reliance on plants for medicinal and domestic purposes. As just one of many examples of the extent of indigenous knowledge about plant species and medicinal herbs, the Hanunoo people of the Philippines can, as Burger (1990, p. 32) points out, distinguish 1600 plant species in their forests, 400 more than scientists working in the region. Deforestation results in soil erosion and loss of soil fertility, affecting and often destroying indigenous farming activities. Climate change and ozone depletion have the potential to affect crops and the viability of the marine food-chain and coastal fishery stocks. Inland waterways may also become polluted through salt-water intrusion resulting from sea-level rises, thereby threatening and undermining traditional hunting and fishing grounds.

The destruction of local environments and indigenous lifestyles is often closely related to the pursuit of development and modernisation. As the Brundtland Report noted, the 'forces of economic development disrupt . . . traditional lifestyles . . . some are threatened with virtual extinction by insensitive development over which they have no control' (WCED, 1987, p. 12). Resource extraction (logging

or mining) or energy programmes (dam-building), which often involve the activities of MNCs, result in loss of land, in soil erosion and
the pollution and sedimentation of streams and rivers which, in turn,
affect indigenous agriculture and fishing. Infrastructure such as road
construction in support of this kind of activity also facilitates the
movement into indigenous lands of non-indigenous peoples, as workers in extractive industries and as colonists, bringing disease and,
often, violence towards local peoples. Internal migrants often contribute to environmental degradation in their use of unsustainable
land management practices. They are also often allocated land which
belongs to indigenous peoples but which is not legally recognised as
such by the state, further contributing to indigenous dispossession. In
the face of environmental degradation, disruption of traditional
lifestyles and marginalisation from the land, indigenous peoples are
often forced into cash-employment, a lifestyle change that also has a
gender dimension in that indigenous women are often left to undertake increasingly difficult subsistence activities and to care for the
welfare of the communities (see, for example, Chai, 1992).

There are any number of examples which provide evidence of the
ways in which the negative synergy of environmental degradation
and development has undermined the security of indigenous communities. In Brazil, the Carajas Dam project has inundated 216 000
hectares of forest and resulted in the displacement of 13 000 people
(Colchester, 1988, p. 450). Military flight testing in Northern Labra-
dor in Canada has affected caribou herds on which the local Innu
peoples rely (Burger, 1990, pp. 112–13). The traditional fishing
grounds of the Huaorani in Ecuador have been contaminated as a
result of oil exploration (see Shutkin, 1991, pp. 493–500), the building of roads has resulted in soil erosion and sedimentation of rivers
and streams which are traditional sources of fish, as well as enabling
the movement of colonists from other parts of the country, further
contributing not only to the spread of disease but also the loss of
autonomy of the indigenous peoples over their lands. Deforestation
in Palawan in the Philippines is 'obliterating the indigenous peoples
who belong to the Tagbanuwa and Batak tribes' (Kennedy Cuomo,
1993, pp. 231–2). In Sarawak, where large tracts of forest are being
felled, not only is deforestation causing damage to the local environment but the traditional land rights of indigenous peoples are being
ignored (see Colchester, 1990). As Colchester observes, logging roads
have been pushed across areas cultivated by the native peoples, the
clearing of forests has resulted in a decline in game and therefore the

protein intake of local peoples. Accelerated forest loss has led to
further soil erosion, rapid surface run-off, pollution of streams,
decline in fish stocks and a further impoverishment of the local diet
(Colchester, 1990, p. 168). Diseases such as measles and whooping
cough, transported by forest and other workers, have brought death
to Yanomami peoples in Venezuela and Brazil (see Burger, 1990,
p. 88; Shutkin, 1991, pp. 496–7; Wiggins, 1993, p. 350).

Programmes designed to include and/or benefit indigenous peoples
have often been imposed rather than being driven by the concerns and
values of indigenous communities. As Davis (1993b, p. 2) observes,
rural development and conservation programmes directed at indigenous peoples tend to be designed by outsiders and they seldom
promote the autonomy or self-reliance of the communities or peoples
they are intended to benefit. Evaristo Nugkuag Ikanan (then President of COICA) has characterised this approach thus: 'there are
many who want to intervene in the destiny of indigenous peoples,
doing it externally and from "above" us' (cited in Wiggins, 1993,
p. 347). This criticism is not just directed towards governments.
COICA, in an open letter to the environmental community, makes
it clear that while indigenous peoples appreciate the efforts of
environmentalists, they are concerned at the way in which indigenous
peoples have been left 'out of the political process', noting that 'we
never delegated any power of representation to the environmentalist
community' (COICA, n.d., p. 304). Indeed, it has been something of
an irony that in some countries conservation programmes or the
establishment of biosphere reserves have also marginalised indigenous
communities. Clad observes that the establishment of national parks
in areas of 'traditional settlement' is more likely to be 'feared as
taking something away rather than welcomed for the protection it
bestows' (1988, p. 324). He provides the examples of the Shakilla
peoples being driven from the Lake Rukana Park in Kenya, or the
Kidepo National Park in Uganda from which the Ik were expelled
(Clad, 1988, p. 330).

Strategies for the economic empowerment of indigenous peoples
and local communities, often intended as a means of dealing with the
impacts of environmental degradation, have been subject to much
criticism. Shiva (1990) and Chatterjee and Finger (1994) are strongly
critical of social forestry programmes launched under the Tropical
Forestry Action Plan. Social forestry was intended 'to raise the
standard of living of the rural dweller, to involve him [sic] in the
decision-making process . . . and to transform him [sic] into a

dynamic citizen capable of contributing to a wide range of activities' (FAO cited in Chatterjee and Finger, 1994, p. 147). Yet social forestry is criticised for 'tak[ing] forestry away from the control of communities . . . and neglect[ing] the economics of tribal and peasant life' (Shiva cited in Chatterjee and Finger, 1994, p. 147). Other strategies have also been questioned, particularly those which emphasise the marketing or harvesting of the rainforest as a means not only of reversing deforestation, but also as a way of providing an economic resource for indigenous peoples (on the 'trade not aid' principle). Corry (1993) argues that, so far, harvesting has done little to empower indigenous peoples or to protect the forests and may, in fact, further undermine indigenous autonomy in that they become reliant on foreign intermediaries, have little control over the marketing process and are vulnerable to price fluctuations and the exigencies of Western consumer demand. Gray (1990, p. 226) suggests that, if such economic empowerment is to succeed, marketing should be firmly under the control of indigenous communities and that full recognition of any related intellectual property rights should accompany such economic activity.

The impact of environmental degradation and development projects on indigenous communities is further exacerbated by state policies which, either by commission or omission, continue to undermine the viability of indigenous cultures. In many parts of the world, governments simply do not recognise indigenous land rights and thus indigenous land is claimed as crown or state land. Gray notes, for example, that less than 30 per cent of the lands belonging to the nearly 500 indigenous nations in the Amazon are 'titled' (1990, p. 224). Indigenous peoples therefore often have little authority over their own lands and there is little recognition within formal government structures of their rights to land and to cultural self-determination. As the executive summary of a World Bank discussion paper acknowledges, 'indigenous peoples face serious problems in gaining official recognition of their customary land and territorial rights' (see Davis, 1993a, p. x). Not only does this further marginalise indigenous peoples from their land but, in doing so, it often contributes further to environmental degradation as new land-holders engage in unsustainable practices. The process of state-building in post-colonial states, built on integrationist or assimilationist principles, often resists self-determination for peoples or nations within states. Indigenous peoples are cast as backward, as pre-modern, as standing in the way of development and the construction of a national identity, and their resistance is deemed to be obduracy. The Transmigration Programme in Indonesia, which has 'caused environmental havoc on an unprecedented scale' (Colchester, 1988, p. 463), and disrupted indigenous communities, is motivated in part by a government desire to de-indigenise the less-populated regions of the country. Mario Vargas Llosa, a candidate in the 1990 presidential election in Peru, argued that 'modernisation is only possible with the sacrifice of the Indian [indigenous] cultures' (cited in Wiggins, 1993, p. 347). In Borneo (Malaysia) where deforestation has threatened the livelihoods and lives of the Dayak peoples, the state minister for the environment (Datuk James Wong) articulated the view that 'there is too much sympathy for the Dayaks. Their swidden lifestyle must be stamped out' (in Durning, 1989, p. 167). Ekins also cites one D. A. J. Wong, Minister of Tourism and Environment in Sarawak (and, one assumes, perhaps the same person) who has argued also that the 'nomadic Penans . . . have always posed a problem . . . They pose a dilemma to the government' (in Ekins, 1992, p. 83).

Participation and Appropriation?

The close reliance of indigenous communities on the land and related ecosystems (rivers, streams, coastal regions) has resulted in traditional practices which have allowed time for land regeneration and enabled the maintenance of ecosystem stability. Indigenous peoples are the original sustainable developers and have often been able to live well in what others might consider marginal environments. Marshall Sahlins calls them the original affluent societies (see Colchester, 1988, p. 445). Maurice Strong has called indigenous peoples the 'guardians of the extensive and fragile ecosystems that are vital to the wellbeing of the planet' (1990, p. 6). Nevertheless this view can also be simplistic and unhelpful. Clad is wary of what he terms 'enforced primitivism' (1988, p. 325) or what Brenton (1994, p. 152) refers to as an almost 'mythical construction' (of forest peoples in this case). Wiggins, a Miskito Indian from Nicaragua, argues that 'it would be a mistake to take too romantic a view' (1993, p. 348). He points out that 'Indians, like all other humans, survive by killing and consuming plants and animals . . . like other peoples they have utilised and developed their territories' (Wiggins, 1993, p. 348). Wiggins also points out that some indigenous peoples have permitted environmentally dangerous practices, such as the dumping of toxic wastes or mining activities on their lands, although he characterises this as an exception rather than a rule (1993, p. 349). Indigenous communities are rarely voluntarily environmentally destructive to the point of ecosystem collapse and such activities are often a response to increasing poverty. Indigenous peoples are also not necessarily anti-development (see Colchester, 1989, p. 249) but rather resistant to culturally and ecologically inappropriate forms of development which are imposed upon them and which are a source of their marginalisation and dispossession as well as destructive of local environments.

It is, however, this historical emphasis on sustainable lifestyles which has engendered the view of indigenous peoples as saviours of humankind, a view sometimes expressed in technocratic or managerialist tones and sometimes in rather more mystical language. In the foreword to a World Bank report, Andrew Steer, then Deputy Director of the Bank's Environment Department, argues that 'indigenous peoples can make a major contribution to the appropriate design and successful implementation of Bank-funded natural resource management and biodiversity conservation programmes' (1993, p. iii). Steer continues, somewhat grudgingly that 'indigenous peoples . . . possess *quite* sophisticated environmental knowledge and are *frequently* excellent resource managers' (1993, p. iii; emphasis added). Thus, as the editor of the report suggests, 'rather than being obstacles to societal progress, the world's remaining indigenous peoples . . . may provide the key to the successful management of these regions' (Davis, 1993a, p. ix). The Brundtland Report, also adopting something of a managerialist tone, suggested that indigenous peoples' lifestyles 'can offer modern societies many lessons on the management of resources in complex forest, mountain and dryland ecosystems' (WCED, 1987, p. 12). The reason for this, the Commission argued, is because 'these communities are the repositories of vast accumulations of traditional knowledge and experience that links humanity with its ancient origins. Their disappearance is a loss for the larger society which could learn a great deal from their traditional skills in sustainably managing very complex ecological systems' (WCED, 1987, pp. 114–15).

The rationale for involving or even empowering indigenous peoples is therefore often couched in terms of the benefit to industrial society and to sustainable development rather than, necessarily, to the interests and rights of indigenous peoples. Thus, to quote Strong again, indigenous peoples are 'indispensable partners as *we* try to make a successful transition to a more secure and sustainable future on our precious planet' (1990, p. 6; emphasis added). The World

Bank report mentioned above suggests that 'it is in *our* interests and those of the planet to open a permanent space for these peoples and their values' in the debate over environment and development (Davis, 1993a, p. xi; emphasis added).

The formal structures of environmental governance, and the UNCED process in particular, have begun to emphasise the imperatives for including indigenous communities in environmental governance on both democratic and efficiency grounds. The IUCN first established a Task Force on Traditional Lifestyles in 1975. At its 1990 General Assembly, the IUCN passed a resolution requiring that all documents, including the World Conservation Strategy and various national conservation strategies, should include specific recognition of the role in environmental management of indigenous communities and particularly indigenous women. The UN Working Group on Indigenous Populations first met in 1982 and has been preparing a Draft Declaration on the Rights of Indigenous Peoples (still not adopted at the time of writing). In 1989 the International Labour Organisation (ILO) adopted the *Convention Concerning Indigenous and Tribal Peoples in Independent Countries* (ILO, 169) which rejects the assimilationist policy of earlier ILO conventions and places some emphasis on the safeguarding of indigenous rights, especially participation and rights to the natural resources of their lands (see Wiggins, 1993, p. 353). The Brundtland Report, as already indicated, paid some attention to the rights of indigenous peoples arguing that their traditional rights 'should be recognised and they should be given a decisive voice in formulating policies about resource development in their areas' (WCED, 1987, p. 12). The Commission recommended that 'the starting point for a just and humane policy for such groups is the recognition and protection of their traditional rights to land and the other resources that sustain their way of life' recognising also that such rights may be defined in terms that 'do not fit into the standard legal systems' (WCED, 1987, p. 115).

The Rio Declaration establishes, in the twenty-second of its principles, that

Indigenous people and their communities and other local communities have a vital role in environmental management and development because of their knowledge and traditional practices. States should recognise and duly support their identity, culture and interests and enable their effective participation in the achievement of sustainable development. (UNCED, 1992a)

Chapter 26 of Agenda 21, in support of this principle, is entitled 'Recognising and Strengthening the Role of Indigenous People and their Communities'. It emphasises the importance of indigenous knowledge deriving from an 'historical relationship with their lands' and the 'interrelationship between the natural environment and its sustainable development and the cultural, social, economic and physical well-being of indigenous people' (UNCED, 1992b, paragraph 26.1). Indigenous people[s] are to be informed, consulted, allowed to participate (and, in some cases, educated) (UNCED, 1992b, paragraph 26.5(b)). Yet while chapter 24 acknowledged the ways in which women had been disadvantaged, chapter 26 goes no further than to make highly veiled references to any of the ways in which indigenous peoples have been marginalised politically, culturally and ecologically. The Forest Principles also included several references to indigenous people[s], requiring that governments should promote opportunities for their participation (UNCED, 1992b, paragraph 2(d)) although indigenous people[s] are included here in a list of potentially interested parties. The Principles require that national forest policies should recognise and support the identity, culture and rights of indigenous people[s], that appropriate conditions should be promoted for them to have an economic stake in forest use and that such policies should include land tenure arrangements which would serve as incentives for the sustainable management of forests (UNCED, 1992c, paragraph 5(a)). The Forest Principles call also for indigenous capacity and knowledge to be recognised, respected, recorded and developed. The preamble to the Biodiversity Convention acknowledges the 'close and traditional dependence of many indigenous and local communities . . . on biological resources', later urging governments (subject to national legislation) to 'respect, preserve and maintain knowledge, innovations and practices of indigenous and local communities' (UNEP, 1992, article 8).

The Rio Declaration, Agenda 21, the Conventions and the Forest Principles all refer to indigenous peoples in the singular – as indigenous people, implying an emphasis not on communities or indigenous nations with a right to self-determination, but on individual rights. The plural noun was apparently struck from every page of Agenda 21 after lobbying by the Canadian and Brazilian delegations (see Chatterjee and Finger, 1994, p. 58). While the Rio Declaration identifies indigenous people[s] as groups who have 'knowledge to contribute' to environmental management and sustainable development, none of the Rio agreements suggest that they should have authority and autonomy over their own lands and lifestyles. What is also missing from these agreements is any recognition of the fundamental feature of indigenous empowerment, that of land rights. The closest one finds is in chapter 26 of Agenda 21 which calls for the lands of indigenous people and their communities to be protected from activities that are environmentally unsound or that indigenous people consider to be socially and culturally inappropriate and which points out that 'some indigenous people . . . may require, in accordance with national legislation, greater control over their lands' (paragraph 26.4).

While the knowledge base of indigenous peoples is recognised in the UNCED agreements, this has not alleviated concerns about the ways in which that knowledge has been used in the past, and how it might be used in the future. Indigenous knowledge has most often either been discounted as unscientific and uncivilised on the one hand, or appropriated by western science and commercial interests without compensation on the other. The Forest Principles suggest that any benefits arising from the utilisation of indigenous knowledge should be equitably shared. The Biodiversity Convention contains similar provisions on the 'equitable sharing of benefits' arising from the utilisation of indigenous knowledge. The issue of intellectual property rights has been a major theme in the debates over biodiversity. Yet there is nothing in either of these agreements which specifically recognises the intellectual property rights of indigenous peoples or their ownership of their knowledge. Genetic resources, according to the Biodiversity Convention, are owned by the state.

Indigenous Activism

Indigenous peoples are not simply waiting to be empowered from outside or from above, nor are they 'passive victims' of environmental degradation or passive recipients of economic empowerment. There is a growing activism of indigenous peoples within and across political borders, an activism which Clad describes as the 'renewed political assertiveness by (and on behalf of) indigenous peoples' (1988, p. 321). Corry dates the emergence of indigenous peoples' organisations to the 1970s (1993, p. 151). Benavides (1996) explores the emergence of indigenous organisations since the 1960s noting, however, that such organisations are not without weaknesses especially in the limited participation of women in leadership positions. Nevertheless indigenous activism is seen to be a basis for strength. As Kayapó Indian leader Paulinko Paiakan has argued, 'no one of us is strong enough to

win alone [but] together we can be strong enough to win' (cited in
Kennedy Cuomo, 1993, p. 233). Indigenous activism has focused on
preventing environmental destruction at local levels. The Penan in
Sarawak have erected blockades to prevent logging and the Kayapó
peoples have mobilised to oppose the Altimira Dam in Brazil (see
Burger, 1990). Indigenous communities have mobilised and enacted
management programmes to protect their lands. The Keina Indians in
Panama have established and managed a forest park and botanical
reserve (Burger, 1990, p. 166). The Inuit have initiated an Arctic
Conservation Programme (Burger, 1990, p. 174). The Quichua-speak-
ing Indian federation in eastern Ecuador has designed and carried out
a forestry management project (see Davis, 1993b, p. 3). Indigenous
peoples' activism also has a transnational and global dimension, with
the formation of coalitions which work not only to support local
efforts but also to lobby and liaise with governments and intergovernmental organisations and to present their cases to human rights
bodies. The Coordinating Body for the Indigenous Peoples Organisations of the Amazon Basin (COICA), which represents over one
million indigenous peoples in the Amazon region, lobbies institutions
such as the World Bank on indigenous concerns and has organised
environmental summits to meet with national and international
conservation organisations.

Yet, in the final analysis the emphasis for indigenous peoples'
organisations and activism is not simply or even primarily one of
environmental degradation. Rather it runs the gamut of indigenous
rights, with land and cultural rights as the goal and as the most
appropriate way in which to ensure the sustainable development of
their lands and communities. As the COICA agenda for bilateral and
multilateral funders of Amazon Development proclaims, 'the most
effective defense of the Amazonian biosphere is the recognition and
defense of the territories of the region's Indigenous Peoples' (appended to Davis, 1993a). Indigenous activism, as with the activism of
women, is also a reclaiming of power over their own environmental
agenda. As Davis suggests, that '[w]hat is being sought is a new
notion of planetary governance in which indigenous and other local
peoples participate, along with nation-states, in the setting of international environment and development priorities' (1993b, p. 6).

7

The International Political Economy of the Environment

In spite of assertions of a 'common future' (the title of the report of the World Commission on Environment and Development) and the imperatives for building a 'global partnership for sustainable development' (the purpose of Agenda 21) the international political economy of the environment is shaped by differences over how that common future is to be achieved, what principles should inform it and what strategies should be adopted to achieve it. Those issues have been touched upon in earlier chapters but they are given greater attention here and in Chapter 8. The International Political Economy (IPE) of the environment is almost always couched, at some point, in terms of a North–South divide to which this chapter first turns. Tensions arise not only over the principles which should address the relationship between rich and poor countries but also over how those principles should be put into practice. Attempts to articulate the view that all countries have obligations but that those obligations might differ in the light of a range of historical and contemporary factors have been give expression in the notion of 'common but differentiated responsibilities' which is explored later in this chapter. A second major principle which is addressed here, and one which has become a defining motif of contemporary environmental politics, is that of sustainable development. The phrase is often used without further explanation, as if its meaning is undisputed. Yet, as this chapter demonstrates, nothing could be further from the truth.

North and South

The terms 'developed' and 'developing' are commonly used in environmental agreements to distinguish, in effect, the rich countries from the poor(er) ones. The former is now usually taken to mean the OECD countries and sometimes to include the transitional economies of the former Soviet bloc. The latter group of countries – the developing world – is defined, in effect, by its exclusion from the former. Other phrases are used: First and Third Worlds; the North and the South. These are loaded terms, not least of which because (with the possible exception of those based on some kind oɪ ̆ loose geographic determination) they suggest a hierarchy of value. Nevertheless, they are widely used within the literature, even by 'Third World' scholars and are therefore used here, cognisant of Ann Hawkins' observation that 'we all await new ways to speak (and think) of differing countries' (1993, p. 222). As earlier chapters have suggested, it can be misleading to conflate the 'North' and 'South' into two implacably opposed but internally cohesive blocs and it would also be incorrect to suggest that the relationship between the two is one simply of confrontation, with no recognition of shared interests and no commitment by developed countries to the environmental concerns of developing countries. Differences within each group on specifics are, however, often overshadowed by a strong degree of cohesion and agreement among, but not often between, developed and developing countries on fundamental contextual and strategic issues, such as the causes of global environmental degradation, relative vulnerabilities and the relative capacities of rich and poor countries to manage the impact of that degradation.

The industrialised countries of the North have been and continue to be disproportionate users of resources, their own and those of developing countries, and remain a major source of degradation of the commons. Yet the nature of future contributions to environmental degradation means that, without some kind of mitigating action in the South, commitments by developed countries to halt and reverse such degradation will of themselves be insufficient. Countries in the South argue, however, that if they are to meet their responsibilities to develop sustainably they should do so *only* when the North has taken a lead and that they can do so *only* with financial and technological assistance. William Nitze (1993, pp. 39–40) summarises the issues thus. Should the rich countries be required to make substantial reductions in their own emissions and rates of natural resource depletion before the developing countries assume obligations to do likewise? Should the rich countries commit in advance to pay to developing countries the incremental costs of reduction in pollution and resource depletion and, if so, who should decide what those incremental costs are? Should the developing countries have preferential access to Western technologies on non-commercial terms to help their economies develop in a more sustainable manner?

The harmful effects of global environmental change will be felt more immediately and to a greater degree in poorer parts of the world, especially in Africa but also in Asia and Latin America. This is especially so given that 'the exploitation of land, forests and water resources, among other primary natural resources, constitutes the basic means of survival for 60 per cent of the population of the Third World' (Soto, 1992, p. 684). These countries and people, many of whom have contributed little to global environmental degradation, will require assistance to manage the impacts of environmental degradation. The UNDP notes, for example, that the land area of Bangladesh, a country which contributes about 0.3 per cent of global greenhouse emissions, could shrink by as much as 17 per cent with a one metre rise in sea-levels (1996, p. 26). From the perspective of many developing countries, solutions to the global environmental crisis cannot and should not be considered independently of a reform of the international trading system, a revising of international development assistance and a rescheduling (at minimum) of external debt. This is because, as Soto argues, the 'global environmental crisis and the socioeconomic decline in the South are the interconnected result of an inequitable world order, unsustainable systems of consumption and production in the North and inappropriate development models in the South' (1992, p. 679) and because the three primary institutions of global economic interdependence – trade, aid and debt – are seen to have worked systematically to the benefit of the North at the expense of the South (Ekins, 1993, p. 97). Most argue, as Speth does, that the solution lies in a 'new era of heightened cooperation and agreement between industrial and developing countries' (1990, p. 16). This is easier said than done.

The rationale for 'heightened cooperation' is advanced in both ethical and practical terms. Paul Harris argues, for example, that it is 'both morally and practically necessary for governments and citizens of rich countries to help people in poor countries develop their economies in a sustainable fashion' (1994, p. 267). Henry Shue (1992) suggests that justice is unavoidable, again on practical and ethical grounds. Past injustices, through the extractive practices associated with colonialism, have left the poorer countries less able to mitigate environmental degradation and less able to manage the impacts of that degradation, both local and global. The industrialised world, on the other hand, has benefited disproportionately from an unrestricted use of developing country resources. Thus past injustices must be compensated. Speth couches his argument in humanitarian terms as well as pointing out the 'unwitting complicity' (1990, p. 18) of developed countries in environmental degradation in the South, especially through the imposition of development projects which ignore local needs and which have often, therefore, contributed to further poverty and environmental degradation. There are also, because of *mutual* vulnerabilities, practical reasons for developed countries to provide assistance to developing countries. Ecological and economic interdependencies mean that unless developing countries are able to address both proximate causes and impacts of environmental degradation, developed countries will also be increasingly environmentally and economically vulnerable to global environmental degradation.

The extent of mutual vulnerabilities, in the long-term, suggests that developing countries (or at least those which are the most populous) should have a degree of political leverage which they have not had in the past. China and India, for example, initially refused to participate in the ozone depletion negotiations because they felt that the Montreal Protocol did not and would not address the concerns of the developing countries, especially regarding questions of financial and technological assistance. The response of the donor countries involved in the negotiations was to commit to an increase in the fund established under Montreal Protocol if India and China participated, which they have now done, although the funds remain small. However, the degree of leverage is minimised because, although the relative contributions of developing countries to global environmental degradation is likely to increase in the future, they are also the countries which will be affected disproportionately. 'Holding out' on negotiations can therefore be to their disadvantage as well. Unity among developing countries can also be difficult to achieve. Within the developing world some will be affected to a greater degree and more immediately than others. That immediate impact (for example, the impact of sea-level rises on low-lying island states) often translates into less rather than more political leverage, especially if such countries have little to offer by way of bargaining chips.

The ability to bargain and to exert leverage is also determined by the extent of participation in negotiations and the kinds of expertise upon which a country can call. Put simply, intergovernmental conferences are expensive and have become more so with the proliferation of formal conferences, preparatory meetings, ad hoc working groups, intersessional meetings and a range of regional and other fora into which governments are keen to inject their views and to protect their interests. It is now standard practice for voluntary funds to be established with each new global environmental negotiating process to assist developing country participation, although the sums contributed are rarely large. The voluntary fund established for the participation of representatives of small island developing states (SIDS) in the UN Global Conference on Sustainable Development in SIDS provides an example. The secretariat sought $US950 000 but, by mid-September 1993, only $US154 783 had been received from developed countries (Anon., 1994a, p. 6). Developing countries, especially the smaller, poorer ones, often have a limited range of technical, scientific, legal and economic expertise upon which to call, expertise that is therefore likely to be quite thinly stretched. At the early meetings of the IPCC, for example, only 11 of the G77 countries were able to send climatological experts, restricted by cost and expertise. That number had increased to 33 by February 1990 after the IPCC established a Special Committee on the Participation of Developing Countries, intended specifically to 'promote the full participation' of developing countries in IPCC activities (see Lunde, 1991, p. 209).

Yet this participation has not been able to overcome differences over how best to interpret or understand concepts such as sustainable development, in spite of the frequently-adopted principle of common but differentiated responsibilities, both of which are explored in this chapter. The differences arise, as suggested above, from tensions over the interpretation of what is supposed to be a common agenda.

Whose Common Agenda?

At the Stockholm Conference in 1972, the head of the Kenyan delegation made a distinction between the 'environmental problems of poverty' and environmental problems resulting from the 'excesses of affluence' (cited in Ntambirweki, 1991, pp. 907–8). Developing countries argue that it is the environmental interests of the affluent North rather than the developmental interests of the South which continue to define the global environmental agenda. Concern is expressed about the way in which the 'resources' of the developing world, such as tropical forests or species and biodiversity, are now determined to be the 'common heritage of humankind', resources which the developing countries are now supposed to manage for the good of all. As Soto argues, 'efforts to extend the concept of the global commons to nationally based resources are a threat to Southern sovereignty over Southern resources and consequently the right of the Third World to benefit economically from indigenous resources' (1992, p. 694). Vandana Shiva sums it up this way: she says that the North's slogan at UNCED and other global negotiation fora seems to be 'what's yours is mine. What's mine is mine' (1993, p. 152).

This is argued to be inequitable on two counts: first, because in the past, developing world resources were exploited by and for the benefit of Northern countries and, second, because (as earlier chapters have shown) when it comes to issues such as desertification, the causes and consequences of which may also have global implications, the Northern countries resist attempts to have these defined as 'global' concerns (and thus as concerns for which, for example, financial assistance through the GEF should be made available). Tariq Banuri (1993, p. 48), executive director of the Sustainable Development Policy Institute in Islamabad, Pakistan, suggests that many from the South fear in the UNCED process the emergence of a new imperialism, of new conditionalities, and of new obstacles to the alleviation of poverty and oppression. For many Northern countries, on the other hand, demands for financial assistance, debt rescheduling and trade reform as a means of mitigating environmental degradation are reminiscent of 1960s and 1970s demands for a new international economic order and are therefore seen to be part of a larger political agenda that, in their view, has little to do with environmental concerns.

The Stockholm Declaration paid some attention to these issues. It confirmed that in developing countries most of the environmental problems are caused by underdevelopment and that, therefore, developing country needs included access to aid, technology and other assistance (principles 9 to 12). The Stockholm Declaration also acknowledged, in principle 23, that the standards set by industrialised countries might not be appropriate for developing countries. Differences between the developed and developing countries were in evidence from the beginning of the UNCED process. That the conference was devoted to environment and development, not as separate issues but as concerns that were inextricably tied, was an attempt to reconcile the major concerns of both developing and developed countries.

The Rio agreements reflect that compromise. The Rio Declaration reaffirms the right to development in principle 3. It emphasises the importance of eradicating poverty (principle 5) and requires that the 'special needs' of developing countries be given priority (principle 6). Many of the chapters of Agenda 21 reflect, in their generalities if not in their specificity, developing country concerns. Thus there are chapters on the importance of eradicating poverty, on changing consumption patterns (with an emphasis on action in the North), on financial resources and mechanisms and technology transfer (although, as explored further in Chapter 8, these issues were highly contentious). These general principles have been reasserted in a number of other environmental agreements, many of which have been discussed in Chapters 2 and 3 of this book. The Montreal Protocol, for example, acknowledged in the preamble that 'special provision is required to meet the needs of developing countries' for substances that might be ozone-depleting and provided, under article 5, for a ten-year grace period for developing countries to comply with restrictions as long as certain requirements were met (see Chapter 3). The Framework Convention on Climate Change emphasises the right for a country to determine its own development priorities and acknowledges that 'the specific needs and special circumstances' of developing countries 'should be given full consideration' (UN INC/FCCC, 1992, article 3.2). It recognises the need for equitable burden-sharing and for developed country parties to mobilise financial resources, and to provide 'new and additional' financial assistance to assist vulnerable developing countries to meet their obligations and to prepare for and adapt to adverse effects of climate change. The Forest Principles also state that access for developing countries to technology in support of forest management and conservation should be 'promoted, facilitated and financed, as appropriate' (UNCED, 1992c, article 11) although the provision is so vague as to be potentially meaningless. Both the Convention on Biodiversity and the Desertification Convention (to use its short title) contained provisions protecting sovereign rights to resources and emphasising the importance of technology and financial resource transfer between developed and developing countries.

Common but Differentiated Responsibilities

Attempts to address the issue of 'who is to blame' or, in more moderate tones, that of relative contributions and obligations has been articulated through the concept of 'common but differentiated responsibilities', in an attempt to meet Northern concerns that all countries have obligations and Southern concerns that those obligations are not the same. Developed countries prefer to focus mainly on proximate causes of environmental degradation. Developing countries, on the other hand, seek also to address the systemic causes of environmental degradation in the functioning of the global economy, the nature of development assistance, inequitable trade and debt, issues addressed further in the next chapter. Southern countries have tended to argue that the *primary* cause of the global environmental crisis has been Northern development and consumerism and that it is therefore incumbent on Northern countries to take the lead in making commitments to reverse environmental degradation. In this view, as Sanders argues, 'a program for economic sustainability . . . must properly begin with the North and particularly the United States' (1990, p. 398). The response of developed countries, again with variations, is that developing countries cannot be free-riders with respect to the mitigation of global environmental problems. Northern demands for comparable action to be taken in the South are interpreted as one more example of Northern imperialism which may place further constraints on economic growth in the South and further exacerbate inequities between rich and poor countries.

There is no doubt that there are inequities in global resource use and in contribution to environmental degradation. The Northern industrialised countries account for about 25 per cent of the world's population but about 80 per cent of the world's resource use. The United States alone accounts for about 25 per cent of commercial energy consumption, with developed countries accounting for about three-quarters of the world's commercial energy consumption. US per capita energy consumption is about 20 times that of India and about 80 times that of sub-Saharan Africa (Fairclough, 1991, p. 82). Former World Bank economist Herman Daly calculates that were the entire global population to consume resources at the current US per capita rate, then annual extraction of non-renewable resources would have to increase by a factor of about seven (cited in Peet, 1992, p. 217). Relativities between developed and developing countries with respect to resource use and contributions to environmental degradation is, however, changing. While developed countries accept that they have been more resource intensive in the past, they point out that developing country contribution to the problem at a global level will increase in the future. They argue, for example, that much of the projected population increase (as much as 90 per cent) will occur in the developing world. As a result of this, and as a result of projected economic growth, estimates suggest that, by 2025, energy consumption in the developing world will have increased from about 23 per cent in the late 1980s to about 44 per cent of world demand (see Porter and Brown, 1991, p. 95). On global commons issues, especially the degradation of the atmosphere, industrialised developed countries argue that any action which they take will have little effect without action from Southern countries given their future contribution to degradation of the commons. On issues such as desertification, deforestation and loss of biodiversity, many developed countries argue that developing countries must take responsibility for proximate degradation and must therefore be prepared to make commitments, especially if they also expect financial and technological assistance.

The climate change issue provides a good example of the complexities of the 'common but differentiated responsibilities' principle and debates on the nature and extent of individual country commitments to reduce emissions. The calculation of greenhouse gas emissions is controversial. If emissions are counted on a total output basis, then a developing country such as China, for example, is the fourth largest emitter in the world (Grubb, 1990, p. 73). If, on the other hand, emissions are calculated on a per capita basis, China emits only one-tenth of all OECD emissions (Paterson and Grubb, 1992, p. 297). China, therefore, would favour commitments based, in the first instance, on past per capita emissions. If, however, China utilises fossil-fuel energy as the basis of its targetted annual growth rate of 6 per cent over the next ten years, then the carbon dioxide produced would cancel out almost all GHG emission reductions in the OECD countries. Northern developed countries argue, therefore, that projected future emissions should also be factored into the negotiations for targets and commitments. The issue is further complicated by the mix of gases. The relative contribution to radiative forcing of methane (a very efficient greenhouse gas) is projected to increase and much of this increase will come from agricultural processes in developing countries. Developed countries such as the United States and Australia have therefore argued that a comprehensive approach is required to reduce emissions, taking methane and the relative contribution of developing countries into account and focusing on the enhancement of sinks as well as reductions in sources. Developing country response is twofold: first that developed country carbon dioxide emissions remain the major source of radiative forcing and, second, that methane is a 'survival' emission arising from basic subsistence activities (animal husbandry, rice farming) whereas carbon dioxide emissions are luxury emissions arising from, for example, wasteful energy use and excessive use of fossil-based fuel.

In 1991, the World Resources Institute developed a 'Greenhouse Index' which set out to rank countries in terms of their relative contribution to greenhouse gas emissions. The Index was hailed as one which, in its apparent measure of national accountability, would be 'ideal for diplomatic (as opposed to scientific) purposes' (Hammond *et al.*, 1991, p. 12). This index ranked China (on 1988 figures) third behind the United States and the then Soviet Union (even though its per capita emissions were only 0.6 carbon equivalent tonnes compared with 5.4 for the US and 3.6 for the USSR). According to the WRI calculations the developing countries contributed 46 per cent of world total, a 'far larger proportion than generally has been recognised' (Hammond *et al.*, 1991, p. 13). The Index was challenged by Third World commentators and scientists, who disputed the basis of the calculations and what they argued to be the political motivation behind them as 'an excellent example of environmental colonialism' (Agarwal and Narain, 1991, p. 1; see also McCully, 1991a).

The Rio Declaration restates the idea of 'common but differentiated responsibilities' (UNCED, 1992a, principle 7). The UNFCCC refers to the 'common but differentiated responsibilities and respective capabilities' of developed and developing countries (UN INC/ FCCC, 1992, article 3.1). It notes, in the preamble, that the largest share of historical and current global emissions comes from the developed countries, but notes also that developing countries' share will increase as they pursue social and development needs. Developed countries are required to take the lead in addressing greenhouse gas emissions and climate change. As Chapter 3 has shown, however, the question of relative commitments remains a contentious one on the Berlin Mandate agenda. The Desertification Convention, on the other hand, is quite specific in its references to complementarity of commitments, requiring affected parties (primarily developing countries) to give priority to desertification and to enact or to strengthen laws, policies and action programmes and for developed countries to provide support, financial resources and facilitate access to technology. The latter group of countries were insistent that there be a degree of complementarity of commitments. There are, therefore, different interpretations of the practical implications of common but differentiated responsibilities: for developing countries, this is a principle which requires the North to take a lead; for developed countries, the principle acknowledges different contributions to environmental degradation but does not (or should not) absolve developing countries of commitments as well.

Sustainable Development

Sustainable development is a key concept in the global politics of the environment and one of the most contested ideas in global environmental discourse. The first site of contestation is definitional. That is, how is sustainable development to be defined and operationalised? What is to be sustained? What kind of development in envisaged? The second is ideational. That is, what are the embedded normative assumptions of the concept? Is sustainable development locked into a development discourse and ideology of growth or is it informed by an ecological ethic? Redclift (1987, p. 32) suggests that the term was first used at the time of the Cocoyoc declaration on environment and development in the early 1970s. The idea of sustainable development was embraced by the International Union for the Conservation of Nature in its 1980 World Conservation Strategy although at that stage, Pearce and Warford (1993, p. 41) suggest, it was a concept limited to the arena of conservationist dialogue, rather than making inroads into the discourse of governments and aid agencies. While the use of the term sustainable development clearly predates the World Commission on Environment and Development (see Chapter 1 for more on the Commission), it was however the report of that Commission which established the phrase firmly in the lexicon of environmental politics.

World Commission on Environment and Development

The Declaration issued by the Commission at its final meeting in Tokyo in February 1987 argued that it was possible to build a future that was 'prosperous, just and secure' (WCED, 1987, p. 363) but that this required all countries to adopt the objective of sustainable development as the overriding goal of national policy and international cooperation. Sustainable development, the Commission argued, is in the 'common interest' because 'ecological interactions do not respect the boundaries of individual ownership and political jurisdiction' (WCED, 1987, p. 46). The Earth's resource base has to be conserved and enhanced, not only in order to meet development goals, but also as part of 'our moral obligation to other living beings and future generations' (WCED, 1987, p. 57). The Report emphasised the importance of multilateralism, the imperatives of addressing social concerns and the need for institutional reform. It urged new norms of behaviour and changes in attitudes, social values and aspirations as necessary (but perhaps not sufficient) conditions for achieving sustainable development.

The Brundtland Report defines sustainable development as 'development that meets the needs of the present without compromising the ability of future generations to meet their own needs' (WCED, 1987, p. 43). Two principles underpin this. The first is that sustainable development must emphasise needs (although those needs are not defined) and give special priority to the essential needs of the poor. The second is that sustainable development must recognise the limits imposed by technology and social organisation on the ability of the environment to meet present and future needs. For the Commission, those limits were not necessarily limits to growth, but limitations placed on resource use in pursuit of that growth. The ecological dimension of sustainable development is not explicitly articulated, and has to be inferred from the Report. For example, the Commission observes that many of us live beyond the world's ecological means, that, at a minimum, sustainable development must not endanger the natural systems that support life on Earth (1987, p. 44) and that the overall integrity of the ecosystem is important (1987, p. 46).

The conservation and enhancement of resource capacity can, the Report argues, be achieved through scientific assessment to ensure better productivity without ecological damage, through energy efficiency, through anticipating the impacts of industrialisation on the biosphere and through encouraging the use of low-waste technologies (1987, pp. 59–60). To do this, technology, which is the 'key link between humans and nature' (WCED, 1987, p. 60), has to be reoriented, technological capacity in developing countries has to be enhanced, and greater attention has to be paid to environmental factors in the development and use of technology. Technology is thus a source of risk *and* a means to managing those risks (WCED, 1987, p. 365). While the expansion of knowledge and technological advances can, the Report suggests, enhance the carrying capacity of the resource base, it cannot extend it indefinitely and therefore it is important that steps be taken long before the limits are reached. Renewable resources must be used within the limits of regeneration and natural growth, taking into account the 'system-wide effects of exploitation' (WCED, 1987, p. 45). Land should not be degraded beyond 'reasonable recovery' (1987, p. 46). The use of non-renewable resources should take into account a variety of factors, including the criticality of the resource and the availability of technology for minimising depletion and for providing substitutes. At very least, a resource should not run out until substitutes are available (WCED, 1987, p. 46). Plant and animal species should be conserved and adverse impacts on the quality of air, water and other natural elements should be minimised (WCED, 1987, p. 46).

The fundamental emphasis in the Commission's report is on growth. Growth, or achieving 'full growth potential' or 'high levels of productive activity' (WCED, 1987, p. 44), has to be revived because it is crucial to overcoming poverty which the Commission identified as a major cause of environmental degradation and a barrier to sustainable development. Poverty and inequity can, the Commission suggested, be overcome by growth and efficiency, as long as that growth is sustainable. The Commission recommends an annual growth rate of about 3 per cent per capita (or, taking population increases into account, something in the vicinity of 5 to 6 per cent per annum in the developing world). Growth, however, has to be less material- and energy-intensive (1987, p. 52), that is it has to be sustainable. It should take into account full environmental costs (for example, the costs of regenerating forests, rather than determining forestry income in terms of the value of timber minus the costs of extraction) (1987, p. 52) and should not increase vulnerability to crises (WCED, 1987, p. 53). Indeed, for the Commission, a measure of progress might be the *abandonment* of a development project for such long-term social and ecological reasons (1987, p. 54). There is an extra incentive for developing countries to pursue 'sustainable growth' according to the Commission. As developed countries pursue their own growth in a more sustainable way (that is, less energy- and material-intensive and more material and energy efficient (WCED 1987, p. 51)), they will provide smaller markets for commodities and minerals from the developing countries. This should provide an extra incentive for developing countries to pursue growth with a focus on equity and basic human needs because such growth will increase the domestic demand for products, goods and services.

Growth strategies followed in developing countries will be less than sustainable, the Commission predicts, if they are not also accompanied by a reorientation of international economic relations. Trade, capital and technology flows must be more equitable and take greater account of environmental imperatives. Market access, technology transfer and international finance must be improved in order to help developing countries to diversify economic and trade bases and to build self-reliance (WCED, 1987, p. 365). The achievement of recommended levels of growth, and therefore of sustainable development, might require, the Commission suggests, the resolution of the debt crisis in Latin America (WCED, 1987, p. 50) and the 'correction of short-term imbalances . . . and the removal of deep-rooted constraints on the growth process' in Africa (WCED, 1987, p. 51).

Growth and sustainable development cannot be separated from issues of social justice and equity within and between generations. Growth and development therefore require a social costing which recognises the impact on 'disadvantaged groups' (WCED, 1987, p. 53) as well as on vulnerable ecosystems. If it does not, then it is not sustainable. The Report acknowledges that 'our inability to promote the common interest in sustainable development is often a product of the relative neglect of economic and social justice within and amongst nations' (WCED, 1987, p. 47) noting that the poor and marginalised are disproportionately disadvantaged by environmental degradation, yet often lack both the political and economic means to address these concerns. Growth has to meet essential human needs, for employment, food (or, more importantly, nourishment), energy, housing, water supply, sanitation and health care (WCED, 1987, pp. 54–5). Growth must be balanced by a sustainable level of population, that is, where 'population size is stabilised at a level consistent with the productive capacity of the ecosystem' (1987, p. 56). While the Commission recognises that the question of population cannot be separated from patterns of consumption, much of the focus is on reducing fertility rates in the developing world, acknowledging the social dimension of this as well as the importance of education of women, health care and expansion of the livelihood base of the poor (WCED, 1987, p. 56).

'Sustainable development' as elaborated by the Brundtland Commission, is, in the final analysis, also about governance. For the Commission, the pursuit of sustainable development requires

> a political system that secures effective citizen participation . . . an economic system that is able to generate surpluses and technical knowledge on a self-reliant and sustained basis, a social system that provides for solutions for the tensions arising from disharmonious development, a production system that respects the obligation to preserve the ecological base for development, a technological system that can search continuously for new solutions, an international system that fosters sustainable patterns of trade and finance and an administrative system that is flexible and has the capacity for self-correction (WCED, 1987, p. 65).

The WCED report provided the basis for subsequent discussions on and debates over the pursuit of sustainable development, discussions and debates which were central to the UN Conference on Environment and Development.

UNCED and Sustainable Development

The Rio Summit was explicitly about managing the links between environment and development and creating, in the words of the preamble to Agenda 21, a 'global partnership for sustainable development' (UNCED, 1992b). In the Rio agreements, sustainable development is not defined – its content is assumed – but it echoes the basic principles and emphases of the Brundtland Report. Principle 1 of the Rio Declaration places human beings at the centre of concerns for sustainable development. Principle 4 provides that 'in order to achieve sustainable development, environmental protection shall constitute an integral part of the development process and cannot be considered in isolation from it' noting also that 'eradicating poverty is an indispensable requirement for sustainable development' (UNCED, 1992a). Sustainable development is not defined in Agenda 21, but the focus of this programme for action seems to suggest that, for the most part, it is in developing countries that sustainable development is absent. Chapter 2 of Agenda 21, the first substantive chapter, is headed 'international cooperation to accelerate sustainable development in developing countries and related domestic policies'. It calls for development to be reactivated and accelerated, suggesting that a supportive international climate for achieving environment and development goals can be attained through trade liberalisation, making environment and trade mutually supportive, providing adequate financial resources to developing countries, dealing with international debt and encouraging macroeconomic policies conducive to environment and development. Chapter 3, on combating poverty, suggests (echoing the Brundtland Report) that an anti-poverty strategy is one of the basic conditions for ensuring sustainable development. Chapter 4 focuses on changing patterns of consumption in the pursuit of sustainable consumption and sustainable economic growth.

Critiques and challenges

While sustainable development may seem to have been generally accepted into the lexicon of global environmental politics, there continues to be much criticism of its content and practice. The grounds for concern include the haziness of the concept, its continued emphasis on growth strategies, its articulation of poverty as a cause of unsustainable development, and the way in which sustainable development seems simply to reinforce the development status quo.

Despite the efforts of the Brundtland Commission and the rather tortuous and technocratic content of Agenda 21, sustainable development has been criticised as an idea which is not well-articulated in practice. Lipschutz, for example, takes the view that Brundtland 'fails to define the concept further in an operational fashion' (1991, p. 193) and Peet argues that the Brundtland Report's definition of sustainable development is so general that it could probably be met via several, mutually exclusive strategies (1992, p. 208). Sustainable development has often been reduced to tautology. The 1990 Business Charter for Sustainable Development, produced by the International Chamber of Commerce, said this: 'economic growth provides the conditions in which protection of the environment can best be achieved, and environmental protection, in balance with other human goals, is necessary to achieve [economic] growth that is sustainable' (cited in Ekins, 1993, p. 92). El-Ashry argues that a 'healthy resource base is necessary for long-term sustainable development' and, in turn that, 'development provides the means for effective environmental protection' (1993, p. 83). Thus Finger argues that what he calls the 'sustainable development slogan' has come simply to mean that 'ecological sustainability is good for economic development and economic development is good for ecological sustainability' (1993, pp. 42–3). All this does, he suggests, is promote fuzzy thinking. Others imply that too much is expected of the concept: Sandbrook, for example, suggests that sustainable development has had to account for the 'problems of poverty, equity, progress *and* human aspiration' (1991, p. 403; emphasis added).

One of the major points of contestation is the extent to which a continued emphasis on economic growth (albeit sustainable growth) is or should be a fundamental component of sustainable development. As noted above, the Brundtland Report calls for the revitalisation of global economic growth, for 'more rapid economic growth in both industrial and developing countries' (WCED, 1987, p. 89). Indeed, the goal is sometimes quite explicitly identified as 'sustainable *economic* development' (see El-Ashry, 1993, p. 87; emphasis added). Growth is important in this formulation because it is seen as the only effective antidote to the poverty which is articulated as a major cause of environmental degradation *and* a measure of underdevelopment. Poverty reduction will increase 'people's ability to invest in environmentally sustainable activities' and decrease their 'propensity to engage in environmentally destructive patterns of behaviour' (El-Ashry, 1993, p. 84). Therefore rather than perceiving environmental policies as a restriction on development, in the manner of traditional neo-classical economics, this modified perspective suggests that development which fails to take account of environmental damage will prove inefficient and often ineffectual in terms of raising incomes and well-being (that is, eradicating poverty) (El Ashry, 1993, p. 84). Martin-Brown suggests that sustainable development is about the 'need to retain or recover the capacity of ecosystems to support *economic* systems and life' (1992b, p. 1100; emphasis added). What is therefore needed is the 'right' kind of development, and that is development which takes account of environmental costs or, as the World Bank's 1992 *World Development Report* defines it, sustainable development is 'development that lasts' (cited in Sachs, 1993b, p. 10).

For many critics, however, this continued emphasis on growth, as a fundamental principle in the world political economy and as a precondition for sustainable development and a successful measure of it, precludes any debate about the need for an intelligent restraint of growth. William Rees argues that the pursuit of sustainable development should 'force a reconsideration of the entire material growth ethic, the central pillar of industrial society' (1990, p. 21), what Sanders calls the 'gospel of export-led growth' (1990, p. 396). Yet it does not do so. Sustainable development legitimises the growth ethic. In contrast to the Brundtland Commission, critics argue that growth is *not* the solution to poverty or environmental degradation. Sachs suggests that the argument that 'growth will alleviate poverty' is the 'single most important pretension of the development ideology' (1991, p. 254). As Lipschutz notes, 'the maximising of economic growth does not ensure that the benefits will be equitably distributed' (1991, p. 192). There is now, as Sanders points out, a substantial body of evidence to support the proposition that 'unrestrained economic growth is incompatible with environmental stability and balance' (1990, p. 395). He goes on to argue that 'the hoped-for benefits of limited growth will be cancelled out by less environmentally sensitive paths of production' (1990, p. 396). World economic growth, he argues, is becoming more uneven rather than less and is showing signs of slowing – a shrinking world market with declining terms of trade will serve to accelerate environmental degradation as nations seek to maximise agricultural, mining and other commodity exports in a losing effort to stay even (Sanders, 1990, p. 397). Braidotti *et al.* argue that, in effect, under the principles of sustainable development, 'growth for environmental recovery itself leads to further environmental degradation' (1994, p. 133).

The objection to this approach is that poverty rather than its underlying causes is cast as the problem, which makes it easier to hold poor people responsible for environmental degradation and to require action on their part. Further, it defines unsustainable development as primarily a developing country problem. Yet, as Pearce and Warford point out, 'rich countries use more resources and emit more waste than poor ones' (1993, p. 6). It is, critics suggest, therefore too simplistic a view of the relationship between poverty and environmental degradation and one which tends to gloss over any recognition that 'poverty is structurally determined' (Redclift, 1984, p. 59). What it ignores, Griffen argues, is 'capitalist development, the profit motive, government promotion of foreign investment and the activities of transnational companies as part of the problem' (cited in Asian and Pacific Women's Resource Collection Network, 1992, p. 10).

Reliance on GNP as a measure of sustainable growth is also viewed with considerable discomfort. American economist Hazel Henderson suggests that trying to measure an economy on indicators such as GNP is like trying to fly a jumbo jet with only one gauge on the instrument panel (in Peet, 1992, p. 209). GNP does not measure 'external costs' such as environmental degradation or resource depletion. The results of timber felling, for example, are usually treated as a net contribution to capital growth, even when it might lead to long-term deforestation and loss of resources (Pearce, cited in Redclift, 1987, p. 16). Thus the benefits of forestry are measured, but not the possible long-term costs of either regeneration or of non-regeneration. Von Weizsäcker (1991, p. 426) refers to studies in (then) West Germany suggesting that the external costs of environmental damage could be as high as 10 per cent of GNP. Studies on Indonesia by economist Robert Repetto indicate that, taking environmental costs into account, the annual growth rate (for the period 1971 to 1984) was effectively 4.0 per cent rather than 7.1 per cent, and that the average growth of domestic investment was 1.3 per cent rather than 11.4 per cent (cited in von Moltke, 1991, pp. 981–2). Measures of the quality of 'growth' are, of course, changing – the World Bank's annual World Development Report now uses a number of indicators (see Redclift, 1987, p. 17) such as average annual rates of inflation and adult literacy and there have been attempts to incorporate natural resources into national income accounts (see Repetto, 1992) – yet GNP is still considered to be a major indicator of growth and, therefore, quality of life. Yet while GNP measures income flows (see Jacobs, 1990, p. 3) it provides no information on how that income is generated. It makes no distinction between different kinds of production, between, for example, that which is spent on arms expenditure, high levels of dirty industrialisation or cleanup after environmental disaster, and that which is spent on the maintenance of education and health. GNP measures only certain kinds of formal, 'productive' economic activity and provides no accurate measure of inequity, injustice or wealth distribution, all of which are relevant to the issue of environmental sustainability. Indeed, Postel and Flavin (1991, p. 187) advance the argument that a move to environmentally sustainable practices could actually be accompanied by a *decrease* in GNP.

Sustainable development has been characterised as 'a radical departure from the conventional objectives of economic policy' because it incorporates welfare, distributive justice and an element of 'futurity' (Jacobs, 1990, p. 3). For Hartshorn, as well, because 'sustainable development attempts to improve the quality of life for humans without depleting renewable and non-renewable natural resources [it] contrasts with traditional development models that stress increasing GNP through economic growth that is often based on rapid depletion of the natural-resource base' (1991, p. 398). Others are less comfortable with assertions that sustainable development is a radical idea. Braidotti and her colleagues argue that the Report's elaboration of sustainable development did not 'fundamentally threaten the status quo' and that this, in turn, has made it easy for it to be accepted by 'mainstream economic, development and political institutions' (1994, p. 133). Rees takes this argument further, suggesting that as the term has 'been embraced by the political mainstream, so it has been stripped of its original concern with ensuring future ecological stability' (1990, p. 18). Thus, he argues, sustainable development is no longer a challenge to a conventional economic paradigm but another excuse for continued economic growth. Chatterjee and Finger argue that the Brundtland Report 'basically reformulates the by-now old development myth' (1994, p. 27) and that it strengthens the old development discourse (1994, p. 28). Sustainable development, they suggest, is simply another term for modernity. David Pearce and Jeremy Warford argue that sustainable development was a 'convenient phrase for rallying support [for development] rather than an agent for forcing environmental change' (1993, p. 41). Governments at UNCED were, Hildyard suggests, 'unwilling to question the desirability of economic growth, the market or the development process itself' (1993, p. 22). Braidotti (and others) take up this point, arguing that at UNCED a 'fundamental thinking of the Western development model and the global economic system as such did not take place' (1994, p. 128).

The failure of sustainable development to challenge the modernisation paradigm is viewed as inherently problematic because it reinforces a form of development which relies on capital injection, transfer of technology and the cultural transformation of old or traditional ways that are considered to be obstacles to development, a process that Sachs refers to as the 'unfettered hegemony of Western productivism' (1993b, p. 4). What has not occurred, in this critical view, is any sufficient analysis of the political and economic reasons behind resource depletion or the failure of development or modernisation models. Braidotti *et al.* argue that the logical consequence of the economic growth model has been 'environmental degradation and resource depletion' (1994, p. 131). Critics take the view that rather than providing a solution to poverty and environmental degradation, development has resulted in *greater* inequities because it has entrenched an exploitative relationship between the industrialised countries and the developing world, and because it has engendered a misplaced belief in the 'linearity of progress' (Braidotti *et al.*, 1994, p. 131). Concerns are therefore expressed that development has come to be seen as the therapy for the injuries caused by development (Sachs, 1993b, p. 9).

For many critics, the test of sustainable development is also applied differently and inequitably in different parts of the world. Chatterjee and Finger (1994, p. 27) argue, for example, that the sustainable development paradigm suggests that if some (developing) societies have not yet achieved sustainable development, it is basically because they lack the financial, human, technological and organisational capacity to do so. If other more developed societies do not do well in terms of sustainable development, so goes the argument, this is due to a lack of economic, technological and organisational efficiency. Indeed, El-Ashry argues that 'economic inefficiencies are a major cause of environmental damage' (1993, p. 85). Michael Redclift observes that 'development' in the US, as its economy is currently organised, requires 370 times as much energy per capita as it does in Sri Lanka (1987, p. 17). Does this then suggest, he asks, that the US cannot achieve sustainability given its economic structure, or does it imply that Sri Lanka cannot achieve development given *its* economic structure?

At best, then, for those who are wary of the way in which sustainable development has been elaborated, the idea provides only alternatives within development rather than alternatives to development (Sachs, 1993b, p. 11). Protection of the environment, or ecological sustainability, is not ignored, but becomes a means to an end, rather than the end in itself. As principle 4 of the Rio Declaration proclaims, environmental protection is to constitute an integral part of the development process – thus environmental protection is 'added on' to the development idea. Where environmental degradation occurs in the wake of development processes, the critical argument goes, this is perceived as not as a flaw in the development process, but as a lack in the development capacity of the relevant country, for which the solution is another strategy of development – thus the efficacy of development remains impervious to any counter-evidence (Sachs, 1993b, p. 9).

Beyond 'Sustainable Development'?

Herman Daly distinguishes between sustainable development, which he argues is about quality, and sustainable growth, which is about quantity (see Peet, 1992, p. 208). For critics of sustainable development as elaborated in the Brundtland Report and the UNCED process, there has been a failure to distinguish the two or, if the distinction has been made, either the emphasis on growth and quantity has overridden the emphasis on quality, or the view that growth supports development which then supports more growth is accepted without any serious questioning as to whether this is indeed so. What is required, in this critical perspective, is a reclaiming of a quality- rather than quantity-driven concept. Some scholars prefer the term 'eco-development' although the phrase has been used in a variety of ways (see Redclift, 1987, p. 34) from a planning concept which emphasises local and regional input (advocated by UNEP) to an 'ethically committed, integrated approach' (Redclift, 1987, p. 34) which explicitly incorporates social and cultural processes, and which is shaped by those processes and basic human needs, rather than assuming that those needs will automatically be fulfilled by something called sustainable development.

Some return to sustainable development as an ethical or moral principle. Baines claims that 'sustainability is not something to be defined, but to be declared' (in Peet, 1992, p. 210). It is an 'ethical guiding principle' (de Vries cited in Peet 1992, p. 209). Jacobs argues that sustainable development has, first and foremost, to be a 'moral concept, not one derived from market behaviour' (1990, p. 9). Others focus more on elaborating a principle that emphasises equity, justice and a reclaiming of the local. Griffen argues that sustainable development has to mean more than 'economic growth without ecological disaster' (cited in Asian and Pacific Women's Resource Collection Network, 1992, p. 10). Rees argues that in its original ecological formulation, sustainable development 'contained a long-awaited call for political recognition of global environmental decay, economic injustice and limits to material growth' and that it should 'represent an opportunity for humanity to correct an historical error and develop a gentler, more balanced and stable relationship with the natural world' (1990, p. 18). Sustainability, Chambers argues, should be 'bottom-up' and people-oriented (cited in Braidotti *et al.*, 1994, p. 134). Lipschutz (1991, p. 193), focusing also on the local, elaborates a 'development without growth' model (or at least, he suggests, development with slow growth). What this means, he suggests, is making available to a society 'the means of production and levels of income that can make local and regional markets largely self-sustaining' (1991, p. 193).

In whatever way these principles – common but differentiated responsibilities and sustainable development – are understood and defined, they have to be put into practice. The question of strategies is the focus of the next chapter. Not surprisingly, given the themes of this book so far, the nature of those strategies and the means of implementing them have been contentious.

8

Strategies for Sustainable Development

Strategies designed to give effect to sustainable development and to the idea of common but differentiated responsibilities have focused on transfer mechanisms, on the reform of existing structures and processes within the globalised political economy, and on the application of economic instruments to environmental protection. These are, however, not simply technical exercises where the problems to be solved are ones of modality. They involve political and social issues which relate to questions about the distribution of costs and benefits, the management of competing interests and to debates not just over how to implement such strategies but also over whether they are of any value in the first place. Thus the underlying structures and processes of the international political economy are called into question.

Enhancing the Flow of Resources to Developing Countries

As noted in the previous chapter, the responsibility question has been finessed in the phrase 'common but differentiated responsibilities' and its application in any specific context left open to further negotiation. Nevertheless, for developing countries, the responsibilities of developed countries should include financial and technology transfer or, in the words of the Brundtland Report, 'enhancing the flow of resources to developing countries' (WCED, 1987, p. 76). The G77 countries sought to have these concerns given priority in the UNCED process by tabling proposals for a separate working group on North–South economic issues at the first preparatory committee. They were unsuccessful. However, debates over new and additional financial resources and about technology transfer were central to the UNCED process, to the agreements adopted at Rio and to subsequent negotiations on the pursuit of sustainable development.

New and Additional Financial Resources

Developing countries' claims for financial assistance are based on the argument that without such assistance they are unable easily (if at all) to meet the costs of mitigating environmental problems and, given that industrialised countries have been the cause of much global environmental degradation, those countries now have a responsibility on equity and mutual vulnerability grounds to meet the incremental costs of addressing environmental insecurity in developing countries. Major differences arise between developed and developing countries over the related issues of additionality and conditionality. For developing countries, the financial resources provided should be additional to those already given through existing bilateral and multilateral development programmes. The reasons? First, because the funds already available for development assistance are small – approximately $US60 billion per annum in concessional loans (that is, at non-commercial rates) and second, because additional funds will be required to address the sources and impacts of environmental degradation. Few donor countries reach the UN target of a commitment of 0.7 per cent of GNP for official development assistance (ODA) and some have not accepted that target at all. Donor countries, on the other hand, are generally concerned about additionality on the grounds that there are no guarantees on how money will be spent and that, without those guarantees, additional resources are simply another form of transfer with no certainty of mutual benefit. Donor countries argue that financial assistance should be conditional – that is it should be tied to particular requirements and actions, such as reductions in military spending, expenditure on poverty alleviation programmes, or tied in such a way as to ensure that the funding is appropriately targetted at global concerns rather than being used for local problems. Recipient countries are reluctant to accept such conditions, seeing them as undermining sovereignty and reminiscent of IMF structural adjustment programmes. The Conference of the Non-Aligned Movement (NAM) in September 1989 noted 'with concern a growing tendency towards external impositions and increased conditionalities on the part of some developed countries in dealing with environmental issues' (cited in Porter and Brown, 1991, p. 127).

Various suggestions have been made for appropriate levels of financial resources and the kinds of multilateral financial mechanisms required to manage transfers. At the 1988 Toronto Conference on the Changing Atmosphere, proposals were made for a World Atmosphere Fund to be financed in part by a levy on fossil fuel consumption in industrialised countries. The Commonwealth Heads of Government Meeting in October 1989 discussed a funding proposal made by then Indian Prime Minister Rajiv Gandhi which called for amounts in the order of $US15 to $20 billion. At the fourth UNCED PrepComm, the G77 (following a lead from China which is not a member of the group) proposed the creation of a new Green Fund, on which each country (whether donor or recipient) would have one vote, to administer the funding of the Rio agreements. Papua New Guinea and the AOSIS have called for a global climate insurance fund which would help with disaster relief in developing countries (see McCully, 1991b, p. 245).

The issue of financial resources was addressed in chapter 33 of Agenda 21 (Financial Resources and Mechanisms). Agenda 21 did not provide a total funding assessment (rather the programmes in each chapter were costed), but the Secretariat determined that the cost to the developing countries of implementing Agenda 21 would be in the vicinity of $US600 billion per annum, of which $125 billion should come from the donor countries. This is twice the amount of concessional loans which presently flow from donor to recipient countries and it takes no account of the net reverse flows of funds from recipient to donor countries (in the form of debt servicing for example) which amounts to about $US50 billion per annum. There was no firm commitment to funding anywhere near this amount at UNCED – developed countries reaffirmed their commitment to 0.7 per cent GNP as ODA but there were no deadlines and no new commitments. Pledges from heads of state or government were estimated to add up to approximately $US2 billion (Chatterjee and Finger, 1994, p. 139) but little of that has yet been forthcoming. Jordan calls chapter 33 'an adroitly crafted diplomatic compromise that fails to bind anyone to anything' (1994a, p. 27).

Technology Transfer

The rationale for technology transfer is that if developing countries are to meet obligations under various international environmental agreements, then they will require the technology to do so, technology that is often not easily available to them. Townsend argues, for example, that 'transfer and development of technology is an *essential* component of a successful strategy of sustainable development' (1993, p. 66; emphasis added). Technology is required to mitigate the causes of environmental degradation, to adapt to and manage to the impacts of that degradation where it occurs and to improve monitoring and measuring. Technology transfer involves not only specific technologies (such as waste management, pollution reduction, or energy and agricultural efficiency technologies) but also the transfer of scientific and technical expertise and know-how. Technology transfer is not without difficulties, particularly with respect to the cost, the adaptability or suitability of Northern technology for Southern economies, the mechanisms for transfer (such as joint ventures or subsidiaries) and the contentious issue of intellectual property rights.

The main point of contention between the sources of technology (usually the developed countries) and those who do not have it (usually the developing countries) is whether technology should be transferred at concessional or commercial rates – that is, should it be a kind of development assistance or should it be a commercial transaction. The 'concessional rates' argument is that developing countries simply cannot afford the technology, but that its use is of benefit to all and that, in light of past exploitations and contributions to global environmental insecurities, technology transfer is a form of redistributive justice. The 'commercial rates' argument is one favoured by the US in particular, on the grounds, first, that technology is held not by governments but by private companies which should be fully compensated for their investment and, second, that technology transfer will enable developing countries to 'leapfrog', thus providing them with commercial competitive advantage. There are also differences over whether environmental agreements should include a guarantee that developed countries *will* facilitate access to technology. India attempted, for example, to have language included in Montreal Protocol amendments that would make the obligations of developing countries to phase out CFCs subject to the private transfer of technology. In the end developing countries had to settle for language which simply noted that their ability to meet obligations would depend on such transfers but did not make that transfer obligatory nor make any developing country commitment conditional upon such transfer. While Agenda 21 included a chapter on 'transfer of environmentally-sound technology, cooperation and capacity building' (chapter 34) it invokes no firm commitments. Rather, access to technology is to be promoted, facilitated and financed as appropriate (UNCED, 1992b, paragraph 34.14(b)) with an emphasis on technology cooperation and capacity building rather than outright transfer. This emphasis also underpins principle 9 of the Rio Declaration.

Solutions or Flawed Strategies?

Not everyone accepts the proposition that an increase in financial resources, development assistance and the transfer of technology are appropriate strategies. Critics of these strategies argue that they rely on the 'same old problem-solving techniques and technologies' (Chatterjee and Finger, 1994, p. 58). That is, they propose 'more information, more data, more training, more science and technology, especially technology transfer for the South [and] more money' (Chatterjee and Finger, 1994, p. 58) rather than grappling with issues of structural change. Hildyard (1993, p. 31) argues that in effect environmental problems have been defined in terms of solutions (money and technology) which only the North can provide, thus increasing rather than decreasing Southern dependency. He argues that underpinning Agenda 21 is the view that environmental and social problems are primarily the result of insufficient capital, for which the solution is to increase Northern investment in the South; of outdated technology, for which the solution is to open up the South to Northern technologies; of a lack of expertise, for which the solution is to bring in Northern-educated managers and experts; and faltering economic growth, for which the solution is a push for an economic recovery in the North.

Chatterjee and Finger (1994, p. 141) suggest that the transfer of financial resources to support commitments in developing countries enables sustainable development in the South to be paid for by continued unsustainable development in the North. In their view, this simply allows Northern countries to avoid the issue of their own unsustainability, and conveys a message that environmental problems and unsustainable practices are to be found primarily in the South and that they can be overcome if only enough money and technology is given. This, for example, was one of the main objections to the Joint Implementation procedures foreshadowed in the FCCC. Those strategies were seen as potentially inequitable in that they could allow the continuation of unsustainable practices in developed countries and curtail opportunities for developing countries (see Chapter 3). McCully (1991b, p. 244) argues that an emphasis on the transfer of money and machinery obscures the urgent need for radical changes in First World consumption patterns and global economic and political structures. Rich echoes this, arguing that 'what is needed is not "more" but "different" – a different approach to economic development in the South and the North' (1994c, p. 313).

A second objection to transfer strategies is that substantial flows of new and additional financial resources to developing countries may well exacerbate rather than solve global environment and development problems and, at the same time, increase global inequities. Loans, even at concessional rates and with a grace period, still have to be repaid with interest. There is, then, a likelihood of a continuation of environmentally unsustainable activities to provide income to service new debt on top of existing debt which is already estimated to be about $US1 trillion. McCully, for example, is unconvinced that 'a massive influx of new aid to . . . developing countries . . . would do anything other than exacerbate the plight of the impoverished Third World' (1991b, p. 246). Concerns are also expressed that 'very little of the aid money disbursed to developing countries by governments and international lending institutions supports ecologically sound development' (Postel and Flavin, 1991, p. 171). To date, the 'scale of economic assistance efforts do not fully reflect [environmental] interdependence and environmental needs do not yet receive sufficient priority' (Williams, 1992, p. 23). Existing aid and development assistance does not go to those most in need of it, suggesting less of a commitment to poverty alleviation than to other priorities. The UNDP's 1992 *Human Development Report* demonstrated that the ten countries in which were found 72 per cent of the developing world's poor received only 27 per cent of ODA (UNDP, 1992, p. 44). McCully argues further that aid and development assistance programmes are rarely responsive to or accountable to the concerns of local communities and often undermine the security of those communities (1991b, p. 247) and that the past legacy of development assistance has been neo-colonialism, debt, dependency, corruption and failure (1991b, p. 244).

Similar arguments about Northern advantage, Southern dependency, inadequate past practice and potential future exacerbation of environmental degradation are made about technology transfer. Transferring technology will, in this view, simply entrench reliance on Northern technology and is, therefore, another form of neo-colonialism. For example, the non-ozone-depleting substances and production processes which are the subject of transfer under the Montreal

Protocol are owned by Northern chemical companies. Chatterjee and Finger (1994, p. 51) suggest that technology transfer from the North to the South might be good for development, but to claim that it will make development more sustainable is an unproven assertion. They question a belief in technology as a solution when technology has been the cause of much environmental degradation in the first place (1994, p. 59). They argue that proponents of a 'more technology' strategy ignore the disastrous social, cultural and environmental damage caused by technology. Past experience shows also that the technology that is transferred is not always appropriate to local needs or concerns and has been less than successful in assisting local communities towards what is often a reclaiming of self-sufficiency and meeting basic human needs. Green Revolution technology was designed to increase agricultural efficiency and yield. Yet it resulted in environmental degradation through extensive fertiliser and water use, land aggregation (and thus increased poverty for those engaged in subsistence agriculture) and introduced seed types which had to be purchased anew each year, replacing so-called 'inefficient'-yield seeds which could be harvested, stored and replanted, thus minimising costs for poor rural dwellers (see, *inter alia*, McCully, 1991b; Shiva, 1989, pp. 135–40). The move to the so-called appropriate technology of the 1970s has also been criticised: a former Director of one of Canada's voluntary aid agencies calls appropriate technology 'perhaps one of the greatest wrongs in the misguided lexicon of international development' (cited in McCully, 1991b, p. 247).

The Global Environment Facility and the World Bank

The question of who should manage financial transfers has been another area of dispute. Developing countries have tended to argue that financial mechanisms should be established under the control of the parties to any convention, separate from existing institutions such as the World Bank which, with its weighted voting system, is seen to favour the donor countries. While there was some initial support for this approach, evidenced in the establishment of the interim fund under the Montreal Protocol, the developed countries have generally supported the use of existing institutions. Under the amended Montreal Protocol, the UNFCCC and the Biodiversity Convention, this financial mechanism is to be the Global Environment Facility.

The GEF was established by the World Bank, the UNDP and UNEP, at a meeting in Paris in November 1990 as a pilot programme to finance projects and training programmes that would aim to limit the negative global environmental impact of development projects (Rowlands, 1992, p. 214). The purpose of the GEF, in the words of its first head (a former analyst with the WRI), is to provide 'grant funding for innovations that protect the global environment – through investment, technical assistance . . . and, to some extent, research' (El-Ashry, 1993, p. 91). The Facility's terms of reference restrict it to funding environmental projects which are of global rather than local significance and which are therefore assumed to be of benefit to the world at large. Its four priorities are the protection of biodiversity, the mitigation of global warming, the control of pollution in international waters and the management of stratospheric ozone depletion. It is in this last capacity that the Interim Multilateral Fund established under the Montreal Protocol has become linked to the GEF. The three year pilot phase of GEF was funded to the tune of $US1.411 billion, through core funding and co-financing, for projects in countries with a per capita income of less than $4000 per annum.

Each of the agencies plays a specific role in the functioning of the GEF (see El-Ashry, 1993, p. 92). The UNDP focuses on technical assistance, institutional capacity and project preparation (as well as administering the NGO small-grant programme). UNEP provides secretariat support for the expert group, the Scientific and Technical Advisory Panel (STAP), convened to elaborate eligibility criteria and priorities for selecting GEF projects. The STAP also reviews project proposals and coordinates research and data collection (El-Ashry, 1993, p. 92). The World Bank administers the Facility, is the repository for the Trust Fund that is the GEF's core fund, and also implements investment projects. El-Ashry suggests that the establishment of the GEF points to a 'willingness on the part of the world's wealthier states to safeguard the inheritance of future generations by helping developing countries to mitigate their growing contribution to global environmental degradation' (1993, p. 93). Tickell and Hildyard, on the other hand, refer to the GEF as the 'North's little helper' (1992, p. 82) suggesting that it determines what is a global problem in the interests of the donor countries of the North. In doing so, Hildyard (1993, p. 34) argues, the GEF has been able to override the local claims of those who rely on local commons. Rich suggests that the GEF also 'serves to propagate the profound fallacy that addressing global environmental problems is a matter of industrialised nations contributing an additional few billion dollars for more projects' (1994a, p. 313).

While there have been a number of criticisms of the GEF, it is the central and authoritative role played by the World Bank that has generated the most opposition from developing countries and from environment and development NGOs. Developing countries were reluctant to accept the GEF as the funding mechanism because of their concerns about the closed and undemocratic nature of the World Bank, an organisation in which they have had little influence as borrowers, and which they have perceived as dominated by developed country interests. According to Tickell and Hildyard (1992, p. 82), early discussions about the GEF were held only among Northern countries (primarily the G7) with a select group of Southern governments being included only after the World Bank had been selected as the lead agency. Werksman (1993, p. 82) points out that developed countries dominated decision-making in the pilot phase of the GEF, when membership was restricted to those countries which could contribute $US4 million to the Facility's Trust Fund. Developing countries accepted the GEF as the funding mechanism reluctantly and only on the grounds that it be restructured to make its processes more transparent and to give them equal representation in the decision-making processes (see UNCED, 1992b, paragraph 33.16(a)(iii)). That has been a slow process. Early discussions broke down at a meeting in Cartagena in 1993 and agreement on the restructured GEFII was not reached until March 1994. Even then, as earlier chapters demonstrate, there have been difficulties in adopting the various Memoranda of Understanding between the GEF and the conferences of parties established under those environmental conventions for which it is the interim financial mechanism because developed countries in particular have been reluctant to accept any agreement which might seem to abrogate decision-making authority on funding to the GEF.

Environmental NGOs and grassroots movements were concerned not only about the non-participatory and, at best, opaque decision-making nature of the World Bank but also its poor environmental record. While Piddington is adamant that 'there [is] nothing marginal about the environment in the World Bank's policy process' (1992, p. 219) NGOs have remained sceptical about the Bank's attempts to 'green' itself, referring to it as 'greenwashing' (see Chatterjee and

Finger, 1994, p. 154), and about its newly adopted mandate to 'assist its borrowers to achieve sustainable development' (Piddington, 1992, p. 216). The Bank appointed its first environmental adviser in 1970 and established an Office of Environmental Affairs in 1973. By 1977, however, there were still only three full-time environmental advisers, a number which had increased to five by the mid-1980s (see El-Ashry, 1993, p. 86). Mikesell argues that there was 'little effort to formulate environmental standards or tie them to the Bank's lending operations until the latter part of the 1980s' (1992, p. 93). In 1987, under pressure from NGO campaigns which documented and publicised the poor environmental record of Bank lending projects, Bank President Barber Conable established a central Environment Department and four regional environment divisions. In October 1992, a new Vice-President for environmentally sustainable development was appointed to the Bank and by 1993 there were approximately 100 staff working on environmental issues in the Environment Department and in five environmental divisions linked to regional operations. Environmental assessments are now required for all Bank projects (this became mandatory in October 1989 under the Operational Directive on Environmental Assessment) a policy adopted by other multilateral development banks as well. The Environment Department is presently part of the Policy, Research and External Affairs complex within the Bank although the Bank is undergoing internal restructuring on the initiative of its new president, James Wolfensohn.

The Bank's *past* environmental record is well known. Over the years, and drawing on their own research and field experience as well as the Bank's own reports and those commissioned of independent experts, NGOs have publicised a number of Bank funded projects which have resulted in environmental degradation and in the dislocation of large numbers of people. Such a list would include the Carajas iron ore project, the Singrauli coal mine and coal-fired electricity generation project, the Narmada Valley Dams (the Sardar Sarovar and Narmada Sagar) as well as the Bank-funded transmigration programmes in Brazil (the Polonoereste) and Indonesia. The environmental impact of Bank projects has been direct and indirect. Plater (1988) points not only to direct environmental degradation such as deforestation and threats to rare and endangered wildlife, but to archaeological losses and displacement of peoples who are often then forced to utilise the marginal lands to which they are moved in an unsustainable manner. Rich suggested in 1994 that in that year approximately two million people would be forcibly resettled as a result of Bank funded projects, compared with 450 000 in 1983 (1994b, pp. 1–2). Infrastructure support such as road construction also contributes to the negative environmental impact of projects. World Bank funding for TFAP, Rich suggests, has revealed a 'shocking . . . gap between the rhetoric and reality in the Bank's self-proclaimed greening' (1990, p. 309). The independent Morse Report, commissioned by the World Bank, found that, as Werksman summarises it, 'Bank management had abused and neglected stated Bank policies on environment and resettlement, and that this attitude pervaded the Bank's hierarchy of decision-making and project implementation' (1993, pp. 73–4).

This past record has given rise to concerns about the Bank's (and therefore the GEF's) present and future environmental record. Environmental impact assessments (EIAs), for example, are the responsibility of the government of the borrowing country, not the Bank (although the Bank may provide advice) and a full EIA is not prepared if a preliminary report determines that there is likely to be no significant environmental impact associated with the project. Nor has there been any provision for 'meaningful public participation' in the assessment process (Werksman, 1993, p. 70) although there is some evidence that this could change under the new Wolfensohn regime. Mikesell raises concerns about the limited focus of EIAs, suggesting they are not able to account for social costs of environmental damage and resource depletion, nor to anticipate unforseen environmental impacts or to take into account whether the project, once completed, will function in accordance with environmental conditions (1992, p. 93–7).

In the not too distant past, the Bank has been criticised for its underfunding of environmental lending priorities in areas such as energy efficiency, for example (see Postel and Flavin, 1991, p. 174) and for its lack of 'a coherent vision of a sustainable economy' (Postel and Flavin, 1991, p. 171). Concern has also been expressed that the majority of projects funded in the first period of the GEF were tied to existing World Bank projects, that decisions were made by existing World Bank staff and that the funds were to be disbursed through existing agencies, some of which had a less than satisfactory record as far as development projects were concerned (see McCully, 1991b, p. 247; Imhof, 1996). According to Rich the first tranche of projects was approved before STAP project selection guidelines were developed (1993, pp. 16–17). Tickell and Hildyard (1992, p. 83) argue that some of those early projects, in Nepal and the Congo, for example, have had environmentally negative impacts. El-Ashry argues, however, that 'loans for environmental management have been the most rapidly growing segment of the Bank's portfolio' (1993, p. 93). He does not provide figures, but Piddington (1992, p. 225) observes that in fiscal year 1991 approximately 7 per cent of Bank lending went to environmental projects (1992, p. 225). Projects are deemed primarily environmental, according to the Bank's 1991 *Report on the Environment*, 'if either the costs of environmental protection measures or the environmental benefits accruing from the project exceed 50 per cent of total costs or benefits' (cited in Piddington, 1992, p. 225). Rich (1993, p. 3) counters this with his suggestion that Bank project funding continues to marginalise environmentally sustainable projects, noting that on the Bank's own figures only 1 per cent of its energy-lending for the period 1992–5 went to support end-use energy efficiency. Porter and Brown (1996, p. 48) point out, for example, that in 1992 the Bank gave China a $US2 million for GHG reduction and, at the same time, proposed $630 million in loans to China for fossil fuel development.

In a critical view, greening the World Bank and, through it the GEF, requires not simply procedural mechanisms such as Environmental assessments (EAs) and an increase in staff but, at minimum, a reorienting of the World Bank culture, a greater commitment to integrating environmental concerns into development and lending priorities (and to implementing those priorities), a greater acknowledgment of the social and environmental costs of project assistance, increased transparency and accountability and opportunities for local, community and NGO participation. Werksman (1993) suggests that the UNCED process and the principles adopted there, as well as the requirements of the UNCED conventions, provide a basis for just this kind of redirection of the World Bank and the GEF. At time of writing, the World Bank is undergoing further internal restructuring which is intended to improve transparency and to facilitate consultation with NGOs, local communities and other stakeholders who have, in the past, often been marginalised in the Bank's relationships with client governments. This new emphasis is designed to take greater account of poverty alleviation and the social and environmental costs of development assistance. The GEF has also provided funding which is intended to cover the incremental costs and thereby reduce the risks of alternative energy programmes, technology and capital costs that are often too high for developing countries to meet without assistance. Recent GEF projects have, for example, included solar-thermal projects in Rajistan with projects due in Morocco and Mexico, and wind energy projects in India with projects forthcoming in Costa Rica.

Debt and the Environment

The Brundtland Report argued that the extent of Third World debt was a factor in environmental damage and that it constrained developing countries in their move to sustainable development. In 1989, Third World external debt was $US1.2 trillion, 44 per cent of the total GNP of indebted countries (Postel and Flavin, 1991, p. 171). In the same year, the developing countries paid to donor countries and institutions $US77 billion in interest and repaid $US85 billion in capital, figures which contributed to a net flow of financial resources from the South to the North of about $US50 billion. By 1993, developing countries' external debt had risen to $US1.8 trillion, with debt servicing accounting for almost one-quarter of export earnings (UNDP, 1995, p. 14). Growing debts have impelled a further 'selling off' of natural resources. In the 1980s, as Sanders notes, developing countries, which are highly dependent on a primary resource base, were 'caught between rising debt and falling commodity prices' (1990, p. 398). As a result, they turned to increased primary production for export (to pay debt and to maintain national income), strategies which resulted in overlogging, overgrazing and, in turn, ecosystem exhaustion. Speth points out that 'half of the Third World external debt and more than two-thirds of global deforestation occur in the same 14 developing countries' (1990, p. 20). Debt servicing is not only a drain on a country's economy but much of the burden of debt servicing falls on the poor.

The Brundtland Commission called for 'urgent action . . . [to] alleviate debt burdens' (WCED, 1987, p. 18) but did not specify how this should be done. The UNCED process paid some but not a great deal of attention to the debt issue. Chapter 2 of Agenda 21 does note that the 'development process will not gather momentum if . . . the developing countries are weighted down by external indebtedness' (UNCED, 1992b, paragraph 2.2) and that a supportive international economic climate would include 'dealing with international debt' (UNCED, 1992b, paragraph 2.3(c)). Paragraphs 2.27 to 2.30 effectively encouraged further debt renegotiation, commended the actions of low-income countries who continue to service their debt burdens at great cost (and thus 'safeguard their creditworthiness') and called for 'serious attention' to be given to 'growth-oriented solutions' to the debt-burden. Von Moltke says of such an emphasis on debtor countries policies that it is 'economically acceptable [but] it is doubtful that it is politically prudent' (1991, p. 977). For many, debt rescheduling is a short-term answer and growth-oriented strategies simply reinforce the problem. Postel and Flavin argue that 'turning the debt crisis around will require more than rescheduling payments or issuing new loans' (1991, p. 176). What is required, in this view, is a writing off of both public and private debt, a strategy that is most unlikely to be adopted by commercial or multilateral lending institutions. Recently announced plans by the IMF and the World Bank to relieve a component of debt of the world's poorest countries remain subject to strict structural adjustment and economic reform conditions (see Henderson, 1996, p. 8).

Debt-for-Nature-Swaps (DFNS)

In the face of the growing debt burden and its impact on continued environmental degradation, one innovative proposal has been the swapping of a component of a country's debt for conservation or environmental repair programmes such as maintenance or expansion of national parks and reserves, and environmental training and research programmes. The idea was first proposed by Thomas Lovejoy, a Vice-President of WWF–US in 1984. Put briefly and simply, a debt-for-nature-swap (DFNS) involves the purchase of part of a country's debt (usually a very small part) at a discount price by a non-governmental organisation (usually) or a government (occasionally), with the debtor country's permission. Effectively, then, the NGO or third country is now the creditor (that is, it owns the debt) although sometimes the debt is then donated to an affiliated NGO in the debtor country. The debt is then effectively 'swapped' for conservation or environmental programmes in the debtor country, usually for more than the 'purchase price' and sometimes at the full face value of the debt. In other words, the debtor 'pays' its debt in internal environmental action, although this usually involves the issuance of local currency or bonds to either the creditor organisation or to an environmental/conservation organisation in the debtor country. Between 1987 and early 1992, nineteen DFNS were executed, involving ten debtor countries (including Poland) and, as purchasers, nine organisations, one official aid agency and two governments (see table in Mahony, 1992, p. 98). A 1990 agreement of the Paris Club of creditor states mandated what Von Moltke (1991) calls second-generation DFNS, those which are debt conversions involving sovereign (that is government) creditors.

At first glance, the strategy seems to be a win–win situation. A debtor country has part of its debt relieved and environmental protection or repair is funded when it might otherwise not have been. The debt is effectively repaid in local currency which relieves foreign exchange pressures on the debtor country. As Webb (1994, p. 225) points out, both creditor- and debtor-country NGO also benefit, the former by acquiring local currency funds greater than the outlay of its purchase of the debt, and the latter by gaining access to conservation funds and to further programme experience.

Nevertheless, DFNS have not been universally praised. First, they involve a possible diminution of sovereignty in cases where the agreement involves restrictions on the use of resources or lands, or where it effectively directs funding decisions. Those restrictions or directions are claimed to reflect the interests of Northern NGOs or countries (a charge which could also, of course, be made of MDB project aid and structural adjustment loans to which many indebted countries are subject). Environmental organisations involved in swaps have been criticised for the way in which they have disregarded local communities (often indigenous communities) in making often arbitrary decisions about the environmental component of the swap, programmes which may undermine indigenous lifestyles and land rights struggles (see Webb, 1994, pp. 227–8; Mahony, 1992; and Patterson, 1990). COICA has made the point on South American DFNS, for example, that the debt involved was not Indian debt while the 'nature' involved was Indian land that the Indians had not agreed to trade for anything (cited in Wiggins, 1993, p. 350).

In this critical view DFNS do little to relieve the debt burden of developing countries (although the *primary* purpose of the swap is environmental protection rather than debt relief) because the amounts involved are small. Instead they legitimise debt and divert attention from debt relief and the structural problems which lead to debt. The extent of environmental protection is also disputed. Von Moltke and DeLong suggest that 'the resulting conservation programs have had a major impact on environmental protection' (1990, p. 10). Mahony queries this, noting, for example, that 'parks in . . . beneficiary countries are being invaded by loggers, miners or the landless' (1992, pp. 97, 100–3). She points out that there is no guarantee that the debtor country will honour its financial agreement with the foreign or local NGO (especially if long-term bonds are involved) or that it can simply cut funding to other environmental programmes or to other programmes, such as welfare programmes, which will affect poor communities. The injection of local currency can also have a potential inflationary effect or, in an inflationary economy, the value of the swaps can diminish quickly (see Patterson, 1990, p. 10). Indeed, Mahony (1992, pp. 99–100) argues that the only ones who can be sure of benefitting, in the long run, are the creditor banks who get something for a debt that otherwise might never have been repaid.

Despite these limitations, most commentators argue that DFNS can be 'useful and creative' (Patterson, 1990, p. 11) and that their limitations can be partially overcome, especially if expectations of swaps are 'realistic'. Mahony (1992, p. 103) points out that some environmental groups have sought to incorporate social development assistance and reform into the environmental component of their DFNS projects. Webb (1994, p. 231) suggests that many problems can be mitigated with the use of sovereignty clauses and enforceability clauses and greater involvement of indigenous peoples and local communities (1994, p. 228).

Trade and the Environment

While Berlin and Lang (1993, p. 35) suggest (and they are not alone) that the trade and environment communities were ill-prepared to address the interrelationship between the two, the trade–environment nexus has recently been taken up in earnest by international financial and trade bodies, including the OECD, the General Agreement on Tariffs and Trade (GATT) and the new World Trade Organisation (WTO) (in accordance with the Marrakesh Decision on Trade and Environment), and by environmental NGOs. The OECD and the WTO both have working groups on trade and environment issues. The WTO group is the heir to an environmental working group established by the GATT in 1972 after the Stockholm Conference: it did not meet until 21 January 1992 as the GATT Group on Environmental Measures in International Trade (EMIT). In 1994, the UNCTAD (United Nations Conference on Trade and Development) also established an ad hoc working group on Trade, Environment and Development.

In conventional trade logic, a progressive freeing up of trade will assist environmental protection and the management of global environmental insecurities, a belief often incorporated, albeit as something of an affirmation, in environmental agreements. Principle 12 of the Rio Declaration provides that 'states should cooperate to promote a supportive and open international economic system' and that 'trade policy measures for environmental purposes should not constitute a means of arbitrary or unjustifiable discrimination or a disguised restriction on international trade' (UNCED, 1992a). The principle goes on to proclaim that 'unilateral actions to deal with environmental challenges outside the jurisdiction of the importing country should be avoided', an injunction, in effect, against extraterritoriality (that is, the effective imposition of one country's domestic environmental standards on another). Chapter 2 of Agenda 21 (entitled 'International cooperation to accelerate sustainable development in developing countries and related domestic policies') provides similar guidance on the relationship between trade and the environment. It suggests that the 'development process will not gather momentum . . . if barriers restrict access to markets and if commodity prices and the terms of trade of developing countries remain depressed' (UNCED, 1992b, paragraph 2.2). Thus trade liberalisation (paragraph 2.3(a)) and 'making trade and environment mutually supportive' (paragraph 2.3(b)) are necessary. The chapter goes on to provide considerable detail on the basis for action and means of implementation of these broad goals.

Agenda 21 accepts that international trading relationships between rich and poor countries are inequitable, an inequity that has contributed directly and indirectly to environmental degradation and to underdevelopment. It also accepts without question that trade liberalisation and environmental protection are compatible goals. There is, however, a dissenting view on this. The issue of the compatibility or otherwise of trade and environment agenda engages with several questions. Can environmental protection issues be accommodated within the logic of trade liberalisation? Can trade liberalisation contribute to overcoming environmental degradation or is free(r) trade likely to contribute further to environmental degradation? Is it possible, in trade liberalisation discourse, to distinguish between environmental protection and environmental protectionism? Are trade restrictions, to borrow from Schoenbaum, 'a legitimate way to retaliate for inadequate environmental standards' (1992, p. 702). These are important questions because, as Postel and Flavin argue, 'trade rules and agreements are a major determinant of how natural resources are used, what pressures are placed on the environment and who benefits from the huge money flows . . . that cross borders with the exchange of goods' (1991, p. 180). Berlin and Lang suggest that different answers to these questions arise from different views of the word 'protection'. In the trade community, they suggest, protection is a 'pejorative term' yet it is an 'exemplary one in the environmental community' (1993, p. 35). Both communities seek also to enhance welfare, the first through the expansion of trading relations and the second through the enhancement of ecological sustainability. In a specific sense, much of the discussion has been about the environment-related provisions of the General Agreement on Tariffs and Trade (the GATT), and the extent to which this agreement (and its successor organisation, the WTO) can accommodate environmental concerns. The analysis here focuses not so much on the GATT or WTO as institutions, but on the *ideas* of trade liberalisation which inform the international trade regime.

For most in the trade community and some in the environmental community, trade and environment objectives are compatible and can be made mutually supportive. The broad propositions are threefold: first, that trade liberalisation is good for the environment; second, that non-liberalised trade (that is, protectionism) is bad for the environment and, third (given the emphasis on *mutual* support) that environmental protection can be bad for free trade because it can mask protectionism. In this view, present inequities in the international trading system which arise from trade barriers disadvantage developing countries to the extent of $US500 billion per annum (UNDP, 1992, p. 6). Freeing international trade, therefore, will increase economic welfare for the developing countries and also improve the efficiency of resource use. This is because trade liberalisation will encourage the removal of environmentally unsound subsidies and because the pressures on unsustainable resource use as a means to generate income will be reduced. This increase in economic welfare and rise in incomes will also, in this view, lead to increased expenditure on the environment (see Esty, 1993, p. 35; Schoenbaum, 1992, p. 702). Continued protectionism (non-free trade) on the other hand can, as the Brundtland Commission suggested, raise barriers against manufactured exports from developing countries, thus limiting their opportunities to diversify from commodity-based exports which rely on the unsustainable use of non-renewable resources (WCED, 1987, p. 79). Protection of domestic markets can result in degradation because it supports unsustainable processes and reinforces disincentives to diversification (see Pearce and Warford, 1993, p. 297). Thus a range of environmental protection measures, including subsidies, are perceived not only as trade-distorting because they provide a country or industry with a subsidised competitive advantage, but raise concerns that countries might adopt protection-ist measures under the guise of environmental protection.

The critique of this approach is that it leaves the logic of trade liberalisation untouched and seeks only to explore how environmen-tal concerns can be added *on* to the trade agenda, rather than asking whether trade liberalisation might be inappropriate as a environmen-tal protection strategy and, indeed, whether it might not exacerbate the situation of environmental decline. Free trade, so the critical argument goes, can engender further environmental degradation precisely because it encourages economic activity which takes no account of external environmental costs. Berlin and Lang observe that even in classical economic welfare analysis there is some doubt as to whether

> trade and trade liberalisation [will] benefit a country's general welfare if the cost of goods sold or produced . . . does not fully reflect the environmental cost of the goods and where, as a consequence, the benefits from increased trade are not sufficient to outweigh the negative effects of the reduction in environmental quality (1993, p. 37).

Thus trade liberalisation may not necessarily be accompanied by a full internalising of externalities especially given that GATT rules apply to the products traded, not the conditions under which they were produced. As Pearce and Warford summarise this position, 'trade liberalisation can be expected to increase market failure' (1993, p. 300). This critical position also takes issue with economic welfare claims suggesting, first, that many developing countries engage in trade not to improve economic welfare but to service debt – what Arden-Clarke calls 'desperation production' (1992, p. 123; see also Opschoor, 1989, p. 138) – and that even if further income were generated there is no guarantee that it would be used for environ-mental protection (Esty, 1993, p. 35). As Postel and Flavin argue

> freer trade . . . would not necessarily help the poorest people in the Third World, nor be a net benefit to the environment. Much

depends . . . on who gains from the added export revenue – peasant farmers or wealthy landowners. Much depends, too, on whether opening world markets would cause scarce land and water to be diverted from subsistence to export crops at the expense of the poor and of food self-sufficiency (1991, p. 180).

Jordan (1994a, p. 27) cites World Bank and OECD studies which calculate that increases in world trade under the GATT would add $213 billion to global income, but that sub-Saharan Africa would be $2.6 billion worse off. Many environmentalists are concerned also that a continued emphasis on trade and trade liberalisation might encourage developing countries to perceive a comparative advantage in pollution intensive industries and that free(r) trade will simply enable some countries (usually the developed ones) to maintain the integrity of their own environments by using the raw materials (especially non-renewables) of other countries.

The practical issues which arise from this debate are just how trade and environment might be made mutually supportive, a debate that focuses on the relevance of the GATT provisions to environmental protection purposes. The analysis here, which is necessarily brief, does not engage with the complexities of the GATT provisions and the nature of international trade law. Those debates, as they apply to environmental issues, address concerns such as the purpose of extra-territoriality, the understanding of a 'legitimate' trade restriction, interpretation of the 'necessity' provisions and the meaning of an 'arbitrary' action under the Agreement, the definition of 'like products' and the issue of harmonisation of standards as well as the implications of a range of trade test cases and GATT panel decisions such as the Mexican Tuna/Dolphin case. For some, the trade regime as it stands simply cannot accommodate environmental concerns, the GATT is not a useful instrument for environmental protection in its present form and the 'mutually supportive' injunction will require, at minimum, adjustments to the GATT. They point out, for example, that the GATT has not been able to prevent trade in goods, such as hazardous waste, which have potentially severe environmental consequences (see Shrybman, 1990, p. 31) and that trade in goods such as tropical timber has contributed to further consumer demand and therefore further unsustainable resource use. Thompson argues that the restrictions on extraterritoriality are a 'major barrier to the use of life cycle assessment as a tool to control global environmental impacts' (1992, p. 765). Therefore, Cameron argues, it is 'necessary to re-orient the General Agreement on Tariffs and Trade so that . . . [it can] . . . lend its support to the resolution of the global environmental problem', a reorientation he believes is possible (1993, p. 100). The GATT, he goes on to argue, 'cannot escape its environmental responsibilities' (1993, p. 100).

Making environment and trade mutually supportive, then, means adjusting the GATT/WTO rules and ensuring, as Weiss exhorts, that trade becomes a means to an end, where that end is 'environmentally sustainable economic development' (1992, p. 728). Weiss argues that '[m]easures needed to protect the environment [such as trade restrictions] cannot be forsworn simply because they may adversely affect trading relationships' (1992, p. 728). In this view, then, it should be possible to use trade restrictions and sanctions for environmental ends. Pearce and Warford argue, for example, that 'trade *should* be restricted when it creates environmental degradation either by importing products that pollute the importing country or by encouraging production that may incur damages to both exporting and importing country' (1993, p. 297; emphasis added). A WWF discussion paper also calls for amendments to the GATT to permit the use of unilateral trade measures where multilateral ones do not exist and to enable trade measures to discriminate on the basis of production methods (Rae, 1993, p. 1).

The counter argument is that GATT *can* accommodate environmental protection concerns in its present form and that any amendments to the Agreement would undermine its free trade principles and, therefore, its primary objective. In this view, as Yu (1994) argues, environmentalists can (and should) use the GATT to pursue environmental protection. Esty points out that the 'GATT is not hostile to the environment but agnostic' (1993, p. 85). Trade liberalisation under GATT rules, Schoenbaum (1992, p. 702) argues, can foster common standards, terminate subsidies and ensure economic growth. Others point out that while the GATT is generally opposed to unilateral environmental trade measures (ETMs) (see Charnovitz, 1993), it does not preclude the use of eco-labelling procedures (see Cameron, 1993, p. 108) although this appears to hold only if there are already internationally accepted norms with respect to the production process. For example, the GATT panel on the Mexican Tuna/Dolphin case would seem to uphold eco-labelling given that there are international norms on the incidental taking of dolphins. However, an Austrian attempt to enforce a sustainability labelling requirement for tropical timber products was challenged because there was no internationally accepted criteria on the determination of sustainable logging. As noted in Chapter 2, arguments have been offered to the effect that trade in protected species (such as the elephant) might actually *enhance* conservation efforts by providing revenue (for example through commercial harvesting fees) for conservation efforts, revenue which might otherwise not be available.

Trade restrictions have been used for environmental purposes without recourse to the GATT disputes resolution procedures. The rule seems to be, first, that such restrictions are acceptable if there is international consensus on their inclusion in an environmental agreement (see Thompson, 1992, pp. 755–6) and, second, that the Vienna *Convention on the Law of Treaties* provides adequate guidance on incompatible provisions between treaties. In the event of a dispute between two countries over incompatible provisions between two treaties, the provisions of the later treaty apply if both countries are parties to both treaties, otherwise the provisions of the treaty to which both are parties take precedence (see Schoenbaum, 1992, p. 719; Lallas *et al.*, 1992, p. 307). There are at least 18 international environmental agreements in place which employ some kind of restriction on trade as a protection provision or compliance mechanism. The most often-cited is the *Convention on International Trade in Endangered Species* (CITES) which seeks to protect wildlife through the regulation of international trade (see Chapter 2). Other conventions, such as the Montreal Protocol or the Basel Convention, place restrictions on trade between parties and non-parties. According to von Moltke (1991, p. 979) (following a personal communication with Richard Benedick), a ruling on the Montreal Protocol trade restrictions to the effect that the provisions were acceptable under article XX of the GATT was obtained from the GATT secretariat.

There is much debate about whether article XX of the GATT, which provides for trade restrictions in the case of overriding public concerns, is amenable to environmental protection. While this article refers to 'measures necessary to protect human, animal or plant life or health' (article XX(b)) and 'measures relating to the conservation of exhaustible natural resources' (article XX(g)), its provisions are usually taken to have been included for quarantine purposes. Charnovitz argues, however, that the history of article XX shows that it '*was* designed to encompass environmental measures' (1991, p. 55) and can therefore be used for such purposes. Decisions by GATT panels would seem to support this interpretation, although not when such restrictions are pursued unilaterally or as coercive measures (see

Commonwealth of Australia, 1995, pp. 6–9). Lallas and colleagues point also to the potential for standards harmonisation under the GATT, arguing that 'harmonisation efforts can be a powerful force in support of higher environmental standards worldwide' (1992, p. 317). The harmonisation debate is a response to concerns about the impact on trade of differential environmental standards. Pearce and Warford (1993, p. 208) raise the possibility that high environmental standards in an importing country could be construed as a non-tariff barrier to protect domestic markets. Those wary of the impacts of freer trade on environmental quality, and concerned about the modalities of free trade, argue that low pollution regulations are themselves a kind of subsidy. Shrybman (1990, p. 31) suggests that while advocates of trade liberalisation have perceived subsidised pollution control measures as a non-tariff barrier, they have not perceived a lack of regulation (in effect the competitive advantage of being able to produce unsustainably) as a subsidy. The potential for migration of industry and production to countries with lesser environmental standards was also an issue during the negotiation of the North American Free Trade Agreement (NAFTA) (see Berlin and Lang, 1993, p. 49). There is some concern also as to whether standardisation will occur at a level adequate for environmental protection. Freer trade, Postel and Flavin (1991, p. 180) suggest, could draw countries into least common denominator standards of environmental protection and thereby undermine conservation efforts (see also Berlin and Lang, 1993, p. 41).

Polluter Pays Principle

One of the advantages claimed for free(r) trade is that it will result in a progressive internalising of externalities (that is, ensuring that the full environmental costs of traded goods, including production, transportation and disposal, will be taken into account). This will occur, so that argument goes, because of an emphasis on removal of subsidies and other non-tariff barriers which distort trade and environmental costs and which also act as disincentives to sustainable extraction and production and to development of alternative technologies. As suggested earlier in the chapter, not everyone accepts this argument on the benefits of free trade with respect to the internalising of external costs. This proposition has, however, been given force in the polluter pays principle (PPP), a principle which Saunders (1992, p. 727) argues is a useful means of balancing environment and trade concerns and which Arden-Clarke suggests offers 'an important adjunct and in some cases the only feasible option for internalising costs' (1992, p. 130). PPP has its genesis in OECD concerns about the allocation of costs of pollution prevention and control measures (see Chapter 4). In 1972, that concern resulted in a formal pronouncement elaborating the principle. In effect, the principle states that the cost of such measures should be met by the polluter, without public subsidy, as a means of encouraging the internalisation in the price of goods of the full costs of pollution abatement. It is, therefore, intended to 'promote efficient resource use' and to 'avoid trade and investment distortions' (Gaines, 1991, pp. 469, 470). PPP is, however, just one of a number of market-based mechanisms which many economists claim are useful tools in the pursuit of sustainable development.

Market-Based Financial Mechanisms

Much attention has been paid to the possible use of a range of financial mechanisms which would act as incentives for reducing environmental degradation. Much of this analysis, grounded as it is in environmental economics (and often with a domestic focus) is beyond the scope of this text, but some brief coverage is helpful in elaborating the direction of this debate. So-called 'command-and-control' or regulatory mechanisms are posited as unwieldy and costly, spawning cumbersome bureaucratic mechanisms. David Pearce, whose work has been central to this debate, suggests that command-and-control is more expensive and less effective in the long-run, especially when it comes to 'technology forcing' (1990, p. 373), that is providing an incentive for the development of new technology. The advantage that is claimed for financial mechanisms, which employ the forces of the market by making use of pricing signals, is that they can address issues of the externality problem (market failure) by providing a realistic valuing of environmental services and that they will address pollution sources rather than 'end-of-pipe' discharges by providing pricing incentives for conservation and technological change. The issue of a monetary valuing of environmental services raises the issue of the limitations of such a valuing. As Peet puts it, 'to impose market valuation mechanisms on what are in many cases reflections of deep human social, cultural, or spiritual needs is to debase and risk destroying that which is being measured' (1992, p. 122).

The purpose of such financial mechanisms is two-fold, although the distinction is not always clearly made. First, such mechanisms are incentives to alter behaviour, to encourage firms and individuals away from environmentally unsustainable practices and towards alternatives. Second, taxes and other mechanisms are proposed as national and international revenue-gathering exercises, the latter as a possible source of 'new and additional financial resources'. Jacobs notes of such instruments, however, that their purpose is not to determine 'the level of pollution or resource consumption. The target must be set first. The instrument is simply the method used to achieve it' (1990, p. 15). Therefore the setting of the target will involve political decisions and choices. A range of mechanisms has been explored including environmental taxes, tradeable pollution permits and tradeable resource quotas (see, for example, Pearce and Warford, 1993; Swanson, 1991). The discussion here touches briefly on two of the most widely canvassed financial mechanisms – taxes and tradeable permits.

Taxes, Postel and Flavin argue, 'are appealing because they offer an efficient way of correcting for the market failure to value environmental services' (1991, pp. 181–2), suggesting that they are 'among the most promising' of tools available to governments to 'reorient economic behaviour' (1991, p. 172). Green taxes, they claim, not only have a role in reshaping national economies, but they can 'raise funds for global initiatives that require transfers from rich countries to poorer ones, transfers that would begin to pay back the ecological debt industrial countries have incurred by causing most of the damage to the global environment thus far' (Postel and Flavin, 1991, p. 185). In this view, then, market forces can be used for ethical ends. There is, however, a range of equity issues to be considered. Domestic taxes may well impact heavily on the poorer sections of the community. McCully argues that global taxes, such as a carbon tax, levied on all countries would be 'unfair and unworkable' (1991b, p. 245). He favours, instead, a tax on energy in the OECD countries. The imposition of any kind of global tax would also, Jain suggests, have to incorporate a 'formula for fair reductions that accounts for diverse national needs' (1990, p. 549). Indeed Soto doubts whether a climate tax *would* 'encourage conservation and wise use' and wonders at what he calls the 'sanity of using consumption to pay for a move to non-consumption' (1992, p. 699). Fears are also raised that governments and institutions would become reliant on any revenue raised, which would thus act as a disincentive to further pollution abatement and ensuing revenue reduction.

Under a permit trading scheme, rights to pollute are allocated in accordance with a predetermined pollution 'target' and are then available to be traded on the open market, thus allowing the market to determine the value of a unit of pollution. The incentive structure for companies (or countries) to reduce abatement costs arises through efficiency measures or alternative technology, to the extent that it then benefits them to sell their permits or to not have to continue purchasing them. As Pearce puts it, 'basically a firm that finds it comparatively easy to abate pollution will find it profitable to sell its permits to a firm that finds it expensive to abate pollution (1990, p. 376). Costs are internalised to the extent that the company (or country) passes them on to the consumer although this can raise equity issues not only for poorer consumers but also for companies and countries for whom both permits and abatements costs are expensive. Pearce points to the potential 'reduction in costs of compliance' (1990, p. 377) as a benefit of tradeable permits. However, such a scheme may have little impact on levels of pollution or resource use, because it is based on an overall 'acceptable' level of pollution or resource use, unless a ratcheting of the overall target or the pollution-unit value of a permit is built into the permit scheme. While much of the analysis in the literature about the use of tradeable permits has focused on domestic applications, they have been discussed in the context of strategies for greenhouse gas reduction. Van Bergeijk, for example, suggests that 'application of the permit approach . . . might be especially promising in an international setting' (1991, p. 112) although he also acknowledges potential difficulties if governments engage in what he terms 'strategic behaviour' to work the system to advantage themselves at the possible cost of overall gains (1991, p. 113).

Conclusion

While there has been much debate in policy circles about a range of possible strategies to give effect to sustainable development (in whatever form it is understood) and to meet the local and global imperatives of reversing environmental decline, much remains at the level of debate and rhetoric. No serious attempt has yet been made to meet commitments on transfer of resources, either financial or technological. Serious relief of debt (as opposed to restructuring of existing debt) remains a topic for discussion rather than a programme for action despite recent IMF announcements. The mutual support between trade and the environment continues, for the most part, to be driven by the trade regime rather than the environmental one, agreements like CITES and the Montreal Protocol notwithstanding. Proposals for international taxes and permit trading schemes remain contentious. The common theme in these strategic debates is cost – who pays and where will the money come from. One answer is not to emphasise *more* money, but to require a reassessment of national and global spending priorities and a potential redirection of existing funds. In this context, attention is often drawn to the impact of high levels of global military spending and the lost opportunity costs and misallocation of resources involved therein. These issues are explored in the next chapter.

9

Environmental Security

Introduction

The phrase 'environmental security' is a relatively new one in the lexicon of global environmental politics. Perhaps because of this, the meaning of the term, the processes it describes and the policy prescriptions it engenders are contested. Brock argues that the idea of environmental security might lead to either a militarisation of environmental politics or a demilitarisation of security thinking (1991, p. 407) and the literature and policy debates tend generally to follow one of these two paths. The first might be characterised as the 'environment-*and*-security' approach in which, as Finger notes, 'the ecological crisis now confronting us [is] increasingly . . . defined as a threat to national security' (1991b, p. 220). The primary referent for security is the state and the primary security concern is the potential for violence, conflict or military action as a result of and in response to environmental degradation. Thus environmental threats are added on to a traditional, geopolitical national security agenda. The second approach emphasises 'securing the environment', by which the integrity of the environment is both security referent and security goal and in which environmental degradation is to be taken at least as seriously as traditional military threats. In this view, the state-centric emphasis of the environmental conflict approach reinforces and legitimises a militaristic mindset which is cast as a cause of environmental degradation and a barrier to the effective pursuit of solutions to environmental decline. Thus the concept of environmental security 'challenges established frames of mind and political conduct' (Lodgaard cited in Brock, 1991, p. 418).

Militarising Environmental Politics: The Environment and Security

Much attention has been paid in both the scholarly literature and the policy community to the potential for conflict to arise as a result of environmental degradation. In this view, the major concern is the 'potential [for] major environmental changes to generate and intensify conflict between and within states' (Soroos, 1994a, p. 318). The environmental security project is therefore one which seeks to identify the kinds of environmental degradation which might present threats to national security, particularly through interstate war or violence. The problem is not environmental degradation *per se*. Rather such degradation is a security problem *only* to the extent that it poses a challenge to either the security of the state or to international peace and security, where there is a demonstrable link with violence or conflict, or when military intervention might be required or can be justified. The questions which inform this approach are those which seek to identify how environmental degradation is likely to become a threat to security – either to internal political security, to the security of the state against incursion or threat by other states, or to international peace and security.

For some, the relationship between conflict and environmental degradation, especially resource scarcity, is axiomatic. This analysis often looks to historical experience as the basis for predictions about future environmental conflict. The World Commission on Environment and Development observed, for example, that 'nations have often fought to assert or resist control over raw materials, energy supplies, land, river basins, sea passages and other key environmental resources. Such conflicts are likely to increase as these resources become scarcer and competition for them increases' (WCED, 1987, p. 290). Neville Brown identifies 'burgeoning ecological threats to peace and security' (1989b, p. 520), a concern echoed in the UN Secretary-General's *Agenda for Peace* which identifies 'ecological damage' as a new risk for stability (Boutros-Ghali, 1992, p. 5). A recent report produced under the auspices of the Strategic Studies Institute at the US Army War College claims, in its opening sentence, that 'international environmental issues can lead to instability and conflict' (Butts, 1994a, p. iii). Westing also claims that 'global deficiencies and degradation of natural resources . . . coupled with the uneven distribution of these raw materials, can lead to . . . national rivalries and, of course, to war' (cited in Deudney, 1990, p. 469).

There is, then, no shortage of predictions about the potential for future environmental conflict.

Resource Conflict

The control of resources for strategic purposes has long been associated with the security of the state, integral to that security and important in denying a source of power to potential or actual enemy states. Thus 'the environment' has been a strategic resource. As Brock notes, 'throughout history, the utilisation of natural resources by humans has meant . . . fighting between social entities . . . over access and distribution' (1991, p. 409). Mische notes that some historians have linked the rise of organised warfare in the Bronze Age to environmental degradation. She suggests that food shortages resulted in raiding and plundering which became institutionalised where it 'paid off in the form of food, material goods and . . . power and prestige' (1992, p. 106). Gleick recalls the resource interests identified by Thucydides as a contributory factor in the Peloponnesian War (1991, p. 19). In more contemporary terms, Rowlands suggests that Paraguay's annexation of Bolivia's Gran Chaco wilderness in the early 1930s was sparked by the former's (misplaced) belief that the region contained oil deposits. Leggett suggests that access to oil infrastructure was a major reason for German advance into the Caucasus and for Japan's invasion of Burma and what was then the Dutch East Indies in World War Two (1992, p. 70). Resource access has been claimed as one reason for US intervention in Korea, to 'prevent the loss . . . of Korean tungsten, Malaysian tin and rubber, New Caledonian nickel and Indonesian oil' (Lipschutz and Holdren, 1990, p. 121). Natural resources (in this case minerals and fish stocks) were also a factor in the Falkland/Malvinas conflict between Britain and Argentina (see Rowlands, 1992, p. 289). Drawing on this historical evidence, scholars argue that future scarcity of resources could exacerbate this tendency to conflict. That conflict is expected to take one of two forms – direct conflict over already scarce resources or military intervention to ensure access to resources which might become scarce at some time in the future. The apparent imperative of access to Kuwaiti oil reserves as one reason for the involvement of the coalition forces, under US leadership, in the Gulf War of 1990–1, would seem to bear out this prediction even though, as Lipschutz and Holdren note, the US was, in fact, minimally reliant on Middle Eastern oil supplies (1990, p. 123).

These confident predictions about resource scarcity and environmental degradation as proximate causes of conflict or war are not universally accepted. Brock cautions that 'a military conflict which involves resources is not necessarily a struggle *over* resources' (1991, p. 410; emphasis added). Johan Holst, a former Norwegian Defence Minister, takes the view that environmental degradation is 'seldom if ever the only cause of major conflict within or among nations' (1989, p. 125). Deudney (1990, p. 461) goes somewhat further when he argues that it is unlikely that environmental degradation will ever lead to conflict. Jessica Mathews' position is that environmental decline only occasionally results in conflict. For Mathews (1989, p. 166) it is more likely that the impact of resource scarcity on national security will arise through overall economic decline.

Defining 'scarce' resources also requires a rethinking of what resources are determined to be 'strategic' and therefore important not only to national security, in traditional discourse, but also to the security of peoples and communities. The irony is that the new strategic resources may well be those which have for so long been thought of as being in plentiful supply, either because they were renewable or because they were, at least, non-depletable – resources such as water, arable land and the services those resources supply. Both water and land are subject to continuing degradation through pollution, soil erosion, the depletion of acquifers, desertification and deforestation as well as from the impacts of global environmental change in the form, especially, of climate change.

Water is forecast to be one of the major causes (perhaps even the most likely cause) of inter- and intrastate tension and possibly outright conflict in the future. In 1994, according to the UNDP (1994, p. 29), the world's per capita water supply was only one-third of that of 1970, although this statistic says little about disparities in per capita use between developed and developing countries. Global water use doubled between 1940 and 1980 and was expected to double again in the remaining two decades of the century (Swain, 1993, p. 429). By the late 1980s, 80 countries with 40 per cent of the world's population were already facing water shortages (WCED, 1987, p. 293). The UNDP identifies 'water scarcity' as an increasing factor in 'ethnic strife and political tension' within countries (1994, p. 29). Concern is evinced not only for stresses *within* countries but also for anticipated cross-border conflict over shared rivers and waterways. As Gleick argues, rapidly growing populations, greater irrigation demands and future climate changes may increase international tensions over shared fresh water resources' (1991, p. 17). One hundred and fifty-five major river systems are shared by two countries and a further 59 are shared by between three and twelve countries (Myers, 1989, p. 29). The Niger, for example, runs through ten countries, for example. Both the Nile and the Congo are shared by nine countries, the Zambesi by eight and the Chad and the Volta each runs through six countries (Holst, 1989, p. 128). Oswald (1993, p. 124) points out that almost 40 per cent of the world's population lives in multi-national river basins.

The Middle East, where scarce water not plentiful oil is the strategic resource, is one part of the world where such conflict is thought likely. As Porter and Brown note, 15 countries compete for the 'rapidly diminishing waters of the Euphrates, Jordan and Nile Rivers' (1991, p. 100). Control over the water resources of those three rivers has been a factor in strategic posturing in the region and remains a likely source of tension. In the mid-1970s, Syria and Iraq came close to hostilities over Syria's al-Thawrah Dam on the Euphrates (see Myers, 1989, p. 29). Turkey's plans to construct a series of dams on the Euphrates River – the Great Anatolia project – have been perceived by Iraq and Syria as a threat to their strategic interests because it would reduce water supplies to both countries (see Homer-Dixon, 1991, p. 108; Butts, 1994a, p. 14). Gleick (1991, p. 20) suggests that Turkey has threatened to restrict the flow of the Euphrates to put political pressure on Syria, a country already short of water, because it suspects the Syrian government of providing support for Kurdish separatists. Control over the Jordan River, upon which Israel relied for almost 60 per cent of its water, was one factor in the 1967 Arab–Israeli war. Israel feared that Syria and Jordan were planning to divert the waters of the Jordan River. After the war, Israel controlled most of the water resources of the Jordan basin (see Myers, 1989, p. 28; Homer-Dixon *et al.*, 1993, pp. 22–3). When Ethiopia announced a dam construction project for the headwaters of the Blue Nile, President Anwar Sadat of Egypt warned, in the light of his country's 'one hundred percent' dependence on the Nile that 'if anyone, at any moment, thinks to deprive us of our life we shall never hesitate to go to war' (cited in Gleick, 1991, pp. 19–20). In 1985, Egypt's then foreign minister (and, more recently, UN Secretary-General) Boutros Boutros-Ghali predicted that the 'next war in [the] region will be over the waters of the Nile, not politics' (cited in Gleick, 1991, p. 20). Inequities in water use further exacerbate these tensions.

Israel's per capita water consumption, for example, is five times that of its regional neighbours (Myers, 1989, p. 28).

Tensions and possible conflict over water resources are not confined to the Middle East. A US government report in the mid-1980s identified ten locations where water scarcity conflicts could be anticipated, only half of them in the Middle East (Porter and Brown, 1991, p. 110). 'Tensions and violence over water-use rights', as Gleick puts it (1991, p. 29) have arisen in the Mekong River basin (shared by Laos, Thailand, Cambodia and Vietnam), the Paraná and Lauca rivers in South America (the former shared by Brazil and Argentina and the latter by Bolivia and Chile) and the Medjerda River which flows through Tunisia and Libya (see also WCED, 1987, p. 293). Political tensions between India and Bangladesh have been exacerbated by disputes over the waters of the Ganges (Swain, 1993; Homer-Dixon *et al.*, 1993, p. 19). The transnational pollution of rivers and coastal waters is another possible source of conflict with the seas, Tickell suggests, 'a potent source of trouble in the future' (1993b, p. 19).

Land, particularly arable land, is now under pressure from environmental degradation, including deforestation, desertification, climate change and over-use. In the 1980s the total amount of cropland in the developing world grew by only 0.25 per cent a year, a growth rate half that of the 1970s; per capita arable land dropped by almost 2 per cent a year (Homer-Dixon, 1991, p. 93). That decline was also unevenly distributed. Predictions suggested that the 1992 global per capita average of 0.28 hectares would decline to 0.17 hectares by 2025. In Asia, that figure was projected to drop as low as 0.09 hectares of arable land per person (Moss, 1993, p. 32). Whether these are conservative figures or whether they overstate the case, there seems little doubt that arable land will continue to become an increasingly scarce resource, on absolute and per capita figures, a scarcity that is likely to occur predominantly in those parts of the world which are already poor and where land is under increasing environmental pressure. Land as territory has always been a geopolitical or strategic resource for states, provided they were able to maintain control and authority over it. The extent of possible future cross-border conflict over arable land (either between local communities or between governments) is not clear. However the possibility that states might seek either to acquire or reclaim arable land, or that arable land inequities might be an exacerbating factor in other kinds of tensions, is not to be completely discounted. Land degradation and depleted water supplies have been identified by a number of scholars as one factor in the so-called Soccer (or Football) War between El Salvador and Honduras in 1969 (although political repression and inequities in land tenure and wealth in El Salvador were also contributory factors) (see Homer-Dixon, 1991, p. 82; Myers, 1989, pp. 32–4).

Environmental Inequities

As the Brundtland Report observed, environmental stress is seldom the only cause of conflict within or among nations but it can be an 'important part of the web of causality' (WCED, 1987, p. 291). The Commission noted that we need to understand how 'poverty, injustice, environmental degradation and conflict interact in complex and potent ways' (1987, p. 291). The proposition that a decline in environmental services might be a threat to national security and a cause for military intervention or conflict rests not only on the possible future exigencies of resource access. Environmental degradation is also cast as a possible cause of increased national and international tensions through the exacerbation of sociopolitical tensions and environmental inequities both within and between states. Lipschutz and Holdren suggest, for example, that it is not access to resources but degradation of the planetary environment and the 'effects that this may have on the well-being and stability of many Third World countries' which is the greater likely threat to international security (1990, p. 121).

Environmental decline may exacerbate already-existing disputes between rich and poor countries and between rich and poor peoples, resulting in what Homer-Dixon refers to as 'relative deprivation conflicts' (1991, p. 109). This relationship is speculative and, as Gleick (1991, p. 20) suggests, its consequences are less well understood. However, inequities in the global distribution and use of resources, in the causes of environmental degradation and resource depletion, in disproportionate impacts and relative vulnerabilities and in response capacities have been identified as possible sources of conflict. Brock suggests, for example, that disparities in the ability of countries to respond to global environmental change are 'likely to become more important as a source of conflict over environmental issues than the relative scarcity of non-renewable resources' (1991, p. 411). The kinds of resentments that might result, according to Lipschutz and Holdren, 'can hardly fail to aggravate international tensions' (1990, p. 128). The World Commission on Environment and Development also expressed concern on this score. The Commission identified 'differences in environmental endowment' as a factor which could 'precipitate and exacerbate international tension and conflict' especially as poorer countries reached the limits of their environmental sustainability (1987, pp. 292–3). Yet, as Ullman (1983, p. 143) has argued, poor countries are unlikely to confront the militarily well-resourced countries over relative deprivation. What is perhaps more likely, in the short term at least, is that relative deprivation could lead to conflict between neighbouring countries, especially in the poorer parts of the world, or to tension and violence within countries as governments and peoples attempt to adjust to the local impacts of local and global environmental stress.

Another outcome of environmental degradation (particularly desertification, soil erosion and a decline in arable land) which is further complicated by inequities between peoples and countries is food insecurity. The problem of food scarcity is exacerbated by inequitable land tenure, especially within developing countries, but also because food surpluses and scarcities are unevenly distributed. Many developing countries which used to be net food exporters are now net food importers, a problem made worse by cash mono-cropping to service not the domestic market but the global market and the imperatives of economic growth. The world's fish catch is also declining as stocks are overfished by long-distance fishing fleets and local commercial fishing industry. The relative scarcity of fish stocks may be further exacerbated by the impacts of ozone depletion and climate change (see Chapter 3). Fish is an important source of protein for a large proportion of the world's population, especially in the developing world. A decline in the food resources of the oceans is a further possible source of conflict as countries compete over fisheries or seek to protect their access to such resources. Oswald argues, for example, that the 'issue of the policing and protection of the world's fish stocks is likely to be one of growing importance in the future' (1993, p. 120). The cross-border conflict potential in fisheries resources is exacerbated because marine ecosystems and the migratory patterns of straddling stocks are not restricted by the Exclusive Economic Zones of coastal states. Overfishing outside a coastal state's EEZ (that is, the 200 nautical mile zone over which states have sovereign rights to resources under the provisions of the UN Convention on the Law of the Sea) can affect the health of stocks within the EEZ. Recent tensions between Canada and Spain over the impact of Spanish fishing outside Canada's EEZ on fish stocks within the EEZ is a case in point.

Climate change provides one example of global inequities and the tensions that arise therefrom. Indeed, climate change has been claimed as the 'moral equivalent of war', in that 'a failure to meet it would have catastrophic consequences for international security' (Brown, 1989b, p. 527). Those countries which are likely to be worst affected by the impact of climate change – by temperature change, by rising sea levels, by changes in agriculture zones, by possible increases in extreme weather conditions, by water shortages or variations in rainfall supply – are the world's poorer countries whose ecosystems are already marginal and whose economies and infrastructures are less flexible and less adaptive in the face of environmental degradation (see Chapter 3). Yet those countries are also less complicitous in the causes of climate change – high levels of fossil fuel burning or energy-consumption – on both a per capita and gross basis and much of the source of past and present radiative forcing is located in the industrialised world. One must nevertheless be cautious in drawing too long a bow in predicting that tensions over climate change could result in actual conflict.

Social and Political Unrest

The social and economic consequences of environmental degradation and resource scarcity, especially food scarcity, may also contribute to a disruption in what Homer-Dixon calls 'legitimised and authoritative social relations' (1991, p. 91). Myers argues that the 'two concurrent trends' (that is, environmental impoverishment and internal social upheaval) 'can hardly be coincidental' (1989, p. 33). The impacts of environmental decline, such as increasingly limited access to food or potable water, will exacerbate the misery and despair which already exists in the poorer parts of the world. Already about one billion of the world's people do not have regular access to clean water, for example. Environmental degradation, especially in rural areas in poorer countries, generates internal migration, either to other rural areas or to the cities, as people move in search of better land or work. Competition for land or for work, environmental pressures on land that is already marginal, or on scarce urban infrastructure can contribute to tensions. In turn, frustrations, tensions and resentments, the consequences of people drawing upon relatively diminished or poorly distributed resources, can result in domestic unrest. 'All too often', in Myers' view, 'the result is civil turmoil and outright violence, either within a country or with neighbouring countries' (1989, p. 24). Gleick also takes the view that environmental decline will 'inevitably [lead to] social and political unrest' (1991, p. 19). This is not necessarily a contemporary phenomenon. Environmental degradation is thought, for example, to have been a major cause of acute conflict in fifteenth century Castille (MacKay cited in Homer-Dixon, 1991, p. 81).

In its 1994 *Human Development Report*, the UNDP identified Afghanistan, Haiti, Angola, Iraq, Mozambique, Burma, the Sudan and Zaire as countries in which internal crises could be linked to environmental degradation and food insecurity (often compounded by inequitable internal resource distribution) (UNDP, 1994, pp. 41–3). Deforestation, loss of arable land (along with rapid population increases) are often identified as major contributory factors to internal instability in Haiti (although, curiously, those analyses often make little or no reference to the former repressive regime in that country) (see, for example, Butts, 1994a, p. 16; Holst, 1989, p. 125; WCED, 1987, p. 292). Food scarcity in Egypt – the result of desert encroachment, salinisation and loss of soil fertility – has been linked to internal tensions and food riots (see Myers, 1989, p. 30). The impact of environmental degradation and loss of land is often an important factor in a range of broader political and social grievances for peoples fighting for various forms of self-determination. Byers (1991, p. 70) points to Sri Lanka, Somalia and Ethiopia as countries in which pressures on the environment have exacerbated internal ethnic tensions. Environmental decline is one of a number of factors which have contributed to the struggle in Bougainville for independence from Papua New Guinea. In South Africa, environmental degradation and relative environmental deprivation, one outcome of the homelands policies which characterised the political and social violence of the apartheid regime, was one factor in the fight for freedom in that country. Homer-Dixon and his colleagues cite studies which indicate that resource scarcity, including access to land, is also an 'increasingly powerful force behind . . . Communist led insurgency' in the Philippines (1993, p. 20).

Environmental Refugees

Both environmental decline and internal instability result in movement of peoples. There is little disagreement that the category of displaced persons now includes environmental refugees, although this is still a rather loosely defined category and one not formally recognised in international refugee law. The numbers of environmental refugees are uncertain but those numbers do seem to be on the increase (see Tickell, 1993b, p. 21). As Mathews points out, '[n]o one knows the true numbers, but in Indonesia, Central America, northern and sub-Saharan Africa, millions have been forced to leave their homes in part because the loss of plant cover and the consequent disappearance of soil have made it impossible to grow food' (1993, p. 30). Environmental stresses have often been discounted as a cause of enforced movement of peoples. Yet as Holst observes, while refugees may be seen to be fleeing 'political upheaval and military violence', the underlying causes of the mass movements of people 'often include the deterioration of the natural resource base' (1989, p. 125). Population displacement, as people go in search of 'more benevolent environmental and social conditions' (Gleick, 1991, p. 17), is a further cause of tension and conflict. The 'conflict-stimulating potential', Byers argues, 'of such massive numbers of refugees is obvious' (1991, p. 70) although too simplistic an analysis can cast environmental refugees as the cause of tension rather than as the victims of environmental degradation. As people move within countries, as noted earlier, greater environmental and social stresses can result. When those people move across (or transgress) territorial borders, environmental refugees are then defined as a threat to national security (and perhaps to international peace and security), illuminating state-based concerns about encroachment and the difficulty of protecting borders.

Many of the examples of the conflict potential of environmental degradation explored in the literature focus on the developing world. The social and political tensions, and possible conflict, which might arise from environmental decline in the Third World are made cause for concern for developed countries (or their governments) because they might require intervention, contribute to international instability or undermine the stability, to cite Butts of 'newly formed democratic regimes' (1994a, p. v). Holst suggests that the 'breakdown of natural support systems' can place 'pressures on national institutions' (1989, p. 123) or, as he puts it, 'soil erosion leads to political erosion' (1989, p. 125). Mathews also raises these concerns: countries suffering from environmental degradation and beset by internal conflict as a result are considered to be potentially ripe for 'authoritarian government or external subversion' (1989, p. 168). This then becomes an issue for developed countries, not on humanitarian grounds but because the '[security] interests of the North may be directly threatened' if countries develop in the direction of extremism (Homer-Dixon, 1991, p. 113).

Military Responses to Non-Military Threats

Environmental threats are therefore identified as 'non-military' threats to national and international peace and security, a position formally adopted by the 1992 summit meeting of Security Council heads of state (see Baker, 1993, p. 356). NATO has also acknowledged environmental problems as security threats. As Butts notes, NATO's Strategic Concept now states that '[r]isks to Allied security are less likely to result from calculated aggression against the territory of the Allies [than from] the adverse consequences of instabilities . . . [and that] security and stability have [*inter alia*] environmental elements as well as the indispensable defence dimension' (1994a, p. 29). But even though environmental stress is identified as a 'non-military' threat, environmental politics are militarised because the 'threat' element is defined, in the final analysis, not by the impact on human security or even economic security but by its relationship, through the potential for conflict, with the military and geopolitical security of the state.

This raises, then, the question of a role for the defence forces. Some of the analysis on this issue suggests a precautionary role such as environmental data gathering or disaster relief (see, for example, McClement, 1992). In other cases a more 'traditional coercive task' (Oswald, 1993, p. 118) is anticipated for the military. Thus defence forces might engage in defensive or pre-emptive action in cross-border resource conflict, to gain control over scarce resources or to maintain control over resources against the threat of incursion from another state. Defence forces might be used to secure borders against environmental refugees or to maintain internal security in the event of environment-related (and often other kinds of) instabilities. States, Brock argues, 'could use military force in order to protect themselves from [the] social consequences of global environmental decay' (1991, p. 410). Mische also raises the possibility that 'governments may . . . resort to increased use of military power to protect or seize vital resources or to quell rebellion and maintain law and order' (1992, p. 110). Military capabilities or the threat of their use could be employed to prevent activities, in or by another country, which could have a transboundary environmental impact. Military power might be garnered on behalf of the international community against environmental renegades, or as a means of enforcing international environmental law, a kind of environmental collective security. Sir Crispin Tickell, a former British diplomat, predicts that 'environmental problems in one country affecting the interests of another could easily come within the purview of the Security Council with its mandate for maintaining international peace and security' (1993b, p. 23). Oswald canvases the possibility that 'poor environmental behaviour from the nations of the world' could require a 'direct active response' from military forces (1993, p. 129). Finger also draws attention to the possible use of 'military force or other coercive means to force recalcitrant states or other bodies to comply with international . . . agreements' (1991b, p. 223). The consequence of such analysis is that use of force is legitimised as a response to environmental decline.

Demilitarising Security: Securing the Environment

In what Finger calls the 'military model' (1991b, p. 223), environmental degradation, resource scarcity and the impacts of differential endowment or relative deprivations are analysed in strategic terms. Environmental (in)security becomes synonymous with environmental threats to the state. Strategic and defence bureaucracies continue to define both the threat to national security and appropriate responses to those threats. Some have suggested that this focus on environmental threat reflects a search by strategic and defence establishments for new assignments in a post-Cold War world. Lipschutz and Holdren, for example, are trenchant in their criticism of 'strategic analysts . . . busy combing the planet for new threats to be countered' by military forces (1990, p. 126). Thus the term environmental security is 'interpreted narrowly to refer to situations in which environmental and resource conflicts heighten the probability of armed conflict. Such a definition is consistent with the conventional notions of military security' (Soroos, 1994a, p. 319). For many, however, this interpretation of environmental security is a problem. It is a problem because it narrows policy options by focusing on symptoms rather than causes, because it engenders inappropriate responses to the problems of environmental degradation and because it reinforces a mindset which continues to be a direct and indirect cause of the very problems (environmental degradation and resource depletion) to which it purports to respond. Myers argues, for example, that 'this conventional approach to security interests surely reflects an overly narrow perception of security problems and of available responses' (1989, p. 41). In short, militarising environmental politics is argued to be inappropriate and antithetical to the real problems of environmental security.

The UN Group of Governmental Experts on the Relationship between Disarmament and Development cautioned, in its 1982 report, against moves to militarise or seek military solutions to non-military threats such as environmental degradation. Otherwise, the Group argued, 'there is a grave risk that the situation will deteriorate to a point of crisis where . . . the use of force could be seen as a way to produce results quickly' (cited in WCED, 1987, p. 300). Yet there are, as the Brundtland Commission argued, 'no military solutions to environmental insecurity' (WCED, 1987, p. 301). The threat-to-state approach also discourages any serious consideration of the extent to which militarisation or militarism contributes to environmental degradation. As Finger argues, because environmental decline is defined as a 'threat to national security, the military is seen by many as part of the solution to the crisis rather than one of its major causes' (1991b, p. 220).

Militarism and Environmental Degradation

The military, and military activities, contribute directly and indirectly to environmental degradation in a number of ways. One of the most obvious is through the environmental consequences of war. Arthur Westing, who has written widely on this, argues that the 'wanton disruption of the environment by armed conflict is a common occurrence in many ecogeographical regions of the world' (1989a, p. 131). So-called 'scorched earth' strategies, involving the 'manipulation of the environment for hostile military purposes' (Finger, 1991b, p. 220) or the 'destruction of the environment for "active" military purposes' (Leggett, 1992, p. 68) are not new. Contemporary examples would include the use of defoliants by US and other forces in Vietnam to deny cover to the Viet Cong (area denial), a strategy which destroyed 14 per cent of Vietnam's forests and severely damaged economically important mangrove swamp ecosystems (see Leggett, 1992, p. 69) as well, of course, as directly affecting the non-combatant population. Other examples include Afghanistan, Southern Sudan, Ethiopia and El Salvador (see Leggett, 1992). During the 1990 Gulf conflict, an estimated three to six million barrels of oil per day were burnt (compared with an average daily consumption of oil in all of Western Europe of 12 million barrels (Barnaby, 1991, p. 168). This deliberate burning of Kuwaiti oil wells by Iraqi troops not only caused economic damage but resulted in changes in temperature, damage to local ecosystems, air pollution through the emission of sulfur dioxide and environment-related health trauma in local populations (see Goldblat, 1993, p. 402; Barnaby, 1991; Leggett, 1992, p. 70). Oil spills into the waters of the Gulf (deliberate and accidental) also caused damage to marine and coastal ecosystems (see Barnaby, 1991, p. 170).

The conduct of war results also in environmental 'collateral damage' as the unintended consequences of conflict. Leggett, in his analysis of the environmental consequences of the Gulf conflict, points to the damage to local ecosystems caused by bombs (and bomb craters), the impact of military vehicles on fragile desert ecosystems and the problems of waste management and excessive water consumption demands (1992, p. 74). Fighting also contributed to extensive bird and animal mortality (Funke, 1994, p. 336). The millions of land mines scattered throughout the world as a result of conflict also contribute to environmental degradation, long after the war has finished. In places like Cambodia, for example, as well as causing extensive trauma to local peoples, unmarked landmines prevent the rejuvenation of land for agriculture, thus requiring what land is available to be used intensively and often, therefore, unsustainably.

Environmental degradation in wartime has been subject to little or no accountability and is poorly covered, in practice, in international law. The basic injunctions against environmental impact in wartime are found in the 1977 Environmental Modification Convention (ENMOD – in full the *Convention on the Prohibition of Military or any other Hostile Use of Environmental Modification Techniques*). The provisions of ENMOD are, Holst argues, 'ambiguous and limited' (1989, p. 124). The Convention places restrictions only on environmental modification techniques which have 'widespread, long-lasting or severe effects' (see Goldblat, 1991, p. 401). Protocol I to the 1949 Geneva Convention 'explicitly requires combatants to limit environmental destruction' (Drucker, 1989, p. 145) even though the Protocol's primary purpose is the protection of victims of conflict. The Protocol incorporates a threshold clause similar to that of ENMOD, banning practices which cause 'widespread, long-term *and* severe damage' (thus requiring all three conditions to be met before the injunction is to be invoked). Drucker calls the language 'vague and permissive' (1989, p. 145) and Goldblat notes its limitations in cases where states are not signatories as, for example, neither the United States nor Iraq were during the Gulf War (1991, p. 400). Other international conventions have some relevance to the environmental impact of wartime, wartime-related or general military activities. Goldblat (1991), for example, discusses the environmental interpretations of the 1963 *Partial Test Ban Treaty*, the 1974 *Threshold Test Ban Treaty*, the 1976 *Peaceful Nuclear Explosions Treaty* and the 1980 *Inhumane Weapons Convention* and its protocols (which cover, among other things, the use of landmines).

However, military's war on the environment goes beyond wartime. There is little doubt that, globally, the military has been and remains a major polluter of the environment and a disproportionate user of resources. Renner observes, for example, that in the US the Pentagon (that is, the Department of Defence) produces more toxics than the top five US chemical companies combined (cited in Finger, 1991b, p. 221). The Pentagon has recently identified over 15 000 toxic waste sites at over 1600 military bases in the United States alone. The German government has listed 4000 sites potentially contaminated by military waste (Anon., 1993f). A 1991 study by the organisation Medical Association for Prevention of War (MAPW) draws on reports which estimate that up to 10 per cent of the former East Germany may have been contaminated by the Soviet military (MAPW, 1991, p. 5). The costs of cleaning up the environmental legacy of the Cold War are extensive. The Pentagon estimates that something between $US11 and $US15 billion (Pirages, 1991, p. 132; Schneider, 1991) will be needed to deal with military-related toxic waste sites in the United States. The costs of permanent and environmentally-safe disposal of Cold War nuclear by-products – 'an estimated 257 tons of weapons-grade plutonium and at least 1300 tons of Highly Enriched Uranium' (Renner, 1994, p. 141) – is, Taylor (1989, p. 158) suggests, likely to cost much more than it cost to make the plutonium in the first place.

The military is also a disproportionate user of world energy and mineral resources using, for example, about 25 per cent of all jet fuel (Renner, cited in Finger, 1991b, p. 221). Mische (1994, p. 280) calculates that an F-16 fighter jet consumes almost twice as much fuel in one hour as the average US motorist does in a year. Brock

(1991, p. 411) points out that the military also often has an important role in decision-making on resource use – he uses the Amazon as an example. Harbinson (1992) describes how the military-dominated State Law and Order Restoration Council (SLORC) which rules Burma has sold oil and mineral exploration rights and logging concessions to pay for its campaign against the democracy movement and the Karen tribal resistance movement. The cost and impact of the struggle against SLORC has also placed pressure on the Karen to abandon their traditional slash-and-burn agriculture in order to survive as well as to fund their struggle (see Harbinson, 1992). The MAPW (1991, p. 4) suggests that, until recently, the largest single holder of agricultural land in the Philippines (land which was often left idle) was the US military. In the then Soviet republic of Kazakhstan, according to the Association, the Soviet military controlled 200 000 square kilometres of land, more than was given over to the cultivation of wheat (MAPW, 1991, p. 4).

The contribution of militaries and military activity to environmental degradation is measured also in lost opportunity costs and a misallocation of resources. Global military spending totals approximately $US1 trillion, with spending in some countries close to 50 per cent of GNP. The level of military spending declined in the late 1980s, driven primarily by economic necessity rather than any normative commitment to disarmament or reduction in defence spending but, as Wulf (1992, p. 2) notes, the rate of that decline slowed again by 1990. The US defence budget is still higher in real terms than it was before the Reagan 'buildup' (Ball, 1994, p. 392) and defence spending in the developing world continues to grow (see, for example, Gill, 1994, p. 557; Young, 1992). Tolba, El-Kholy *et al.* (1992, p. 592) remind us that UNEP's expenditure in the decade 1982–92, a sum of $US450 million, was the equivalent of less than five hours of global military spending for the same period of time. Funds absorbed by the military are therefore denied to other areas of spending, including environmental repair, a view summed up in President Eisenhower's oft-quoted aphorism 'Every gun that is made, every warship launched, every rocket fired represents, in the final analysis, a theft from those who hunger and are not fed, who are cold and are not clothed' (cited in Renner, 1989, p. 137). The Brundtland Commission expressed its concern about this misallocation of resources when it noted that 'arms competition and armed conflict create major obstacles to sustainable development' (WCED, 1987, p. 294). UN Secretary-General Boutros Boutros-Ghali also took up this theme, observing in his

Agenda for Development that 'preparation for war absorbs inordinate resources . . . which diminish the prospects for development' (1994, paragraph 17).

Opportunity costs are calculated not just in terms of direct military spending. Lipschutz and Holdren (1990, p. 130) suggest that up to 40 per cent of the world's scientific and technological capabilities are directed towards military-related activities and Thee (1988, p. 47) provides figures which suggest that, as a percentage of military spending, research and development (R&D) is actually increasing in a post-Cold War world. Renner details reports which conclude that even where spin-offs are available, they could have been achieved more efficiently and effectively with direct civilian investment (1989, pp. 139–41). Seymour Melman, among others, challenges the idea that 'military goods and services are a source of wealth' (1988, p. 55) a proposition which has been supported by a number of studies which, using neo-classical economic growth models, show that 'military spending is a drain on the economy' (see Ward and Davis, 1992).

The analysis of the impact of militarism on the environment points also to the closed nature of military activity and the extent to which such impact is often subject to little or no scrutiny, often in the name of national security. Finger (1991b, p. 222) notes, for example, that in the build-up to the Gulf War, the Pentagon was exempted from having to conduct Environmental Impact Assessments on its projects. Boulding (1991, p. 80) describes the practice of militaries in constructing 'sacrifice areas' for the conduct of military exercises or weapons testing, practices that are damaging to both the environment and people. French testing at Mururoa Atoll, US testing in the Marshall Islands, or the British use of Maralinga in Australia for its atomic tests would all fall into this category.

Flawed Discourse?

The security discourse which informs militarism and the environmental threat literature is argued to be both inappropriate and antithetical to the pursuit of environmental security for three reasons. First, it engenders policy responses that are inadequate as responses to the impacts of environmental 'threats', even in a narrow conflict sense. Second, the discourse is inappropriate for addressing environmental insecurities in a broader sense. Third, it entrenches a mindset and practice that contributes to continued environmental degradation.

There is a strong argument that military action of some kind is an ineffective response to resource scarcity. Lipschutz and Holdren (1990) argue, in effect, that resource conflict is not a rational policy response. In their investigation of the costs and benefits of military action to secure access to resources they suggest that there is little evidence to support the proposition that 'trying to defend resources access militarily pays off' (Lipschutz and Holdren, 1990, p. 122). Deudney concurs. He suggests that it is increasingly difficult to exploit foreign resources through territorial conquest (1990, p. 470). All three take the view that the international trading system is now so robust that it should not be necessary for states to fight to gain access to resources (although the degree of robustness of the trading system may itself be open to question). Indeed, they suggest that resource scarcity (and they are talking here about non-renewable resources such as minerals and hydrocarbons) is unlikely, especially in the absence of effective resource cartels. Even OPEC has had limited success in establishing a monopoly on hydrocarbon reserves, in part because not all petroleum exporters are members of OPEC and because many of the industrialised countries which are heavily reliant on hydrocarbons (such as Japan) have instituted efficiency measures to reduce that dependence. OPEC's attempts in the early 1970s to control the price and supply of oil were directed primarily at industrialised countries, yet there is strong evidence to suggest that the developing countries were affected even more (see Rosecrance, 1994, pp. 233–8).

It is therefore suggested that, for developed countries at least, non-renewable resources are unlikely to reach a point of strategic scarcity, such that national security is considered to be at stake, because technological and financial capacity, along with public concerns about the increasing profligate use of resources, should ensure that substitutes are developed long before a state of scarcity is reached. However, this does require us to consider what determines and defines scarcity in a resource context. Scarcity is often determined by politics rather than, as Brock puts it, the '*physical* limitations of natural resources' (1991, p. 410; emphasis added). He notes, for example, with respect to oil, that there is 'no scarcity as such: it exists only in specific political, socio-economic and cultural contexts' (Brock, 1991, p. 410). Finger suggests that defining scarcity in strategic terms runs the risk of transforming 'every single resource into a potentially strategic one' (1991a, p. 5). In turn, if what is considered strategic is linked to the pursuit of national security, then any resource defined as strategic or scarce becomes a potential source of conflict.

Traditional security discourse is also based on the assumption that threats to national security and identity come from 'others', usually other states or groups of states. Secure states, through the protection of borders, make (in theory) for a secure world and for secure citizens. Security against other states is to be pursued through military-related strategies, either unilaterally, through the deterrent acquisition of military capability or through alliance strategies and confidence building. Yet, as explored in Chapter 4, environmental degradation does not fit comfortably with this geopolitical, state-centric analysis. Environmental degradation does not respect state borders and states cannot take unilateral action to attain and maintain the security of their own environment. Traditional security responses which focus on military capability cannot ensure the security of the state and its people against environmental degradation. In the face of ecological insecurities, states and peoples cannot be secure unless the ecosystem is secure. Neither is it helpful to identify an enemy 'other', whose intent is the violation of territorial integrity and state sovereignty. The 'enemy', the source of the threat, is not the environment but the everyday activities of humans and corporations, the former primarily in pursuit of quality of life and the latter in pursuit of profit. State-centric and national security interpretations of environmental security have also restricted who can contribute to the 'security' discourse. Defining and providing security is determined to be the responsibility of state actors, nationally and internationally. When this is joined with 'environmental' threats, it can preclude ideas and concepts which do not have states as the key structures. Thus traditional security discourse is not only inappropriate as a basis for environmental security but it may also stand in the way of creative and successful solutions to environmental insecurity.

The expansion of the national security discourse to include economic security concerns provides some space for incorporating environmental concerns but, for those working within a critical perspective, it remains limited and problematic. These issues have, in effect, been canvassed in Chapters 7 and 8 and are therefore revisited only briefly here. The 'economic security' agenda was a recognition that the survival of the state over the longer term depends as much (and perhaps more) on economic capability as on military capacity. However, the pursuit of economic security, through growth strategies, can itself result in environmental degradation. Thus, for both military and economic securities, we have the environmental equivalent of the classic security dilemma. As states seek either territorial or economic security through unilateral initiatives and often unrestricted development and consumption, the less secure they become through the pressures of environmental decline.

The traditional security discourse also engenders a focus on symptoms rather than causes. As Mathews notes, the 'underlying cause of turmoil is often ignored, instead governments address the . . . instability that . . . results' (1989, p. 166). Yet it is failure to take action on environmental degradation that is 'likely to lead to escalating insecurity and instabilities in which the forces of traditional security will be heavily engaged' (Oswald, 1993, p. 113). The solution, Porter and Brown argue, is 'international cooperation . . . not futile conflict over the degraded resource itself'. The real problem, they argue, is the 'mismanagement of the resource' (1991, p. 110) in the first place. Therefore, rather than a focus on conflict as an outcome of resource scarcity, attention should be given to *preventing* resource scarcity. Rather than anticipating the extent to which internal tensions and conflict as a result of environmental degradation may spill over into neighbouring countries and pose a threat to international peace and security, greater attention should be given to mitigating the causes of that environmental degradation.

There is some resistance to use of the term 'environmental security' from within both the traditional security community and the environmental community, albeit for quite different reasons. In the former case, security scholars are concerned at what they consider to be a weakening of 'real' security with the addition of what they often define as welfare concerns. Gleick, for example, argues that it is not a 'redefinition of international or national security' that is required but a 'better understanding of the nature of certain threats' (1991, p. 17). Scholars such as Brock and Deudney, on the other hand, caution against a claiming of the term security for the environmental discourse because in their view, it sends us off in the wrong direction and because it locks environmental concerns into an inappropriate, state-centric framework (see Brock, 1991, p. 418; Deudney, 1990). Thus Deudney argues, the 'environmental crisis is not a threat to national security, but it does challenge the utility of thinking in "national" terms' (1990, p. 468). Brock asks whether 'it make[s] sense at all to talk about environmental matters in terms of aggression and security' (1991, p. 408). Deudney is concerned that 'efforts to harness the emotive power of nationalism', which he sees as a logical outcome of the use of a security discourse, 'may prove counterproductive' (1990, p. 461). Mische (1992, pp. 103–6), on the other hand, argues that there is a sound philosophical and politically practical basis for the term precisely because it invokes deep feelings and portrays environmental concerns as ones which are crucial to the pursuit of safety and survival.

Revisiting Environmental Security

The achievement of environmental security requires two things. First, because traditional security discourse is inappropriate for environmental security issues, non-traditional approaches to environmental security must be adopted, approaches which do not seek to identify the enemy 'other', and which do not seek to identify security only in terms of states, conflict, and military and territorial security. However, establishing a separate discourse for environmental insecurity is insufficient if the assumptions and practices of the traditional security agenda, which are antithetical to the pursuit of environmental security, are left unchallenged. Therefore achieving environmental security requires a demilitarising of security, the second of Brock's propositions outlined at the beginning of this chapter. Security has to be demilitarised by reducing global military expenditure, by taking the planning and implementation of global security away from strategists who cannot or are unwilling to accept this broader vision, and by encouraging new ways of thinking about what it means to be secure. The UNDP (1994, pp. 22–5) urges that environmental security should be part of a comprehensive approach to security, one that moves away from a narrow military and defensive meaning of security to one which is integrative and focuses on human security. The Brundtland Report advocates and urges turning away from the 'destructive logic of an "arms culture"', a process which should include reductions in both military spending and arms trading, and acting 'in concert to remove the growing environmental sources of conflict' (WCED, 1987, p. 304). Soroos (in what may be an unintended appropriation of the language of traditional security) calls for an 'assault on business-as-usual practices' (1994a, p. 320). It is worthwhile also heeding Prins' words. He argues that environmental security is 'not something in the here and now. It is a *goal*' (Prins, 1993, p. xiv; emphasis added). What we have, he reminds us, is environmental insecurity!

In this view, environmental security stands for security of the environment, valuable in its own right and as a crucial component of human security. Buzan argues that 'environmental security concerns the maintenance of the local and planetary biosphere as the essential support system on which all other human enterprises depend' (1991, p. 433). Thus, as a report by UNEP and the Peace Research Institute in Oslo (PRIO) has argued, 'in the context of comprehensive international security, the significance of environmental security extends far beyond the environmental sector itself' (PRIO, 1989, p. 13). It also extends far beyond what has usually been defined and claimed as the security sector in international politics.

10

The Global Politics of the Environment

There has clearly been no lack of attention to the global environment in the years since the Rio Conference. Thousands of committed people have worked hard to keep environmental issues on the agenda. Since June 1992, negotiation and debate on environment-related issues have continued apace. There are, within the UN system and outside it, any number of committees, working groups, expert panels, subsidiary bodies, workshops, commissions and other fora, convened by governments, intergovernmental organisations and NGOs, which have focused and continue to focus on a wide range of transboundary and global environmental issues. Much has also been made in those years of the imperative for a global partnership (as Agenda 21 has it) in support of our common future (as the World Commission on Environment and Development described it). As the President of the Republic of the Maldives reminded the industrialised countries in a speech in 1995, 'environmental security is a common good that we share together or forfeit forever' (Gayoom, 1995, p. 10).

Yet there are serious grounds for arguing that while we have seen considerable activity, we have yet to see the decisive action that the world's seven most industrialised countries (the G7) thought imperative when, in 1989, they stated that 'decisive action' on global environmental issues was urgently needed. Indeed they have themselves not heeded their own injunction. As Richard Falk reminds us, the 'geopolitical leadership of the world is not meeting the environmental challenge in a responsible fashion' (1995, p. 32). There is little evidence that the much-vaunted New World Order is becoming a green world order. Nearly a quarter of a century after the Stockholm Conference and almost five years after Rio, the United Nations Environment Programme reported that the global environment – air, water, ocean and forests – continued to deteriorate (see Lever,

1996, p. 6). For many there has been 'precious little global sharing' (Agarwal and Narain, 1991, p. 1). We continue to suffer from 'green planet blues' (Conca *et al.*, 1995).

In the view of many, then, the ecological confidence which was proclaimed after UNCED has yet to be justified and may well be misplaced. Caroline Thomas has argued, for example, that 'at the most fundamental level, the *causes* of environmental degradation have not been addressed and . . . efforts to tackle the crisis are bound to fail' (1993, p. 1; emphasis added). Many scholars claim, as Marc Williams does, that what is therefore required to tackle this environmental crisis is a 'rethinking of fundamental concepts and assumptions' (1996, p. 43). However, others whose views have also been explored here have cautioned against unrealistic expectations of decision-making processes that, while not perfect and perhaps slower than would be ideal, still represent progress in international environmental governance, the development of international environmental law and better practice in the pursuit of sustainable development. In other words, this is a position which fears that the demands for radical change would be, to coin a phrase, akin to throwing babies out with the bathwater.

These two, broadly based positions – which Torgerson characterises as radical transformation on the one hand and incremental reform on the other (1995, p. 3) – have increasingly come to characterise the global politics of the environment.

Problem-Solving and Critique

An important distinction which helps make sense of the different views and strategies which have been explored in this text is that which Robert Cox makes between problem-solving and critical approaches. For Cox, problem-solving

> takes the world as it finds it, with the prevailing social and power relationships and the institutions into which they are organised, as the given framework for action. The general aim of problem-solving is to make these relationships and institutions work smoothly (1986, p. 208).

This characterises the reformist tradition, one which not only accepts but reinforces and helps to maintain the dominant social paradigm.

At the risk of simplifying the views which have been explored in earlier chapters, reformist approaches share a general understanding of the environmental crisis and the search for solutions as primarily managerial or technical problems which can be solved through making the existing political and economic order, which is not itself at fault, work more effectively and efficiently. For those of this persuasion, a system of international governance based primarily on sovereign states (of the kind explored in Chapter 4) is a reality and it is, therefore, simply unhelpful or unrealistic either to advocate or expect extensive change. Rather, the environmental problematic – and the energies of those involved in environmental decision-making – should focus on finding ways of strengthening institutional competence, particularly through the United Nations which, in this view, offers the best hope for progress. This problem-solving approach also views the principles and institutions of the liberal international economic order as fundamental to any attempts to mitigate and reverse global environmental degradation. Thus an open and supportive trading system can only contribute to the overall goal of sustainable development, and economic growth, albeit pursued in a sustainable manner, remains a basic condition for managing the environmental crisis. Nevertheless, these views are not, as various chapters in this book have demonstrated, simply business-as-usual strategies. If sustainable development is to be achieved, environmental concerns must, as the Brundtland Report urged or as Maurice Strong argued at UNCED, be factored into the very centre of economic decision-making; environmental governance must be democratised; the poverty, misery and despair faced by such a large proportion of the world's people must be addressed and overcome.

At a rhetorical level, there is little disagreement with these propositions among many policy-makers and commentators. However, as explored in this book, there is frequently a chasm (some would suggest one of insurmountable proportion) between statements of principle and subsequent commitments to act on such principles. For those who continue to advocate reform of the contemporary system of governance and political economy, the problem lies not in the strategies themselves but in the fact that those strategies have not yet been effectively operationalised because of the intervention of political and economic interests.

This is hardly an explanation to satisfy those who adopt a critical approach. As Cox elaborates it, such an approach stands apart from the prevailing order . . . [it] does not take institutions and social and power relations for granted but calls them into question by concerning itself with their origins . . . [it appraises] the very framework for action which problem-solving accepts as its parameters (1986, p. 208).

Critical approaches, Cox argues, are 'directed to the social and political complex as a whole rather than to the separate parts' (1986, p. 208). Environmental issues are explored, therefore, not in isolation but as a manifestation of and intimately connected in their causes with a range of historical and contemporary social and political relationships. Rather than reinforcing the dominant social paradigm, these are the views which 'challenge established frames of mind and political conduct' (Lodgaard cited in Brock, 1991, p. 418).

In calling the prevailing order into question, critical approaches extend the environmental problematic from one which focuses primarily on institutions and cooperation, the effective functioning of the market and processes of transfer and exchange to one which explores the environmental crisis in the context of questions about equity and justice, the importance of what Thomas describes as 'social forces above and below the state' (1993, p. 4) and the negative synergies between militarism and environmental degradation. In this view, economic and political interests are not simply intervening factors in an otherwise value-free and effective process as the problem-solvers would have it. Rather they are intricately and inextricably bound up with the ways in which environmental problems are articulated and understood, with the causes of the environmental crisis and with the dysfunctions of the contemporary political and economic world order. Prevailing power relationships, which reflect and constitute the contemporary world order, are perceived as an ecological 'double-assault' – as a cause of the environmental crisis and a barrier to its resolution. Thus strategies which continue to emphasise primarily state-centric governance (even if mediated through 'collective sovereignty' and democratisation), or the more effective implementation of the liberal international economic order, are considered to be ineffective in the final analysis because they do not embody the kinds of fundamental normative change which, in a critical view, are necessary for a sound ecological future.

Smith, along with others of a critical view, argues that a further consequence of the problem-solving approach is the 'exclusion of normative debate from social and political life' (1996, p. 25). Thus, for example, little attention is paid to power relationships of the kind embodied in gender or the marginalisation of local and indigenous voices. Problems of ecology become cast as 'problem[s] of technology transfer and finance' (Shiva, 1993, p. 153). Prevailing inequities in resources are identified primarily as a statement of geography rather than, as Soroos argues, a 'consequence of centuries of colonialism as well as [of] contemporary forms of international economic domination' (1986, p. 356).

Critical perspectives are grounded also in an increasingly widely-held perception that it has become 'impossible to comprehend the causes of environmental concern' and the problems of environmental change within contemporary disciplinary orthodoxies (see Vogler, 1996, p. 13). In other words, our theoretical frameworks are inadequate for thinking about the environmental crisis and, therefore, for offering strategies and solutions. Benton and Redclift argue that 'the social sciences are not equipped to play [an] enlarged imaginative and practical role' in 'understanding and responding to the environmental crisis' without a 'radical rethink of their *own* inherited assumptions' (1994, p. 2; emphasis in original). They continue that 'serious attempts to come to terms with issues posed by our environmental crisis expose to critical examination some very basic 'settled' assumptions of the "mainstream" traditions of the social sciences' (Benton and Redclift, 1994, p. 2). Benton makes a similar point about what he calls the 'technological environmental ideology' (1994, p. 37). Such an ideology is, he argues, flawed for two reasons: first because it cannot 'contemplate qualitatively different lines of sociocultural and economic change' and second because it tends to 'undertheorise the social, legal and political processes of environmental regulation' (Benton, 1994, p. 37). One finds, therefore, demands for a serious investigation of the ways in which theories 'might need to be broadened, recast or transformed in order to understand global environmental problems and the ways in which these can, or should be, tackled' (Hurrell, 1995, p. 136).

While a detailed investigation of those theories, and what is termed 'green theory' in particular, is beyond the scope and purpose of this chapter, it is worth at least identifying many of the shared purposes in those theoretical debates which span disciplines: concerns about the relationship between humans and non-human species, important debates about the values and normative imperatives which should inform policy-making, about social goals, about the ideologies of industrialism and anthropocentrism and about democratisation, decentralisation and appropriate forms of political practice.

The divergence between those ideas which have been described in this book as reformist and those which have been identified as critical is manifest in approaches to description and analysis (how can we describe and understand the politics of this process?), to prescription (what policies will best meet the goals of reversing environmental decline?) and to epistemological and normative framework (what unquestioned assumptions do we bring to the study and practice of the global politics of the environment and what kinds of norms and values are most appropriate for the goals we set ourselves?). This chapter turns now to draw those themes together.

The different analytical traditions which are the basis for the reformist and critical approaches give rise to some quite different perspectives on just what constitutes the global politics of the environment. In reformist or problem-solving terms, politics is understood primarily as a process of arbitration between competing interests. Thus the global politics of the environment can be understood by identifying the actors and their interests, and by describing and analysing negotiations on environmental degradation as a collective action problem. As Sheldon Kamieniecki suggests in the introduction to his edited collection, 'global environmental issues can best be understood by studying environmental movements, ecological parties, international organisations and regimes, international law and the problems and policies of specific nations in different regions of the world' (1993, p. 1). From a critical perspective, with its emphasis on underlying power structures, politics also arises (and is implicated in) the disenfranchisement of the powerless and the means by which particular environmental (and other) ideologies are reproduced. Thus, for example, Conca and Lipschutz argue that the global environment is something more than an issue area. Rather it is 'an arena in which fundamental conflicts over power, wealth and control are played out' (1993, p. 3). They go on to raise the possibility that 'environmental problems . . . are part of a larger process of systemic transformation' (Conca and Lipschutz, 1993, p. 3) and suggest that the politics of global environmental change is 'grounded in [and] related to the economic, social and political structures of the current world order' (Conca and Lipschutz, 1993, p. 5).

A second point of divergence about global environmental politics which arises from the competing reformist and critical analytical traditions is their understanding not just of the causes of global environmental degradation but the kinds of strategies that are likely to be most effective in mitigating and reversing the environmental crisis. At a more fundamental level, this question of effective strategies is related to the degree of confidence or otherwise in the 'basic assumptions of modern western society' (Sessions, cited in Paehlke, 1994, p. 350) and the 'capacity of western institutions to redress or reverse the environmental crisis' (Fischer and Black, 1995a, p. xiii). Those assumptions are based on a commitment to the market and industrialism, international institutions based on the state, decision-making informed by democratic pluralism, and a belief in the importance of objective science and technology. For those of a reformist persuasion, while a modern western society characterised by governance based on democratic pluralism and a liberal economic order might have some previously unforeseen side effects which need to be managed and overcome, it still holds out the best promise for progress for humanity and for managing the environmental crisis. For others, the consequences for the environment of these practices and assumptions of the contemporary world order 'have been devastating' (Doran, 1995, p. 194).

Evaluating the Contemporary World Order

One of the major characteristics of the post-Cold War and post-Rio era has been the continued globalisation of a neo-liberal international economic order and the spread (some would claim the triumph) of capitalism (see Little, 1995), engendering what Paterson describes as the 'hegemony of neo-liberal economic assumptions' (1995, p. 216). As Chapters 7 and 8 have indicated, for many whose positions can be characterised as reformist or problem-solving, this is to be welcomed. In this view, free(r) trade along with the free movement of capital, supported by limited interference in the market, provides the basis for increased economic welfare, greater equity and, as a welcome consequence, the potential for greater environmental protection. Environmental values and costs will be internalised and major economic players will be encouraged, through competition and market-based mechanisms, to act in a more environmentally sustainable and sound manner. The problem of sustainability is here located 'within the context of a global economy of mutually interdependent actors' whereby nature becomes a commodity and in which a properly functioning market will determine the most 'efficient use of resources' (Williams, 1996, p. 53). This is a position which generally 'assumes that the pursuit of market efficiency and free trade can achieve the necessary balance with a minimum of political management' (Devlin and Yap, 1994, pp. 49–50). Therefore there is no questioning of the assumption that economic growth *per se* is a good thing nor, indeed, that sustainable growth can be pursued within the contemporary international economic order.

In contrast to this general optimism, critical positions raise 'doubts about the compatibility of an increasingly globalised world economy with any notion of global ecological rationality . . . [giving] rise to an emerging radical ecological critique of the world economy' (Hurrell, 1995, p. 143). This is a tradition which, as explored in Chapters 7 and 8, challenges the 'predominantly market-liberal assumptions that characterise Northern policies and attitudes' (Hurrell, 1995, p. 144). In this critical view, the framework and assumptions of the existing global economy are implicated in the causes of environmental degradation in the way that they 'intensify environmental degradation' (Hurrell, 1995, p. 144). As Caroline Thomas states bluntly, the 'causes of environmental degradation are fundamentally rooted in the processes of globalisation' (1993, p. 3). Globalisation of the liberal world economy thus comes to be characterised not as the basis for overcoming the environmental crisis but as extractive of 'resources from the natural world and local communities', destructive of 'communities and environments', complicitous in 'world wide impoverishment and a growing polarisation between rich and poor' and undermining of true participatory democracy (see Anon., 1993a, pp. xi–xiii).

This is so *precisely* because of the continuing emphasis on resource-intensive growth and trade, the maintenance of debt and global inequities, and the powerful and central role played by global corporate and business interests. Rather than providing the basis for global economic growth and increased welfare, this globalisation of industrialism which has become a defining feature of the contemporary economic order has enabled major centres to draw on the ecological capital of other countries (see MacNeill *et al.*, 1991, pp. 58–61) and, through the processes of 'global trading and direct investment', to export pollution directly and indirectly (see Maull 1992). The very institutions which are advantaged by a globalised world economy – multinational corporations and the multinational development banks – are those which continue to pose 'major environmental threats' (see Shiva, 1993, p. 149).

Differences over the capacity of the practices and values of the contemporary world to address the causes of environmental degradation also engenders, at minimum, some ambivalence about the value of existing international state-centric institutions. The crisis of state legitimacy and capacity has been explored in Chapter 4. In a globalised world, the state is under siege territorially from environmental degradation and institutionally from the forces of globalisation, especially the globalised world economy. As Linklater argues, 'globalisation has seriously reduced [states'] scope for independent action' (1995, p. 250). The state is also under challenge because it is increasingly unable to fulfil the social contract to provide citizens with security: its normative appeal is, as Hurrell (1994, p. 147) notes, diminishing. Thus we have a process of deterritorialisation: the territorial integrity of the state is increasingly precarious and vulnerable to a range of challenges, including environmental ones, and the normative appeal of the state as the primary referent for identity is weakened. Yet, as Mische (1989) argues, if international environmental agreements are to be implemented and if environmental commitments are to be put into practice, then the paradox is that a strong state may be required. Saurin further elaborates the paradox of the state when, drawing on Raymond Williams, he observes that 'contemporary states are too large to deal with the local problems of modern life and too small to deal with the global problems of modernity' (1996, p. 92).

Despite concerns about the adequacy and capacity of the state (and the state-system), a general reformist optimism claims that the increase in multilateral environmental agreements and international institutions and the development of a web of environmental norms, including sustainable development, is evidence that governance based on the state as the major legitimate site of policy-making, while not perfect, is working reasonably well. This problem-solving emphasis on efficiency and effectiveness also engenders, as Chapter 6 suggested, a commitment to pluralism and the participation of a range of stakeholders. There can be little doubt that this is a precondition for addressing environmental concerns. Yet a reformist emphasis on democratic efficiency tends still to focus on elite dynamics and, as Marc Williams notes, has 'tended to have little to say about non-elite social movements' (1996, p. 51). Advocating participation as a strategy in the problem-solving tradition reveals little about the power relationships which determine the extent or nature of that participation. Its assumptions about democratic outcomes are open to question.

From a critical perspective the pluralism of reformist approaches and the commitment to international institutions based on cooperative sovereignty establishes and reinforces political processes which represent the privileged interests of the few rather than the democratic interests of the many. International institutions and the processes of environmental governance are not, in this view, democratised despite the participation (some would suggest the incorporation) of NGOs. Rather environmental governance continues, from this critical perspective, to 'represent a coalition of the rich and powerful political regimes, their corporations and their military establishments' (Aigbokhan, 1993, p. 32). As earlier chapters have suggested, one of the consequences of the commitment to state-centric institutions, regardless of demands for reform, has been to move the debate about solutions to the environmental crisis, and the implementation of those solutions, out of the hands of those who are most directly affected. What exists, according to Shiva, is not a 'democratic distillation of all local and national concerns worldwide but the imposition of a narrow group of interests from a handful of nations on a world scale' (1993, p. 154), a condition Sachs calls the 'hegemony of globalism' (1993b, p. 17) and which Fischer and Black argue 'inherently privilege[s] the view of elite industrialists' (1995a, p. xvi).

A reformist or problem-solving emphasis on this particular form of global governance also ensures that environmental concerns which do not meet the privileged criteria of global are excluded from the arena of responsibility of the world community of states, thereby narrowing rather than expanding the global environmental agenda. Yet, to paraphrase Conca and Lipschutz (1993, p. 3), there are multiple meanings of the global. Local concerns may be global in that they occur in many parts of the world (that is, global issues may be a cluster of local issues) but they have not been defined as *international* because they have been excluded from the definition of transboundary or multilateral collective action problems. As Lipschutz and Conca point out, 'phenomena such as soil erosion and land degradation that are depicted as "local" – and thus relegated to a lesser sense of urgency – are . . . linked by economic, political and social institutions of much broader, and often global, extent' (1993b, p. 331). Some environmental problems, Sachs suggests, also become more global than others in terms of whose interests dominate: did Senegalese peasants, he asks, 'ever pretend to have a say in Europe's energy consumption, or did the people of Amazonia ever rush to North America to protect the forests in Canada and the North-West Pacific' (1993a, p. xvii). The 'global', then, is not simply a geographic term appropriated to describe increasing environmental interdependence, as it is most often used in the reformist tradition. Rather it is a political term and one which, according to scholars such as Shiva (1993, p. 154), provides the North with a new political space in which to control the South, thus creating the moral base for green imperialism.

Reformist traditions tend also to be characterised by a growing confidence in scientific knowledge as an essential basis for action, one which accepts explicitly or implicitly, that 'increased scientific understanding of environmental problems will . . . facilitate international cooperation' (Hurrell, 1995, p. 134). Critical scholars, while recognising the imperatives for agreement, cooperation and the growth of knowledge, are cautious about an unbridled commitment to and belief in technology and science as the solution to the environmental crisis. This wariness arises, first, from concern about the impact of science and technology which has, Sachs argues, 'successfully transform[ed] nature on a vast scale, but so far, with unpleasant as well as unpredictable consequences' (1993b, p. 20). It arises also because of a perception that the 'ascendant ideology of global environmental management' which characterises this position is not value-free but reproduces the 'values and interests of existing international institutions and their most powerful members' (Doran, 1995, p. 193).

Critical scholars are concerned that this reformist faith in science and technology as the basis for environmental progress has also closed any 'serious consideration of alternatives' (Torgerson, 1995, p. 16). In particular, it marginalises and disenfranchises 'diverse and competent communities of knowledge which embrace numerous ways of understanding, perceiving, experiencing and defining reality, including relations between people and people and their environment' (Doran, 1995, p. 201). Attempts to incorporate indigenous knowledge and indigenous communities, or declarations that women have a vital role to play in environmental management, are viewed therefore with some concern, perceived not as democratisation but as examples of the mining of competing knowledge systems as and when necessary and appropriate in order to shore up the central reformist paradigm.

Future Conditional?

For some, the twenty-first century is a turning point and we must now be certain that we make the right choice. For others, the problem is no longer one of deciding which way to turn: rather we have *lost* our direction. Lynton Caldwell suggests that we are in an 'historical discontinuity . . . wandering between the modern world of the past half-millennium and a different world if civilisation and perhaps humanity is to survive' (1990, p. xiii). Wolfgang Sachs characterises this as a 'civilisational impasse' (1991, p. 257) and Jerry Sanders acknowledges only that we are 'slouching towards a new world order' (1990, p. 399).

The problems are, at one level, clear. This book has identified the difficulties of securing effective environmental protection in a decentralised world of sovereign states, while also pointing out problems with increasing centralisation of environmental governance. It has drawn attention to the gap between statements of principle and rhetoric, on the one hand, and political and financial commitments on the other. It has teased out the ways in which global environmental degradation is embedded in the global political economy and explored, therefore, the imperatives for reform (at minimum) and, perhaps, a radical reorienting of the international economic order. It has suggested, as have many before, that the hopes ignited at Rio remain largely unfulfilled.

There is no shortage of general prescriptions for an environmentally secure future. Shiva calls for a 'new global order for environmental care' (1993, p. 155). Caldwell (1990) demands a new planetary paradigm. Cropper seeks a 'new vision of the future' (1992, p. 316). Ernst von Weizsäcker, a member of the Club of Rome, suggests that 'we need to enter and to create a new era of human history' (1994, p. 5). The new century, he argues, should be a 'Century of the Environment' and will need a 'compelling new vision' (1994, p. 176). Lester Brown, from the WorldWatch Institute, argues that we need nothing short of an environmental revolution to rival the agricultural and industrial revolutions in scope as 'one of the greatest economic and social transformations of human history' (1992, p. 174). Even Gro Harlem Brundtland, in a speech in 1990, urged that a 'new environmental ethic must enter our consciousness' (cited in Starke, 1990, p. 157).

Yet, as suggested throughout this book, there is a considerable divergence between the kinds of strategies advocated by those who look to a better and more effective functioning of the contemporary world order to provide solutions to the environmental crisis and those who argue that the contemporary world order is not only inappropriate for reversing ecological decline but is, in the long run, antithetical to that purpose. Can we address, halt and reverse global environmental degradation and its social and economic impacts through, as Torgerson asks, better 'policy planning or management' or does it require a 'process of basic social change' (1995, p. 3)?

These issues of political practice and appropriate strategies illuminate differences between reformist and critical positions over the question of agency. At the risk of simplifying the intellectual debates over agency (which are themselves beyond the scope of this text), the reformist or problem-solving approaches explored in earlier chapters tend to look to the collective actions of individuals as the basis for solutions to the environmental crisis on the grounds that it is human action (whether individual, collective or corporate) that is at the root of the environmental crisis. For critical scholars, this is rather too simple and rather too easy. Saurin argues, for example, that environmental change is not so much just the outcome of human agency, whether deliberative or otherwise, but the 'cumulative or systematic consequences of a set of structured practices and processes' (1996, p. 85), which for Saurin at least are further embedded in capitalism. Therefore, in this view, simply changing human behaviour is inadequate as a solution to the environmental crisis if those 'structured practices and processes' remain. It becomes, to borrow a much-used phrase, a necessary but not sufficient condition for overcoming environmental insecurity.

Critical approaches call, implicitly and sometimes explicitly, for a 'fundamentally different approach' (Thomas, 1993, p. 2) to political practice. If the critical position that the causes of the environmental crisis are to be found in the structures of the contemporary world order is right, then 'unless these structures are overturned, sustainable development will remain an aspiration rather than a practical goal' (Williams, 1996, p. 55). Paterson argues that what is required is a challenge to 'prevailing power relationships, between states, within states, within capitalist economies and within patriarchal forms of power' (1995, p. 212).

What is common to these alternative paths is an emphasis on humane governance, globalisation from below (rather than a globalisation characterised by further centralisation of power and authority) and a reclaiming of the local and of different ways of knowing and understanding. A major theme of this critical tradition has been the 'empowerment of both individuals and communities, combined with a strong emphasis on decentralised forms of political organisation' (Hurrell, 1994, p. 158). There is a fundamental concern with equity and social justice, and for ecological values to inform decision-making, issues which have been explored in earlier chapters in this text. As a minimum requirement, the imperatives of a truly participatory democracy and the empowerment of those who are presently disempowered cannot be gainsaid on either environmental or human rights grounds. In this sense, rather than simply questions of strategy and efficiency, the debate about solutions to the problems of global environmental change becomes one of 'informed ethics and morality' (Caldwell, 1990, p. xiii).

This would involve a stronger recognition of ecological responsibility, environmental stewardship, an emphasis on welfare and human rather than state security, equity and respect for the diversity of cultures and traditions. The values and institutions of governance need to recognise ecological interdependence as the force which shapes political and economic interdependence. In the face of concerns about continuing and possibly worsening environmental degradation, many look to a reclaiming of 'people-centred and ecologically mindful' development as a 'better approach to . . . human and global survival' (Asian and Pacific Women's Resource Collection Network, 1992, p. 10). Demands for radical transformation are accompanied by hopes for a 'return to small-scale technologies, decentralised bioregions and participatory democracy' (Fischer and Black, 1995a, p. xiv). Shiva argues that the reversal of ecological decline will only be achieved with a strengthening of local rights, including the right to information and prior consent along with recognition of the rights of non-human nature (1993, pp. 155–6). A new global order for environmental care would see local communities equipped with rights and obligations, rather than the current trend which is to move rights further upwards to centralised agencies (such as the World Bank) in which local concerns are rarely heard. In this view, the global must accede to the local, and must be informed by the right to information and the right of prior consent. Yet the paradox of the state explored in Chapter 5 and revisited earlier in this chapter is matched, as Chapter 6 hinted, by the paradox of civil society. While some, such as Breyman, argue that 'ecology movements, despite their imperfections, inspire hope for the future' (1993, p. 124), others are cautious about this confidence in civil society and a concommitant decentralisation of governance. Hurrell, for example, questions whether there is a 'degree of romanticisation about the potential capabilities of such movements to define a new pattern of politics' (1995, p. 146).

The prospects for even a reformed, green world order are not looking good on present performance as earlier chapters have suggested. If enthusiasm over the prospects for reform is muted then the prospects for a transformed world order must be even more constrained. It seems clear, as Falk argues, that 'environmental security requires a willingness to make . . . fundamental changes' (1995, p. 169). There is, however, much in the world to make us cautious about any fundamental change in the short term. It is unclear quite how we are to achieve such transformations in a world characterised by continued high levels of military spending, parlous levels of development assistance, continued inequities between rich and poor, centralisation of decision-making and, paradoxically, the crisis of the capacity of the state in the absence, at this stage, of widely accepted decentralised sites of decision-making and implementation.

The agenda of global environmental politics is likely to continue much as it has since Rio (indeed, since Stockholm). On the one hand the emphasis on sectoral issues will ensure continued debate and discussion on particular environmental problems, the status of scientific knowledge, the kinds of targets that should be established and how best to ensure implementation of those agreements. If past experience is a guide, however, progress on sectoral issues may not keep pace with the environmental problems themselves. This is in large part because of a lack of political will in addressing fundamental *cross*-sectoral concerns – issues of funding and technology transfer, trade, debt, poverty and inequities in wealth, the nature of international environmental institutions and the role of actors such as multinational corporations and non-governmental organisations. Many of those issues were on the agenda at Stockholm in 1972. They were addressed by the World Commission on Environment and Development in 1987 and were on the agenda again in Rio in 1992. At the Stockholm Conference in 1972, one observer suggested that activities there amounted to little more than 'fighting a fire with a thermometer' (in Rowland, 1973, p. 33). It is doubtful whether we can claim to have moved in any significant way to dealing with the fire in the years since, despite the many activities described in this book.

At the end of the United Nations Conference on Environment and Development in 1992, the then United Nations Secretary-General Boutros Boutros-Ghali reminded, indeed cautioned his audience, that 'one day we will have to do better' (cited in Brenton, 1994, p. 231). We would do well to heed his words.

Further Reading

The growing interest in global environmental issues among political scientists and international relations scholars has been reflected in a developing corpus of literature. Many of those works are cited in various chapters of this book and are listed in the bibliography. This guide to further reading is therefore brief, suggesting only some *starting* points for those who want to delve more deeply into some of the issues which have been covered in this book. There is still a bias in the literature towards edited texts (some of which are uneven in content) rather than single-authored works although that is changing. Some of the issue-specific texts are mentioned below. Good general surveys would include Thomas (1992b) (although it is now a little dated and lacks both an index and the critical analysis of some of the author's more recent work), Brenton (1994) and Porter and Brown (1996).

Keeping up-to-date on environmental issues is time-consuming, which is why the Internet has become such a boon to researchers. One of the best journals for information, although less so for analysis, is *Environmental Policy and Law*. The journal *Environment* provides a useful balance of commentary and analysis, as does *Global Environmental Change: human and policy dimensions* but probably one of the best analytical journals with a disciplinary focus is *Environmental Politics*. For a more radical or critical perspective on environmental issues, *The Ecologist* is worth exploring.

1 From Stockholm to Rio

Little has been written on the politics of the Stockholm Conference. Rowland (1973) provides a readable and what was then a contemporary commentary although for a briefer (and more recent) analysis, see Brenton (1994, pp. 35–50). The UNCED conference, on the other hand, has generated a flurry of publishing activity. Halpern (1992), Johnston (1993) and Grubb *et al.* (1993) are worth consulting on the detail and, in some respects, the analysis of the conference. Chatterjee and Finger (1994) offer a more critical approach to UNCED and its achievements (or lack thereof). Campiglio *et al.* (1994) covers UNCED and the post-Rio agenda.

2 The Transboundary Agenda: Conservation and Pollution

Some of the introductory texts on these issues are now a little dated and there seems to have been less attention paid to many of these issues in contemporary writing, in favour of environmental concerns with a more global focus. Haas *et al.* (1993) contains a number of chapters on the transboundary agenda, including Levy (1993) on long-range air pollution, Mitchell (1993) on oceans pollution and Peterson (1993) on fisheries. The collection edited by

Carroll (1988) contains several chapters each on acid rain and marine pollution. Kummer (1995) explores hazardous waste issues. Burke (1994) provides a good grounding for understanding recent debates over fisheries resources.

3 The Emergence of a Global Agenda

One of the difficulties with literature on the global agenda – in particular the 'big five' which are addressed in this chapter – is the time-lag between the events and the publication of commentaries. While there are many detailed articles on specific meetings, it is only recently that one finds more comprehensive analysis of the international politics of particular environmental issues. Benedick (1991) is of interest on the ozone negotiations, given his 'insider' status as head of the US delegation. Litfin (1994) and Rowlands (1995a) both tackle the ozone issue in the context of broader theoretical questions related to global politics concerns and Paterson (1996b) does likewise with respect to climate change. Rowlands (1995a) is helpful also on the climate change issue although one of the most interesting texts here is Mintzer and Leonard (1994a) which views the climate negotiations from a range of participant perspectives. Humphreys (1996b) is helpful on international cooperation on forests and McConnell (1996) provides a negotiating history of the Biodiversity Convention from the perspective of someone closely involved with those negotiations.

4 The State and Global Institutions

The whole issue of environmental governance is so broad that almost all books on global environmental issues, and a goodly number of articles as well, touch on this at some stage. The problem of the inadequate state is well covered in Hurrell (1994). Susskind (1994) provides the best treatment of the difficulties of environmental diplomacy (and offers solutions as well). While the history of international environmental law can be found in any number of international law texts, Birnie (1992) provides a short but readable (and fairly orthodox) introduction for the lay-person. Weiss (1988) is probably still the seminal work on intergenerational equity. O'Riordan and Cameron (1994) focus on the precautionary principle. Aaron Sachs (1996) succinctly explores the issue of human rights and environmental justice. While most of the chapters in Haas *et al.* (1993) are specific to particular environmental problems, the overall theme is one which attempts to tease out questions about what effective international environmental institutions might look like. Other texts include Young (1994) and Werksman (1996b). The critical perspective on debates about global governance and international institutions, including the UN, is explored in the various chapters in Sachs (1993c) and in Chatterjee and Finger (1994). Elliott (1998) provides a concise summary of the main debates. For a more detailed but immensely readable study of contemporary environmental governance in the United Nations, Imber (1994) is probably the best.

5 Non-State Actors: Science, Commerce and Global Civil Society

There is not yet a strong analytical *political* literature on either the scientific community or MNCs. Andresen and Østreng (1989) set out some of the basic issues regarding science and politics. There is now some useful work documenting and analysing the role of non-governmental organisations. Wapner (1996) explores the activism and contribution to global environmental politics of Greenpeace, Friends of the Earth and WorldWide Fund for Nature. Princen and Finger (1994) also explore NGOs in the context of theory and practice.

6 Voices from the Margin: Women and Indigenous Peoples

The issue of women, gender and environmental degradation has most often been dealt with in the broader context of the impact of development on women, particularly in the developing world. For more on the way women are directly and indirectly affected by environmental degradation, see, *inter alia*, Shiva (1989b), Momsen (1991), Jacobson (1992) and Braidotti *et al.* (1994). Seager (1993) is also useful. Tickner (1992) includes a very good chapter on gendered perspectives on ecological security in the context of a feminist investigation of international relations. Much of the book-length work on indigenous peoples and environmental destruction has focused on particular regions of the world or on particular issues such as biodiversity – see, for example, Colchester (1994b). Wilmer (1993) provides a general introduction to indigenous peoples in world politics. See also the Winter 1994 issue of the *Colorado Journal of International Environmental Law and Policy* on indigenous rights and the environment.

7 The International Political Economy of the Environment

Most books on the global politics of the environment examine, at some stage, the International Political Economy (IPE) of the environment. On the relationship between developed and developing countries from a critical perspective, see the chapters in Sachs (1993c). Miller (1995) provides a more conventional interpretation. Shue (1992) and (1993) is good on the ethical and moral aspects of the North–South relationship. The Brundtland Report (WCED, 1987) remains the key work on sustainable development. See de la Court (1990) for a specific critique of the Report or Redclift (1987) for a more general analysis of the concept of sustainable development. Pearce *et al* (1994) examine sustainable development in a Third World context. Daly and Cobb (1994) is also useful.

8 Strategies for Sustainable Development

Much of the literature related to the strategies discussed in this chapter is to be found in journal articles and book chapters (many of which are already cited in this chapter) rather than in full-length works. Little of it as yet engages with political questions. The main exception to this is work on trade and environment: see Esty (1994) for an introduction to these issues. Rich (1994c) also provides a strongly political critique of the World Bank. Jacobs (1990) provides a brief summary of the limitations of price incentives and Roodman (1996) examines the idea of using the market for environmental protection.

9 Environmental Security

As the chapter suggests, there is an extensive journal-based literature which addresses the potential for conflict over particular resources and debates over the usefulness of the term environmental security. Two useful edited collections which cover reformist and critical positions on the environmental security issue are Käkönen (1992 and 1994). Dalby (1994) provides a good coverage of the debates about the politics of environmental security. Westing (1988) examines the relationship between the conduct of war and environmental degradation. See also Plant (1992) on the elaboration of international law to protect the environment from the impact of warfare.

10 The Global Politics of the Environment

There is now a growing literature which locates the environmental agenda within particular disciplinary debates. Doran (1995) and Vogler and Imber (1996) – the latter an edited collection – are particularly useful on International Relations and the environment. Another edited collection – Lipschutz and Conca (1993a) – focuses on the state and social power in global environmental politics. Benton and Redclift (1994) cover social theory more generally. These issues are also examined in Fischer and Black (1995b) and, particularly, Torgerson (1995) in that collection.

Bibliography

Abate, Dejen and Shahid Akhtar (1994) 'Information and knowledge inputs: combatting desertification in Africa and transboundary air pollution in Europe', *Environmental Policy and Law*, vol. 24, no. 2/3, June, pp. 71–84.

Agarwal, Anil and Sunita Narain (1991) *Global Warming in an Unequal World: a case of environmental colonialism* (New Delhi: Centre for Science and Environment).

Aigbokhan, Ben E. (1993) 'Peaceful, people-centred and ecologically sensitive development' in Jeremy Brecher, John Brown Childs and Jill Cutler (eds), *Global Visions: beyond the New World Order* (Boston: SouthEnd Press).

Åkerman, Nordal (ed.) (1990) *Maintaining a Satisfactory Environment: an agenda for international environmental policy* (Boulder: Westview Press).

Anderson, Kym (1994) 'The entwining of trade and environmental policies', *Agenda*, vol. 1, no. 1, pp. 55–62.

Andresen, Steinar and Willy Østreng (eds) (1989) *International resource management: the role of science and politics* (London: Belhaven Press).

Anon. (1989) 'WWF's 25 steps in conservation progress', *Transnational Associations*, no. 3, pp. 124–7.

Anon. (1991a) 'International environmental law', *Harvard Law Review*, vol. 104, no. 7, May, pp. 1484–639.

Anon. (1991b) 'Just what is conservation?', *Cultural Survival Quarterly*, vol. 15, no. 4, Fall, pp. 20–9.

Anon. (1992a) 'The systemic challenges facing UNCED', *Development*, no. 2, pp. 3–4.

Anon. (1992b) NGO and social movements alternative treaty process, unpublished typescript (Montevideo: NGONET/INGOF).

Anon. (1993a) 'Introduction' in Jeremy Brecher, John Brown Childs and Jill Cutler (eds), *Global Visions: beyond the New World Order* (Boston: South-End Press).

Anon. (1993b) 'Small Island Developing States: Prepcom meets', *Environmental Policy and Law*, vol. 23, no. 1, February, pp. 5–8.

Anon. (1993c) 'Basel Convention: more action?', *Environmental Policy and Law*, vol. 23, no. 1, February, pp. 12–14.

Anon. (1993d) 'Eagerly awaited Commission established', *Environmental Policy and Law*, vol. 23, no. 2, April, pp. 58–60.

Anon. (1993e) 'UNEP: 17th Governing Council', *Environmental Policy and Law*, vol. 23, no. 3/4, June/August, pp. 118–42.

Anon. (1993f) 'Germany faces expensive world war military waste cleanup', *The Canberra Times*, 29 July, p. 9.

Anon. (1994a) 'Small Island Developing States: Prepcom meets', *Environmental Policy and Law*, vol. 24, no. 1, February, pp. 5–8.

Anon. (1994b) 'INC/Desertification: convention proposals discussed', *Environmental Policy and Law*, vol. 24, no. 1, February, pp. 8–12.

Anon. (1994c) 'GEF restructuring: discussions postponed', *Environmental Policy and Law*, vol. 24, no. 2/3, April/June, pp. 57–8.

Anon. (1994d) 'INCD: more than halfway', *Environmental Policy and Law*, vol. 24, no. 2/3, April/June, pp. 60–4.

Anon. (1994e) 'Ozone layer: budgets approved', *Environmental Policy and Law*, vol. 24, no. 2/3, April/June, pp. 67–8.

Anon. (1994f) 'ITTA successor agreement', *Environmental Policy and Law*, vol. 24, no. 2/3, April/June, p. 69.

Anon. (1994g) 'Intersessional ad hoc working groups', *Environmental Policy and Law*, vol. 24, no. 2/3, April/June, pp. 148–50.

Anon. (1994h) 'Chainsaw massacres', *The Economist*, 25 June, p. 29.

Anon. (1994i) 'Export of hazardous wastes', *Environmental Policy and Law*, vol. 23, no. 4, pp. 147–8.

Anon. (1994j) 'Sustainable development and international law', *Environmental Policy and Law*, vol. 24, no. 5, September, pp. 218–25.

Anon. (1994k) 'Small island developing states: programme of action adopted', *Environmental Policy and Law*, vol. 24, no. 5, September, pp. 226–9.

Anon. (1994l) 'Desertification convention finalised', *Environmental Policy and Law*, vol. 24, no. 5, September, pp. 229–30.

Anon. (1994m) 'Sulphur Protocol adopted', *Environmental Policy and Law*, vol. 24, no. 5, September, p. 231.

Anon. (1994n) 'Biodiversity convention ratified', *Environmental Policy and Law*, vol. 24, no. 5, September, p. 265.

Anon. (1994o) 'Intergovernmental working group on global forests: report of first meeting', *Environmental Policy and Law*, vol. 24, no. 5, September, pp. 289–90.

Anon. (1994p) 'International wildlife task force', *Environmental Policy and Law*, vol. 24, no. 6, December, p. 307.

Anon. (1995a) 'Ozone Protocol: sixth meeting of the Parties', *Environmental Policy and Law*, vol. 25, no. 1/2, February/April, pp. 21–3.

Anon. (1995b) 'Biological diversity: first meeting of the Conference of the Parties to the Rio Convention', *Environmental Policy and Law*, vol. 25, no. 1/2, February/April, pp. 38–9.

Anon. (1995c) 'Carbon emissions update', *Climate Change Newsletter*, vol. 7, no. 2, May, pp. 3–4.

Anon. (1995d) 'CITES: 9th Conference of the Parties', *Environmental Policy and Law*, vol. 25, no. 3, Spring [sic], pp. 88–90.

Anon. (1995e) 'Commission on Sustainable Development: third session', *Environmental Policy and Law*, vol. 25, no. 4/5, August/September, pp. 163–77.

Anon. (1995f) 'UNEP: land-based marine pollution', *Environmental Policy and Law*, vol. 25, no. 4/5, August/September, pp. 177–8.

Anon. (1995g) 'UN/GA: fourth Fisheries conference', *Environmental Policy and Law*, vol. 25, no. 4/5, August/September, pp. 178–80.

Anon. (1995h) 'International agreement on fish stocks', *Environmental Policy and Law*, vol. 25, no. 6, November, pp. 294–5.

Anon. (1995i) 'INC/Desertification: preparations for the first COP', *Environmental Policy and Law*, vol. 25, no. 6, November, pp. 295–7.

Anon. (1995j) 'Climate Change Convention: COP1 follow-up to the Berlin Mandate', *Environmental Policy and Law*, vol. 25, no. 6, November, pp. 297–9.

Anon. (1996a) 'UN/CSD: Intergovernmental Panel on Forests', *Environmental Policy and Law*, vol. 26, no. 1, January, pp. 6–8.

Anon. (1996b) 'Rio follow-up: marine environment', *Environmental Policy and Law*, vol. 26, no. 1, January, pp. 11–13.

Anon. (1996c) 'Montreal Protocol: the Vienna meeting', *Environmental Policy and Law*, vol. 26, no. 2/3, May, pp. 66–71.

Anon. (1996d) 'INC/Desertification: eighth session', *Environmental Policy and Law*, vol. 26, no. 2/3, May, pp. 76–8.

Anon. (1996e) 'UN/CSD: one year before the review', *Environmental Policy and Law*, vol. 26, no. 4, June, pp. 138–54.

Anon. (1996f) 'Climate report criticised', *Environmental Policy and Law*, vol. 26, no. 4, June, p. 175.

Arden-Clarke, Charles (1992) 'South-North terms of trade: environmental protection and sustainable development', *International Environmental Affairs*, vol. 4, no. 2, Spring, pp. 122–38.

Arrhenius, Erik and Thomas W. Waltz (1990) *The Greenhouse Effect: Implications for Economic Development* (Washington, DC: The World Bank).

Arts, Bas and Wolfgang Rüdig (1995) 'Negotiating the Berlin Mandate: reflections on the First Conference of Parties to the UN Framework Convention on Climate Change', *Environmental Politics*, vol. 4, no. 3, Autumn, pp. 481–7.

Asian and Pacific NGO Working Group (1993) *Draft Plan of Action: Women, Environment and Development*, Asian and Pacific Symposium of non-governmental organisations of women in development, Philippines, November 1993 (convened by the UN Economic and Social Commission for Asia and the Pacific (ESCAP) and the National Commission on the Role of Filipino Women (NCRFW)).

Asian and Pacific Women's Resource Collection Network (1992) *Environment* (Kuala Lumpur: Asian and Pacific Development Centre).

Bäckstrand, Karin, Annica Kronsell and Peter Söderholm (1996) 'Organisational challenges to sustainable development', *Environmental Politics*, vol. 5, no. 2, Summer, pp. 209–30.

Baker, Betsy (1993) 'Legal protection for the environment in times of armed conflict', *Virginia Journal of International Law*, vol. 33, no. 2, pp. 351–83.

Ball, Nicole *et al.* (1994) 'World military expenditure', *SIPRI Yearbook 1994* (Oxford: Oxford University Press).

Banuri, Tariq (1993) 'The landscape of diplomatic conflicts' in Wolfgang Sachs (ed.), *Global Ecology: a new arena of political conflict* (London: Zed Books).

Barbier, Edward B. (1995) 'Elephant ivory and tropical timber: the role of trade interventions in sustainable management', *Journal of Environment and Development*, vol. 4, no. 2, Summer, pp. 1–32.

Barnaby, Frank (1991) 'The environmental impact of the Gulf War', *The Ecologist*, vol. 21, no. 4, July/August, pp. 166–72.

Barnes, J. (1984) 'Non-governmental organisations: increasing the global perspective', *Marine Policy*, vol. 8, no. 2, April, pp. 171–81.

Beitz, Charles (1979) *Political Theory and International Relations* (Princeton: Princeton University Press).

Benavides, Margarita (1996) 'Amazon indigenous peoples: new challenges for political participation and sustainable development', *Cultural Survival Quarterly*, vol. 20, no. 3, Fall, pp. 50–3.

Benedick, Richard (1991) *Ozone Diplomacy: new directions in safeguarding the planet* (Cambridge, Mass.: Harvard University Press).

Benton, Ted (1994) 'Biology and social theory' in Michael Redclift and Ted Benton (eds), *Social theory and the environment* (New York: Routledge).

Benton, Ted and Michael Redclift (1994) 'Introduction' in Michael Redclift and Ted Benton (eds), *Social theory and the environment* (New York: Routledge).

Bergesen, Helge Ole and Georg Parmann (eds) (1996) *Green Globe Yearbook* (Oxford: Oxford University Press).

Berlin, Kenneth and Jeffrey M. Lang (1993) 'Trade and the environment', *The Washington Quarterly*, vol. 16, no. 4, Autumn, pp. 35–51.

Bilderbeek, Simone (ed.) (1992) *Biodiversity and international law* (Amsterdam: IOS Press).

Biggs, Gonzalo (1994) 'Latin America and the Basel Convention on hazardous wastes', *Colorado Journal of International Environmental Law*, vol. 5, no. 2, Summer, pp. 333–68.

Birnie, Patricia (1992) 'International environmental law: its adequacy for present and future needs' in Andrew Hurrell and Benedict Kingsbury (eds), *The International Politics of the Environment* (Oxford: Clarendon Press).

—— (1993) 'The UN and the environment' in Adam Roberts and Benedict Kingsbury (eds), *United Nations, Divided World* (Oxford: Oxford University Press).

Birnie, Patricia W. and Alan E. Boyle (1992) *International Law and the Environment* (Oxford: Clarendon Press).

Bleicher, Samuel A. (1972) 'An overview of international environmental regulation', *Ecology Law Quarterly*, vol. 2, no. 1, Winter, pp. 1–90.

Boardman, Robert (1990) *Global Regimes and Nation-States: environmental issues in Australian politics* (Ottawa: Carleton University Press).

Bodansky, Daniel (1994) 'Prologue to the Climate Change Convention' in Irving M. Mintzer and J. Amber Leonard (eds), *Negotiating Climate Change: the inside story of the Rio Convention* (Cambridge: Cambridge University Press).

Bosso, Christopher J. (1994) 'After the movement: environmental activism in the 1990s' in Norman J. Vig and Michael E. Kraft (eds), *Environmental policy in the 1990s*, 2nd edn (Washington, DC: CQ Press).

Boulding, Elise (1991) 'States, boundaries and environmental security in global and regional conflicts', *Interdisciplinary Peace Research*, vol. 3, no. 2, October/November, pp. 78–93.

Boutros-Ghali, Boutros (1992) *An Agenda for Peace*, Report of the Secretary General pursuant to the Statement adopted by the Summit Meeting of the Security Council on 31 January 1992, 47th Session, Security Council S/24111; General Assembly A/47/277, 17 June.

Boutros-Ghali, Boutros (1994) *Development and International Economic Co-operation: An Agenda for Development*, Report of the Secretary General, 48th session, A/48/935, 6 May.

Bowman, Michael (1991) 'Global warming and the international protection of wildlife' in Robin Churchill and David Freestone (eds), *International law and Global Climate Change* (London: Graham & Trotman).

Boyle, Alan E. (1994) 'The Convention on Biological Diversity' in Luigi Campiglio *et al.* (eds), *The Environment After Rio: International Law and Economics* (London: Graham & Trotman).

Brack, Duncan (1995) 'Balancing trade and the environment', *International Affairs*, vol. 71, no. 3, July, pp. 497–514.

Bragdon, Susan H. (1992) 'National sovereignty and global environmental responsibility: can the tension be reconciled for the conservation of biological diversity?', *Harvard International Law Journal*, vol. 33, no. 2, Spring, pp. 381–92.

Braidotti, Rosi *et al.* (1994) *Women, the Environment and Sustainable Development: towards a theoretical synthesis* (London: Zed Books).

Brecher, Jeremy, John Brown Childs and Jill Cutler (eds) (1993) *Global Visions: beyond the new world order* (Boston: SouthEnd Press).

Brenton, Tony (1994) *The greening of Machiavelli: the evolution of international environmental politics* (London: Royal Institute of International Affairs/Earthscan).

Breyman, Steve (1993) 'Knowledge as power: ecology movements and global environmental problems' in Ronnie D. Lipschutz and Ken Conca (eds), *The State and Social Power in Global Environmental Politics* (New York: Columbia University Press).

Brock, Lothar (1991) 'Peace through parks: the environment on the peace research agenda', *Journal of Peace Research*, vol. 28, no. 4, November, pp. 407–23.

—— (1992) 'Security through defending the environment: an illusion?' in Elise Boulding (ed.), *New Agendas for Peace Research* (Boulder: Lynne Rienner Publishers).

Brown, Chris (1995) 'The idea of world community' in Ken Booth and Steve Smith (eds), *International Relations theory today* (Oxford: Polity).

Brown, Lester, Christopher Flavin and Sandra Postel (1989) 'Our world at risk', *Habitat*, vol. 17, No 5, October, pp. 9–12.

Brown, Lester R. (1992) 'Launching the environmental revolution' in Lester R. Brown *et al.* (eds), *State of the world 1992* (London: Earthscan).

Brown, Lester R., Hal Kane and Ed Ayres (1993) *Vital Signs 1993: the trends that are shaping our future* (New York: W. W. Norton & Co.).

Brown, Neville (1989a) 'The "greenhouse effect": a global challenge', *The World Today*, vol. 45, no. 4, April, pp. 61–4.

—— (1989b) 'Climate, ecology and international security', *Survival*, vol. XXXI, no. 6, November/December, pp. 519–31.

Brown, Robin (1995) 'Globalisation and the end of the national project' in John MacMillan and Andrew Linklater (eds), *Boundaries in Question: new directions in International Relations* (London: Pinter Publishers).

Brundtland, Gro Harlem (1993) 'The environment, security and development' in *SIPRI Yearbook 1994* (Oxford: Oxford University Press).

Bull, Hedley (1977) *The Anarchical Society: a study of order in world politics* (London: Macmillan).

Burger, Julian (1990) *The Gaia Atlas of First Peoples* (London: Robertson McCarta).

Burke, Tom (1982) 'Friends of the Earth and the conservation of resources' in Peter Willetts (ed.), *Pressure Groups in the Global System: the transnational relations of issue-oriented non-governmental organisations* (London: Frances Pinter).

Burke, William T. (1994) *The New International Fisheries: UNCLOS 1982 and Beyond* (Oxford: Clarendon Press).

Butts, Kent Hughes (ed.) (1994a) *Environmental security: a DOD Partnership for Peace*, Strategic Studies Institute Special Report, US Army War College.

—— (1994b) 'Why the military is good for the environment' in J. Käkönen (ed.), *Green Security or Militarised Environment* (Aldershot UK: Dartmouth Publishing).

Buzan, Barry (1991) 'New patterns of global security in the twenty-first century', *International Affairs*, vol. 67, no. 3, pp. 431–51.

Byers, Bruce (1991) 'Ecoregions, state sovereignty and conflict', *Bulletin of Peace Proposals*, vol. 22, no. 1 pp. 65–76.

Caldwell, Lynton Keith (1990) *Between Two Worlds: science, the environmental movement and policy choice* (Cambridge: Cambridge University Press).

—— (1991) 'International responses to environmental issues', *International Studies Notes*, vol. 16, no. 1, Winter, pp. 3–7.

Cameron, James (1993) 'The GATT and the environment' in Philippe Sands (ed.), *Greening International Law* (London: Earthscan).

Campiglio, Luigi, Laura Pineschi, Domenico Siniscalo, Tullio Treves (eds) (1994) *The Environment after Rio: international law and economics* (London: Graham & Trotman).

Caron, David D. (1991) 'Protection of the stratospheric ozone layer and the structure of international environmental lawmaking', *Hastings International and Comparative Law Review*, vol. 14, no. 4, Summer, pp. 755–79.

Carroll, J. E. (ed.) (1988) *International Environmental Diplomacy* (Cambridge: Cambridge University Press).

Chadwick, Michael J. (1994) 'Foreword' in Irving M. Mintzer and J. Amber Leonard (eds), *Negotiating Climate Change: the inside story of the Rio Convention* (Cambridge: Cambridge University Press).

Chai, Michael (1992) 'The "other indigenous" peoples of Sarawak', *Development*, no. 2, pp. 56–61.

Charnovitz, Steve (1991) 'Exploring the environmental exceptions in GATT article XX', *Journal of World Trade*, vol. 25, no. 5, October, pp. 37–55.

—— (1993) 'Environmental trade measures: multilateral or unilateral', *Environmental Policy and Law*, vol. 23, no. 2/3, June/August, pp. 154–9.

—— (1996) 'Multilateral Environmental Agreements and trade rules', *Environmental Policy and Law*, vol. 26, no. 4, June, pp. 163–9.

Chatterjee, Pratap and Matthias Finger (1994) *The Earth brokers* (London: Routledge).

Childers, Erskine B. (1990) 'The future of the United Nations: the challenges of the 1990s', *Bulletin of Peace Proposals*, vol. 21, no. 2, pp. 143–52.

Churchill, Robin and David Freestone (eds) (1991) *International Law and Global Climate Change* (London: Graham & Trotman).

Cicin-Sain, Biliana and Robert W. Knecht (1993) 'Implications of the Earth Summit for ocean and coastal governance', *Ocean Development and International Law*, vol. 24, no. 4, pp. 323–53.

Clad, James C. (1988) 'Conservation and indigenous peoples: a study of convergent interests' in J. Bodley (ed.), *Tribal Peoples and Development* (Mountain View: Mayfield Publishing).

Clapp, Jennifer (1994) 'The toxic waste trade with less-industrialised countries: economic linkages and political alliances', *Third World Quarterly*, vol. 15, no. 3, September, pp. 505–18.

Colchester, Marcus (1988) 'The global threat to tribal peoples: strategies for survival' in Asia-Pacific Peoples Environmental Network (ed.), *Global Development and Environment Crisis: has humankind a future?* (Penang: Sahabat Alam Malaysia).

—— (1989) 'Indian development in Amazonia: risk and strategies', *The Ecologist*, vol. 19, no. 6, November/December, pp. 249–54.

—— (1990) 'The International Tropical Timber Organisation: kill or cure for the rainforests?', *The Ecologist*, vol. 20, no. 5, September/October, pp. 166–73.

—— (1994a) 'The new sultans: Asian loggers move in on Guyana's forests', *The Ecologist*, vol. 24, no. 2, March/April, pp. 45–52.

—— (1994b) *Salvaging Nature: indigenous peoples, protected areas and biodiversity conservation* (Geneva: UN Research Institute for Social Development).

Committee for International Environmental Programs (1972) *Institutional Arrangements for International Environmental Cooperation: a report to the Department of State* (Washington DC: National Academy of Sciences).

Commonwealth of Australia, Department of Foreign Affairs and Trade (1995) *The Relationship Between the Provisions of the Multilateral Trading System and Trade Measures Pursuant to Multilateral Environmental Agreements: a discussion paper*, prepared by the GATT Projects Section, Multilateral Trade Organisations Branch, Trade Negotiations and Organisations Division, 3 February 1995.

Commonwealth of Australia, Office of the Chief Scientist (1995) *Australia's Ocean Age: science and technology for managing our ocean territory* (Canberra: Australian Government Publishing Service/Prime Minister's Science and Engineering Council).

Conca, Ken (1994a) 'Peace, justice and sustainability', *Peace Review*, vol. 6, no. 3, Fall, pp. 325–31.

—— (1994b) 'Rethinking the ecology–sovereignty debate', *Millennium*, vol. 23, no. 3, Winter, pp. 701–11.

—— (1995) 'Greening the United Nations: environmental organisations and the UN system', *Third World Quarterly*, vol. 16, no. 3, September, pp. 441–57.

Conca, Ken and Ronnie D. Lipschutz (1993) 'A tale of two forests' in Ronnie D. Lipschtuz and Ken Conca (eds), *The State and Social Power in Global Environmental Politics* (New York: Columbia University Press).

Conca, Ken, Michael Alberty and Geoffrey D. Dabelko (eds) (1995) *Green Planet Blues: environmental politics from Stockholm to Rio* (Boulder: Westview Press).

Convention to Combat Desertification (1996) *Down to Earth – CCD Newsletter*, no. 2, August (http://www.unep.ch/incd/bull2–96.html).

Coordinating Body for the Indigenous Peoples Organisation of the Amazon Basin (COICA) (n.d.) '[A letter] To the Community of Concerned Environmentalists' [reproduced in] Ken Conca, Michael Alberty and Geoffrey D. Dabelko (eds) (1995) *Green Planet Blues: environmental politics from Stockholm to Rio* (Boulder: Westview Press).

—— (1991) 'Statement to the XIth session of the International Tropical Timber Council', *ECO*, Issue 1, Article 3 (http://bioc09.uthscsa.edu/natnet/archive/nl/9202/0161.html).

Corry, Stephen (1993) 'The rainforest harvest: who reaps the benefits?', *The Ecologist*, vol. 23, no. 4, July/August, pp. 148–53.

Cox, Robert W. (1986) 'Social forces, states and world orders: beyond International Relations theory' in Robert O. Keohane (ed.), *NeoRealism and its Critics* (New York: Columbia University Press).

Cropper, Angela (1992) 'Unsaid '92', *Review of European Community and International Environmental Law*, vol. 1, no. 3, pp. 314–16.

Dalby, Simon (1994) 'The politics of environmental security' in Jyrki Käkönen (ed.), *Green Security or Militarised Environment* (Aldershot, UK: Dartmouth Publishing).

Daly, Herman E. and John B. Cobb Jr (1994) *For the Common Good: redirecting the economy toward community, the environment and a sustainable future,* 2nd edition (Boston: Beacon Press).

D'Amato, Anthony (1990) 'Do we owe a duty to future generations to preserve the global environment?', *American Journal of International Law*, vol. 84, no. 1, January, pp. 190–8.

Dankelman, Irene and Joan Davidson (1988) *Women and the environment in the Third World: alliance for the future* (London: Earthscan).

Davis, Shelton H. (ed.) (1993a) *Indigenous Views of Land and the Environment*, World Bank Discussion Paper no. 188 (Washington, DC: The World Bank).

—— (1993b) 'Introduction' in Shelton H. Davis (ed.), *Indigenous Views of Land and the Environment*, World Bank Discussion Paper no. 188 (Washington, DC: The World Bank).

Davison, Aidan and Ian Barns (1992) 'The Earth Summit and the ethics of sustainable development', *Current Affairs Bulletin*, vol. 69, no. 1, June, pp. 4–12.

de la Court, Thijs (1990) *Beyond Brundtland: green development in the 1990s* (London: Zed Books).

Deudney, Daniel (1990) 'The case against linking environmental degradation and national security', *Millennium*, vol. 19, no. 3, Winter, pp. 461–76.

Devlin, John F. and Nonita T. Yap (1993) 'Structural adjustment programmes and the UNCED agenda: explaining the contradictions', *Environmental Politics*, vol. 2, no. 4, Winter, pp. 65–79.

Devlin, John F. and Nonita T. Yap (1994) 'Sustainable development and the NICs: cautionary tales for the South in the New World (Dis)Order', *Third World Quarterly*, vol. 15, no. 1, pp. 49–62.

Diaz, Ayesha (1994) 'Permanent sovereignty over national resources', *Environmental Policy and Law*, vol. 24, no. 4, June, pp. 157–73.

Dobson, Andrew (1990) *Green Political Thought* (London: Harper Collins Academic).

Doran, Peter (1995) 'Earth, power, knowledge: towards a critical environmental politics' in John MacMillan and Andrew Linklater (eds), *Boundaries in Question: new directions in International Relations* (London: Pinter Publishers).

—— (1996) 'The UN Commission on Sustainable Development, 1995', *Environmental Politics*, vol. 5, no. 1, Spring, pp. 100–7.

Drucker, Merrit P. (1989) 'The military commander's responsibility for the environment', *Environmental Ethics*, vol. 11, no. 2, Summer, pp. 135–52.

Durning, Alan B. (1989) 'Mobilising at the grassroots' in Lester R. Brown *et al.* (eds), *State of the World 1989* (New York: W.W. Norton & Co).

Dyer, Hugh C. (1993) 'EcoCultures: global culture in the Age of Ecology', *Millennium*, vol. 22, no. 3, pp. 483–504.

—— (1996) 'Environmental security as a universal value: implications for international theory' in John Vogler and Mark F. Imber (eds), *The Environment and International Relations* (London: Routledge).

Eckersley, Robyn (1992) *Environmentalism and Political Theory: towards an ecocentric approach* (London: UCL Press).

Ehrlich, Paul (1968) *The Population Bomb* (New York: Ballantine Books).

Ekins, Paul (1992) *A New World Order: grassroots movements for global change* (London: Routledge).

—— (1993) 'Making development sustainable' in Wolfgang Sachs (ed.), *Global Ecology: a new era of political conflict* (London: Zed Books).

Elliott, Lorraine M. (1994) *International Environmental Politics: protecting the Antarctic* (London: Macmillan).

—— (1996a) 'Environmental conflict: reviewing the arguments', *Journal of Environment and Development*, vol. 5, no. 2, June, pp. 149–67.

—— (1996b) 'Women, gender, feminism and the environment' in Jennifer Turpin and Lois Ann Lorentzen (eds), *The Gendered New World Order: militarism, development and the environment* (New York: Routledge).

—— (1998) 'Greening the United Nations: future conditional?' in A. Paolini, A. Jervis, C. Reus-Smit (eds) (in press), *Between Sovereignty and Global Governance: the United Nations, the state and civil society* (London: Macmillan).

El-Ashry, Mohamed T. (1993) 'Development assistance institutions and sustainable development', *The Washington Quarterly*, vol. 16, no. 2, Spring, pp. 83–95.

Esteva, Gustavo and Madhu Suri Prakash (1994) 'From global to local thinking', *The Ecologist*, vol. 24, no. 5, September/October, pp. 162–3.

Esty, Daniel C. (1993) 'GATTing the Greens not just greening the GATT', *Foreign Affairs*, vol. 72, no. 5, November/December, pp. 32–6.

—— (1994) *Greening the GATT: trade, environment and the future* (Washington, DC: Institute for International Economics).

Evans, Senator Gareth (1994) *Reintegrating the United Nations*, Statement to the 49th General Assembly of the United Nations, 3 October.

Fairclough, A. J. (1991) 'Global environmental and natural resource problems – their economic, political and security implications', *The Washington Quarterly*, vol. 14, no. 1, Winter, pp. 81–98.

Fairman, David (1994) 'Report of the Independent Evaluation of the GEF Pilot Phase', *Environment*, vol. 36, no. 6, July/August, pp. 25–30.

Falk, Richard (1972) *This Endangered Planet: prospects and proposals for human survival* (New York: Random House).

—— (1992) *Explorations at the Edge of Time: the prospects for world order* (Philadelphia: Temple University Press).

—— (1995) *On Humane Governance: toward a new global politics* (Cambridge: Polity Press).

Favre, David (1993) 'Debate within the CITES community: what direction for the future?', *Natural Resources Journal*, vol. 33, no. 4, Fall, pp. 875–918.

Finger, Matthias (1991a) *Unintended Consequences of the Cold War: global environmental degradation and the military*, Occasional Paper No. 10 (Syracuse, NY: Programe on the Analysis and Resolution of Conflict, Maxwell School of Citizenship and Public Affairs, Syracuse University).

—— (1991b) 'The military, the nation-state and the environment', *The Ecologist*, vol. 21, no. 5, September/October, pp. 220–5.

—— (1992) 'New horizons for peace research: the global environment' in Jyrki Käkönen (ed.), *Perspectives on environmental conflict and international relations* (London: Pinter).

—— (1993) 'Politics of the UNCED process' in Wolfgang Sachs (ed.), *Global ecology: a new arena of political conflict* (London: Zed Books).

—— (1994a) 'NGOs and transformation: beyond social movement theory' in Thomas Princen and Matthias Finger (eds), *Environmental NGOs in world politics: linking the local and the global* (London: Routledge).

—— (1994b) 'Environmental NGOs in the UNCED process' in Thomas Princen and Matthias Finger (eds), *Environmental NGOs in world politics: linking the local and the global* (London: Routledge).

Fischer, Frank and Michael Black (1995a) 'Introduction' in Frank Fischer and Michael Black (eds), *Greening Environmental Policy: the politics of a sustainable future* (New York: St Martin's Press).

Fischer, Frank and Michael Black (eds) (1995b) *Greening Environmental Policy: the politics of a sustainable future* (New York: St Martin's Press).

Fletcher, Susan R. (1992) *Earth Summit Summary: United Nations Conference on Environment and Development (UNCED), Brazil 1992*, Congressional Research Service Report 92–347 ENR (Washington, DC: The Library of Congress).

Foundation for International Environmental Law and Development (FIELD) (1993) *Foundation for International Environmental Law and Development* [information booklet] (London: FIELD).

Freestone, David (1991) 'International law and sea level rise' in Robin Churchill and David Freestone (eds), *International Law and Global Climate Change* (London: Graham & Trotman).

French, Hilary F. (1992) 'Strengthening global environmental governance' in Lester R. Brown *et al.* (eds), *State of the World 1992* (London: Earthscan).

Funke, Odelia (1994) 'National security and the environment' in Norman J. Vig and Michael E. Kraft (eds), *Environmental Policy in the 1990s*, 2nd edition (Washington, DC: CQ Press).

Gaines, Sanford E. (1991) 'Taking responsibility for transboundary environmental effects', *Hastings International and Comparative Law Review*, vol. 14, no. 4, Summer, pp. 781–809.

Gardner, Richard N. (1972) 'The role of the UN in environmental problems' in David A. Kay and Eugene B. Skolnikoff (eds), *World Eco-Crisis: international organisations in response* (Madison: University of Wisconsin Press).

Gayoom, H. E. Maumoom Abdul (1995) *A warning from the Small Island States: our fate will be your fate*, Address by the President of the Republic of the Maldives to the Second Municipal Leaders' Summit on Climate Change, Berlin, 27 March.

Gehring, Thomas and Sebastian Oberthür (1993) 'The Copenhagen meeting', *Environmental Policy and Law*, vol. 23, no. 1, February, pp. 6–13.

George, Jim (1994) *Discourses of Global Politics: a critical (re)introduction to International Relations* (Boulder: Lynne Rienner Publishers).

Gerlach, Luther P. (1991) 'Global thinking, local acting: movements to save the planet', *Evaluation Review*, vol. 15, no. 1, February, pp. 120–48.

Gill, Bates (1994) 'Arms acquisition in East Asia' in *SIPRI Yearbook 1994* (Oxford: Oxford University Press).

Gilpin, Robert (1981) *War and Change in World Politics* (Cambridge: Cambridge University Press).

—— (1987) *The Political Economy of International Relations* (Princeton: Princeton University Press).

Gleick, Peter H. (1991) 'Environment and security: the clear connections', *Bulletin of Atomic Scientists*, April, pp. 17–21.

Glover, David (1994) 'Global institutions, international agreements and environmental issues' in Richard Stubbs and Geoffrey R. D. Underhill (eds), *Political Economy and the Changing Global Order* (London: Macmillan).

Glowka, Lyle (1996) 'Convention on Biological Diversity: Second Conference of the Parties', *Environmental Policy and Law*, vol. 26, no. 2/3, May, pp. 71–5.

Godwin, Diana L. (1993) 'The Basel Convention on Transboundary Movements of Hazardous Wastes: an opportunity for industrialised nations to clean up their acts?', *Denver Journal of International Law and Policy*, vol. 22, no. 1, Fall, pp. 193–208.

Goldblat, Jozef (1991) 'Legal protection of the environment against the effects of military activity', *Bulletin of Peace Proposals*, vol. 22, no. 4, pp. 399–406.

Goodland, R. J. A. (1991) 'The World Bank's environmental assessment policy', *Hastings International and Comparative Law Review*, vol. 14, no. 4, Summer, pp. 811–30.

Gore, Al (1993) *Earth in the balance: ecology and the human spirit* (New York: Penguin Books USA Inc.)

Gray, Andrew (1990) 'Indigenous peoples and the marketing of the rainforest', *The Ecologist*, vol. 20, no. 6, November/December, pp. 223–27.

Gray, Denis (1996) 'How Asia's logging companies are stripping the world's forests', *Sydney Morning Herald*, 31 August, p. 20.

Gray, Mark Allan (1990) 'The United Nations Environment Programme: an assessment', *Environmental Law*, vol. 20, no. 2, pp. 291–319.

Greene, Owen (1993) 'International environmental regimes: verification and implementation', *Environmental Politics*, vol. 2, no. 4, Winter, pp. 156–73.

Groom, A. J. R. and Dominic Powell (1994) 'From world politics to global governance: a theme in need of a focus' in A. J. R. Groom and Margot Light (eds), *Contemporary International Relations: a guide to theory* (London: Pinter Publishers).

Grubb, Michael (1990) 'The greenhouse effect: negotiating targets', *International Affairs*, vol. 66, no. 1, January, pp. 67–89.

—— (1995) 'Seeking fair weather: ethics and the international debate on climate change', *International Affairs*, vol. 71, no. 3, July, pp. 463–96.

Grubb, Michael *et al.* (1993) *The Earth Summit Agreements: a guide and assessment* (London: RIIA/Earthscan).

Gudynas, Eduardo (1989) 'The challenge to recover "El Dorado" ', *Transnational Associations*, no. 4, pp. 197–9.

—— (1993) 'The fallacy of Ecomessianism: observations from Latin America' in Wolfgang Sachs (ed.), *Global ecology: a new arena of political conflict* (London: Zed Books).

Gündling, Lothar (1990) 'Our responsibility to future generations', *American Journal of International Law*, vol. 84, no. 1, January, pp. 207–12.

—— (1991) 'Protection of the environment by international law: air pollution' in Winfried Lang, Hanspeter Neuhold and Karl Zemanek (eds), *Environmental protection and international law* (London: Graham & Trotman).

Gupta, Joyeeta (1995) 'The Global Environment Facility in its North–South context', *Environmental Politics*, vol. 4, no. 1, Spring, pp. 19–43.

Haas, Peter M. (1990) 'Obtaining international environmental protection through epistemic consensus', *Millennium*, vol. 19, no. 3, Winter, pp. 347–63.

—— (1993) 'Protecting the Baltic and North Seas' in Peter M. Haas, Robert O. Keohane and Marc A. Levy (eds), *Institutions for the Earth: sources of effective environmental protection* (Cambridge, Mass.: The MIT Press).

—— (1994) 'United Nations Environment Program', *Environment*, vol. 36, no. 6, July/August, pp. 43–5.

Haas, Peter M., Robert O. Keohane and Marc A. Levy (eds) (1993) *Institutions for the Earth: sources of effective environmental protection* (Cambridge, Mass.: The MIT Press).

Haas, P., Marc A. Levy and Edward A. Parson (1992) 'Appraising the Earth Summit: how should we judge UNCED's success?', *Environment*, vol. 34, no. 8, pp. 6–11; 26–33.

Haggard, Stephan and Beth A. Simmons (1987) 'Theories of international regimes', *International Organisation*, vol. 41, no. 3, Summer, pp. 491–517.

Hahn, Robert W. and Kenneth R. Richards (1989) 'The internationalisation of environmental regulation', *Harvard International Law Journal*, vol. 30, no. 2, Spring, pp. 421–46.

Hall, Charles A. S. (1990) 'Sanctioning resource depletion: economic development and neo-classical economics', *The Ecologist*, vol. 20, no. 3, May/June, pp. 99–104.

Halliday, Fred (1991) 'International Relations: is there a new agenda?', *Millennium*, vol. 20, no. 1, Spring, pp. 57–72.

Halpern, Shanna (1992) *The United Nations Conference on Environment and Development: process and documentation* (Providence, RI: Academic Council on the United Nations System) (http://www.ciesin.org/docs/008–585/unced-home.html).

Hammond, Allen L., Eric Rodenburg and William R. Moomaw (1991) 'Calculating national accountability for climate change', *Environment*, vol. 33, no. 1, pp. 11–15; 33–5.

Hampson, Fen Osler (1989–90) 'Climate change: building international coalitions of the like-minded', *International Journal*, vol. XLV, no. 1, Winter, pp. 36–74.

Handelman, John R., Howard B. Shapiro and John A. Vasquez (1974) *Introductory Case Studies for International Relations: Vietnam/the Middle East/the environmental crisis* (Chicago: Rand McNally).

Hanisch, Ted (1992) 'The Rio Climate Convention: real solutions or political rhetoric?', *Security Dialogue*, vol. 23, no. 4, December, pp. 63–73.

Harbinson, Rod (1992) 'Burma's forests fall victims to war', *The Ecologist*, vol. 22, no. 2, March/April, pp. 72–3.

Hardin, Garrett (1968) 'The tragedy of the commons', *Science*, vol. 162, no. 3859, 13 December, pp. 1243–8.

—— (1974) 'Living on a lifeboat', *BioScience*, vol. 24, no. 10, October, pp. 561–8.

Harris, Paul G. (1994) 'Global equity and sustainable development', *Peace Review*, vol. 6, no. 3, Fall, pp. 267–73.

Harris, Stuart (1991) 'International trade, ecologically sustainable development and the GATT', *Australian Journal of International Affairs*, vol. 45, no. 2, November, pp. 196–212.

Hartshorn, Gary S. (1991) 'Key environmental issues for developing countries', *Journal of International Affairs*, vol. 44, no. 2, Winter, pp. 393–402.

Hawkins, Ann (1993) 'Contested ground: international environmentalism and global climate change' in Ronnie D. Lipschutz and Ken Conca (eds), *The State and social power in global environmental politics* (New York: Columbia University Press).

Hazlewood, Peter T. (1989) 'Expanding the role of non-governmental organisations in national forestry programs', *Transnational Associations*, no. 4, pp. 186–96.

Helman, Udi (1990) 'Environment and the national interest: an analytical survey of the literature', *The Washington Quarterly*, vol. 13, no. 4, Autumn, pp. 193–206.

Helmich, Henny and Shamita Sharma (1992) 'Partnership towards global sustainable development', *Development*, no. 2, pp. 80–1.

Henderson, Ian (1996) 'Bank to ease Third World debt', *The Australian*, 2 October, p. 8.

Hendrickx, Frederic, Veit Koesler and Christian Prip (1993) 'Convention on Biological Diversity – access to genetic resources: a legal analysis', *Environmental Policy and Law*, vol. 23, no. 6, December, pp. 250–8.

Henry, Reg (1996) 'Adapting United Nations agencies for Agenda 21: programme coordination and organisational reform', *Environmental Politics*, vol. 5, no. 1, Spring, pp. 1–24.

Hey, Ellen (1995) 'Increasing accountability for the conservation and sustainable use of biodiversity: an issue of transnational global character', *Colorado Journal of International Environmental Law and Policy*, vol. 6, no. 1, pp. 1–29.

Hildyard, Nicholas (1993) 'Foxes in charge of the chickens' in Wolfgang Sachs (ed.), *Global Ecology: a new arena of political conflict* (London: Zed Books).

Hoffman, Mark (1994) 'Normative international theory: approaches and issues' in A. J. R. Groom and Margot Light (eds), *Contemporary International Relations: a guide to theory* (London: Pinter Publishers).

Hoffmann, Stanley (1981) *Duties Beyond Borders: on the limits and possibilities of ethical international politics* (Syracuse: Syracuse University Press).

Holmberg, Johan (1992a) 'Whither UNCED?', *IIED Perspectives*, no. 8, Spring, pp. 8–9.

—— (1992b) 'Judgement on Rio', *People and the Planet*, vol. 1, no. 3, p. 4.

Holst, Johan Jørgen (1989) 'Security and the environment: a preliminary exploration', *Bulletin of Peace Proposals*, vol. 20, no. 2, June pp. 123–8.

Homer-Dixon, Thomas F. (1991) 'On the threshold: environmental changes as causes of acute conflict', *International Security*, vol. 16, no. 2, Fall, pp. 76–116.

—— (1994) 'Environmental scarcities and violent conflict: evidence from cases', *International Security*, vol. 19, no. 2, Summer, pp. 5–40.

Homer-Dixon, Thomas F., Jeffrey H. Boutwell and George W. Rathjens (1993) 'Environmental change and violent conflict', *Scientific American*, vol. 268, no. 2, February, pp. 38–45.

Hontelez, John (1988) 'Friends of the Earth International: an international movement to fight for environment and a better future for humankind' in Asia-Pacific Peoples' Environmental Network (ed.), *Global Development and Environment Crisis* (Penang: Sahabat Alam Malaysia).

Houghton, J. T., G. J. Jenkins and J. J. Ephraims (eds) (1990) *Climate change: the IPCC scientific assessment*, Final Report of Working Group I, IPCC (Cambridge: Cambridge University Press).

Howard, Kathleen (1990) 'The Basel Convention: control of transboundary movement of hazardous wastes and their disposal', *Hastings International and Comparative Law Review*, vol. 14, no. 1, Fall, pp. 223–46.

Hulme, Mike and Mick Kelly (1993) 'Exploring the links between desertification and climate change', *Environment*, vol. 35, no. 6, July/August, pp. 4–11; 39–45.

Humphreys, David (1996a) 'The global politics of forest conservation since the UNCED', *Environmental Politics*, vol. 5, no. 2, Summer, pp. 231–56.

—— (1996b) *Forest politics: the evolution of international cooperation* (London: Earthscan).

Hurrell, Andrew (1992) 'The 1992 Earth Summit: funding mechanisms and environmental institutions', *Environmental Politics*, vol. 1, no. 4, Winter, pp. 273–79.

—— (1994) 'A crisis of ecological viability? global environmental change and the nation state', *Political Studies*, XLII, pp. 146–65.

—— (1995) 'International political theory and the global environment' in Ken Booth and Steve Smith (eds), *International Relations Theory Today* (Cambridge: Polity Press).

Hurrell, Andrew and Benedict Kingsbury (eds) (1992a) *The International Politics of the Environment* (Oxford: Clarendon Press).

Hurrell, Andrew and Benedict Kingsbury (1992b) 'Introduction' in Andrew Hurrell and Benedict Kingsbury (eds), *The International Politics of the Environment* (Oxford: Clarendon Press).

Ikeda, Daisaku (1992) 'A renaissance of hope and harmony', *Bulletin of Peace Proposals*, vol. 23, no. 2, June, pp. 123–8.

Imber, Mark (1993) 'Too many cooks? the post-Rio reform of the United Nations', *International Affairs*, vol. 69, no. 1, January, pp. 55–70.

—— (1994) *Environment, Security and UN Reform* (London: Macmillan).

Imhof, Aviva (1996) 'World banking', *The Australian*, 15 October, p. 23.

Intergovernmental Panel on Climate Change (1990) *Impacts Assessment of Climate Change: the policy-makers summary of the Report of Working Group II* (Canberra: Australian Government Publishing Service).

Intergovernmental Panel on Climate Change (1995) *IPCC Second Assessment: synthesis of scientific technical information relevant to interpreting article 2 of the UN Framework Convention on Climate Change 1995* (Geneva: UNEP, http://www.unep.ch/ipcc/syntrep.html).

International Institute for Sustainable Devlopment (1993a) 'Desertification and the UN system', *Earth Negotiations Bulletin*, ENB:04:01 (Winnipeg: International Institute for Sustainable Development, http://www.iisd.ca/linkages/vol04/0401018e.html).

—— (1993b) 'A brief history of the Convention on Biological Diversity', *Earth Negotiations Bulletin*, ENB:09:28 (Winnipeg: International Institute for Sustainable Development, http://www.iisd.ca/linkages/vol09/0928002e.html).

—— (1995a) 'Second meeting of the Conference of the Parties to the Convention on Biological Diversity: 6–17 November 1995', *Earth Negotiations Bulletin*, ENB:09:39 (Winnipeg: International Institute for Sustainable Development, http://www.iisd.ca/linkages/vol09/0939000e.html).

—— (1995b) 'A brief analysis of COP-2', *Earth Negotiations Bulletin*, ENB:09:39 (Winnipeg: International Institute for Sustainable Development, http://www.iisd.ca/linkages/vol09/0939011e.html).

—— (1996a) *The Montreal Process* (Winnipeg: International Institute for Sustainable Development, http://www.iisd.ca/linkages/forestry/mont.html).

—— (1996b) *The Helsinki Process* (Winnipeg: International Institute for Sustainable Development, http://www.iisd.ca/linkages/forestry/hel.html).

—— (1996c) *The Malaysian/Canadian Initiative: Intergovernmental Working Group on Forests* (Winnipeg: International Institute for Sustainable Development, http://www.iisd.ca/linkages/forestry/iwgf.html).

—— (1996d) *Global Forest Policy* (Winnipeg: International Institute for Sustainable Development, http://www.iisd.ca/linkages/forestry/forest.html).

—— (1996e) 'Summary of the ninth session of the INC for the Convention to Combat Desertification: 3–13 September 1996', *Earth Negotiations Bulletin*, ENB:04:95 (Winnipeg: International Institute for Sustainable Development, http://www.iisd.ca/linkages/vol04/0495001e.html).

—— (1996f) 'A brief analysis of INCD-9', *Earth Negotiations Bulletin*, ENB:04:95 (Winnipeg: International Institute for Sustainable Development, http://www.iisd.ca/linkages/vol04/0495020e.html).

—— (1996g) 'Third session of the Conference of the Parties to the Convention on Biological Diversity' *Earth Negotiations Bulletin*, ENB:09:65 (Winnipeg: International Institute for Sustainable Development, http://www.iisd.ca/linkages/vol09/0965001e.html).

—— (1996h) 'A brief analysis of COP-3', *Earth Negotiations Bulletin*, ENB:09:65 (Winnipeg: International Institute for Sustainable Development, http://www.iisd.ca/linkages/vol09/0965028e.html).

Jacobs, Michael (1990) *Sustainable Development: greening the economy* (London: The Fabian Society).

—— (1994) 'The limits to neoclassicism: towards an institutional environmental economics' in Michael Redclift and Ted Benton (eds), *Social Theory and the Environment* (New York: Routledge).

Jacobson, Jodi (1992) *Gender Bias: roadblock to sustainable development*, WorldWatch Paper no. 110, (Washington DC: WorldWatch Institute).

Jain, Peeyush (1990) 'Proposal: a pollution added tax to slow ozone depletion and global warming', *Stanford Journal of International Law*, vol. 26, no. 2, Spring, pp. 549–72.

Johnson, Brian (1972) 'The United Nations institutional response to Stockholm: a case study in the international politics of institutional change' in David A. Kay and Eugene B. Skolnikoff (eds), *World Eco-Crisis: international organisations in response* (Madison: University of Wisconsin Press).

Johnson, Stanley P. (1993) *The Earth Summit: the United Nations Conference on Environment and Development (UNCED)* (London: Graham & Trotman).

Johnston, Barbara R. (1994) 'Human rights and the environment', *Practising Anthropology*, vol. 16, no. 1, Winter, pp. 8–12.

Jordan, Andrew (1994a) 'Financing the UNCED agenda: the controversy over additionality', *Environment*, vol. 36, no. 3, April, pp. 16–20; 26–33.

—— (1994b) 'Paying the incremental costs of global environmental protection: the evolving role of the GEF', *Environment*, vol. 36, no. 6, July/August, pp. 12–20; 31–6.

Jowkar, Forouz (1994) 'Women bear the brunt', *Our Planet*, vol. 6, no. 5, pp. 16–17.

Käkönen, Jyrki (ed.) (1992) *Perspectives on Environmental Conflict and International Relations* (London: Pinter Publishers).

—— (ed.) (1994) *Green Security or Militarised Environment* (Aldershot: Dartmouth Publishing).

Kamieniecki, Sheldon (1991) 'Political mobilisation, agenda building and international environmental policy', *Journal of International Affairs*, vol. 44. no. 2, Winter, pp. 339–58.

—— (1993) 'Emerging forces in global environmental politics' in Sheldon Kamieniecki (ed.), *Environmental Politics in the International Arena: movements, parties, organisations and policy* (Albany, NY: State University of New York Press).

Karno, Valerie (1991) 'Protection of endangered gorillas and chimpanzees in international trade: can CITES help?' *Hastings International and Comparative Law Review*, vol. 14, no. 4, pp. 989–1015.

Kay, David A. and Eugene B. Skolnikoff (eds) (1972) *World Eco-Crisis: international organisations in response* (Madison: University of Wisconsin Press).

Kay, David A. and Harold K. Jacobson (1983) *Environmental Protection: the international dimension* (Totowa, NJ: Allenheld, Osmun).

Kelly, P. M. and J. H. W. Karas (1989) 'The greenhouse effect', *Capital and Class*, no. 38, Summer, pp. 17–27.

Kennedy Cuomo, Kerry (1993) 'Human rights and the environment: common ground', *Yale Journal of International Law*, vol. 18, No.1, Winter, pp. 227–33.

Keohane, Robert O. (1989) *International Institutions and State Power* (Boulder: Westview Press).

Keohane, Robert O., Peter M. Haas and Marc A. Levy (1993) 'The effectiveness of international environmental institutions' in Peter M. Haas, Robert O. Keohane and Marc A. Levy (eds), *Institutions for the Earth: sources of effective international environmental protection* (Cambridge, Mass.: The MIT Press).

Keohane, Robert O. and Joseph S. Nye, Jr. (1977) *Power and Interdependence: World Politics in Transition* (Boston: Little Brown & Co).

Khor Kok Peng, Martin (1988) 'The Third World environmental crisis: a Third World perspective' in Asia-Pacific Peoples Environmental Network (ed.), *Global Development and Environment Crisis: has humankind a future?* (Penang: Sahabat Alam Malaysia).

Kildow, Judith T. (1992) 'The Earth Summit: we need more than a message', *Environmental Science and Technology*, vol. 26, no. 6, pp. 1077–8.

King, Ynestra (1983) 'Towards an ecological feminism and a feminist ideology' in Joan Rothschild (ed.), *Machina ex Dea: feminist perspectives on technology* (New York: Pergamon Press).

Kirwin, Joe (1994) 'Rio two years on: a strong reaction', *Our Planet*, vol. 6, no. 2, pp. 24–8.

Kiss, Alexander (1991) 'The international control of transboundary movement of hazardous waste', *Texas International Law Journal*, vol. 26, no. 3, Summer, pp. 521–39.

Kowalok, Michael E. (1993) 'Common threads: research lessons from acid rain, ozone depletion and global warming', *Environment*, vol. 35, no. 6, July/August, pp. 13–20; 35–8.

Krasner, Stephen D. (ed.) (1983a) *International Regimes* (Ithaca: Cornell University Press).

Krasner, Stephen D. (ed.) (1983b) 'Structural causes and regime conse-
quences: regimes as intervening variables' in Stephen D. Krasner (ed.),
International Regimes (Ithaca: Cornell University Press).
—— (1985) *Structural Conflict: the Third World against global liberalism*
(Berkeley: University of California Press).
Kummer, Katharina (1995) *International management of hazardous
wastes: the Basel Convention and related legal rules* (Oxford: Clarendon
Press).
Laferrière, Eric (1996) 'Emancipating International Relations theory:
an ecological perspective', *Millennium*, vol. 25, no. 1, Spring,
pp. 53–75.
Lafferty, William M. (1996) 'The politics of sustainable development: global
norms for national implementation', *Environmental Politics*, vol. 5, no. 2,
Summer, pp. 185–208.
Lallas, Peter L., Daniel C. Esty and Daniel J. van Hoogstraten (1992)
'Environmental protection and international trade: towards mutually
supportive rules and policies', *Harvard Environmental Law Review*,
vol. 16, no. 2, pp. 271–342.
Lang, Winfried (1991a) 'The international waste regime' in Winfried Lang,
Hanspeter Neuhold and Karl Zemanek (eds), *Environmental Protection and
International Law* (London: Graham & Trotman).
—— (1991b) 'Negotiations on the environment' in Victor A. Kremenyuk
(ed.), *International Negotiation: analysis, approaches, issues* (San Francisco:
Jossey-Bass Publishers).
Lawrence, Peter M. (1990) 'International legal regulation for protection of
the ozone layer: some problems of implementation', *Journal of Environmental Law*, vol. 2, no. 1, pp. 17–52.
Leggett, Jeremy (1992) 'The environmental impact of war: a scientific analysis
and Greenpeace's reaction', in Glen Plant (ed.), *Environmental Protection
and the Law of War* (London: Belhaven Press).
Leggett, Jeremy and Paul Hohnen (1992) 'The Climate Convention: a
perspective from the environmental lobby', *Security Dialogue*, vol. 23,
no. 4, December, pp. 75–81.
Leubuscher, Susan (1996) 'Ozone depletion: seventh meeting of the Parties to
the Montreal Protocol', *Review of European Community and International
Environmental Law*, vol. 5, no. 2, pp. 186–7.
Lever, Rob (1996) 'World environment on steep slide, says UN report card',
The Canberra Times, 21 April, p. 6.
Levy, Marc A. (1993) 'European acid rain: the power of tote-board diplo-
macy' in Peter M. Haas, Robert O. Keohane and Marc A. Levy (eds),
*Institutions for the Earth: sources of effective international environmental
protection* (Cambridge, Mass.: The MIT Press).
——, Peter M. Haas and Robert O. Keohane (1992) 'Institutions for the
Earth: promoting international environmental protection', *Environment*,
vol. 34, no. 4, pp. 12–17, 29–36.
Linklater, Andrew (1995) 'Neo-realism in theory and practice' in Ken Booth
and Steve Smith (eds), *International Relations Theory Today* (Cambridge:
Polity Press).

Lipschutz, Ronnie D. (1991) 'One world or many? global sustainable economic development in the 21st century', *Bulletin of Peace Proposals*, vol. 22, no. 2, pp. 189–98.

―― (1993) 'Learn of the green world: global environmental change, global civil society and social learning', paper presented at the Annual Conference of the International Studies Association, 23–27 March.

―― (1994) 'Who are we? Why are we here? Political identity, ecological politics and global change', paper presented to the Annual Meeting of the International Studies Association, 28 March to 1 April.

Lipschutz, Ronnie D. and John P. Holdren (1990) 'Crossing borders: resource flows, the global environment and international security', *Bulletin of Peace Proposals*, vol. 21, no. 2, pp. 121–33.

Lipschutz, Ronnie D. and Ken Conca (eds) (1993a) *The State and Social Power in Global Environmental Politics* (New York: Columbia University Press).

―― (1993b) 'The implications of global ecological interdependence' in Ronnie D. Lipschutz and Ken Conca (eds), *The State and Social Power in Global Environmental Politics* (New York: Columbia University Press).

Litfin, Karen (1993) 'Ecoregimes: playing tug of war with the nation-state' in Ronnie D. Lipschutz and Ken Conca (eds), *The State and Social Power in Global Environmental Politics* (New York: Columbia University Press).

―― (1994) *Ozone Discourses: science and politics in global environmental cooperation* (New York: Columbia University Press).

Little, Richard (1995) 'International relations and the triumph of capitalism' in Ken Booth and Steve Smith (eds), *International Relations Theory Today* (Cambridge: Polity Press).

Livernash, Robert (1992) 'The growing influence of NGOs in the developing world', *Environment*, vol. 34, no. 5, June, pp. 12–20, 41–3.

Lohmann, Larry (1990) 'Whose common future?', *The Ecologist*, vol. 20, no. 3, May/June, pp. 82–4.

―― (1991) 'Who defends biological diversity? conservation strategies and thecase of Thailand', *The Ecologist*, vol. 21, no. 1, January/February, pp. 5–13.

Lunde, Leiv (1991) 'North/South and global warming – conflict or cooperation?', *Bulletin of Peace Proposals*, vol. 22, no. 2, pp. 199–210.

McClement, T. P. (1992) 'The environment, green issues and the military', *The Naval Review*, vol. 80, no. 3, July, pp. 201–8.

McConnell, Fiona (1996) *The Biodiversity Convention: a negotiating history* (London: Kluwer Law International).

McCormick, John (1989) *The Global Environment Movement* (London: Belhaven Press).

―― (1993) 'International nongovermental organisations: prospects for a global environmental movement' in Sheldon Kamieniecki (ed.), *Environmental Politics in the International Arena* (Albany, NY: State University of New York Press).

McCully, Patrick (1991a) 'Discord in the greenhouse: how WRI is attempting to shift the blame for global warming', *The Ecologist*, vol. 21, no. 4, July/August, pp. 157–65.

McCully, Patrick (1991b) 'The case against climate aid', *The Ecologist*, vol. 21, no. 6, November/December, pp. 244–51.

McManus, Phil (1996) 'Contested terrains: politics, stories and discourses of sustainability', *Environmental Politics*, vol. 5, no. 1, Spring, pp. 48–73.

McNeely, Jeffrey A., Martha Rojas and Caroline Martinet (1995) 'The Convention on Biological Diversity: promise and frustration', *Journal of Environment and Development*, vol. 4, no. 2, Summer, pp. 33–53.

MacNeill, Jim (1989–90) 'The greening of international relations', *International Journal*, vol. XLV, no. 1, Winter, pp. 1–35.

MacNeill, Jim, Pieter Winsemius and Taizo Yakushiji (1991) *Beyond interdependence: the meshing of the world's economy and the Earth's ecology* (New York: Oxford University Press).

Maddox, John (1972) *The Doomsday Syndrome* (London: Macmillan).

Makhijani, Arjun, Amanda Bickel and Annie Makhijani (1990) 'Beyond the Montreal Protocol: still working on the ozone hole', *Technology Review*, vol. 93, no. 4, May/June, pp. 53–9.

Mahony, Rhona (1992) 'Debt-for-Nature Swaps: who really benefits?', *The Ecologist*, vol. 22, no. 3, May/June, pp. 97–103.

Malik, Michael (1988) 'Fear of flooding', *Far Eastern Economic Review*, vol. 142, no. 51, 22 December, pp. 20–1.

Mann, Dean (1991) 'Environmental learning in a decentralised political world', *Journal of International Affairs*, vol. 44, no. 2, Winter, pp. 301–37.

Martens, Todd K. (1989) 'Ending tropical deforestation: what is the proper role for the World Bank?', *Harvard Environmental Law Review*, vol. 13, No.2, pp. 485–515.

Martin-Brown, Joan (1992a) 'Women in the ecological mainstream', *International Journal*, vol. XLVII, Autumn, pp. 706–22.

—— (1992b) 'Rethinking technology in the future', *Environmental Science and Technology*, vol. 26, no. 6, pp. 1100–2.

Mathews, Jessica Tuchman (1989) 'Redefining security', *Foreign Affairs*, vol. 68, no. 2, pp. 162–77.

—— (ed.) (1991) *Preserving the Global Environment: the challenge of shared leadership* (New York: W. W. Norton).

—— (1993) 'Nations and nature: a new view of security' in Gwyn Prins (ed.), *Threats Without Enemies* (London: Earthscan).

Maull, Hanns W. (1992) 'Japan's global environmental politics' in Andrew Hurrell and Benedict Kingsbury (eds), *The International Politics of the Environment* (Oxford: Clarendon Press).

Meadows, Donella *et al.* (1972) *The Limits to Growth* (London: Earth Island Ltd).

Medical Association for Prevention of War (1991) *Environmental Effects of Warfare* (Canberra: MAPW).

Melman, Seymour (1988) 'Law for economic conversion: necessity and characteristics', *ENDPapers*, no. 18, Summer/Autumn, pp. 54–60.

Merchant, Carolyn (1983) 'Mining the earth's womb' in Joan Rothschild (ed.), *Machina ex Dea: feminist perspectives on technology* (New York: Pergamon Press).

Mikesell, Raymond F. (1992) *Economic Development and the Environment* (London: Mansell Publishing).

Milbrath, Lester L. (1984) *Environmentalists: vanguard for a new society* (Albany, NY: State University of New York Press).

Miller, David (1995) 'Montreal Protocol: Open-ended Working Group', *Environmental Policy and Law*, vol. 25, no. 4/5, August/September, pp. 181–4.

Miller, Kenton R. (1983) 'The Earth's living terrestrial resources: managing their conservation' in David A. Kay and Harold K. Jacobson (eds), *Environmental protection: the international dimension* (Totowa, NJ: Allenheld, Osmun).

Miller, Marian A. L. (1995) *The Third World in global environmental politics* (Boulder: Lynne Reinner).

Mintzer, Irving M. and J. Amber Leonard (eds) (1994a) *Negotiating Climate Change: the inside story of the Rio Convention* (Cambridge: Cambridge University Press).

—— (1994b) 'Visions of a changing world' in Irving M. Mintzer and J. Amber Leonard (eds), *Negotiating climate change: the inside story of the Rio Convention* (Cambridge: Cambridge University Press).

Mische, Patricia M. (1989) 'Ecological security and the need to reconceptualise sovereignty', *Alternatives*, no. XIV, pp. 389–427.

—— (1992) 'Security through defending the environment: citizens say yes!', in Elise Boulding (ed.), *New Agendas for Peace Research* (Boulder: Lynne Rienner).

—— (1994) 'Peace and ecological security', *Peace Review*, vol. 6, no. 4, Fall, pp. 275–84.

Mitchell, Ronald (1993) 'International oil pollution of the oceans' in Peter M. Haas, Robert O. Keohane and Marc A. Levy (eds), *Institutions for the Earth: sources of effective environmental protection* (Cambridge, Mass.: The MIT Press).

Mol, Arthur P. J. (1996) 'Ecological modernisation and institutional reflexivity: environmental reform in the late modern age', *Environmental Politics*, vol. 5, no. 2, Summer, pp. 302–23.

Molina, Mario J. and F. S. Rowland (1974) 'Stratospheric sink for chlorofluoromethanes: chlorine atom-catalysed destruction of ozone', *Nature*, vol. 249, no. 5460, 28 June, pp. 810–12.

Momsen, Janet Henshall (1991) *Women and Development in the Third World* (London: Routledge).

Moody-O'Grady, Kristin (1995) 'Nuclear waste in the oceans: has the Cold War taught us anything?', *Natural Resources Journal*, vol. 35, no. 3, Summer, pp. 695–709.

Morris, David (1990) 'Free trade: the great destroyer', *The Ecologist*, vol. 20, no. 5, September/October, pp. 190–5.

Morrisette, Peter M. (1989) 'The evolution of policy responses to stratospheric ozone depletion', *Natural Resources Journal*, vol. 29, no. 3, Summer, pp. 793–820.

Moss, Richard H. (1993) 'Resource scarcity and environmental security', *SIPRI Yearbook 1994* (Oxford: Oxford University Press).

Muller, Frank (1996) 'Mitigating climate change: the case for energy taxes', *Environment*, vol. 38, no. 2, March, pp. 13–20, 36–43.

Munson, Abby (1993) 'Genetically manipulated organisms: international policy-making and implications', *International Affairs*, vol. 69, no. 3, July, pp. 497–517.

Murphy, Sean D. (1993) 'The Basel Convention on hazardous wastes', *Environment*, vol. 35, no. 2, March, pp. 41–4.

—— (1994) 'Prospective liability regimes for the transboundary movement of hazardous wastes', *American Journal of International Law*, vol. 88, no. 1, January, pp. 24–75.

Murray, Martyn (1993) 'The value of biodiversity' in Gwyn Prins (ed.), *Threats without enemies* (London: Earthscan).

Myers, Norman (1989) 'Environment and security', *Foreign Affairs*, no. 74, Spring, pp. 23–41.

—— (1992) 'The anatomy of environmental action: the case of tropical deforestation' in Andrew Hurrell and Benedict Kingsbury (eds), *The International Politics of the Environment* (Oxford: Clarendon Press).

Nanda, Ved P. (1989a) 'Stratospheric ozone depletion: a challenge for international environmental law and policy', *Michigan Journal of International Law*, vol. 10, no. 2, Spring, pp. 482–525.

—— (1989b) 'Global warming and international environmental law – a preliminary inquiry', *Harvard International Law Journal*, vol. 30, no. 2, Spring, pp. 375–92.

—— (1991) 'International environmental protection and developing countries' interests: the role of international law', *Texas International Law Journal*, vol. 26, no. 3, Summer, pp. 497–519.

Native Peoples of Sarawak (1991) 'Statement by representatives to the 11th meeting of the ITTO', *ECO*, Issue no. 1, Article 4 (http://bioc09.uthscsa. edu/natnet/archive/nl/9202/0163.html).

Ndi, George K. (1993) 'Cooperation towards sustainable development in the African ACPs', *Environmental Policy and Law*, vol. 23, no. 1, February, pp. 18–33.

Newsom, David D. (1988–89) 'The new diplomatic agenda: are governments ready?', *International Affairs*, vol. 65, no. 1, Winter, pp. 29–41.

Nitze, William A. (1993) 'Swords into Ploughshares: agenda for change in the developing world', *International Affairs*, vol. 69, no. 1, January, pp. 39–53.

Ntambirweki, John (1991) 'The developing countries in the evolution of an international environmental law', *Hastings International and Comparative Law Review*, vol. 14, no. 4, Summer, pp. 905–28.

Nye, Joseph S., Jr. (1993) 'Foreword' in Peter M. Haas, Robert O. Keohane and Marc A. Levy (eds), *Institutions for the Earth: sources of effective environmental protection* (Cambridge, Mass.: The MIT Press).

Oberthür, Sebastian (1993) 'Discussions on Joint Implementation and the financial mechanism', *Environmental Policy and Law*, vol. 23, no. 6, December, pp. 245–9.

—— (1996a) 'UN/FCCC: sign of progress', *Environmental Policy and Law*, vol. 26, no. 4, June, pp. 158–60.

—— (1996b) 'UNFCCC: the second Conference of the Parties', *Environmental Policy and Law*, vol. 26, no. 5, October, pp. 195–201.

Oberthür, Sebastian and Hermann Ott (1995) 'UN Convention on Climate Change: the first Conference of the Parties', *Environmental Policy and Law*, vol. 24, no. 4/5, August/September, pp. 144–56.

Opschoor, Johannes B. (1989) 'North–South trade, resource degradation and economic security', *Bulletin of Peace Proposals*, vol. 20, no. 2, June, pp. 135–42.

Organisation for Economic Cooperation and Development (1992) *Climate Change Policy Initiatives* (Geneva: OECD/International Energy Agency).

O'Riordan, Timothy (1991) 'The new environmentalism and sustainable development', *The Science of the Total Environment*, no. 108, pp. 5–15.

O'Riordan, Tim and James Cameron (eds) (1994) *Interpreting the precautionary principle* (London: Cameron May).

Orrego Vicuña, Francisco (1993) 'Toward an effective managment of high seas fisheries and the settlement of the pending issues of the Law of the Sea', *Ocean Development in International Law*, vol. 24, pp. 81–92.

Oswald, Julian (1993) 'Defence and environmental security' in Gwyn Prins (ed.), *Threats without enemies* (London: Earthscan).

Paarlberg, Robert L. (1993) 'Managing pesticide use in developing countries', in Peter M. Haas, Robert O. Keohane and Marc A. Levy (eds), *Institutions for the Earth: sources of effective environmental protection* (Cambridge, Mass.: The MIT Press).

Paehlke, Robert (1994) 'Environmental values and public policy' in Norman J. Vig and Michael K. Kraft (eds), *Environmental Policy in the 1990s: toward a new agenda*, 2nd edition (Washington DC: CQ Press).

—— (1995) 'Environmental values for a sustainable society: the democratic challenge' in Frank Fischer and Michael Black (eds), *Greening Environmental Policy: the politics of a sustainable future* (New York: St Martin's Press).

Pallemaerts, Marc (1993) 'International environmental law from Stockholm to Rio: back to the future?' in Philippe Sands (ed.), *Greening International Law* (London: Earthscan).

Palmer, Geoffrey (1992) 'New ways to make international environmental law', *American Journal of International Law*, vol. 86, no. 2, April, pp. 259–83.

Park, Jacob (1996) 'Climate change: Joint Implemention under the UN Framework Convention on Climate Change', *Review of European Community and International Environmental Law*, vol. 5, no. 2, pp. 188–9.

Parson, Edward A. (1993) 'Protecting the ozone layer' in Peter M. Haas, Robert O. Keohane and Marc A. Levy (eds), *Institutions for the Earth: sources of effective environmental protection* (Cambridge, Mass.: The MIT Press).

Parson, Edward A., Peter M. Haas and Marc A. Levy (1992) 'A summary of major documents signed at the Earth Summit and the Global Forum', *Environment*, vol. 34, no. 8, pp. 12–15, 34–6.

Paterson, Matthew (1992) 'The Convention on Climate Change agreed at the Rio conference', *Environmental Politics*, vol. 1, no. 4, Winter, pp. 267–73.

—— (1993) 'The politics of climate change after UNCED', *Environmental Politics*, vol. 2, no. 4, Winter, pp. 174–90.

Paterson, Matthew (1995) 'Radicalising regimes? ecology and the critique of IR theory' in John MacMillan and Andrew Linklater (eds), *Boundaries in Question: new directions in International Relations* (London: Pinter Publishers).
—— (1996a) 'IR theory: neorealism, neoinstitutionalism and the Climate Change Convention' in John Vogler and Mark F. Imber (eds), *The Environment and International Relations* (London: Routledge).
—— (1996b) *Global Warming and Global Politics* (New York: Routledge).
Paterson, Matthew and Michael Grubb (1992) 'The international politics of climate change', *International Affairs*, vol. 68, no. 2, pp. 293–310.
Pathak, R. A. and Akshay Jaitly (1992) 'Rio Declaration – economic issues for developing countries', *Review of European Community and International Environmental Law*, vol. 1, no. 3, pp. 267–9.
Patterson, Alan (1990) 'Debt-for-Nature Swaps and the need for alternatives', *Environment*, vol. 32, no. 10, December, pp. 5–13, 31–2.
Peace Research Institute Oslo (1989) *Environmental Security: a report contributing to the concept of comprehensive international security* (Oslo: Peace Research Institute, Oslo/United Nations Environment Programme).
Pearce, David (1990) 'Economics and the global environmental challenge', *Millennium*, vol. 19, no. 3, Winter, pp. 365–87.
Pearce, David W. and Jeremy J. Warford (1993) *World Without End: economics, environment and sustainable development* (New York: Oxford University Press).
Pearce, David, Edward Barbier and Anil Markandya (1994) *Sustainable development: economics and environment in the Third World* (London: Earthscan).
Pearce, Fred (1991) *Green Warriors: the people and politics behind the environment revolution* (London: The Bodley Head).
Peet, Gerard (1994) 'The role of (environmental) non-governmental organisations at the Marine Environment Protection Committee (MEPC) of the International Maritime Organisation (IMO) and at the London Dumping Convention (LDC)', *Ocean and Coastal Management*, vol. 22, no. 1, pp. 3–18.
Peet, John (1992) *Energy and the ecological economics of sustainability* (Washington, DC: Island Press).
Peters, Margot B. (1989–90) 'An international approach to the greenhouse effect: the problem of increased atmospheric carbon dioxide can be approached by an innovative international agreement', *California Western International Law Journal*, vol. 20, no. 1, pp. 67–89.
Peterson, M. J. (1988) *Managing the Frozen South: the creation and evolution of the Antarctic Treaty system* (Berkeley: University of California Press).
—— (1993) 'International fisheries management' in Peter M. Haas, Robert O. Keohane and Marc A. Levy (eds), *Institutions for the Earth: sources of effective environmental protection* (Cambridge, Mass.: The MIT Press).
Piddington, Kenneth (1992) 'The role of the World Bank' in Andrew Hurrell and Benedict Kingsbury (eds), *The International Politics of the Environment* (Oxford: Clarendon Press).
Pirages, Dennis Clark (1978) *The New Context for International Relations: global ecopolitics* (North Scituate, Mass.: Duxbury Press).

Pirages, Dennis Clark (1983) 'The ecological perspective and the social sciences; [extracted in] Charles W. Kegley and Eugene R. Wittkopf (eds) (1984) *The global agenda: Issues and Perspectives*, 2nd edn (New York: Random House).

—— (1991) 'The greening of peace research', *Journal of Peace Research*, vol. 28, no. 2, May, pp. 129–33.

Plant, Glen (1990) 'Institutional and legal responses to global climate change', *Millennium*, vol. 19, no. 3, Winter, pp. 413–28.

—— (ed.) (1992) *Environmental protection and the law of war: a fifth Geneva convention on the protection of the environment in time of armed conflict* (London: Belhaven Press).

Plater, Zygmunt J. B. (1988) 'Damming the Third World: multilateral development banks, environmental diseconomies and international reform pressures on the lending process', *Denver Journal of International Law and Policy*, vol. 17, no. 1, Fall, pp. 121–53.

Porras, Ileana M. (1993) 'The Rio Declaration: a new basis for international cooperation' in Philippe Sands (ed.), *Greening International Law* (London: Earthscan).

Porritt, Jonathon (1984) *Seeing Green: the politics of ecology explained* (Oxford: Basil Blackwell).

Porter, Gareth and Janet Welsh Brown (1991) *Global Environmental Politics* (Boulder: Westview Press).

—— (1996) *Global Environmental Politics*, 2nd edn (Boulder: Westview Press).

Posey, Darrell A. (1996) 'Protecting indigenous peoples' rights to biodiversity', *Environment* vol. 38, no. 8, pp. 7–9, 37–45.

Postel, Sandra and Christopher Flavin (1991) 'Reshaping the global economy' in Lester R. Brown *et al.* (eds), *State of the World 1991* (New York: W. W. Norton & Co.).

Postiglione, Amedeo (1990) 'A more efficient international law on the environment and setting up an international court for the environment within the United Nations', *Environmental Law*, vol. 20, no. 2, pp. 321–8.

Preston, Shelley (1994) 'Electronic global networking and the NGO movement: the 1992 Rio Summit and beyond', *Swords and Ploughshares*, vol. 3, no. 2, Spring (http://www.american.edu/academic.depts/sis/sword/spring94/preston).

Princen, Thomas (1994) 'NGOs: creating a niche in environmental diplomacy' in Thomas Princen and Matthias Finger (eds), *Environmental NGOs in World Politics: linking the global and the local* (London: Routledge).

Princen, Thomas and Matthias Finger (1994) 'Introduction' in Thomas Princen and Matthias Finger (eds), *Environmental NGOs in world politics: linking the global and the local* (London: Routledge).

Prins, Gwyn (1990) 'Politics and the environment', *International Affairs*, vol. 66, no. 4, pp. 711–30.

—— (1993) 'Putting environmental security in context' in Gwyn Prin (ed.), *Threats without enemies* (London: Earthscan).

Puckett, Jim (1994) 'Disposing of the waste trade: closing the recycling loophole', *The Ecologist*, vol. 24, no. 2, March/April, pp. 53–8.

Pulvenis, Jean-François (1994) 'The Framework Convention on Climate Change' in Luigi Campiglio *et al.* (eds), *The environment after Rio: international law and economics* (London: Graham & Trotman).

Rae, Michael (1993) *The Integration of Trade and Environmental Policy to Achieve Ecologically Sustainable Development* (Sydney: WWF Australia).

Ramakrishna, Kilaparti (1990) 'North–South issues, common heritage of mankind and global climate', *Millennium*, vol. 19, no. 3, Winter, pp. 429–45.

Raustiala, Kal and David G. Victor (1996) 'Biodiversity since Rio: the future of the Convention on Biological Diversity', *Environment*, vol. 38, no. 4, May, pp. 17–20, 37–45.

Reader, Melvyn (1993) 'The International Whaling Commission (IWC)', *Environmental Politics*, vol. 2, no. 1, Spring, pp. 81–5.

Redclift, Michael (1984) *Development and the Environmental Crisis* (London: Methuen).

—— (1987) *Sustainable Development: exploring the contradictions* (London: Methuen).

—— (1989) 'Turning nightmares into dreams: the Green movement in Eastern Europe', *The Ecologist*, vol. 19, no. 5, September/October, pp. 177–83.

—— (1993) 'Sustainable development: needs, values, rights', *Environmental Values*, vol. 2, no. 1, Spring, pp. 3–20.

Redclift, Michael and Ted Benton (1994) (eds), *Social theory and the environment* (New York: Routledge).

Redclift, Michael and Graham Woodgate (1994) 'Sociology and the environment: discordant discourse?' in Michael Redclift and Ted Benton (eds), *Social Theory and the Environment* (New York: Routledge).

Redgwell, Catherine (1992) 'Has the Earth been saved? a legal evaluation of the 1992 United Nations Conference on Environment and Development', *Environmental Politics*, vol. 1, no. 4, Winter, pp. 262–7.

Rees, William E. (1990) 'The ecology of sustainable development', *The Ecologist*, vol. 20, no. 1, January/February, pp. 18–23.

Reid, Walter V. (1992) 'Conserving life's diversity: can the extinction crisis be stopped?', *Environmental Science and Technology*, vol. 26, no. 6, June, pp. 1090–5.

Reinstein, R. A. (1993) 'Climate negotiations', *The Washington Quarterly*, vol. 16, no. 1, Winter, pp. 78–95.

Renner, Michael (1989) 'Enhancing global security' in Lester R. Brown *et al.* (eds), *State of the World 1989* (New York: W. W. Norton & Co.).

—— (1991) 'Assessing the military's war on the environment' in Lester R. Brown *et al.* (eds), *State of the World 1991* (New York: W. W. Norton & Co.).

—— (1994) 'Cleaning up after the arms race' in Lester R. Brown *et al.* (eds), *State of the World 1994* (New York: W. W. Norton & Co.).

Repetto, Robert (1992) 'Earth in the balance sheet: incorporating natural resources in national income accounts', *Environment*, vol. 34, no. 7, September, pp. 13–20; 43–5.

Rich, Bruce (1989) 'The 'greening' of the development banks: rhetoric and reality', *The Ecologist*, vol. 19, no. 2, pp. 44–52.

Rich, Bruce (1990) 'The emperor's new clothes: the World Bank and environmental reform', *World Policy Journal*, vol. 7, No.2, Spring, pp. 305–29.

—— (1993) Statement on behalf of the Environmental Defense Fund, National Wildlife Federation and Sierra Club before the Subcommittee on Foreign Operations, Committee on Appropriations, US Senate, 15 June.

—— (1994a) 'The cuckoo in the nest: fifty years of political meddling by the World Bank', *The Ecologist*, vol. 24, no. 1, January/February, pp. 8–13.

—— (1994b) *Memorandum: forcible resettlement in World Bank Projects* (Washington, DC: Environmental Defense Fund).

—— (1994c) *Mortgaging the Earth: the World Bank, environmental impoverishment and the crisis of development* (London: Earthscan).

Richardson, Elliot L. (1992) 'Climate change: problems of law-making' in Andrew Hurrell and Benedict Kingsbury (eds), *The International Politics of the Environment* (Oxford: Clarendon Press).

Ricupero, Rubens (1993) 'Chronicle of a negotiation: the financial chapter of Agenda 21 at the Earth Summit', *Colorado Journal of International Environmental Law and Policy*, vol. 4, no. 1, pp. 81–101.

Robinson, Nicholas A. (1993) 'Universal and national trends in international environmental law', *Environmental Policy and Law*, vol. 23, no. 3/4, June/August, pp. 148–54.

Rodda, Annabel (1991) *Women and the environment* (London: Zed Books).

Roodman, David Malin (1996) 'Harnessing the market for the environment' in Lester R. Brown *et al.* (eds), *State of the World 1996* (New York: W. W. Norton & Co.)

Rosecrance, Richard (1994) 'Trade and power' in Richard K. Betts (ed.), *Conflict after the Cold War: arguments on causes of war and peace* (New York: Macmillan).

Rosenau, James (1993) 'Environmental challenges in a turbulent world' in Ronnie D. Lipschutz and Ken Conca (eds), *The State and Social Power in Global Environmental Politics* (New York: Columbia University Press).

Rosencranz, Armin and Christopher L. Eldridge (1992) 'Hazardous waste: Basel after Rio', *Environmental Policy and Law*, vol. 22, no. 5/6, November/December, pp. 318–22.

Rosswall, Thomas (1991) 'Greenhouse gases and global change: international collaboration', *Environmental Science and Technology*, vol. 25, no. 4, April, pp. 567–73.

Rowland, Wade (1973) *The Plot to Save the World: the life and times of the Stockholm Conference on the Human Environment* (Toronto: Clarke Irwin & Co).

Rowlands, Ian (1991) 'The security challenges of global environmental change', *The Washington Quarterly*, vol. 14, no. 1, Winter, pp. 99–114.

—— (1992) 'The international politics of environment and development: the post-UNCED agenda', *Millennium*, vol. 21, no. 2, Summer, pp. 209–24.

—— (1995a) *The Politics of Global Atmospheric Change* (Manchester: Manchester University Press).

—— (1995b) 'The climate change negotiations: Berlin and beyond', *Journal of Environment and Development*, vol. 4, no. 2, Summer, pp. 145–63.

Rummel-Bulska, Iwona (1994) 'The Basel Convention: a global approach for the management of hazardous waste', *Environmental Policy and Law*, vol. 24, no. 1, February, pp. 13–18.

Sachs, Aaron (1996) 'Upholding rights and environmental justice' in Lester R. Brown *et al.* (eds), *State of the World 1996* (New York: W. W. Norton & Co.).

Sachs, Wolfgang (1991) 'Environment and development: the story of a dangerous liaison', *The Ecologist*, vol. 21, no. 6, November/December, pp. 252–7.

—— (1993a) 'Introduction' in Wolfgang Sachs (ed.), *Global ecology: a new arena of political conflict* (London: Zed Books).

—— (1993b) 'Global ecology and the shadow of "development"' in Wolfgang Sachs (ed.), *Global ecology: a new arena of political conflict* (London: Zed Books).

—— (ed.) (1993c) *Global ecology: a new arena of political conflict* (London: Zed Books).

Sand, Peter H. (1993) 'International environmental law after Rio', *European Journal of International Law*, vol. 4, no. 3, pp. 377–89.

Sandbrook, Richard J. (1986) 'Towards a global environmental strategy' in Chris C. Park (ed.), *Environmental policies: an international review* (London: Croom Helm).

—— (1991) 'Development for the people and the environment', *Journal of Interntional Affairs*, vol. 44, no. 2, Winter, pp. 403–20.

Sander-Regier, Renate (1989) 'Last chance for the black rhino', *Alternatives*, vol. 16, no. 1, March/April, pp. 18–19.

Sanders, Jerry W. (1990) 'Global ecology and world economy: collision course or sustainable future', *Bulletin of Peace Proposals*, vol. 24, No.1, December, pp. 395–401.

Sands, Philippe J. (1989) 'The environment, community and international law', *Harvard International Law Journal*, vol. 30, no. 2, Spring, pp. 393–420.

—— (1992a) 'The role of environmental NGOs in international environmental law', *Development*, no. 2, pp. 28–31.

—— (1992b) 'The United Nations Convention on Climate Change', *Review of European Community and International Environmental Law*, vol. 1, no. 3, pp. 270–7.

—— (1993) 'Enforcing environmental security: the challenges of compliance with international obligations', *Journal of International Affairs*, vol. 46, no. 2, Winter, pp. 367–90.

Sanwal, Mukul (1992) 'The sustainable development of all forests', *Review of European Community and International Environmental Law*, vol. 1, no. 3, pp. 289–94.

Saunders, J. Owen (1992) 'Trade and environment: the fine line between environmental protection and environmental protectionism', *International Journal*, vol. XLVII, Autumn, pp. 722–50.

Saurin, Julian (1993) 'Global environmental degradation, modernity and environmental knowledge', *Environmental Politics*, vol. 2, no. 4, Winter, pp. 46–64.

Saurin, Julian (1996) 'International relations, social ecology and the globalisation of environmental change' in John Vogler and Mark F. Imber (eds), *The Environment and International Relations* (London: Routledge).

Schachter, Oscar (1983) 'International equity and its dilemmas' in Martin I. Glassner (ed.), *Global Resources and Challenges of Interdependency* (New York: Praeger).

—— (1991) 'The emergence of international environmental law', *Journal of International Affairs*, vol. 44, no. 2, Winter, pp. 457–93.

Schmidheiny, Stephan (1992) *Changing Course: a global business perspective on environment and development* (Cambridge, Mass.: The MIT Press).

Schneider, Keith (1991) 'US escalates war on waste', *Financial Review* [Australia], 20 September, p. 30.

Schneider, Stephen (1991) 'Global warming: climate at risk' in Jonathon Porritt (ed.), *Save the Earth* (Sydney: Angus and Robertson).

Schoenbaum, Thomas J. (1992) 'Free international trade and protection of the environment: irreconcilable conflict?', *American Journal of International Law*, vol. 86, no. 4, October, pp. 700–27.

Schrijver, Nico (1989) 'International organisation for environmental security', *Bulletin of Peace Proposals*, vol. 20, no. 2, pp. 115–22.

Schultz, Jennifer (1995) 'The GATT/WTO Committee on Trade and the Environment – toward environmental reform', *American Journal of International Law*, vol. 89, no. 2, April, pp. 423–39.

Schwarzer, Gudrun (1993) 'The international long-range air pollution regime', *Aussenpolitik*, vol. 44, no. 1, pp. 13–22.

Seager, Joni (1993) *Earth follies: feminism, politics and the environment* (London: Earthscan).

Sebenius, James K. (1994) 'Towards a winning climate coalition' in Irving M. Mintzer and J. Amber Leonard (eds), *Negotiating Climate Change: the inside story of the Rio convention* (Cambridge: Cambridge University Press).

Shea, Cynthia Pollock (1989) 'Protecting the ozone layer' in Lester Brown *et al.* (eds), *State of the World 1989* (New York: W. W. Norton and Co).

Shelton, Dinah (1991) 'Human rights, environmental rights and the right to environment', *Stanford Journal of International Law*, vol. 28, no. 1, Fall, pp. 103–38.

Sher, Michael S. (1993) 'Can lawyers save the rain forest? Enforcing the second generation of Debt-for-Nature Swaps', *Harvard Environmental Law Review*, vol. 17, no. 1, pp. 151–224.

Shine, Clare and Palitha T. B. Kohona (1992) 'The Convention on Biological Diversity: bridging the gap between conservation and development', *Review of European Community and International Environmental Law*, vol. 1, no. 3, pp. 278–88.

Shiva, Vandana (1989a) 'Strategies for environmental protection in Asia', *Transnational Associations*, no. 4, pp. 200–203.

—— (1989b) *Staying Alive: women, ecology and development* (London: Zed Books).

—— (1990) 'Biodiversity, biotechnology and profit: the need for a people's plan to protect biodiversity', *The Ecologist*, vol. 20, no. 2, March/April, pp. 44–7.

Shiva, Vandana (1993) 'The greening of the global reach' in Wolfgang Sachs (ed.), *Global Ecology: a new arena of political conflict* (London: Zed Books).

Shrybman, Steven (1990) 'International trade and the environment: an environmental assessment of the General Agreement on Tariffs and Trade', *The Ecologist*, vol. 20, no. 1, January/February, pp. 30–4.

Shue, Henry (1992) 'The unavoidability of justice' in Andrew Hurrell and Benedict Kingsbury (eds), *The International Politics of the Environment* (Oxford: Clarendon Press).

—— (1993) 'Subsistence emissions and luxury emissions', *Law and Policy*, vol. 15, no. 1, January, pp. 39–59.

—— (1995) 'Ethics, the environment and the changing international order', *International Affairs*, vol. 71, no. 3, pp. 453–61.

Shutkin, William Andrew (1991) 'International human rights and the Earth: the protection of indigenous peoples and the environment', *Virginia Journal of International Law*, vol. 31, no. 3, Spring, pp. 479–511.

Simms, Andrew (1993) 'If not then, when? non-governmental organisations and the Earth Summit process', *Environmental Politics*, vol. 2, no. 1, pp. 94–100.

Simon, Julian and Herman Kahn (eds) (1984) *The Resourceful Earth: response to Global 2000* (Oxford: Basil Blackwell).

Simonds, Stephanie N. (1992) 'Conventional warfare and environmental protection: a proposal for international legal reform', *Stanford Journal of International Law*, vol. 29, no. 1, Fall, pp. 165–221.

Sitarz, Daniel (ed.) (1994) *Agenda 21: the Earth Summit strategy to save our planet* (Boulder: Earthpress).

Slocombe, D. Scott (1989) 'CITES, the wildlife trade and sustainable development', *Alternatives*, vol. 16, no. 1, pp. 20–9.

Smith, Richard (1996) 'Sustainability and the rationalisation of the environment', *Environmental Politics*, vol. 5, no. 1, Spring, pp. 25–47.

Smith, Steve (1993) 'Environment on the periphery of International Relations: an explanation', *Environmental Politics*, vol. 2, no. 4, Winter, pp. 28–45.

Solomon, Lewis D. and Bradley S. Freedberg (1990) 'The greenhouse effect: a legal and policy analysis', *Environmental Law*, vol. 20, no. 1, pp. 83–110.

Soroos, Marvin S. (1986) *Beyond Sovereignty: the challenge of global policy* (Columbia: University of South Carolina Press).

—— (1991) 'Introduction', *International Studies Notes*, vol. 16, no. 1, Winter, pp. 1–2.

—— (1992) 'Conflict in the use and management of international commons' in Jyrki Käkönen (ed.), *Perspectives on Environmental Conflict and International relations* (London: Pinter).

—— (1994a) 'Global change, environmental security and the Prisoner's Dilemma', *Journal of Peace Research*, vol. 31, no. 3, August, pp. 317–32.

—— (1994b) 'From Stockholm to Rio: the evolution of environmental governance' in Norman J. Vig and Michael E. Kraft (eds), *Environmental policy in the 1990s*, 2nd edn (Washington, DC: CQ Press).

Soto, Alvaro (1992) 'The global environment: a Southern perspective', *International Journal*, vol. XLVII, Autumn, pp. 679–705.

Speth, James Gustave (1990) 'Toward a North–South compact for the environment', *Environment*, vol. 32, no. 5, June, pp. 16–20, 40–3.

—— (1992) 'On the road to Rio and to sustainability', *Environmental Science and Technology*, vol. 26. no. 6, pp. 1075–6.

Springer, Allen L. (1983) *The International Law of Pollution: protecting the global environment in a world of sovereign states* (Westport, Connecticut: Quorum Books).

Stairs, Kevin and Peter Taylor (1992) 'Non-governmental organisations and the legal protection of the oceans: a case study' in Andrew Hurrell and Benedict Kingsbury (eds), *The International Politics of the Environment* (Oxford: Clarendon Press).

Starke, Linda (1990) *Signs of Hope: working towards our common future* (Oxford: Oxford University Press).

Steer, Andrew (1993) 'Foreword' in Shelton H. Davis (ed.), *Indigenous Views of Land and the Environment*, World Bank Discussion Paper no. 188 (Washington, DC: The World Bank).

Stevens, Candice (1994) 'Interpreting the Polluter Pays Principle in the trade and environment context', *Cornell International Law Journal*, vol. 27, no. 3, pp. 577–90.

Stone, Christopher D. (1992) 'Beyond Rio: "insuring" against global warming', *American Journal of International Law*, vol. 86, no. 3, July, pp. 445–88.

Strong, Maurice (1972a) Opening statement by Secretary-General of the United Nations Conference on the Human Environment, Stockholm, Sweden, 5 June (Association for Progressive Communications: gopher://infoserver.ciesin.org/00/human/domains/political-policy/intl/confs/conf72/SGs_Open_72.

—— (1972b) Statement by Secretary-General of the United Nations Conference on the Human Environment to Closing Plenary Meeting, Stockholm, Sweden, 16 June (Association for Progressive Communications: gopher://infoserver.ciesin.org/00/human/domains/political-policy/intl/confs/conf72/SGs_Close_72.

—— (1973) 'Introduction' to Wade Rowland, *The plot to save the world: the life and times of the Stockholm Conference on the Human Environment* (Toronto: Clarke, Irwin & Co.).

—— (1990) 'Foreword' in Julian Burger, *The Gaia Atlas of First Peoples* (London: Robertson McCarta).

—— (1991) 'ECO '92: critical challenges and global solutions', *Journal of International Affairs*, vol. 44, no. 2, Winter, pp. 287–300.

Subrahmanyam, K. (1990) 'Alternative security doctrines', *Bulletin of Peace Proposals*, vol. 21, no. 1, pp. 77–85.

Susskind, Lawrence E. (1994) *Environmental Diplomacy: negotiating more effective global agreements* (New York: Oxford University Press).

—— and Connie Ozawa (1992) 'Negotiating more effective international environmental agreements' in Andrew Hurrell and Benedict Kingsbury (eds), *The International Politics of the Environment* (Oxford: Clarendon Press).

Swain, Ashok (1993) 'Conflicts over water: the Ganges water dispute', *Security Dialogue*, vol. 24, no. 4, December, pp. 429–39.

Swanson, Timothy M. (1991) 'Environmental economics and regulation' in Owen Lomas (ed.), *Frontiers of Environmental Law* (London: Chancery Law Publishing).

—— (1992) 'The evolving trade mechanisms in CITES', *Review of European Community and International Environmental Law*, vol. 1, no. 1, pp. 57–63.

Szekely, Alberto (1994) 'The legal protection of the world's forests after Rio '92', in Luigi Campiglio *et al.* (eds), *The Environment after Rio: international law and economics* (London: Graham & Trotman).

Széll, Patrick (1991) 'Ozone layer and climate change' in Winfried Lang, Hanspeter Neuhold and Karl Zemanek (eds), *Environmental protection and international law* (London: Graham & Trotman).

Taylor, Theodore (1989) 'Roles of technological innovation in the arms race' in J. Rotblat and V. I. Goldanski (eds), *Global problems and common security: Annals of Pugwash 1988* (Berlin: Springer-Verlag).

Tegart, W. J. McG., G. W. Sheldon and D. C. Griffiths (1990) *Climate Change: the IPCC Impacts Assessment* Final Report of Working Group II, Intergovernmental Panel on Climate Change (Canberra: Australian Government Publishing Service).

Thacher, Peter S. (1991) 'Multilateral cooperation and global change', *Journal of International Affairs*, vol. 44, no. 2, Winter, pp. 433–55.

—— (1992) 'Evaluating the Earth Summit – an institutional perspective', *Security Dialogue*, vol. 23, no. 3, September, pp. 117–26.

Thee, Marek (1988) 'Recovering research and science', *ENDpapers*, no. 17, Winter/Spring, pp. 38–75.

Theorin, Maj Britt (1992) 'Military resources to the environment', *Bulletin of Peace Proposals*, vol. 23, no. 2, pp. 119–22.

Theys, Jacques (1987) '21st century: environment and resources', *European Environment Review*, vol. 1, no. 5, December, pp. 2–11.

Thomas, Caroline (1992a) 'The United Nations Conference on Environment and Development (UNCED) of 1992 in context', *Environmental Politics*, vol. 1, no. 4, Winter, pp. 250–61.

—— (1992b) *The environment in international relations* (London: Royal Institute of International Affairs).

—— (1993) 'Beyond UNCED: an introduction', *Environmental Politics* vol. 2, no. 3, Winter, pp. 1–27.

Thompson, Dixon (1992) 'Trade, resources and the international environment', *International Journal*, vol. XLVII, Autumn, pp. 751–75.

Thomson, Koy (1992) 'Lowering sights on the road to Rio', *IIED Perspectives*, no. 8, Spring, pp. 3–5.

Tickell, Crispin (1993a) 'The world after the Summit meeting at Rio', *Washington Quarterly*, vol. 16, no. 2, Spring, pp. 75–82.

—— (1993b) 'The inevitability of environmental security' in Gwyn Prins (ed.), *Threats without Enemies* (London: Earthscan).

Tickell, Oliver and Nicholas Hildyard (1992) 'Green dollars, green menace', *The Ecologist*, vol. 22, no. 3, May/June, pp. 82–3.

Tickner, J. Ann (1992) *Gender in International Relations: feminist perspectives on achieving global security* (New York: Columbia University Press).

Timberlake, Lloyd (1989) Speech to the Mining Industry Seminar, 'Minerals: sustaining the future', Australian National University, Canberra, 4 May (unpublished typescript).

Tinker, Catherine J. (1993) 'NGOs and environmental policy: who represents global civil society?', paper presented to the Annual Meeting of the International Studies Association, Acapulco, Mexico.

Tisdell, Clement A. (1990) *Natural Resources, Growth and Development: economics, ecology and resource-scarcity* (New York: Praeger).

Tolba, Mostafa Kamal (1982) *Development Without Destruction: evolving world perceptions* (Dublin: Tycooly International Publishing Limited).

Tolba, Mostafa K., Osama A. El-Kholy *et al.* (1992) *The World Environment: 1972–1992: two decades of challenge* (London: Chapman & Hall).

Tolbert, David (1991) 'Global climate change and the role of international non-governmental organisations' in Robin Churchill and David Freestone (eds), *International Law and Global Climate Change* (London: Graham & Trotman).

Torgerson, Douglas (1995) 'The uncertain quest for sustainability: public discourse and the politics of environmentalism' in Frank Fischer and Michael Black (eds), *Greening Environmental Policy: the politics of a sustainable future* (New York: St Martins Press).

Townsend, Matthew (1993) 'The international transfer of technology', *Environmental Policy and Law*, vol. 23, no. 2, April, pp. 66–9.

Turbayne, David (1993) *To the Summit and beyond*, Development Dossier no. 32 (Canberra: Australian Council for Overseas Aid).

Turner, R. Kerry (1989) 'Economics and environmentally sensitive aid', *International Journal of Environmental Studies*, vol. 35, no. 1/2, pp. 39–50.

Ullman, Richard H. (1983) 'Redefining security', *International Security*, vol. 8, no. 1, pp. 129–53.

UNICE/UNFPA (1991) *Women and Children First*, Report of the symposium on the impact of poverty and environmental degradation on women and children, Geneva, 27–30 May.

UNIFEM (1993) *Agenda 21: an easy reference to the specific recommendations on women* (New York: UNIFEM) (also available at http://iisd1.iisd.ca/women/unifema.htm).

United Nations Centre on Transnational Corporations (1994) *Environmental Disclosures: international survey of corporating reporting practices* E/C.10/AC.3/1994/4, 12 January (New York: UNCTC).

United Nations Conference on Environment and Development (1992a) Report of the UN Conference on Environment and Development: Annex I, *Rio Declaration on Environment and Development*, A/CONF.151/26 (vol. I), 12 August.

United Nations Conference on Environment and Development (1992b) Report of the UN Conference on Environment and Development: Annex II, *Agenda 21*, A/CONF.151/26 (vol. I–III), 12 August.

United Nations Conference on Environment and Development (1992c) *Non-legally binding authoritative statement of principles for a global consensus on the management, conservation and sustainable development of all types of forests*, A/CONF.151/26 (vol. III), 14 August.

United Nations Department for Policy Coordination and Sustainable Development (1995) *Division for Sustainable Development* (New York: United Nations Secretariat) (available at http://www.un.org/DPCSD/ sustdev.html).

United Nations Development Programme (1992) *Human Development Report 1992* (New York: Oxford University Press).

—— (1994) *Human Development Report 1994* (New York: Oxford University Press).

—— (1995) *Human Development Report 1995* (New York: Oxford University Press).

—— (1996) *Human Development Report 1996* (New York: Oxford University Press).

United Nations Economic and Social Council (1993) 'Development: women in extreme poverty; integration of women's concerns in national planning', Commission on the Status of Women. 37th Session, 17–26 March, E/CN.6/ 1993/L.12.

United Nations Environment Programme (1981) *In Defence of the Earth: the basic texts on environment* (Nairobi: UNEP).

—— (1982) *The state of the environment: 1972–1982* (Nairobi: UNEP).

—— (1992) *Convention on Biological Diversity* (Nairobi: UNEP/CBD Secretariat).

—— (1994a) 'Representatives of 14 countries to meet in New Delhi on tiger conservation', Press Release HE/846, 2 March (Nairobi: UNEP) (gopher:// gopher.undp.org:70/00/uncurr/press_releases/HE/94_03/ 846).

—— (1994b) 'UNEP helps Asian states to establish global forum to save tiger', Press Release HE/847, 16 March (Nairobi: UNEP) (gopher:// gopher.undp.org:70/00/uncurr/press_releases/HE/94_03/8 47).

—— (1994c) 'Major progress achieved towards first African wildlife task force', Press Release HE/848, 17 March (Nairobi: UNEP) (gopher:// gopher.undp.org:70/00/uncurr/press_releases /HE/94_03/848).

—— (1994d) 'Experts to meet in Nairobi to finalise agreement for Africa Wildlife Task Force', Press Release HE/853, 27 May (Nairobi: UNEP) (gopher://gopher.undp.org:70/00/uncurr/press_releases/HE/94_ 05/853).

—— (1994e) 'Resolutions on interim arrangements and on urgent action for Africa', INCD, Fifth Session, Paris 6–17 June, Agenda item 2 (available at http://www.unep.ch/incd/resol-e .html).

—— (1994f) 'Bahamas to host first convention of parties to Biodversity Convention', Press Release HE/858, 22 June (Nairobi: UNEP) (gopher:// gopher.undp.org:70/00/uncurr/press_releases/HE/9 4_06/858).

—— (1994g) 'Illegal international trafficking in African wildlife targeted in agreement to set up world's first international task force for action', Press Release HE/866, 12 September (Nairobi: UNEP) (gopher://gopher. undp.org:70/00/uncurr/press_releases/HE/94_09/866).

—— (1994h) *United Nations Convention to Combat Desertification in Countries experiencing serious drought and/or Desertification, especially in Africa* (Nairobi: UNEP/CCD Interim Secretariat).

—— (1995a) *Fact Sheet 1 – An introduction to the Convention to Combat Desertification* (Geneva: Interim Secretariat of the Convention to Combat

Desertification/Information Unit for Conventions of UNEP) (available at http://www.unep.ch/incd/fs1.html).

—— (1995b) *Fact Sheet 2 – The causes of desertification* (Geneva: Interim Secretariat of the Convention to Combat Desertification/Information Unit for Conventions of UNEP) (available at http://www.unep.ch/incd/fs2.html).

—— (1995c) *Fact Sheet 3 – The consequences of desertification* (Geneva: Interim Secretariat of the Convention to Combat Desertification/Information Unit for Conventions of UNEP) (available at http://www.unep.ch/incd/fs3.html).

—— (1995d) *Fact Sheet 8 – Financing action to combat desertification* (Geneva: Interim Secretariat of the Convention to Combat Desertification/Information Unit for Conventions of UNEP) (available at http://www.unep.ch/incd/fs8.html).

—— (1995e) *The United Nations Convention to Combat Desertification: an explanatory leaflet* (Geneva: Interim Secretariat of the Convention to Combat Desertification/Information Unit for Conventions of UNEP) (available at http://www.unep.ch/incd/leaflet.html).

United Nations General Assembly (1983) 'Process of preparation of the Environmental Perspective to the year 2000 and beyond', A/RES/38/161, 19 December (gopher://gopher.undp.org:70/00/undocs/gad/RES/38/161).

—— (1988) 'Protection of global climate for present and future generations of mankind', A/RES/43/53, 70th Plenary Meeting, 6 December.

—— (1989a) 'Protection of global climate for present and future generations of mankind', A/RES/44/207, 85th Plenary Meeting, 22 December.

—— (1989b) 'International cooperation in the monitoring, assessment and anticipation of environmental threats and in assistance in cases of environmental emergency', A/RES/44/224, 85th Plenary Meeting, 22 December.

—— (1989c) 'United Nations Conference on Environment and Development', Resolution 44/228, 85th Plenary Meeting, 22 December.

—— (1990) 'Protection of global climate for present and future generations of mankind', A/RES/45/212, 71st Plenary Meeting, 21 December.

United Nations Information Centre (1992) *Earth Summit Summary* (Sydney: United Nations Information Centre/UNCED Information Programme Department of Public Information).

United Nations INC/FCCC (1991) 'Climate change negotiations set to shift from drafting to political "give and take"', Press Release ENV/DEV/21, 19 December.

—— (1992) *United Nations Framework Convention on Climate Change* (Bonn: Climate Change Secretariat) (http://www.un/ccc.def.fccc/conv/conv-toc.htm).

United States Information Service (1992a) 'Bush environmental actions supporting UNCED: Text of White House Fact Sheet June 1', *Backgrounder* (Canberra: USIS) 4 June.

—— (1992b) 'US proposes survey of Earth's biodiversity' *Backgrounder*, (Canberra: USIS) 16 June.

Van Aelstyn, Nicholas W. (1992) 'North–South controversy mounts around the international movement of hazardous wastes', *Review of European Community and International Environmental Law*, vol. 1, no. 3, pp. 340–5.

Van Bergeijk, Peter A. G. (1991) 'International trade and the environmental challenge', *Journal of World Trade*, vol. 25, no. 6, December, pp. 105–15.

Vavilov, Andrey (1992) 'The challenge of Brazil – environment and development', *Bulletin of Peace Proposals*, vol. 23, no. 2, June, pp. 115–18.

Vidal, John (n.d.) *The GATT effect* (Gland: WorldWide Fund for Nature).

Vogler, John (1995) *The global commons: a regime analysis* (Chichester: John Wiley & Sons).

—— (1996) 'The environment in International Relations: legacies and contentions' in John Vogler and Mark F. Imber (eds), *The Environment and International Relations* (London: Routledge).

Vogler, John and Mark F. Imber (eds) (1996) *The Environment and International Relations* (London: Routledge).

Von Moltke, Konrad (1991) 'Debt-for-Nature: the second generation', *Hastings International and Comparative Law Review*, vol. 14, no. 4, Summer, pp. 973–87.

Von Moltke, Konrad and Paul J. DeLong (1990) 'Negotiating in the global arena: debt-for-nature swaps', *Resolve*, no. 22, pp. 1–10.

Von Weizsäcker, Christine (1993) 'Competing notions of biodiversity' in Wolfgang Sachs (ed.), *Global ecology: a new arena of political conflict* (London: Zed Books).

Von Weizsäcker, Ernst U. (1991) 'Sustainability: a task for the North', *Journal of International Affairs*, vol. 44, No.2, Winter, pp. 421–32.

—— (1994) *Earth politics* (London: Zed Books).

Waltz, Kenneth (1979) *Theory of International Politics* (New York: Random House).

Wapner, Paul (1995) 'The state and environmental challenges: a critical exploration of alternatives to the state-system', *Environmental Politics*, vol. 4, no. 1, Spring, pp. 44–69.

—— (1996) *Environmental Activism and World Civic Politics* (Albany, NY: State University of New York Press).

Ward, Barbara and René Dubos (1972) *Only one Earth: care and maintenance of a small planet* (Harmondsworth: Penguin).

Ward, Michael D. and David R. Davis (1992) 'Sizing up the peace dividend: economic growth and military spending in the United States, 1948–1996', *American Political Science Review*, vol. 86, no. 3, September, pp. 748–55.

Webb, Eileen (1994) 'Debt for Nature Swaps: the past, the present and some possibilities for the future', *Environmental and Planning Law Journal*, vol. 11, no. 3, June, pp. 222–44.

Weber, Peter (1994) 'Safeguarding oceans' in Lester R. Brown *et al.* (eds), *State of the World 1994* (New York: W. W. Norton & Co.).

Weiss, Edith Brown (1988) *In Fairness to Future Generations: international law, common patrimony and intergenerational equity* (Dobbs Ferry, NY: Transnational Publishers).

—— (1990) 'Our rights and obligations to future generations for the environment', *American Journal of International Law*, vol. 84, no. 1, January, pp. 198–207.

—— (1992) 'Environment and trade as partners in sustainable development: a commentary', *American Journal of International Law*, vol. 86, no. 4, October, pp. 728–35.

Werksman, Jacob D. (1992) 'Trade sanctions under the Montreal Protocol', *Review of European Community and International Law*, vol. 1, no. 1, pp. 69–72.

—— (1993) 'Greening Bretton Woods' in Philippe Sands (ed.), *Greening International Law* (London: Earthscan).

—— (1996a) 'The Basel Convention's amendment to ban the shipping of hazardous waste', *Review of European Community and International Environmental Law*, vol. 5, no. 1, pp. 69–70.

—— (ed.) (1996b) *Greening International Institutions* (London: Earthscan).

Westing, Arthur H. (ed.) (1988) Cultural Norms, War and the Environment (Oxford: Oxford University Press).

—— (1989a) 'The environmental component of comprehensive security', *Bulletin of Peace Proposals*, vol. 20, no. 2, pp. 129–34.

—— (1989b) 'Constraints on military disruption of the biosphere: an overview', *Transnational Associations*, no. 3, pp. 160–7.

Wettestad, Jørgen (1995) 'Science, politics and institutional design: some initial notes on the long-range transboundary air pollution regime', *Journal of Environment and Development*, vol. 4, no. 2, Summer, pp. 165–83.

Wexler, Pamela (1990) 'Protecting the global atmosphere: beyond the Montreal Protocol', *Maryland Journal of International Law*, vol. 14, no. 1, Spring, pp. 1–19.

Wiggins, Armstrong (1993) 'Indian rights and the environment', *Yale Journal of International Law*, vol. 18, no. 1, pp. 345–54.

Wijkman, Per Magnus (1982) 'Managing the global commons', *International Organisation*, vol. 36, no. 3, Summer, pp. 511–36.

Wilder, Martijn (1995) 'Quota systems in international wildlife and fisheries regimes', *Journal of Environment and Development*, vol. 4, no. 2, Summer, pp. 55–104.

Williams, Marc (1996) 'International political economy and global environmental change' in John Vogler and Mark F. Imber (eds), (1996) *The Environment and International Relations* (London: Routledge).

Williams, Maurice (1992) 'Guidelines to strengthening the institutional response to major environmental issues', *Development*, no. 2, pp. 22–7.

Wilmer, Franke (1993) *The Indigenous Voice in World Politics* (Newbury Park, CA: Sage).

Woehlcke, Manfred (1992) 'Environmental refugees', *Aussenpolitik*, vol. 43, no. 3, pp. 287–96.

Women's Environment and Development Organisation (n.d.) *The Women's Environment and Development Organisation WEDO* (New York: WEDO) (gopher://gopher.igc.apc.org:70/00/orgs/wedo/about).

—— (1992) *Official Report: World Women's Congress for a Healthy Planet, 8–12 November 1991, Miami, Florida* (New York: WEDO).

Wood, William B., George J. Demko and Phyllis Mofson (1989) 'Ecopolitics in the global greenhouse', *Environment*, vol. 31, no. 7, September, pp. 12–17; 32–4.

Woodliffe, John (1991) 'Tropical forests' in Robin Churchill and David Freestone (eds), *International Law and Global Climate Change* (London: Graham & Trotman).

World Commission on Environment and Development (1987) *Our Common Future* (Oxford: Oxford University Press).

World Rainforest Movement (1990) *Rainforest Destruction: causes, effects and false solutions* (Penang: WRM).

WorldWIDE Network (1992) 'Messages from world leaders on women and environment: Global Assembly of Women and the Environment', *World-WIDE News*, Issue no. 4, July, pp. 3–4.

Wulf, Herbert (1992) 'Disarmament as a chance for human development: is there a peace dividend?', Occasional Paper no. 5 (New York: UNDP Human Development Report Office).

Yamin, Farhana (n.d.) *The United Nations Framework Convention on Climate Change: the need for a protocol on energy efficiency and new and renewable sources of energy* (London: Foundation for International Environmental Law and Development).

—— (1995) 'Biodiversity, ethics and international law', *International Affairs*, vol. 71, no. 3, July, pp. 529–46.

Yap, Nonita (1989–90) 'NGOs and sustainable development', *International Journal*, vol. XLV, no. 1, Winter, pp. 75–105.

Young, Oran R. (1982) *Resource Regimes: natural resources and social institutions* (Berkeley: University of California Press).

—— (1983) 'Regime dynamics: the rise and fall of international regimes' in Stephen D. Krasner (ed.), *International Regimes* (Ithaca: Cornell University Press).

—— (1989) *International Cooperation: building regimes for natural resources and the environment* (Ithaca: Cornell University Press).

—— (1990) 'Global environmental change and international governance', *Millennium*, vol. 19, no. 3, pp. 337–46.

—— (1994) *International Governance: protecting the environment in a stateless society* (Ithaca, NY: Cornell University Press).

Young, P. Lewis (1992) 'Southeast Asian nations see no sign of a "peace dividend"', *Armed Forces Journal International*, vol. 129, no. 7, February, pp. 30–4.

Yu, Douglas (1994) 'Free trade is green: protectionism is not', *Conservation Biology*, vol. 8, no. 4, December, pp. 989–96.

Zacher, Mark (1990) 'Toward a theory of international regimes', *International Organisation*, vol. 41, no. 2, Spring, pp. 173–202.

Index